D1453187

DATE DUE			

THE FREEDOM SCHOOLS

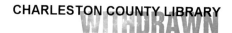
JON N. HALE

THE

FREEDOM

SCHOOLS

STUDENT ACTIVISTS IN

THE MISSISSIPPI

CIVIL RIGHTS MOVEMENT

Columbia University Press / New York

Columbia University Press
Publishers Since 1893
New York   Chichester, West Sussex
cup.columbia.edu

Copyright © 2016 Columbia University Press
All rights reserved

Library of Congress Cataloging-in-Publication Data
Hale, Jon N.
The freedom schools : student activists in the Mississippi civil rights
movement / Jon N. Hale.
pages cm
Includes bibliographical references and index.
ISBN 978-0-231-17568-5 (cloth : acid-free paper)
ISBN 978-0-231-54182-4 (e-book)
1. African Americans—Civil rights—Mississippi—History—20th century.
2. Mississippi Freedom Schools. 3. Civil rights movements—Mississippi—History—
20th century. 4. African American students—Mississippi—History—20th century.
5. Student movements—Mississippi—History—20th century. 6. Political activists—
Mississippi—History—20th century. 7. Education—Political aspects—Mississippi—
History—20th century. 8. Mississippi—Race relations—History—20th century.
I. Title.
E185.93.M6H35 2016
323.1196'0730762—dc23
2015034499

Columbia University Press books are printed on permanent and durable acid-free paper.
This book is printed on paper with recycled content.
Printed in the United States of America

c 10 9 8 7 6 5 4 3 2 1

COVER IMAGE: © Matt Herson, courtesy of Eddie James Carthan
COVER DESIGN: Kathleen Lynch/Black Cat Design

References to Web sites (URLs) were accurate at the time of writing.
Neither the author nor Columbia University Press is responsible for URLs
that may have expired or changed since the manuscript was prepared.

For David J. Dennis Sr., Freedom Fighter, Father Figure, Friend

For Luke Charles Chamberlain, and the generation

to whom the torch of Freedom must now be passed

CONTENTS

Acknowledgments ix

Abbreviations xiii

Introduction: The Mississippi Freedom Schools 1

1. "The Pathway from Slavery to Freedom": The Origins of Education
and the Ideology of Liberation in Mississippi 19

2. "There Was Something Happening": The Civil Rights Education
and Politicization of the Freedom School Students 37

3. "The Student as a Force for Social Change": The Politics
and Organization of the Mississippi Freedom Schools 68

4. "We Will Walk in the Light of Freedom": Attending
and Teaching in the Freedom Schools 108

5. "We Do Hereby Declare Independence": Educational Activism
and Reconceptualizing Freedom After the Summer Campaign 149

6. Carrying Forth the Struggle: Freedom Schools
and Contemporary Educational Policy 196

Epilogue: Remembering the Freedom Schools Fifty Years Later 224

Notes 231

Index 287

ACKNOWLEDGMENTS

Writing this book has been an intellectual and personal journey that has brought me in touch with a network of people whom I am honored to have met and worked with. This book was only possible with institutional support. I am indebted and grateful to the National Academy of Education / Spencer Dissertation Fellowship that provided the support to complete the first stages of this research. Subsequent faculty research development grants from the College of Charleston and the Center for Partnerships to Improve Education at the College of Charleston provided funding to complete the final stages of this manuscript. I am especially grateful to have met and worked with Philip Leventhal, my editor at Columbia University Press, who reached out to me at a conference in New Orleans and has provided invaluable support ever since.

Talented archivists across the country have shared their expertise while I combed through the archival sources used to reconstruct this history. Elaine Hill and Cynthia Lewis of the King Library and Archives at the Martin Luther King Jr. Center for Nonviolent Social Change, Jacky Johnson of the Miami University Archives, Clinton Bagley and the staff at the Mississippi Department of Archives and History, Angela Stewart and the staff at the Margaret Walker Center at Jackson State University, Dan Brenner of the Benjamin J. Rosenthal Library at Queens College, the staff at the McCain Library and Archives at the University of Southern Mississippi, and the staff at the Wisconsin Historical Society have granted access and provided much-needed guidance during the many archival trips this journey entailed.

Acknowledgments

I am indebted to my advisers at the University of Illinois at Urbana-Champaign, Christopher Span, James Anderson, and Yoon Pak, who set a standard of scholarship that I can only hope to emulate in my career. I am appreciative that V. P. Franklin, Clarence Lang, R. Scott Baker, and Derrick Alridge took time to provide feedback on various aspects of my research. The "Growlers"—Bil Kerrigan, Laura Hilton, Vivian Wagner, Jane Varley, and Sandy Tabachnik—provided crucial feedback while I began to draft this manuscript at Muskingum University. Jason Coy, Tammy Ingram, and Joe Renouard provided encouragement and crucial feedback during the final stages, both in and outside of Mellow Mushroom. William Sturkey generously shared sources and his exemplary work on this topic. Mario Perez, Kevin Lam, Michelle Purdy, Robert Chase, Stefan Bradley, Karen Graves, Philo Hutchinson, Wayne Urban, Kate Rousmaniere, Joy Ann Williamson, Dionne Danns, Michael Hevel, Isaac Gottesman, Benjamin Hedin, and the one and only Kevin Zayed are consummate scholars who always encouraged me to complete this project to the best of my ability. Katherine Fleck, Harriet Grimball, and Nicola Hodges provided painstaking technical support by transcribing interviews and tracking down permission forms. I am particularly indebted to Phyllis Jestice, chair of the History Department at the College of Charleston, who read and marked every single line of a draft of this manuscript before it went out for review. I can never thank enough Stanley Thangaraj, an insightful scholar and very dear friend who provided the emotional and professional support needed during the most trying times of balancing research, writing, teaching, and service to our communities. Thank you, Stan, for all that you have done and for all that you do.

I am the youngest of eight, and the standard my family has set is high. My parents, Charles and Karen Hale, instilled a work ethic that made writing a book possible while meeting the demands of a teaching institution. My siblings and their families provided immeasurable support through the years: Veronica, Stuart, and Georgia Parker; Kevin and Ofelia Hale; Brian, Michelle, and Bréanna Hale; Becky, Mark, Kyle, and Luke Chamberlain; Mark and Vivian Hale; Dan, Laura, and Anna Mia Hale; and Alan, Vanessa, William, and Sophia Hale. I am fortunate to have an extended family, too: Steve and Leslie Cavell; Emily and Will Tunstall; Randy and Julie Glau; Justin, Phuong, and Lincoln Petersen; and Andrew, Tiffany, and Charli Gapinski. I cannot thank you enough for being by my side throughout this journey.

Acknowledgments

I cannot begin to express all of my gratitude and love for the one who I am so fortunate to spend the rest of my life with: the very kind, compassionate, and beautiful Claire Dougherty Cavell Hale. I met Claire on July 19, 2012, and was finishing an earlier draft of this book that very same day. Since then, my cosmic match has provided unending and unwavering support with love and patience.

Finally, I am ultimately indebted to the Freedom Fighters, those who sacrificed their lives and livelihood for the notion of freedom that has long been promised but still is unrealized. Meeting the teachers and students of the Freedom Schools has been an incredible honor, and their lives are a genuine inspiration. Dave Dennis, Hymethia Washington Lofton Thompson, Arelya Mitchell, Eddie James Carthan, Hezekiah Watkins, Anthony Harris, Homer Hill, Roscoe Jones, Wilbur Colom, Staughton Lynd, Gwendolyn (Robinson) Simmons, Mark Levy, Chude Allen (Pamela Parker), Liz Aaronsohn, Frances O'Brien, Howard Zinn, Sanford Siegel, and Gloria Xifaras Clark have generously taken the time to share with me their stories, suggestions, and sources. They are heroic civil rights veterans, and I am forever grateful for the opportunity to have met and talked with each of these individuals. This book is a humble token of appreciation for your service to our nation as we struggle to find our path to freedom.

ABBREVIATIONS

AFT   American Federation of Teachers
CCFCO   Coahoma County Federated Council of Organizations
CDF   Children's Defense Fund
CDGM   Children's Development Group of Mississippi
COFO   Council of Federated Organizations
CORE   Congress of Racial Equality
ESEA   Elementary and Secondary Education Act
FOCUS   Freedom of Choice in the United States
KKK   Ku Klux Klan
MFDP   Mississippi Freedom Democratic Party
MSU   Mississippi Student Union
NAACP   National Association for the Advancement of Colored People
NCC   National Council of Churches
OAAU   Organization of Afro-American Unity
SCLC   Southern Christian Leadership Conference
SNCC   Student Nonviolent Coordinating Committee
SSOC   Southern Student Organizing Committee
UFT   United Federation of Teachers

THE FREEDOM SCHOOLS

INTRODUCTION

The Mississippi Freedom Schools

The Freedom Schools shaped my future, my thinking, my outlook on life,
they challenged me to do the things I've done and to the have the mindset
that I have. If I had to attribute anything to my community involvement,
I would attribute it to my attending the Freedom School.

EDDIE JAMES CARTHAN, FREEDOM SCHOOL STUDENT
IN MILESTON, MISSISSIPPI

E ddie James Carthan was born in the Mississippi Delta on October 18,
1949. Many of his memories are set in the small community of Mileston
in Holmes County, whose history and collective memory extends into
the antebellum era when white aristocratic planters reaped the rewards of "King
Cotton." The strain of cotton production still rested upon the backs of entire
communities, like Mileston, Tchula, and other towns across Holmes County.
Especially in the Delta, an area internationally known for its cotton production,
white segregationist landholders after the Civil War maintained their commitment to an economic order that exploited black labor. Whites sustained a system
of total segregation by race, oppressive race relations, and the complete political
disenfranchisement of the local African American population through strictly
enforced racial codes. However, such oppressive race relations were always sites

of resistance, and supremacy never existed free of challenge. Carthan inherited some of these traditions of resistance. His family owned and farmed its own land since the 1930s through a federal New Deal program that spawned a small community of independent black landowners who developed cooperatives, shared decision-making, and laid the foundations for the civil rights movement. As cracks in the overarching racial structure became more visible to those who toiled in the freedom struggles across the state during the 1960s, Carthan and his community connected to a larger statewide and national movement. At the age of fourteen, Carthan and two thousand other students attended Freedom Schools and joined the marches, boycotts, protests, and the front lines of the civil rights movement.

As the American public and an international audience commemorates and remembers the milestones of the civil rights movement, the story of students like Carthan and the Freedom Schools he attended are often lost or marginalized. Yet understanding the significance of Carthan's work and the history of the Freedom Schools fundamentally challenges and necessarily reframes how we understand the history of the nation's greatest social, political, and economic movement for equality. A history of the students who enrolled in Freedom Schools highlights overlooked yet profound truths of the civil rights movement. A history of the Freedom Schools reveals that young people still in middle and high school were on the front lines of the civil rights movement, and in many instances it was the young people—not rebellious college students or established National Association for the Advancement of Colored People (NAACP) card-carrying members—who inspired local movements in their own community. A study of the Freedom Schools illustrates how central education was to the local grassroots civil rights movement. The Freedom School idea started small and was secondary to the voter registration projects that consumed organizers in Mississippi. This civil rights educational project grew in strength because the Freedom Schools organized entrée for thousands of young people into the civil rights movement, and middle and high school students served as both the leaders and foot soldiers at the local level. Examining the Freedom Schools also illustrates the dialectical relationship between the local and national context. Though marginalized within contemporary discourse and typically overlooked by civil rights movement scholars, the local development of the Freedom Schools enabled the growth of federal educational initiatives that transformed public education by the mid-1960s. A history of the Freedom Schools, and the civil rights educational programs these schools exemplify, demonstrates that the civil rights movement was more comprehensive in its reach, more dynamic in its interaction with a larger national context, and much more nuanced in its historic development than popular understandings and public commemorations suggest.

How Carthan and his cohort of students arrived at the front doors of the Freedom Schools, what they experienced inside the schools, and the ways in which the civil rights education they received defined the contours of the civil rights movement is the subject of this book. The processes that led young students to the Freedom Schools reveals much about the nature of the civil rights movement and the capacity of education to affect social change. Children in the Delta and elsewhere across the Deep South experienced the frighteningly efficient system of Jim Crow entrenched within the segregated public schools they attended. As schools are an important battleground of political, economic, and social ideology, it should be no surprise that the dual system of education in this area was governed by hegemonic racial sensibilities and, as such, was a microcosm of the larger segregated society. Simply stated, schooling was used to maintain the social, political, and economic status quo that always worked in favor of white segregationist land and business owners. Many in the state of Mississippi believed the state could only function properly if African Americans generally were laborers and second-class citizens. The segregated system of schooling functioned as it almost always had, reinforcing a tragic truth that historian James D. Anderson once summarized eloquently by stating that "both schooling for democratic citizenship and schooling for second-class citizenship have been basic traditions in American education."[1] While white students received the lion's share of funding and resources, acquired highly valued skills, and enjoyed preferential treatment in the job market after graduation, African American students in Mississippi received far less funding and resources, and a racial code rooted in the days of slavery subverted any aspirations of social mobility. By the time Carthan and his peers came of age in the 1960s, they felt the residual if not quantifiable effects of the Jim Crow system in multifaceted and profound ways.

The Freedom Schools of 1964 were the most recent manifestation of a tradition of education for empowerment, politicization, resistance, and organization that perennially challenged segregationist policy. Such a perspective is clear from Eddie James Carthan's vantage point. When he looked back on the Freedom School experience during the summer of 1964, he connected it to his conceptualization of social relations, his constructed self-identity, and his worldview. Looking back as a local Mississippian, a youth and civic leader, a community businessperson, and an embattled elected politician, Carthan traced his success and, more importantly, his lasting impact on his community to a form of education that was built upon a long tradition of resistance grounded in the principles of the civil rights movement. While the Freedom Schools extended important traditions of education for democratic and participatory citizenship, the schools are also indicative of the rich ideological debate and deep-seated tension that defined the civil rights movement. Civil rights organizers and community members established Freedom Schools across the state of Mississippi while white legislators, school boards, and administrators maintained a segregated system of education ten years after the monumental *Brown v. Board of Education* (1954) decision. Within the Freedom Schools, students, educators, and organizers debated whether to desegregate the public school system, studied the political means to demand greater resources, and protested for more humane treatment in their own schools. Integration, in other words, was not the be-all and end-all of the black community in 1964. The emergence of the Freedom Schools illustrates the diversity of ideology, thought, and opinion about how schools should operate, how the curriculum should be organized, and what paths educational reform should follow during the era of desegregation.

In order to examine the overlooked yet generative role of grassroots education during the civil rights movement, this book reconstructs the history of the Freedom Schools from the perspective of students who attended them. The lived experiences of Eddie James Carthan, Hymethia Washington Lofton Thompson, Homer Hill, Brenda Travis, Arelya Mitchell, Hezekiah Watkins, and other young activists illustrate just how significant education was in the history of the civil rights movement. Freedom Schools continued a long tradition of a revolutionary ideology that stated education was an irrevocable pathway to freedom—a sentiment long embedded in Mississippi communities. But by their very nature the Freedom Schools also stood in stark contrast to the dual system of education provided by the state of Mississippi. Freedom School was physically held outside that system, in church sanctuaries and basements, in local community homes, in storefronts, and in "Freedom Houses" built by civil rights activists (figure I.1). Students studied a humanities-based curriculum that taught political efficacy, social critique, and the organizing strategies employed in the civil rights movement. They discussed the U.S. Constitution and questioned why their parents were not allowed to vote. Students worked in the community, marched on the picket lines, organized boycotts, and desegregated libraries, parks, and schools for the first time in the history of their home communities. Young people were not marginal players in the civil rights struggle. They played an instrumental role during that era and in post-segregated society. Attending Freedom School translated into protest and community-organizing skills; which students applied in the fall of 1964 to demand better resources in their own schools, to protest unjust expulsions, suspensions, and other racially motivated disciplinary actions; and to organize long-term school boycotts. The legacy of the Freedom Schools suggests that despite the best efforts of the architects of the Jim Crow system, community-based efforts taught students to act as historic change agents.

Moreover, an analysis of the Freedom Schools reveals how young the activists were when they were politicized during the civil rights movement.[2] One of the most distinguishing aspects of the Freedom Schools is the fact that they served a K–12 population, a group that generally falls between the ages of six and eighteen, though it was not uncommon for younger students and older adults to attend Freedom Schools as well. But the Freedom Schools generally educated young people in elementary, middle, and high school, and this cohort of students constituted a politically and socially constructed category. By the 1960s educators and activists affirmed G. Stanley Hall and an earlier generation's construction of adolescence as a separate category that was physiologically and cognitively distinct from both childhood and adulthood.[3] Civil rights activists targeted this cohort while building a wider base for the civil rights movement through the Freedom Schools. Charlie Cobb, the Student Nonviolent Coordinating Committee (SNCC) member who first proposed the idea of forming Freedom Schools in Mississippi, and others who organized the 1964

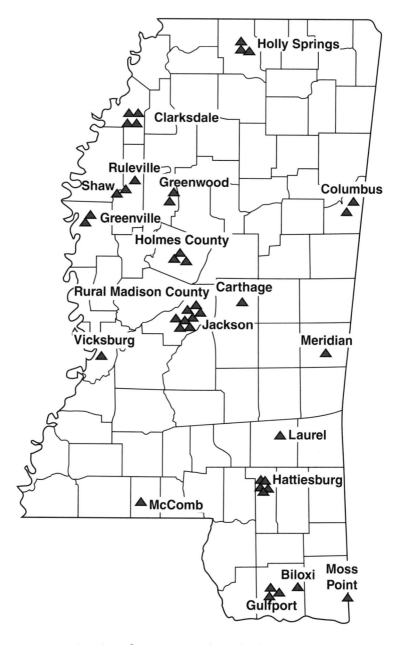

FIGURE I.I   Locations of Mississippi Freedom Schools during the summer of 1964.

summer campaign saw a distinct opportunity and need to reach young people enrolled in elementary, middle, and high school. Students not yet in college or the workforce offered something more appealing to organizers than older adults. Young people were more likely to stay in the state, at least until completing high school, which provided an opportunity to create a more stable and long-term network of activists. Young people were in a formative stage of their lives, and their political consciousness was malleable and could be shaped by the principles of nonviolence and justice. Young people were old enough to understand the injustices embedded within the system of Jim Crow and were fearless enough in their desire to challenge it.

The category of youth, however, has been usurped by collegiate and postsecondary activists, which is evident in the metanarrative and historiography of the civil rights movement. College students and the institutions they attended were indeed central battlegrounds of the movement. The University of California, Berkeley; Northwestern University; the University of Illinois; Columbia University; and southern campuses, including the University of Mississippi, Tougaloo College, and South Carolina State University, to name but a few national exemplars, encapsulated the most defining moments of the civil rights movement for both black and white students across the country. These campuses encompassed a wide spectrum of organization to desegregate public spaces, secure voting rights, protect academic freedom, and reform curricula throughout the 1960s. Protest often evolved from the radical work of college students who comprised SNCC, the Congress of Racial Equality (CORE), the Southern Student Organizing Committee (SSOC), and other organizations at the grassroots level. Focal points that define traditional civil rights narratives and college students' place in it are the sit-ins of 1960, the Freedom Rides in 1961, the integration of the University of Mississippi in 1962, and the Freedom Summer campaign of 1964, all of which involved college-aged students or college campuses.[4] Yet focusing on the college campus limits the categorization of youth activism to the ages of eighteen or older, which fails to attend to the nuances of activism in the Freedom Schools. To focus solely on the college campus is in effect to overlook educational programs of the civil rights movements where many activists learned and practiced the art of resistance.

This history reminds us that the civil rights movement unfolded at all levels of education. Tragically, it also reminds us that young people who elected to join the front lines were not spared the violence associated with challenging social norms. Hardly one year after the monumental *Brown* decision struck down segregation by race, these schoolchildren learned a powerful lesson in the dangers associated with challenging the white establishment. The lesson in subservience came when Emmett Till, a fourteen-year-old African American youth visiting from Chicago, allegedly whistled at a white woman in a store in Money, Mississippi, in 1955. Local whites Roy Bryant and J. W. Milam kidnapped the boy from his uncle's home, brutally beat him to a point of disfiguration, shot him in the head, and threw him into the Tallahatchie River with a cotton-gin fan tied around his neck. The slaying of Emmett Till was extreme even by Mississippi standards. Violent acts such as the murder of Till were sanctioned by and acceptable to whites because an all-white jury acquitted Bryant and Milam in the small Delta town of Sumner, Mississippi.[5] The Till case resonated with those who eventually worked in the Mississippi civil rights movement. "I was shaken to the core by the killing of Emmett Till," said John Lewis, SNCC chairperson and later a U.S. congressman from Georgia, "I was fifteen, black, at the edge of my own manhood just like him. He could have been me. *That* could have been me, beaten, tortured, dead at the bottom of a river."[6]

A history of the Freedom Schools and the young students who attended them is a testament to the courage and conviction needed to join the front lines of the civil rights movement. It is also a testament to the important role education played in the long struggle for freedom in the state of Mississippi. Although activists often sidelined civil rights educational programs to focus on other efforts such as registering voters, the Freedom Schools provided an education that facilitated entrée for thousands of young people into the civil rights movement. In the process, educators and student activists outlined a model of civil rights education that restored American schooling to the ideal of providing an education for democratic, active, and participatory citizenship. The local context of the Freedom Schools facilitated a connection to a larger national context. Head Start, a federally funded early-childhood program that sought to alleviate poverty, was implemented across the Mississippi in 1965. The rapid development of this federal program illustrates how the organic growth of a local movement enabled a national program to develop in a short period of time and appropriate the ideological and political network of the grassroots movement. Although the numbers of schools precipitously declined by 1966, Freedom School teachers and students served on the front lines of other struggles that emerged in the late 1960s such as the black power, antiwar, and women's liberation movements. This dynamic interplay between the local and national context illustrates a dialectical relationship that is often overlooked yet enriches our understanding of the role of civil rights educational projects at the grassroots level. By providing a comprehensive history of the Freedom Schools, this book reinserts education into the civil rights lexicon of American history.

This is not the first study to notice the importance of the Freedom Schools. Educators, activists, and scholars began discussing the Freedom Schools during and immediately following the movement of the 1960s. Howard Zinn, Sally Belfrage, Florence Howe, Sandra Adickes, Staughton Lynd, and Liz Fusco—all white volunteers who volunteered to work with the Freedom Schools during the summer of 1964—expressed a passionate faith in the pedagogy, curriculum, and goals of education that advanced the goals of the freedom movement.[7] These teacher activists dedicated themselves to Freedom School education with the zeal and ardent devotion to social justice that became associated with the youthful activism of the 1960s. Their energetic and idealistic commitment also presents another layer to understand the development of the Freedom Schools. The volunteer teacher corps was mostly white, politically and economically affluent, and from the North or at least outside the state of Mississippi. The white volunteers continued traditions, sometimes problematic, of white benevolence devoted to assisting the South in achieving the ideal of freedom.

These activists and scholars since the summer of 1964 have shaped a larger narrative of the civil rights movement that eclipsed the role of educational programs like the Freedom Schools. As activists began to ask why the revolution never happened, or, rather, why *their* revolution never happened, scholars began to privilege other aspects of the civil rights movement such as voter registration and school desegregation but not the grassroots educational programs that trained a generation of activists. The Freedom Schools have been unjustly overlooked as a result. Today the American public has commemorated the anniversary of the civil rights movement's major milestones and in the process has captured our collective imagination. Popular major motion pictures like *Mississippi Burning*, *The Great Debaters*, *The Help*, *Freedom Writers*, *Remember the Titans*, *42*, *The Butler*, and *Selma* have dramatized, oftentimes inaccurately, this historic movement toward equality. Public television documentaries like *Eyes on the Prize*, *Freedom Riders*, and *Freedom Summer* have replayed footage of protests that questioned a nation's commitment to democratic ideals. Remembering events of the 1960s shape the way we think about the civil rights movement without incorporating the legacy of the Mississippi Freedom Schools.

Some revisionist academic analyses have begun to document overlooked grassroots organizations like those that spawned the Freedom Schools. These interpretations offer competing versions of the national metanarratives of the civil rights movement. Historians and sociologists such as Clayborne Carson, Charles Payne, John Dittmer, and Neil McMillen, among others, analyze the long-organized struggle for equal opportunity among local people in Mississippi.[8] Emilye Crosby, François N. Hamlin, Constance Curry, and Chris Myers Asch examine rural counties and towns within Mississippi that offer a localized perspective to illustrate the complexity, continuity, and differences among various locales across the state.[9] Doug McAdam, Mary Aickin Rothschild, and Bruce Watson examine the Freedom Summer campaign, a highly publicized effort during the summer of 1964 to register voters and focus attention on civil rights violations in Mississippi, thereby dispelling the myth that African Americans would not vote if provided the opportunity.[10] Daniel Perlstein examines the connection between the grassroots organization of SNCC and the Freedom Schools.[11] The Freedom Schools, as these and many other scholars, teachers, students, and activists have noted, played an important yet secondary role within the Freedom Summer campaign and the Mississippi civil rights movement. When thousands of people organized to dismantle Jim Crow in Mississippi in 1964, entrenched racism became visible across the world and the participants learned how to carry forth the struggle for equality. Examined in terms of the organizers' experience, the literature historicizes the legacy of grassroots organization, but it does not comprehensively examine the role and impact of educational programs within the movement.

A number of historians, educators, practitioners, and other scholars of education more extensively develop and elaborate upon the promise of a Freedom

School education and curriculum. These scholars examine the pedagogy and curriculum these schools embraced, a unique feature that also helps explain the significance of the schools. Curriculum theorists George Chilcoat and Jerry Ligon examine the curriculum and modes of instruction in the schools and relate their significance to contemporary educational practice. Sandra Adickes's memoir focuses on her time teaching in a Freedom School and organizing her students during the summer of 1964. John Rachal examines the role of adult education during the Freedom Summer campaign. William Sturkey examines the role of the press and newspaper development in the Freedom Schools to motivate, activate, and connect students as participants in the movement. Kristal Clemons examines the role of black women who taught in the Freedom Schools. These scholars, among others, examine the contributions and attributes of the Freedom Schools and reinforce their importance within the civil rights movement.[12]

While noted in the fields of history, sociology, and education, the Freedom Schools are not the subject of extensive analysis or research, nor is their contribution seriously considered within the larger context of the civil rights movement. Education during the freedom movement is marginalized at the expense of covering the more visible aspects of the struggle that captured national headlines. This book builds upon and further develops the existing literature by providing a comprehensive historical account of the Mississippi Freedom Schools, which, from the perspective of those who participated in the schools, were a phenomenal and inspirational success. This study also builds upon this historiography by closely examining another overlooked though insightful perspective: the experiences of the Freedom School students.

This book follows a number of Freedom School students and their families in several towns and counties across Mississippi to provide a history of the Freedom Schools from various locations across the state. It also follows the teachers and shows how their lives briefly though very profoundly intersected with young people during the civil rights movement. Each of the Freedom School locations in Mississippi covered in this book—Jackson, Clarksdale, Tchula, McComb, Meridian, Holly Springs, Hattiesburg—illustrates a very different and localized movement, but together they represent a statewide movement of education for freedom. Even though communities across the state supported the

Freedom Schools and over two thousand students attended that summer, this book focuses on the history, experience, and legacy of just some of the locations. Not all of the participants were identified for this study, nor did all choose to participate. The students, teachers and locations examined in this book are representative of the Freedom School population in that they represent the age range of the students who attended, they are representative of the four different geographical and congressional divisions of Mississippi, they had similar familial support for their involvement in the movement, and they all remained committed to the principles of the movement in one way or another after the summer of 1964. The student experiences and histories examined in this book demonstrate the commonalities shared among Freedom School participants. At the same time, the participants identified throughout this study illustrate the distinct and unique experiences of the Freedom School population. Students entered the movement at different ages, through different networks, and for different reasons. All participants remained committed to movement principles, yet their activism after 1964 varied widely in scope and content. Moreover, each participant remembers different aspects of the Freedom Schools, which highlights the diversity of thought and curriculum of this civil rights educational program. While many traits are shared across the state, each locale and every student point toward distinguishing aspects that make this history truly unique.

In reconstructing this history, this book builds on three themes that emerge from what has been written about the schools. First, this history begins with the vantage point of the students who attended schools and of the communities in which they lived. This history makes the case that elementary, middle, and high school students have been overlooked, though they are very important historical actors. This perspective also reveals that the students who attended the schools occupied important spaces on the front lines of the civil rights movement prior to the historic Freedom Summer campaign of 1964, thereby challenging a history that emphasizes the role of white organizers or the teachers in the movement. Second, this book is grounded in the fact that the field of education emerged as a crucial battleground of the civil rights movement. The state of Mississippi legally disenfranchised nearly half of its total population, from slavery through the era of Jim Crow. In the years before and during the civil rights movement, activists used education as a way to challenge and

finally dismantle Jim Crow. Through legal challenges to equalize teacher salaries and resource allocation and to acquire the right to attend all-white schools,
activists used the schoolhouse as a front to fight a larger war that eventually
become memorialized as the civil rights movement. Third, this book incorporates the pedagogically distinct aspect of the Freedom Schools and the notion
of civil rights movement education in general into this historical analysis. The
Freedom Schools developed a unique, politically oriented curriculum through
a progressive student-centered pedagogy that differed sharply from education
typically offered to students in Mississippi and across the country. This form of
education and the political activity it engendered revolutionized how students
learned to become active citizens in a changing democracy. By looking at this
history through a normative, organizational, and pedagogical analytical lens,
the history of the Freedom Schools emerges as a unique and profound moment
in the history of the civil rights movement and American education. This analysis is structured in such a way that these themes are incorporated throughout
the book in order to generate a greater historical understanding of the Freedom
Schools.

The history of the Freedom Schools, as noted, is part of a longer tradition
of community and regional organization that equated education with freedom.
Chapter 1 briefly examines the history of education throughout the American
South and the way it was viewed both by southern landowners, who sought
to maintain firm control over a labor force they depended upon, and enslaved
communities, who desired to supplant an entrenched system of oppression,
exploitation, and disenfranchisement through schooling. Education was therefore contested terrain as communities who were enslaved implemented a form
of education within a context of freedom as they transitioned into citizenship in
the United States. The ongoing and historic struggles over the aims and methods of education since Reconstruction provides the backdrop to better understanding the nuances and historic import of the Mississippi Freedom Schools.

The history of the Freedom Schools ultimately originates with the students.
Chapter 2 follows seven students in Jackson, Clarksdale, Tchula, McComb,
Meridian, Holly Springs, and Hattiesburg as they come of age and observe iter-
ations of the national civil rights movement as they materialize in their hometowns. Students study and discuss the sit-ins, the Freedom Rides, and other

protests that occurred in their home communities while they were growing up. Observing the civil rights movement as it unfolded around them at a formative age constituted a form of education that served as an important precursor to the Freedom Schools. The local civil rights organization enabled the larger national movement to take root in Mississippi and, subsequently, motivated youth to become active at a grassroots level within the larger national context. Students shaped by this history were primed to use the Freedom Schools as a space through which to participate actively in the civil rights movement.

Chapter 3 examines how civil rights activists organized the Freedom Schools as part of a larger effort to register disenfranchised black voters. Most histories have focused on the fact that the Freedom Summer campaign of 1964 was the single largest voter registration project in history. The organization of the schools rested on contentious notions of race and gender as well. Civil rights activists relied upon white volunteers to teach in the Freedom Schools, which challenged local leadership, and they also framed teaching as "women's work," which reflected gendered notions of femininity that dictated who could teach. Looking closely at the pedagogical and curricular organization of the schools reveals idealistic intentions, however, which indicates that organizers also saw the schools as a way to build a stronger movement in Mississippi. The organization of the Freedom Schools reflected a commitment to actively inculcate youth with a participatory notion of American citizenship. Organizers accordingly developed a curriculum that focused on developing critical thinking, African American history, leadership skills, and political organizing.

Chapter 4 examines the day-to-day experiences in the Freedom Schools and the pedagogy and curriculum that translated into student protest. Although the Freedom Schools received less publicity from the press and fewer resources from the organizers, the schools were by far the most successful initiative of the Freedom Summer campaign. Teachers implemented a Freedom School curriculum that focused on African American history and culture, local and civil rights movement history, and American government and citizenship. Teachers employed a pedagogy that focused on facilitating critical thinking, engaging the students through discussion, and making the civil rights movement directly relevant to the lives of the students. Additionally, the mostly white teaching force presented an opportunity for interracial dialogue that espoused the values of integration. Students and teachers, often for the first time in their lives, were able to interact openly, honestly, and safely with the racialized "other." Quite remarkably, the pedagogy and curriculum cultivated forms of protest among students in elementary, middle, and high school. Freedom School students used the schools as a way to connect with the marches, protests, and demonstrations of the 1960s. Already exposed to the principles, rhetoric, and strategies of the civil rights movement through lived experiences, the students participated actively in protests, staged demonstrations, and organized their peers to join the front lines of the civil rights movement during the summer of 1964.

Chapter 5 examines how students participated in the movement immediately after the Freedom Summer campaign. Freedom School students organized on their own and in connection with the short-lived Mississippi Student Union. This cohort sustained the struggle by organizing school boycotts, protesting discriminatory policies in their communities, participating in mass demonstrations, and, during the fall of 1964, attempting to desegregate Mississippi public schools for the first time. In short, the students lived up to the intended objective of the Freedom School architects—to develop a student-led network committed to the civil rights movement. The teachers were similarly politicized and they, too, applied the knowledge, networks, and skills developed during the summer. After their work in the Freedom Schools, teachers participated and became key leaders in other social movements of the late 1960s, including the antiwar and feminist movements. For those returning to classrooms in the North, Freedom School teachers sought to improve their own teaching practice and actively worked to provide a quality education to all students. While the Freedom School infrastructure slowly faded during the 1964/1965 school year, the curricular, pedagogical, and political aims of the schools influenced the development of other education programs. Black Panther Liberation Schools exhibited a similar commitment to providing an education for liberation and educated young people to become actors in the ongoing movement throughout the late 1960s and 1970s. The locally organic infrastructure that facilitated the Freedom Schools enabled the rapid growth of the Head Start program, an early-childhood education program that was part of Lyndon B. Johnson's "War on Poverty."

Chapter 6 examines the legacy of the Freedom Schools by following the students and teachers after the 1960s and the influence of the schools on contemporary policy and educational discourse. The students who attended Freedom School were often politicized and carried forth the lessons they had learned into their careers in education, local politics, and community organizing. Fifty years after the inception of the Freedom Schools and despite the struggles of desegregation, resegregation, and the privatization of American public education, educators and reformers continue to use the Freedom School model and to debate its merits in a context of contemporary reform efforts. Direct contemporary implications of this history are found in the Children's Defense Fund's nationwide after-school program the Algebra Project, a mathematics- and humanities-based curriculum reform initiative founded by Freedom Summer organizers Bob Moses and Dave Dennis, and the individual actions of those who attended the Freedom Schools. The legacy is also embodied within numerous school districts that embraced the Freedom School model. Although the context of reform has shifted dramatically in the past half century, the Freedom Schools provide a civil rights model by which to evaluate the progress of educational reform initiatives implemented to provide a quality education for all students.

This book provides a comprehensive history of the Mississippi Freedom Schools. This history is viewed from perspectives that have been overlooked since scholars, educators, and the American public have begun to commemorate the milestones of the civil rights movement. Focusing exclusively on the Freedom Schools corrects a historical record that typically focuses on the direct action protests, boycotts, and the white resistance this inspired. Focusing on the Freedom Schools and the role of education in the civil rights movement demonstrates just how comprehensive, complex, and far-reaching the movement was. The movement sought to register voters and desegregate public spaces as much as civil rights leaders sought to implement quality educational programs that sustained the movement at a local level and challenged statewide systems of public education that disenfranchised students of color. Additionally, this book tells the story of young students who cast aside youthful innocence to join the front lines of the civil rights movement.

By looking at different perspectives, a new understanding of the civil rights movement emerges that enriches the historiography of the greatest social, political, economic, and educational movement of the twentieth century. A history of the Freedom Schools deepens our understanding by looking at the role of young people and the concerted effort among organizers to implement educational programs that looked beyond registering voters and desegregating public spaces. The history of the Freedom Schools, though, is still incomplete. As the teachers and students continue to carry forth this struggle in individualized and nuanced ways, we are reminded that the historical quest for full inclusion, access, and opportunity remains elusive. But we are also reminded that within this history lies a roadmap, a coherent set of historical markers that point toward the potential of civil rights educational reform initiatives in addressing the needs of a rapidly changing and multiracial democracy.

1

"THE PATHWAY FROM SLAVERY TO FREEDOM"

The Origins of Education and the Ideology of Liberation in Mississippi

There were generations of conversations about the situation that we were in, about the absence of political rights, about the absence of economic opportunity, and they were passed from generation to generation.

HOMER HILL, FREEDOM SCHOOL STUDENT IN CLARKSDALE, MISSISSIPPI

As an independent grassroots school system alternative to the state's underfunded and segregated system of public education, the Mississippi Freedom Schools were grounded in a long struggle to secure a quality education by any means necessary.[1] The origins of a school system in the United States can be traced to Puritan or religiously influenced communities in the northern colonies in the seventeenth century. Southern colonies, however, passed laws that explicitly forbade the education of enslaved communities, thereby casting the regions first educational policy in a framework of denial and exclusion.[2] Yet enslaved communities strove to educate themselves through illegal and clandestine means. In this historic struggle for freedom, enslaved communities in the South and their descendants equated education and literacy with freedom and citizenship. Within the context of this larger struggle, oppressed communities articulated an ideology of education for freedom throughout American history and organized schools accordingly. Local black communities educated successive generations by passing down transcripts of resistance in spite of exclusionary policies that students were privy to during the 1960s. The origins of this system and the ideology behind it can be traced to the thousands of freed slaves who demanded an education during the first years of the Civil War.

When civil rights activists developed Freedom Schools in 1964, they acted within established traditions of the local black community that supported education for liberation and freedom. Since southern legislators passed the constitutional provisions for education during Reconstruction, black educators supported a system of education that not only ensured freedom but also provided access to full citizenship. But the black system of education was not a monolithic institution. Especially in the aftermath of the *Brown v. Board of Education* (1954) decision, which desegregated the entire southern school system and threatened professional black teachers with massive displacement and dismissal, black educators often adopted a position that was hostile to notions of freedom. In this sense, the Freedom Schools and their explicit political objectives stood in stark contrast to the education offered to many students in Mississippi. But the Freedom Schools also continued the longer tradition of education for freedom when key actors such as teachers could not. Contextualizing the Freedom Schools in this longer history illustrates the important though largely unrecognized role that education played in advancing the civil rights movement.

AFRICAN AMERICAN EDUCATION
AND FREEDOM IN THE SOUTH

Rebellion and unrest among enslaved communities prompted southern states to pass laws that forbade the education of Africans and African Americans. In September 1739, a band of over twenty slaves outside Charleston, South Carolina, robbed a store that served local plantations, killed the owner, armed themselves, and began marching toward Spanish Florida, whose colonial governors recently granted freedom to the enslaved subjects of the English colonies of North America. They did not make it to St. Augustine, and low country planters crushed the rebellion that same afternoon. But the banners, drums, and colors displayed sent a powerful message that literacy was a dangerous tool. Local planters speculated that slaves had read the news that announced the declaration of freedom in Florida and that a law was recently passed, soon to be enacted, that mandated whites to arm themselves in church. The notion inspired planters in South Carolina and across the southern colonies to establish a powerful precedent, and they passed a law forbidding the education of enslaved communities. Antiliteracy laws and other edicts that explicitly forbade the education of Africans and African Americans comprised the foundation of the "Slave Codes" that sought to regulate, control, and suppress the activities of enslaved and free black communities across the South.[3]

Literacy and education was therefore positioned as a politically volatile tool in antebellum America. Education and the tools of literacy held profound symbolic value. Learning to read in spite of the law was a powerful act of resistance. Literacy opened up new political and spiritual horizons and provided a medium to ideologies alternative to the hegemonic practices of slavery. Education also provided literal and tangible benefits to those who possessed the tools of literacy. In a world governed by strict codes, literate African Americans held the potential to physically write a pass for freedom. Literacy allowed the oppressed to read and connect to abolitionist literature. Literacy and education were the means to freedom for those who did not possess it. As such, the battle for or against education constituted a fundamental struggle that politicized education and defined the contours of American history.

But the codification of laws that sought to ideologically shackle those already enslaved only strengthened a collective desire for education among enslaved communities whose members equated literacy with freedom, liberty, and equality. Frederick Douglass, the great abolitionist of the nineteenth century, is a quintessential example of the individual who, though enslaved, risked life and livelihood to acquire even a rudimentary form of education. Sophia Auld, the wife of Douglass's master, Hugh Auld, began to teach Douglass how to read the Bible, a rare activity even among paternalistic slave owners. However, the epiphany that Douglass experienced once his owner discovered that his wife was teaching her young black charge to read was more illuminating for the young slave. The owner clearly projected the hegemonic views that defined laws governing literacy in antebellum America. "It is unlawful, as well as unsafe," Auld declared, "to teach a slave to read." As Douglass observed, his owner went on to say:

> "If you give a [ni**er] an inch, he will take an ell. A [ni**er] should know nothing but to obey his master—to do as he is told to do. Learning would *spoil* the best [ni**er] in the world. Now," said he, "if you teach that [ni**er] (speaking of myself) how to read, there would be no keeping him. It would forever unfit him to be a slave. He would at once become unmanageable, and of no value to his master." These words sank deep into my heart, stirred up sentiments within that lay slumbering, and called into existence an entirely new train of thought. . . . I now understood what had been to me an almost perplexing difficulty—to wit, the white man's power to enslave the black man. It was a grand achievement, and I prized it highly. From that moment, I understood the pathway from slavery to freedom.[4]

Douglass's response defined a widespread desire for literacy that shaped a system of education for African Americans well into the twentieth century. Upon realizing the liberating and emancipatory potential that education held for freedom, Douglass embarked on a self-directed path toward literacy. As he went on to recall: "The plan which I adopted, and the one by which I was most successful, was that of making friends of all the little white boys whom I met in the street. As many of these as I could, I converted into teachers. With their kindly aid, obtained at different times and in different places, I finally succeeded in learning to read."[5] Douglass's determination to receive an education is indicative of a universal fervent among the slave community to acquire the tools of literacy by any means necessary. In Mississippi, under the cover of darkness, a small though determined portion of the enslaved community in the South taught themselves to read and write through hidden forms of resistance in clandestine locations and through disguised textbooks. This self-directed process elevated education to the "pathway from slavery to freedom."[6]

The antebellum ideology of education for freedom was the foundation from which the first schools developed across the southern states. With the first glimpse of freedom provided by the Civil War, one hundred years prior to the civil rights movement, freed slaves organized grassroots schools to make education for freedom a reality. Indeed, the first schools for blacks in Mississippi were established in the territory occupied by the Union Army. By 1864, freed slaves in northern Mississippi—in Holly Springs, Natchez, Vicksburg, and other towns on the Mississippi River—established schools in conjunction with the Northern army and beneficiary societies, but often of their own accord. African Americans established what Freedmen's Bureau officials called "native schools," educational institutions organized solely by black communities whose children attended them. Freed people established these first schools in the state of Mississippi with a desire to learn and the collective recognition that education would protect their new status of freedom.[7] The Civil War and the prospect of federal troops protecting slaves in their quest for freedom transformed an ideology of education for freedom into a demand for an education, with or without the munificence of the federal government and sympathetic whites.

The understanding that literacy would lead to freedom ultimately provided the political will needed to prompt the southern states to adopt a public system of education. A comprehensive system of public education did not exist in the South, although northern states had embraced a "common school" model since the 1840s. Freed slaves and the newly elected black politicians during Reconstruction were the first architects of public education, and they passed laws creating a public school system in each of the former Confederate states. With the support of elected black officials deeply immersed in the traditions of education for freedom, Mississippi ratified the state constitution adopted in 1868, which codified a publicly funded system of education. John R. Lynch, a Reconstruction-era black politician and the first black Speaker of the House in Mississippi (and later elected to the U.S. House of Representatives), oversaw the ratification of the constitution that inaugurated the state's first system of public education in 1870. These representatives were the first stalwarts and defenders of public and universal education in Mississippi.[8] As freed people carried forth the ideology of education for freedom, black politicians, educators, and civil rights leaders during Reconstruction viewed the schoolhouse as a site of politicization that could be used in the ongoing struggle for freedom.

W. E. B. DuBois and other scholars have since noted, "Public education for all at public expense, in the South, was a Negro idea."[9] Schools for formerly

frican Americans proliferated across the South, and the former Con-
ates reentered the Union with legislative and financial commitment to
the region's first comprehensive public school system. Yet whites that
descended from the antebellum planter and slave owning class had scorned the
idea behind black education since its adoption. They also evaded the deep financial commitment necessary to properly construct a viable system of education.
To offset their own tax payments, whites often used "tax shifting," the process
by which planters, landowners, and business owners could shift or "share" the
initial tax responsibility to others (mostly blacks) in alternative taxation methods, such as excise taxes, poll taxes, sales taxes, civil fines, etc.[10] Black Mississippians were forced to pay a disproportionate share of state-appropriated taxes
yet they received significantly less than they contributed. This precarious situation forced blacks to use a method of "double taxation." African Americans
were thus resigned to elicit private contributions—in essence, another tax—to
pay for their own schools. Double taxation was required as private, missionary,
and northern contributions often required black communities to match their
own contributions. Considering the burden of taxation among the poor and the
subscription of private contributions within black communities, Du Bois was
certainly justifiable in postulating that blacks paid for 113 percent of their own
education.[11]

White segregationists contested the move toward universal education on
every front as part of the larger effort to disenfranchise the newly emancipated
population. A conservatively and violently supported "Mississippi Plan" dramatically limited the participation of freed people in the new social order. Racial
propaganda and statewide terrorism silenced the African American vote during
the elections of 1875 as "Redeemers," largely white militia groups composed
of vigilantes and terrorists, intimidated, harassed, assaulted, and killed African
Americans with impunity in the months leading to the election. After the violent coup d'état during the statewide elections of 1875, white supremacists of the
Democratic Party regained control of Mississippi politics and effectively stymied the strides made in establishing a public system of education. The compromise of 1877, which elected Republican Rutherford B. Hayes as president of the
United States and withdrew federal troops from the South, further weakened
the political positioning of African Americans in the South.[12] Amid this legal

disenfranchisement in the state of Mississippi, formal Jim Crow policies were adopted as early as 1888, initially separating railroad passengers by race but eventually extending to every facet of public accommodations. After the new Mississippi constitution was adopted in 1890, blacks in Mississippi were subject to exclusionary voting requirements such as poll taxes and literacy tests. Additionally, the constitution clarified that education provided by the state would be segregated by race.[13] Support at the federal level precipitously declined, and a series of Supreme Court cases severely limited the application of the equal protection clause of the Fourteenth Amendment that further disenfranchised African Americans throughout the South. The *Plessy v. Ferguson* (1896) decision, which stated that separate facilities were constitutional as long as they were equal, marked the beginning of the Jim Crow era.[14] Governor James K. Vardaman stated in 1899 that black education "only spoils a good field hand and makes a shyster lawyer or a fourth-rate teacher. It is money thrown away."[15] Vardaman's statement in many ways embodied legislators' official resistance to black education that left African Americans on their own accord to provide a quality education.

Schools in the black community reflected intellectual and spirited debates around the purpose and scope of education within the African American community. "The problem of education," W. E. B. Du Bois contended at the turn of the century, "must first of all deal with the Talented Tenth; it is the problem of developing the Best of this race that they may guide the Mass away from the contamination and death of the Worst, in their own and other races."[16] Du Bois advocated a liberal arts college preparatory curriculum that trained students to teach or to advance in professional circles, which often meant preparing teachers in a segregated black context. This potentially presented the greatest threat to the established order. Others, including Booker T. Washington, along with white, northern philanthropists, funded a vocational model of education often aligned with the curriculum taught at Tuskegee Normal and Industrial Institute and the Hampton Normal and Industrial Institute. When the Mississippi Supreme Court in 1910 ruled that the state must provide for black agricultural secondary education, they signified the notion that if black education was to be supported by the state, it should be vocational in nature.[17] Ongoing tensions between vocational and more liberal forms of education illustrate the ideologically rich discourse that surrounded black education during the first half of the twentieth century. What remained constant throughout the history of African American education is the fact that the schoolhouse represented an institution, an ideology, and a collective space through which to achieve full political, economic, and social rights.[18]

Black institutions fashioned a curriculum in the context of discourse that focused on building a more liberal public system of education. As Vanessa Siddle Walker, William Chafe, David Cecelski, and R. Scott Baker have noted, black teachers adopted pedagogies of protest that negotiated the changing politics of education since Reconstruction.[19] Teacher education programs of the 1920s and 1930s facilitated an intellectual climate inspired by northern, urban, Progressive-era educators such as John Dewey and George Counts. The education of teachers during the interwar period was firmly rooted in social critique, critical thinking, and an ardent commitment to democracy. Charles J. Cunningham, a black educator who studied to be a teacher in the 1930s in Mississippi and Tennessee, was deeply immersed in this tradition. Far from the bastions of liberal thought on the East Coast, Cunningham was still part of the Progressive ideology that shaped black educators. A critical assessment like this fueled the ideology of young teachers in segregated schools. "The development of power," Cunningham wrote in his college notes, "is the main business of the school, and all the knowledge obtained should be gained and used in such a way as to be toward this growth of power."[20] For young professionals like Cunningham, providing an education in a segregated context was in and of itself an act of civil rights.

Throughout the 1930s and 1940s, teachers cultivated local and community support to challenge the unjust and unequal education provided by the state. Black educators, lawyers, and organizers targeted the unequal distribution of resources to combat the harmful conditions of segregated education. Beginning with the careful selection and training of an elite legal team from Howard University, Charles Hamilton Houston and his protégée, Thurgood Marshall, mounted the legal assault that resulted in overturning *Plessy v. Ferguson*. One of the first plans of the NAACP was to bankrupt the segregated system by challenging the "equal" portion of the "separate but equal" doctrine. Beginning in 1938, Aline Black, and later Melvin Alston, sued the school board of Norfolk,

Virginia, in a series of court cases that demanded equal salaries between black and white educators. In June 1940, the Supreme Court refused to review this teacher salary equalization case (*Alston v. City School Board of City of Norfolk*), thereby letting the lower court's decision stand, which ruled that the salaries of similarly qualified black and white teachers must be equal.[21] By the 1940s, the all-black Mississippi Teachers Association inquired and petitioned the state for equal salaries and organized legislation of their own accord. In a clandestine meeting held at the Masonic Temple in the capital city of Jackson, Mississippi, in 1948, educators and other NAACP members met and invited Thurgood Marshall to discuss the possibility of filing an equalization suit. Gladys Noel Bates, a science teacher at Smith Robertson Junior High School and a card-carrying member of the NAACP, stepped forward to initiate the lawsuit that prodded the legislature to at least marginally address the growing need for reform through the equalization campaigns. As could be expected, the school district summarily terminated Bates's contract.[22] Although the state eventually acquiesced in principle, such retaliation typified white reaction to challenging the status quo and foreshadowed events of the next decade.

The equalization campaign wrought the first legal victories for the NAACP and educators who supported challenging structural discrimination. The Supreme Court, with the support of a small though influential cadre of federal judges in the Deep South, began to require southern states to equalize funding of black schools in order to fulfill "separate but equal" requirements.[23] As the NAACP aggressively pursued equalization cases to challenge Jim Crow in the courts and experienced success, the organization began to phase out the equalization campaign and shift its legal strategy to address the doctrine of segregation itself. The NAACP experienced gradual success as the Supreme Court began to rule in favor of the desegregation of graduate programs and other institutions of higher education, most notably in *Gaines v. Canada* (1938), *Sweatt v. Painter* (1950), and *McLaurin v. Oklahoma* (1950). These cases provided the legal precedent needed to challenge de jure segregation in K–12 schools through the *Brown v. Board of Education* decision.[24]

Black educators in Mississippi occupied a precarious position as the NAACP pursued desegregation. Stepping forward to demand an equal salary was a radical move among black educators in the South during the 1940s.

Yet equalization suits were conservative and antithetical by comparison to the NAACP's challenge to the doctrine of segregation that was firmly in place by the early 1950s. At the very moment that the NAACP radicalized its assault on de jure segregation, teachers who once radically demanded equalization now demonstrated indifference. Once the NAACP adopted a more aggressive stance in attacking legal segregation, the organization adopted a hardened stance and dismissed teachers as key change agents.[25] Although teachers continued to provide an important foundation for activism that continued to resonate with young people, the NAACP cast educators as a hindrance since many often professionally aligned themselves with administrators and college presidents.[26] Historian Adam Fairclough, in his thorough study of black teachers in the South, concludes that "black teachers' support for integration may have been widespread, but it was shallow."[27] John Dittmer notes in his examination of the Mississippi civil rights movement from the local perspective that "as a group black teachers in the 1950s refused to take a stand and the movement of the early 1960s passed them by."[28] The courageous first attempts to dismantle structural discrimination in education illustrated that teachers were historically supportive of the movement to provide a quality education to all students. But by the time organizers opened the Freedom Schools in 1964, black teachers were often criticized as conservative impediments to the civil rights movement. Organizers in Mississippi would thereafter conclude that teachers outside the public school system were required to instill notions of education for liberation among young activists.

BROWN V. BOARD OF EDUCATION AND THE CONTESTED NATURE OF EDUCATION DURING THE CIVIL RIGHTS MOVEMENT

The *Brown* decision was a watershed moment in American history. The decision to overturn legally mandated de jure segregation fundamentally reconstructed the entire system of education in the South. For those who endorsed education for liberation in their home communities throughout Mississippi, the *Brown* decision actualized the ideal of freedom promised since Reconstruction. Scholars and the American public have valorized the decision. In reference to *Brown*, Pulitzer Prize–winning author Richard Kluger writes, "The outcome of [*Brown*] would change America profoundly. The injustice it sought to end has persisted since the settlement of the New World."[29] James Patterson, in his historical analysis of the decision, regards *Brown* as "the most eagerly awaited and dramatic judicial decision of modern times."[30] As legal scholar Jack Balkin states, "There is no doubt that [the *Brown* decision] is the single most honored opinion in the Supreme Court's corpus. The civil rights policy of the United States in the last half century has been premised on the correctness of *Brown*."[31]

Although the decision holds a special place in American history and memory, white segregationists entrenched in Mississippi met the prospect of integration with fierce resistance and legislators vowed to avoid desegregation at all costs. "If a non-segregated system of school were established," Walter Sillers, Speaker of the House in Mississippi, stated in 1953, "the white race would be mongrelized. [I would] gladly give up my property and my life if necessary to preserve the integrity of segregation. But it isn't necessary; we can do it by law."[32] The timing and content of Sillers's comments reveal that the *Brown* decision did not surprise Mississippi legislators, and that legislators were free to manipulate the law to maintain segregation even before the Supreme Court reached their decision. Because politicians viewed desegregation as a challenge to the very essence of the southern way of life, Mississippi legislators consented to equalization as a lesser evil to desegregation. In a move reflected across the South, the Mississippi legislature made weak gestures toward equalizing its segregated public schools. As early as the late 1940s, particularly after the Bates suit for equal salaries, state policymakers adopted equalization plans and appropriated millions to accomplish just that. Legislators put forth the most ambitious proposal, estimated at approximately $34 million, as late as 1953 when the possibility of desegregation loomed on the legislative horizon.[33] When the Supreme Court ruled in the second *Brown* decision on May 31, 1955, that school districts were to begin desegregation with "all deliberate speed," and at the hands of local courts, Mississippi selected to delay desegregation as long as possible.[34] The state created the Mississippi Legal Education Advisory Committee in 1954, a twenty-five-person board given the task to come up with the legal means to sidestep desegregation. Governor Hugh White led the committee that was made up of leading legislators and, initially, representatives of the black community.[35] The state legislature passed provisions to abolish the public school system if necessary and established the means to support a private school system at public expense.[36]

The hard-fought legal victories of the NAACP and the state's feigned attempt to equalize did little to alter the deep and systemic inequalities that persisted throughout the 1950s and 1960s. Black teachers, for instance, faced enduring inequality. The average salary of a white teacher in Mississippi the year of the *Brown* decision in 1954 was $2,177, while the average salary for a black teacher was $1,244. Ten years later in 1964, when state legislators were "equalizing" education to avoid desegregation, white teachers averaged $4,321 while black educators still only earned $3,566.[37] Students confronted ongoing structural inequality as well. Black students attending segregated schools between 1954 and 1965 comprised 57 percent of school-age students throughout the state of Mississippi yet received only 13 percent of state funds.[38] And although educational funding continued to increase due to pressures to desegregate, it was far from equal. Local officials in Hattiesburg, for instance, appropriated $536,341 yet distributed $157,632 or approximately 29 percent of the total fund for black education.[39] This meant that the city appropriated $61.69 for each black student, which paled in comparison to the $115.96 each white student received. Per county spending on a dual system of education is similarly disproportionate. North Pike County spent $30.89 for each white student and just 79 cents for each black student. In South Pike County, white students were provided $59.55 whereas black students were appropriated on average $1.35.[40] The racially discriminatory distribution of resources supports the assertions of numerous analysts and scholars who have pointed out that the public schools have a lengthy history of slighting their very raison d'être: the preparation of future citizens in a democratic society.[41]

The state enacted structural resistance to ensure that the school system remained segregated, but white Mississippians also endorsed forms of intimidation to secure this end. Segregationists founded the Citizens' Council in 1953, with councils in seventeen Mississippi counties, most often in counties with high black populations or counties where black individuals had challenged segregation in local districts. Within two years of the *Brown* decision, the Citizens' Council—by this time the South's most revered "moderate" organization committed to segregation—enrolled between 250,000 to 300,000 fee-paying members in Mississippi, Alabama, Georgia, Louisiana, and South Carolina.[42] Citizens' Councils employed economic and other modes of intimidation where constitutional resistance did not prevent black families from attempting to desegregate schools. Such tactics were common throughout the state and regularly plagued those who joined the front lines of the civil rights movement. In August 1954, a delegation from the Walthall County NAACP branch filed the first desegregation suit in the state. The petitioners quickly faced grand jury subpoenas on trumped-up charges.[43] The NAACP still encouraged all of its branches to take immediate steps to integrate, especially after the "Brown II" decision was reached (*Brown v. Board of Education*, 349 U.S. 294 [1955]). As a result, black parents filed desegregation petitions in Clarksdale, Jackson, Natchez, Vicksburg, and Yazoo City, only to be countered with fierce Citizens' Council resistance. White segregationists published the names and addresses of the petitioners, and they fired the petitioners who worked for them, and independent business owners lost business to boycotts.[44] Local pressure to desegregate the schools without federal support was not enough to dismantle the segregated system.

At the same time, white school officials made the message clear that open public endorsement of the civil rights movement among teachers and administrators would not be tolerated. School district officials, for instance, never renewed the contracts of educators or principals who publicly demanded an equal salary in the equalization suits of the 1940s.[45] The equalization suits sacrificed a number of teachers and, as in the case of Gladys Noel Bates, teacher associations often organized support for educators they knew would be terminated. In this way the economic hardships of activist educators were mitigated throughout the 1940s. But after the *Brown* decision in 1954, black teachers faced endemic unemployment. Mississippi and other southern states openly dismissed or suspended teachers for open affiliation with the NAACP or other "subversive" associations.[46] The prospects of full-scale desegregation, moreover, threatened tens of thousands of teachers with unemployment. As school districts were reorganized to meet the demands of desegregation, institutional discrimination threatened black teachers with massive layoffs, prospects that threatened a significant portion of the professional class of the black community. Although the numbers are difficult to assess, general patterns emerge that point toward an increase in the number of black children enrolled in public schools at the same time the numbers of black teachers decreased by about 10 percent. Scholars have estimated that 38,000 teachers lost their jobs in the seventeen southern and border states during the decade following the *Brown* decision. The toll was particularly heavy on black leadership. In North Carolina, for instance, over 200 black principals led high schools, but only 3 remained in the leadership position by 1970. In Alabama the number of principals dropped from 250 to 40.[47] Despite such fears, the NAACP attempted to reassure teachers. They viewed that any pain incurred during the desegregation process was necessary if society was to progress.[48]

Students who attended schools in Mississippi in 1964 were inculcated in the tradition of education for freedom in spite of fierce white resistance. "There were generations of conversations about the situation that we were in, about the absence of political rights, about the absence of economic opportunity," recalled Homer Hill, a student at the all-black W. A. Higgins High School in Clarksdale and Freedom School student in 1964, "and they were passed from generation to generation."[49] The notion of a hidden transcript embodied in Hill's statement reflects the private means by which educators across the South passed down the ideology of education for freedom during the 1950s and 1960s. Walter A. Higgins, the principal of the segregated black high school in Clarksdale named in his honor, illustrates the role of black educators in passing down this tradition. Higgins in the early 1950s provided behind-the-scenes support for establishing a chapter of the NAACP in Clarksdale but fell short of publically endorsing the movement.[50] Ineva May-Pittman, an elementary school teacher in Jackson who joined the NAACP in the 1950s, was exceptional in that she joined the organization. As she recalled, "Some [teachers] did join, and they were intimidated and they had to cancel their membership."[51] May-Pittman recalled that more educators supported the movement in other ways. In this capacity, though behind the scenes, Higgins and other educators in the 1950s and 1960s were not unlike Gladys Noel Bates and the educators who stepped forth in previous decades to demand equality.

But Hill, attending school in Clarksdale, much like any other location across Mississippi, learned other truths, too. By 1964 and the advent of the Mississippi Freedom Schools, the public schools that students attended were still segregated. Black educators occupied a complicated space within the education system as well. Higgins, the same person who encouraged the formation of the NAACP, was also listed as a known informant of the Sovereignty Commission, the state-supported reconnaissance group that closely monitored civil rights activity across the state. The commission reported that Higgins was an "opportunist and was agreeing to segregation because he knew his job depended on it." At a community meeting held in Clarksdale in 1959, the commission reported that Higgins was one of several speakers who, much to their approval, "stress the fact that Negroes should want to be segregated from the whites and develop their own culture."[52] Higgins more than likely attempted to negotiate both spaces; while his true intentions are lost to history, his position illustrates the precarious position of black educators at the time of the *Brown* decision. The historically black colleges and universities in Mississippi modeled strict surveillance and punishment of civil rights activity as well. Black college presidents often threatened expulsion for any transgression of the social code and reported such activity to the Sovereignty Commission.[53] Each level of education historically exemplified what historian Carter G. Woodson lamented as the "mis-education" of African American students since the end of Reconstruction through the era of Jim Crow.[54] While students received private or hidden transcripts of resistance through a few notable educators, they also learned that some educators were complicit in maintaining state-supported segregation.

THE FREEDOM SCHOOLS AND THE CIVIL RIGHTS MOVEMENT

The Freedom Schools were both similar and oppositional to the traditions that defined the nature of public education in Mississippi. The Freedom Schools embodied long traditions of an ideology that equated education with freedom and liberation and were therefore ideologically familiar to Mississippi communities. The Freedom Schools were built upon community organization strategies that dated back to Reconstruction. Yet the Freedom Schools were markedly different. They were organized outside of the state's purview, which afforded opportunities to directly combat de jure segregation. Freedom School teachers were independent from the economic system controlled by whites and were therefore free to openly defy the segregated way of life that was cherished in Mississippi. They also adopted a radical and progressive pedagogy and curriculum that cultivated participatory notions of citizenship that were absent from most Mississippi schools. Through both continuity and rupture, the Freedom Schools constitute one of the most unique legacies of the civil rights movement and, indeed, American history.

Civil rights activists embraced the term "Freedom School" and the ideology behind it well before the Mississippi program began in 1964. The term and the concept, therefore, did not originate during the Freedom Summer project of 1964. The term "Freedom Schools" harkens back to the "Freedmen's schools" of the Reconstruction era and, indeed, drew upon the same concepts of education for liberation. Activist-oriented schools directly built on a premise of education for social change were influential as well. Myles Horton, the director of the Highlander Folk School in Monteagle, Tennessee, exerted significant influence on the pedagogical ethos of the civil rights movement. Highlander provided a safe meeting place for interracial planning meetings since 1932, where activists met to discuss strategies and adopt further plans to enact in their home communities. Workshops at Highlander were steeped in problem-based learning grounded in the students' culture. Nearly all civil rights leaders attended workshops at Highlander at one point or another during the movement, and this form of pedagogy for social and political change was adopted widely, most notably in the Citizenship Schools, the grassroots educational program founded in 1955 for adults that guided disenfranchised adults through the cumbersome and discriminatory voter registration process.[55]

The first iteration of the term "Freedom School" in the context of the modern civil rights movement, however, can be found in Mississippi. Activists in Mississippi organized a "Nonviolent High" in 1961 for nearly one hundred students who participated in a student-led protest in McComb. The idea originated in a jail cell but evolved into the state's first Freedom School, held at a local

church and the SNCC office. Activists offered classes in algebra, English, physics, geometry, and French to students expelled from school for protesting.[56] The
United Federation of Teachers (UFT) and Queens College students supported
an "adopt-a-school" program, or, as some referred to it, a "freedom school," in
Prince Edward County, Virginia, in the fall of 1963. The school provided some
form of education for African American students denied an education after the
state shut down the school system in 1959.[57] The term "Freedom School" particularly flourished in a northern and urban context by 1963. Organizers sponsored a network of Freedom Schools throughout the city of Chicago when over
two hundred thousand students boycotted the schools they attended to protest
segregation, discriminatory practices, and other failures of the state to provide
a quality education. Activists also organized Freedom Schools in churches and
community centers throughout Harlem and New York during the 1963/1964
school year as parents, teachers, and students protested unequal education.[58]
Freedom Schools in Boston were a particularly influential example that directly
preceded the schools in Mississippi. Activists organized a "stay out" in June
1963, when over three thousand students boycotted the schools, and a second
walkout in February 1964 in which nearly twenty thousand students boycotted. Noel Day, one of the key organizers in Boston, was heavily involved in
planning the Mississippi Freedom Schools.[59] The Mississippi Freedom Schools
were not the first such schools, either ideologically or in the name they used.
They were, however, the most significant network of schools that illustrated the
extent to which the civil rights movement incorporated education into its overarching goals and organization.

As indicated by the way in which the term and ideology behind the term was
applied, Freedom Schools clearly stood in stark contrast to the perennial conundrum that educators in the Magnolia State faced. Black educators were committed to the ideal of education and freedom yet were shackled by dependency
upon whites for employment. The Freedom Schools were a radical deviation
from the traditional education received in Mississippi because, unlike the black
educators in Mississippi, Freedom School teachers were volunteers and were
completely independent from white school boards and administrators. This
independence facilitated political and social autonomy through which Freedom School educators could openly and publically embrace radical political

notions that challenged entrenched forms of segregation. The fact that the volunteers were largely white, a theme examined in greater detail throughout this book, also differentiated the Freedom Schools from their local counterparts in Mississippi.

Held in untraditional spaces and taught by unorthodox teachers who were mostly white, northern, and liberal, the Freedom Schools looked unlike anything else on the Mississippi landscape in 1964. The Freedom Schools were built upon a history of education for freedom, but the context of the 1960s presented a new opportunity to actualize the promises of democracy. The goals and organization of the Freedom Schools and their place in American history illustrate the tensions, ideals, and promises that posit education for freedom was one the most salient aspects of the civil rights movement.

2

"THERE WAS SOMETHING HAPPENING"

The Civil Rights Education and Politicization
of the Freedom School Students

I knew there was something happening before those people ever came to
Clarksdale, I knew as young as when I was ten years old that there was
something happening.

HOMER HILL, FREEDOM SCHOOL STUDENT IN CLARKSDALE, MISSISSIPPI

It had been going on even before I was involved, they had the movement
going on all the time . . . there were people constantly involved.

HYMETHIA THOMPSON, FREEDOM SCHOOL STUDENT IN
TOUGALOO, MISSISSIPPI

There was something happening then. You never got bored.

BEN CHANEY, HIGH SCHOOL ACTIVIST IN MERIDIAN, MISSISSIPPI

The young people who enrolled in the Freedom Schools were, at most,
in their early teens at the beginning of the tumultuous 1960s. Growing up in Mississippi at such a formative time provided a unique perspective on the civil rights movement. Students watched television and listened
to the radio along with the American public when the Freedom Riders arrived

by an integrated bus in Jackson, Mississippi, in 1961, and when the town of Oxford erupted in flames as James Meredith desegregated the University of Mississippi in 1962. Sit-ins, citywide boycotts, and the assassination of NAACP leader Medgar Evers shook the capital city of Jackson in 1963. Americans read the headlines as over one thousand volunteers joined the Freedom Summer campaign of 1964, the largest voter registration campaign in the history of the civil rights movement. To the American public and historians since then, these events were the defining moments of the Mississippi civil rights movement. These events have received the most attention and have therefore dominated the interpretation of Mississippi civil rights history. Such a narrative situates Mississippi as a staunchly racist and conservative space with little agency for local African Americans. What the American public did not see on television or read in the newspapers was how the dialectical relationship between locally sophisticated civil rights networks and the larger national movement influenced the political socialization of young people across the state of Mississippi. There is a much longer history of locally organized black resistance to white supremacy than is usually supposed.[1] These political actors consisted of a wide spectrum of African Americans in Mississippi, including young people. Understanding how the movement educated young people as students of the civil rights movement leads to a comprehensive understanding that places young people in the center of the struggle.

As can be seen in the statements of Homer Hill, Hymethia Thompson, and Ben Chaney, the students who attended the Mississippi Freedom Schools connected to the civil rights movement through local networks well before the largely northern white volunteers moved to Mississippi during the summer of 1964. Born in the late 1940s or early 1950s, Freedom School students grew up in communities with a history of organizing for political, economic, and social equality. Learning the artful forms of resistance in the age of Jim Crow provided an unorthodox education for these students. Seeing and participating in the movement around them during the early 1960s was a version of "freedom schooling" that consisted of joining and observing major protests across the state such as the sit-ins, frequenting informal meeting spaces in churches and locally owned black businesses with civil rights leaders, and growing up in families sympathetic to the movement. This type of civil rights education formed at the nexus of the national movement and the organizations that enabled its manifestation at the local level was an important intellectual precursor to the Freedom Schools. The Freedom Schools maintained this form of education by cultivating and refining the skills these young activists already possessed.

Interpretations of the "official" civil rights movement in the Magnolia State overlook the dynamic interplay between the national and local context that educated and profoundly shaped the education of the civil right generation. Hymethia Thompson, Homer Hill, Eddie James Carthan, Brenda Travis, Arelya Mitchell, Anthony Harris, Roscoe Jones, and other students developed a political and social consciousness as young students in middle and high school that ultimately led to their decision to enroll in a Freedom School. Attending school during the civil rights movement and participating in the movement itself was a claim to knowledge and creation of critical educational spaces. Through an examination of the lives of these young people, we can see how Homer Hill's assertion that "there was something happening, the local things," situates the larger struggle within the specificity of student experiences across Mississippi. Their stories provide us a rich context with which to understand both the relevance of the Freedom Schools and the larger civil rights movement. The personal histories of the Freedom School students reveal the role of educational spaces outside of formal schools that built politically efficacious, participatory, and activist-oriented definitions of citizenship. This was facilitated through intimate engagement with their social context, their peers, multiple educational and religious institutions, their family histories, and local leaders that connected to the larger national movement and organizations like the NAACP and SNCC. Attending community meetings at local churches, canvassing the neighborhood to discuss voter registration, and marching in protests therefore constituted an informal education that taught middle and high school students how to become American citizens in a country that denied full citizenship to people of color. Examining the histories and contextual factors that led to enrolling in a Freedom School also reveals differences that complicate a monolithic understanding of the Freedom School students.

HYMETHIA WASHINGTON LOFTON THOMPSON: POLITICIZED IN THE CAPITAL CITY

The capital city of Jackson, Mississippi, was a pivotal site of resistance to segregationist policies and inequalities. Within this highly charged city, one would expect the struggle to have been uniformly embodied in African American activists. However, neither the adults nor the larger framework of the movement were so neatly contained. It spilled over and infiltrated into young people's consciousness. An insightful example of this is the story of Hymethia Thompson. She was born on March 24, 1948, in Madison, Mississippi, a small community just north of Jackson, and grew up with her younger brother, Denver. Her father was a deacon at the Missionary Union Baptist Church and also held a position with the federal government working on the Natchez Trace Parkway, which ran through Jackson. Her mother worked as an assistant for a local Native American doctor sympathetic to the movement. Despite the relative position of security, resisting the established Jim Crow culture was perilous. Deacon Washington's church was burned during the movement. As the deeds to the church and the land it rested on were never located after the fire, the city forced the congregation to relocate, uprooting generations of their family who had worshiped and remained buried there.[2] They subsequently moved closer to the capital to the "Tougaloo" neighborhood, which was named after nearby Tougaloo College, a historically black college founded in 1869. Taking advantage of their close proximity to the all-black college and the relative economic independence afforded by their positions, Thompson's parents maintained their support for the civil rights movement. At sixteen years old when the Freedom Schools opened their doors, Washington was already familiar with the nuances of black resistance that were more visibly manifest in Mississippi in the early 1960s.

Hymethia Thompson learned the art of resistance at a very young age through the neighborhood in which she grew up. "Tougaloo College was a different world in itself," Thompson recalled about her childhood neighborhood. Tougaloo College long supported the civil rights movement in Mississippi by providing a relatively safe haven for organizers and students committed fully to the struggle for equality. Because of its distance from the city, Tougaloo College was afforded some protection from white segregationists who sought to violently repress any civil rights activity. As a historically black college, Tougaloo was in a position to lend instrumental support to the movement or to serve, as Aldon Morris described it, as a movement center that could mobilize, organize, and coordinate activity among a particular population aimed at achieving a particular political aim.[3] Tougaloo College, in this instance, "supplied the foot soldiers, intellectual leadership, and safe places to meet and plan civil disobedience."[4]

The college served as a notable point of origin for the most visible aspects of the movement in May 1961 when police arrested nine Tougaloo students for attempting to integrate the Jackson Municipal Public Library. "The Tougaloo Nine" captured local attention, and their action served as an important precursor to the Freedom Rides.[5] The sit-in marked the beginning of direct-action, nonviolent protest in Jackson, and students remained fully committed to building a network of activism. "We too have a commitment and a task to perform," Joyce Ladner, a student activist and leader from Tougaloo, reminded her classmates in January 1963. "We must not only give lip service but we must feel the pressing need to place our bodies, skills and talents in the Struggle."[6] College activists also organized the Mississippi Council on Human Relations, whose purpose was "to carry on an educational program directed toward creating a climate of opinion favorable to an expansion of opportunity for all the people of Mississippi, in economic, civil and cultural areas based on freedom from discrimination on grounds of race, religion or national origin."[7] Moreover, activist administrators at Tougaloo College, including white president Adam Beittel and sociology professor and German-Jewish immigrant Ernst Borinski, fostered a network of local intellectuals that promoted resistance to the status quo.[8] Tougaloo College and the atmosphere of activism it engendered contextualized Hymethia Thompson's childhood, teaching her how to actively challenge the discrimination she encountered.

The fact that Jackson housed three predominantly black colleges figured prominently in the city's civil rights history. The Tougaloo sit-in set a new standard for the black colleges across the capital city. Events at Tougaloo had a strong impact on the black students at Jackson State College and Campbell

College, in addition to a liberal contingent at Millsaps College, an all-white college in the city. In a movement organized and mobilized by youths, the students from these colleges provided crucial input as the movement unfolded. Though initially a conservative campus, Jackson State College eventually took up the banner for civil rights.[9] Both Jackson State and Campbell took on the civil rights cause and pushed each other through competition to "out struggle" one another. As a result of the fortuitous location of these local colleges, student activism was well organized between 1960 and 1964 and tended to focus on library sit-ins, kneel-ins at Jackson churches, pray-ins on federal property to protest police brutality, pickets at the segregated county fair, boycotts of Jackson stores, protests at segregated lunch counters, and organizing civil rights groups like the Cultural and Activist Agitation Committee, which demanded integration of the city's cultural events.[10] The college students in Jackson, in other words, influenced young students like Hymethia Thompson and taught young people an important model to follow.

Civil rights organization was not limited to the institutions of higher learning in Jackson. As a resident of the state capital of Mississippi, Thompson was also exposed to the work of the NAACP. The NAACP gained strength in Mississippi when Medgar Evers became the first NAACP field secretary there in 1954. After returning from service in the Second World War, Evers was the first black applicant to the University of Mississippi Law School in January 1954. His application earned him the respect and notice of the national office, which had a vested interest in building the NAACP presence in Mississippi, a state that was not as organized as others.[11] Appointed as the first NAACP field secretary to Mississippi in December, Evers mobilized the city of Jackson and strengthened the state's NAACP infrastructure. He provided instrumental legal help to activists who were arrested in Jackson and the central part of the state. Evers was responsible for locating attorneys, publicizing activities, lobbying for federal intervention and protection, documenting poverty across the state, getting victims and witnesses to testify and file lawsuits, and supporting local civil rights efforts.[12]

As Evers worked feverishly in Mississippi, he recognized the instrumental role of young people in the organization. "We realize fully that the success of this great organization lies with the men and women of tomorrow. It is our hope that success with the youth will inspire the hearts of others, so that in the ensuing years we will see the dawn of a bright tomorrow as a result of the birth and growth of more Youth Councils in Mississippi." Evers went on to write that "the fine support of the Youth Councils shall be used as a stepping stone toward our goal of first-class citizenship."[13] The youth councils that Evers referred to were the product of the NAACP's organization of young people across the country. Since 1935, the NAACP actively organized youth councils and recruited young people in middle and high school to work with the organization, attend state and national conferences, and raise critical awareness about legal and political solutions to racial discrimination.[14] Youth councils throughout Mississippi provided an informal introduction to the movement through dynamic leaders like Medgar Evers. At the age of twenty-nine, and with a demonstrated record of radical activism, Evers was closer in age and disposition to young people than the more established leadership.[15] For Hymethia Thompson and other young people, Medgar Evers was a role model and, despite his busy schedule, a confidant to her and her peers. She rode to church with Evers the week before Byron De La Beckwith, a local Ku Klux Klan (KKK) and Citizens' Council member, gunned Evers down in the driveway of his home on June 12, 1963.[16]

Hymethia Thompson and her peers also witnessed firsthand the direct-action protests in Jackson that captured national headlines in 1961. The Freedom Ride campaign attempted to desegregate buses and bus terminals along the route through the Deep South, from Washington, D.C., to New Orleans. The Freedom Riders tested the Interstate Commerce Commission's decision to desegregate interstate transportation facilities. The bus never reached New Orleans in its first attempt; it was firebombed and attacked in Anniston, Alabama, and all riders were either beaten or arrested.[17] With national media attention upon them, Freedom Riders organized more bus trips, and the next major stop was Jackson. When the twenty-seven riders landed in Jackson on May 24, 1961, police arrested them immediately and threw the activists in jail from then until late August.[18] But by the time the Freedom Riders had reached Jackson, SNCC had planned to maintain momentum, and by the end of May 1961 police had arrested twenty-five more Freedom Riders for attempting to integrate the Jackson Greyhound bus terminal.[19] As came to be typical of movement activity in Mississippi, all of the riders were arrested and put in jail. Each rider was convicted of a breach of peace, fined two hundred dollars, and sentenced to sixty days in jail. The riders, following an informal "jail, no bail" principle, refused to post bond and opted to stay in jail in order to draw attention to their struggle instead.[20]

Mississippi authorities prided themselves on their quick, quiet, and efficient removal of the agitators from the public eye. They insisted that the Freedom Rides, or "the incidents," occurred with "no attention being paid to them."[21] But contrary to the news reported in the Jackson *Clarion-Ledger*, many people in Mississippi were closely following the Freedom Rides news reports. One such viewer was thirteen-year-old Hezekiah Watkins, who lived in Jackson with his mother and attended Rowan Middle School. "In 1961 when the demonstrators in Alabama were being shown on TV, they were being beaten, hosed by water, spit on, dogs chasing them," Watkins recalled. "We received the nightly news and that was always shown and everybody was saying, 'don't get involved.'"[22] That the Freedom Riders were coming to Jackson generated great excitement among Watkins and his peers. Out of curiosity, Watkins and a friend attended a local meeting at the Masonic Temple in Jackson that discussed supporting the Freedom Riders. In the demonstration that followed, Watkins inadvertently stood in the white-only part of the terminal, and Jackson police arrested him along with the Freedom Riders (figure 2.1). The police escorted Watkins, just thirteen years old, to Parchman Farm, the notorious Mississippi State Penitentiary, where he stayed for a couple of days until the governor, upon learning his age, ordered that he be released. "And believe it or not I did not want to get involved," Watkins recalled just after the fiftieth anniversary of the Freedom Rides. "I was just nosey. I could say being at the wrong place at the wrong time and basically what happened to me was being nosey. Thereafter, after I realized what the cause was all about, I wanted to be a part of it."[23] Demonstrations like the Freedom Rides were very influential in inspiring students still in middle and high school to join the civil rights movement. From this moment on in Mississippi, every activist who worked in the state would be known as a "Freedom Rider" or a "Freedom Fighter," whether he or she were involved in the Freedom Rides or not.[24]

The ongoing national movement influenced young students in Mississippi to organize protests on their own. In May 1963, Hezekiah Watkins and Hymethia Thompson participated in a school walkout with over five hundred of their peers. Students walked out of their schools to protest legal segregation and to

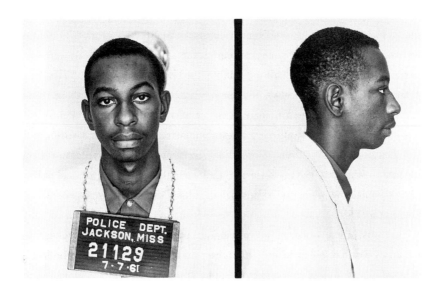

FIGURE 2.1   Hezekiah Watkins, photograph upon arrest, July 7, 1961.
(Courtesy of Eric Etheridge)

join the local efforts connected to organized protests in downtown Jackson. In a coordinated effort, nearly all of the students attending the three black high schools in Jackson—Brinkley, Jim Hill, and Lanier—coordinated a walkout. Hezekiah Watkins, politicized at an early age after his experience at Parchman, remembered the walkout in historic terms:

> We were able to organize the three high schools and at noon we were going to walk out and we did this within less than a week and the word just traveled just like a wildfire. I'm told that we had 90 percent of the student body walk out of the school and we walked down the highway. Some of us were arrested and some of us weren't. Each school did not know what the other school was going to do. . . . But it happened and we made history that day.[25]

The police force was not strong enough to handle the large walkout. City police arrested and placed the young protesters in the livestock pens at the state fairgrounds because the jails were overcrowded and the mayor hesitated to incarcerate youth in Parchman Farm. The experience was dehumanizing for the young protesters. "I remember walking out of Brinkley High School and we were put in a garbage truck and were taken to the fairgrounds down there until our parents came and got us," Hymethia Thompson recalled of a student protest. "Mississippi police wanted our parents to force us to sign a statement saying we would never participate in any more demonstrations."[26] It was not uncommon for Jackson police to arrest demonstrators of any age during the city's largest demonstrations, such as those connected with the Freedom Rides, the school-walk out, and marches with Dr. Martin Luther King Jr. Local police often detained the marchers in the stock pavilions of the county fairgrounds or "temporary jail facilities."[27]

Boycotts, school walkouts, and attempts to integrate the public spaces across the city constituted a form of civil rights education that shaped the budding political consciousness of students in Jackson. The location of three black college campuses in the state capital and a strong black business district ensured that Jackson would be a headquarters of the civil rights movement. What emerged by 1963, then, was a strong local movement that received national attention and housed a critical base within the capital city that included middle and high school students. The protests in Jackson prepared the city's youth and laid important groundwork for planning the Freedom Summer campaign, from which the Freedom Schools developed. The events in Jackson did not define the way of life for the majority of the state, however. Residing in the largest city in the state afforded certain privileges and a degree of safety that was unknown in the most rural parts of the state, particularly in the region to the northwest that was notorious for its hostility toward African Americans—the Mississippi Delta.

HOMER HILL AND EDDIE JAMES CARTHAN: COMING OF AGE IN THE MISSISSIPPI DELTA

Jackson has held a special place in the imagination of the civil rights movement and local Mississippi organizing. The Freedom Rides, the organized protest that stemmed from the cluster of historically black colleges, the NAACP, and other civil rights activity, figured prominently as Mississippi blacks mobilized to challenge Jim Crow. But Jackson was just one fixed point in the history of activism that predated the Freedom Schools. Homer Hill and Eddie James Carthan grew up outside the gaze of the national media and beyond the modicum of tolerance for civil rights activity permitted within the capital. Students who entered the movement in the Delta were introduced to it within a very different context. Students across the Delta also grew up in a region that harbored its own forms of white resistance. This northwestern section of the state, bordered by the Mississippi River on its western edge, was home to the first chapters of the notorious Citizens' Council, a popular segregationist organization formed in 1954 that employed economic intimidation to avoid desegregation.[28] Furthermore, though many were too young to recall personally, white terrorists had kidnapped and brutally murdered Emmett Till in the small town of Money in the southeastern corner of the Delta in 1955. Growing up in a region fraught with terror and distant from the protections offered by the larger urban centers, local leaders played an instrumental role in introducing students in the Delta to the movement.

Homer Hill was born in Clarksdale, Mississippi, on June 29, 1949. His grandmother and mother raised him, along with his younger sister. Hill's mother was a teacher and the daughter of a principal.[29] Hill was mostly raised in a section of Clarksdale called the "Brickyard," several blocks away from the town center. "I lived in a black world that hardly ever intersected with the whites in the city, outside of some forms of employment and patronages to some of the businesses," Hill recalled about his childhood in the Mississippi Delta.[30] Those who grew up in the region recall tight social, political, and economic control. Yet growing up in the small urban center of Clarksdale afforded certain opportunities that, even in the Delta, provided a different way of life. Clarksdale was a larger city of over twenty-four thousand people.[31] Though only half the size of the capital, Clarksdale was a haven of sorts from the most rural parts of the Delta and the long history of terror and segregation associated with them.

Politically, living in the town of Clarksdale provided more exposure to civil rights organization than the Delta's more rural areas. The civil rights movement and organization that unfolded across the Delta occurred under the auspices of local leaders, in particular Aaron Henry, a prominent black pharmacist who owned the Fourth Street Drug Store in Clarksdale and president of the Coahoma County branch of the NAACP, and Vera Pigee, a civic leader in the local branch of the NAACP and local business owner. Their organization generated a plethora of organizations that mobilized the local population to act. Clarksdale was home to both the Coahoma County Progressive Voters League and the Coahoma County Negro Citizens Associations in the early 1950s. Local organizers also established the NAACP in 1952 and elected Henry to serve as the Mississippi state president that same year.[32] Aaron Henry organized a chapter of the Southern Christian Leadership Conference (SCLC) in the Delta and formed the Coahoma County Federated Council of Organizations (CCFCO).[33] The CCFCO was an important precursor to the Council of Federated Organizations (COFO), the umbrella organization that orchestrated the massive Freedom Summer campaign of 1964.[34]

As the events of the civil rights movement were rarely discussed in black segregated public schools, Henry and Pigee served as informal movement teachers. Homer Hill and his peers met Pigee through her organizational work with the NAACP Youth Council in Clarksdale. Beginning in the early 1950s, but increasingly after the death of Emmett Till, Pigee organized for the NAACP in Clarksdale and opened her beauty parlor as a civil rights meeting place and a Citizenship School.[35] Pigee and Henry organized local parents to push for desegregation immediately after the *Brown* decision and spearheaded an effort to file over four hundred desegregation cases in the local courts. Henry's pharmacy and the activity of the NAACP had long been known, especially since he had brought in well-known and popular movement people, such as comedian Dick Gregory, who organized massive donation drives to Clarksdale and Greenwood.[36] Homer Hill, growing up in the midst of movement activity in Clarksdale, worked as a young man in the Fourth Street Drug Store. His mother was a close friend and former classmate of Aaron Henry, further strengthening the bond that Hill developed with the larger civil rights community.[37] Moreover, the spaces Henry and Pigee maintained, the pharmacy and beauty parlor in downtown Clarksdale, created relatively safe places for youth and adults in the community to meet to organize, discuss strategies of ongoing campaigns, and plan upcoming events. These spaces were centrally located and became an important part of the social fabric and life of the community.[38] They were also close to Haven Methodist Church, a congregation that included the Hill family.[39] Under the leadership of the Reverend Theodore Trammell, the church became a regular meeting place for the civil rights movement.[40] Connections like this brought young students across Clarksdale in close proximity to local leaders who reinforced, personified, and connected the larger national movement that unfolded across the country to their own private lives.

The confluence of leadership in Clarksdale translated into several modes of activism available to the students of the movement. For Hill and other youths across the state, the Youth Council of the NAACP meant that students were politically engaged at a young age through an organization outside of school. As Vera Pigee recalled about working with the NAACP Youth Council in Clarksdale: "We worked from 1955 to 1959 [through] unpopular membership campaigning—door to door, beauty shops, barber shops, civil and social groups, individual and churches when possible—to bolster youth memberships in the NAACP."[41] This laid important and instrumental groundwork that facilitated increasing youth participation in the early 1960s. With the influx of white volunteers in the state for the Freedom Vote campaign in 1963, Clarksdale experienced its first sustained experiment in nonviolent direct-action protest. Young students in Clarksdale flocked to the opportunity. "One Saturday," Hill recalled of some of the activity associated with the NAACP Youth Council, "we had demonstrated at the local Woolworths, and it was because of Aaron Henry that they didn't put us in jail."[42] Hill referred to one of the many demonstrations that occurred during the late summer and fall of 1963. Young African Americans organized a sit-in at a segregated lunch counter downtown, organized kneel-ins at local white churches, and marched and distributed leaflets in downtown Clarksdale the year before the summer campaign of 1964. Throughout the waves of direct-action protests that upset the typically quiet and calm city landscape, Clarksdale police arrested and convicted nearly one hundred youthful demonstrators and activists on various charges.[43]

Still, Clarksdale did not epitomize the experience of the Delta in its entirety. "There was some violence," Hill recalled of growing up in Clarksdale, "but nothing like what you would find in a place like Sunflower, or Ruleville, or some of the smaller, former plantations in the area where there was a need to be much more overt in terms of control."[44] These small towns were forty and fifty miles south of Clarksdale, deeper in the Delta interior, and residents there experienced a different form of organization—and terror.

Eddie James Carthan was born in one such town in the Delta, Mileston, Mississippi, on October 18, 1948. The nearest incorporated town is Tchula, six miles to the north, which is a small town of about eight hundred people deep in the Mississippi Delta.[45] When recalling what it was like to grow up in this part of the Delta, a land he still calls home, hard work is an important theme. "We all worked picking cotton, plowed, sunup to sundown. Six years old. Worked like a slave. I thought that it was the way it's supposed to be. Didn't know any better." Mileston closely resembled the land and type of community where Emmett Till was killed. Deeper in the Delta and outside of the small Tchula community, Carthan recalled: "It was hot, no fans, just sitting there and just suffering, some of the poorest conditions that I have ever seen in my life, people living like they were, you know, holes in the floor, standing shotgun houses, some sights were awful. Old people lying in the bed sick. . . . Just laying there sweating, sick, flies, you know, it was quite an experience to see how my folk were living and suffering."[46]

Elsewhere across the Delta, students in Drew, Indianola, and Ruleville similarly observed and experienced firsthand the brutal reality of what it meant to be black in the segregated South. Since the low percentage of black land-ownership guaranteed that large numbers of African Americans across rural Mississippi worked *for* somebody, many blacks were vulnerable to debt accumulation and protracted servitude, as dictated by Jim Crow social customs. In the rural parts of the Delta and, indeed, across the state, black laborers still worked six or seven days a week, usually from early morning until late afternoon or early evening.

Carthan also experienced forms of activism afforded by economic independence. Since 1935, the Mileston community had received support from the federal government through the Farm Security Administration, an antipoverty program established by Congress as part of Franklin Delano Roosevelt's New Deal. Carthan's grandfather was one of over one hundred farmers who purchased their own land with a loan from the program. Land ownership was rare. From the New Deal to the end of the Jim Crow era, only 15 percent of the state's black farmers owned the land they farmed.[47] As a result of the cooperatives that black landowners established during this period, the Mileston community owned its own community center, shops for tools and feed, and a cotton gin, among other businesses.[48] The cooperatives also embraced, by their very nature, a democratic form of governance that Carthan remembered very well. The cooperatives met weekly, and Carthan attended the meetings with his grandfather as a child. The independent landowners in Mileston served as the basis for meetings for the duration of the freedom movement.[49] The rural landscape lent itself to different forms of political activity than the political organization that unfolded in Clarksdale, Jackson and other cities across the state. Carthan and activists in the area met in a rural church on an unpaved road leading out further into the country, a scene quite different from the beauty parlor and pharmacy in Clarksdale.

Because of young people's connections with locally established civil rights leadership like Henry and Pigee, the presence of organizations like the NAACP, and a rich history of cooperatives, organizing and participating in the civil rights movement was a legitimate and viable choice for the civil rights generation as they came of age during the 1960s. As civil rights organizers from outside the state began to organize in Mississippi during the summer of 1964, this local network of activism provided strong social and political networks that facilitated young people's participation on the front lines of the movement.

BRENDA TRAVIS: YOUTH ORGANIZING YOUTH IN SOUTHWEST MISSISSIPPI

As demonstrated in the Mississippi Delta, political organization occurred well outside the networks found in the capital city. Organizations such as those found in the Delta, served interests unique to their respective localities, and they introduced the future Freedom School students to the civil rights movement at an early age. But not every region in Mississippi experienced such a long history of activism. In the southwest corner of the state, young high school students initiated the first attempts to orchestrate a local civil rights movement through direct-action, nonviolent protests. The history of the local civil rights movement in McComb is significant as it illuminates the critical role of youth in the movement, particularly where civil rights organizations did not autonomously organize youth. One student who illustrates the role of youth in facilitating the growth of the civil rights movement is Brenda Travis.

Travis was born on March 16, 1945, in McComb, Mississippi. She was a sixteen-year-old student at Burgland High School, a black school built in 1957 as part of the state's so-called equalization attempts, when she first encountered direct-action protests in August 1961.[50] But Brenda Travis's and her peers' foray into the civil rights movement has deeper roots, and her entrée into the movement illustrates the ways in which college-aged students facilitated direct-action, nonviolent demonstrations through locally established leadership. The events of 1961 that captivated young peoples' imagination were built upon a network of NAACP activity. C. C. Bryant, a local worker on the Illinois Central Railroad, became the NAACP president of the McComb branch in 1955 and boosted membership that had lagged since its inception in 1944. Following patterns across the state, the NAACP members in McComb became active in the mid-1950s by petitioning to enter all-white schools soon after the *Brown* decision, which local whites quickly ended through intimidation.[51] Like other local leaders across the state, Bryant served in many professional capacities and reached a wide audience in a number of ways. He was a preacher at nearby Society Hill Baptist Church, where he introduced many local people to the ideology of organizing. "[C. C. Bryant] prompting people every Sunday was my motivating force," Brenda Travis later recalled of the factors that influenced her activism in the early 1960s.[52]

Bryant was representative of the traditional NAACP leadership in Mississippi, but he was different in that he actively sought and invited younger radical activists to organize in McComb and the surrounding areas. Bryant invited Bob Moses, a twenty-five-year-old Harvard philosophy major and Harlem math educator who sought to organize voters in Mississippi, to McComb after reading about his work in *Jet* magazine. Moses had volunteered with the SCLC and quickly grew frustrated with the pace of change and its ambivalence toward nonviolent direct-action protest, among other issues. Ella Baker, a kindred spirit who understood the frustration of dealing with bureaucracy and interfactional dissonance, introduced Moses to Amzie Moore, then vice president of Mississippi's NAACP branches in neighboring Amite County. Through Amzie Moore, Moses met C. C. Bryant and thereby gained entrée into the local McComb community.[53] By way of Bryant's invitation, Moses entered an entrenched activist community and became privy to the history, traditions, and culture of the movement unique to the area. This was the local network that he was searching for.

Moses represented the direct-action activity associated with and inspired by the sit-ins of 1960 and Freedom Rides of 1961. He was a part of SNCC, the newest civil rights organization that had formed in the wake of the sit-ins. This form of direct action had not emerged yet in McComb, although such protests like the Freedom Riders in Jackson, which was seventy miles to the north, received national attention. Local people were more interested in voter registration, and Moses followed suit. Moses began organizing in the small town of Liberty. After a month of door-to-door canvassing and the support of an NAACP youth group and a voter registration school at the house of E. W. Steptoe, a leader in the local NAACP chapter, about twenty people marched to the courthouse to register. Approximately ten people passed the required literacy tests and other arbitrary examinations imposed upon African American applicants. Moses was badly beaten and thrown in jail as a result, but he managed to frighten local segregationists when he called the Justice Department for support.[54]

Brenda Travis met Moses through C. C. Bryant and was thereby introduced to the civil rights movement during this voter registration drive. As Travis recalled, the voter registration classes reached out to those interested in voting, but the focus of the classes eventually shifted toward organizing for civil disobedience, which included learning how to protect oneself from segregationists during nonviolent demonstrations.[55] Her first form of civil rights education was learning the art of resistance from the established leaders in the area, but this was supplemented with direct-action protest when Hollis Watkins and Curtis Hayes, among other young college students, joined the organizing efforts in McComb in the aftermath of the Freedom Rides. Brenda Travis joined Watkins and Hayes in August 1961 as they sat-in at the local Greyhound bus terminal and the local Woolworths, the first direct-action, nonviolent protests in the area. Local police promptly arrested the young activists, and a judge sentenced them to thirty days in jail.[56]

When local authorities released Travis after she served her sentence, the local school board refused to admit her back into school and the principal subsequently expelled her.[57] The expulsion angered her classmates at Burgland High School. Expelling Travis added fuel to the fire because students were already incensed by the recent murder of Herbert Lee, a local farmer and member of the NAACP who was gunned down by E. H. Hurst of Hattiesburg, a representative in the Mississippi state legislature. Upon word of Travis's expulsion, Burgland students organized a walkout, triggered by her friend Joe Lewis who inquired at a school-wide assembly as to why Travis was expelled. Over one hundred students boycotted, walking out of the school in protest and carrying signs and singing "We Shall Overcome," much to the dismay of local whites.[58] Burgland High School students marched to the local Masonic Temple, demanded action, and the civil rights crowd that soon gathered began the fateful march to City Hall. It was an exhilarating experience for Travis, who felt vindicated for her recent expulsion by her classmates' support. "I felt exhilarated, triumphant, here I had people behind me and it was just a good feeling, it was feeling like someone was embracing me and believing the way I felt, that things needed to change," Travis recalled.[59] As inspiring as it was for Travis, who was already exposed to the terrors of being in prison, some students who entered the movement for the first time through the walkout experienced it differently. Eloise Carter, a Burgland High School student who walked out, experienced this moment of protest as a "nightmare" as she was confronted by "policemen with big chains around their wrists, their weapons drawn, batons and German Shepherd dogs."[60] The march inspired a visceral and violent reaction from local white segregationists. SNNC organizer Bob Zellner in particular, but others as well, was brutally and savagely beaten by the white mob that formed around them.[61]

Local authorities threw the book at the students. The school board expelled those who did not sign a statement against the civil rights movement, and the local courts gave a maximum fine to those arrested. Yet Brenda Travis, at the age of sixteen, fared the worst and bore a heavy punishment for participating in the walkout. Travis's age and status as a legal minor did little to soften the blow levied by local authorities. She was charged as a minor, convicted as a delinquent, and ordered to attend Oakley Training School.

She spent over six months in the reformatory school before moving to Alabama.[62] To be expelled by the local school board, subsequently uprooted, and essentially run out of town was a dramatic experience for Travis, as it would be for any student. The incident sent a powerful message to other young people who put themselves on the front lines of the civil rights movement through the school walkout.

Young people in the first wave of direct-action, nonviolent protests in 1961 also established the first antecedents to the Freedom Schools. Similar to the development of other Freedom Schools across the country, Burgland High School students and their SNCC mentors organized an early precursor of the Freedom Schools for expelled students. Chuck McDew remembered being in the cell with Bob Moses when they "took the responsibility of teaching the kids that were in the jails. I would discuss the history of black people and Jews. Bob gave classes in mathematics."[63] Students in middle and high school were expelled from school after their release from jail, since only a handful signed the statement offered by police that denounced all movement participation. As McDew recalled, the "students had made a decision that they would pay the price." SNCC organizers supported them and opened "Nonviolent High" in a local Baptist church and the SNCC office, which was held in the Masonic Temple. They expanded the lessons taught in the jail cell, with Moses teaching math, Dion Diamond teaching physics and biology, and Chuck McDew teaching history and courses called "Problems of Democracy." As McDew recalled:

> We taught them about the need to vote and the exercise of political power. We tried to politicize them, hoping they would start talking to their parents about the same sorts of things. We introduced to them the idea of the necessity of them teaching older people who couldn't read or couldn't write or couldn't count, and were being cheated [and] to share what they had learned with people who were around them.[64]

Once released from jail, nearly one hundred kids participated in the one-room schoolhouse that offered classes in algebra, English, physics, geometry, and French. Campbell College in Jackson eventually opened its doors to the students to provide a more sustained education.[65] Denied an education by the state of Mississippi, student activists and committed organizers pulled together the resources needed to provide an education to those who went without during the waves of protest that shook McComb. The organizers learned from the process of organizing Nonviolent High as well. "We set up school," McDew recalled, "which was an education for us, too. We recognized how systematic the school system is in messing up the minds of children."[66] When activists organized the Freedom Summer campaign three years later, the experience in McComb made them aware of the sentiment supporting alternative education, knowledge of the importance of setting up Freedom Schools, and, more importantly, traditions of self-help that would support the development of alternative schools such as the Freedom Schools.[67] This model of a Freedom School, a parallel institution that filled the void when students walked out or were denied an education by the public school, emerged as a popular idea during the fall of 1964 after the Freedom Summer campaign.

As high school students, Brenda Travis and her fellow students looked up to Hollis Watkins and Curtis Hayes, who were indeed young at the time of the arrests, just nineteen years old. "We were the old guys," Bob Zellner recalled about a meeting held at the Masonic Temple in McComb before marching to City Hall, "I was all of twenty-one, and maybe [Charles] McDew and [Bob] Moses, a little older."[68] Organizing young people had tremendous implications for the local movement in McComb. Bob Moses and other organizers felt compelled to intervene and stop the student marches. High schoolers were too young, many reasoned, and it was more difficult to gain the trust of parents and cautious adults in McComb when young people were arrested, especially for those unfamiliar with the work of the college-aged students. "We did not want to have the parents alienated," McDew, the SNCC chairperson at the time, recalled. "We didn't want the parents to feel that we were using their kids."[69] However, students in McComb became the energetic force that pushed the movement forward. As McDew recalled, "It was only after we started working with the kids that we got the large groups of people to go down and attempt to register."[70] Similar to the Jackson protests organized by high school students, the McComb protests solidified commitment to the movement and generated fundamental support for further civil rights activity.

ANTHONY HARRIS: RAISED IN THE PRINCIPLES
OF THE HATTIESBURG MOVEMENT

Organizing in Mississippi in the years leading up to the Freedom Summer campaign was not a monolithic enterprise. The level of activity in Hattiesburg in Forrest County, located in southeastern Mississippi, illustrates the groundwork established around voter registration and federal involvement, which were two key factors that shaped the Freedom Summer campaign of 1964. Hattiesburg was neither dominated by a black majority, as was the case in various Delta towns and communities, nor marked by the deep-seated poverty that defined much of rural Mississippi.

Anthony Harris was born on October 26, 1953, and, like all African American children in Mississippi, he grew up learning the evils of segregation as well as the means to challenge it. Harris remembered taking trips "downtown shopping with my granddad, and whenever a white person approached us, we were required to step off to the side more and lower our heads." He went on to recall:

> We went to this dairy place that served ice cream, and they had two windows, one for coloreds and one for whites, and it did not matter if the white line only had one person or there was nobody at the white line and the colored line was maybe eight, nine, or ten people deep. We were not allowed to go to the white lane for service. We had to always stay in the colored line because the laws of Jim Crowism demanded that this was your place.[71]

Harris learned the tragic tale of Clyde Kennard, a Korean War veteran who had been born and raised in Hattiesburg. Kennard attempted to enroll, unsuccessfully, several times at Mississippi Southern College (now the University of Southern Mississippi). State authorities arrested Kennard on fabricated charges of stealing chicken feed and sentenced him to seven years at the state's Parchman Farm. While in prison, doctors diagnosed Kennard with cancer. He was initially refused treatment in prison, and authorities continued to subject him to forced labor. After his health deteriorated further, the state permitted medical attention, and Harris's father helped drive Kennard back to Hattiesburg from a hospital in Jackson. Kennard died in 1963, and Harris was raised hearing the story of Kennard like others learned of the tragic fate of Emmett Till.[72] Harris was thus exposed, like all young people in Mississippi, to the brutal realities of segregation.

Harris's family, like other families across the state, also informally educated their children in the organization of the movement. His mother, Daisy Harris, was a secretary of the NAACP and worked with CORE, SNCC, and SCLC throughout the 1960s. She raised her children in the principles of the movement. "The civil rights movement and Daisy Harris were made for each other," her son Anthony recalled. "She participated in marches, transported marchers, cooked meals for marchers, put marchers up in her homes, and raised bail money to get marchers out of jail."[73] Harris's mother exemplifies the action and commitment of local leaders across the state and, as a significant influence over her children, explains how familial support was critical in ushering young people to the front lines of the movement. Anthony Harris grew up knowing local grassroots leaders such as Vernon Dahmer. Dahmer was a local NAACP leader with a reputation that bordered on militancy. He owned his own farm, a successful sawmill, and a small country store that gave him independence from white employment. Much to the chagrin of established NAACP leadership, after the incident in McComb, Dahmer invited Curtis Hayes and Hollis Watkins of SNCC to live on his farm and to assist in voter registration work in Forrest County.[74]

White resistance in Hattiesburg, much like other locales across the Magnolia State, was visibly located in policies that systematically excluded people of color from voting. For many activists in the movement, the town's registrar, Theron Lynd, a three-hundred-pound former football player and proud Citizens' Council member, epitomized white resistance in the age of Jim Crow. Lynd blatantly refused to register African Americans. He was an oppositional figure who activists organized against, particularly after the Justice Department filed a suit in 1961. The Federal Circuit Court of Appeals issued an injunction against him in the case *United States v. Lynd* (1961), which prohibited Lynd from engaging in further discriminatory practices as a registrar. It was one of the few instances the federal government intervened on behalf of the right of black citizens to vote, but Lynd still failed to comply. Hayes, Watkins, and Dahmer organized the Forrest County Voters League in protest and launched one of the largest voter registration campaigns prior to the Freedom Vote project in the fall of 1963, the organizational precursor to the Freedom Summer campaign. Victoria Gray, a successful business owner, parent-teacher association member, and local church leader who defined local leadership with Dahmer, led the organization, and helped broaden the grassroots support in and around Hattiesburg.[75]

Voting, voter education, and the right to vote became a focal point of organizing in Hattiesburg in the early 1960s. This is exemplified by the fact that Hattiesburg was home to the first "Freedom Day" in Mississippi. Rather than register individually or in small groups, organizers with experience in voter registration reasoned that larger groups could register to vote while others peacefully marched outside the courthouse. The federal injunction made Hattiesburg a logical location for the first Freedom Day, which was held on January 22, 1964. Though the registrar permitted few to take the exam necessary to register, over two hundred people demonstrated outside the courthouse, state and national news outlets covered the event, and activists and clergy from across the nation traveled to Hattiesburg to assist in registering voters.[76] The Freedom Day in Hattiesburg provided a model that was replicated across the state. In particular, the strategic use of whites from outside Mississippi and the national media were distinguishing aspects that organizers sought to use during the summer of 1964. In addition to serving as a precursor to the Freedom Summer campaign, the voter registration project shaped the early politicization of young people growing up in Hattiesburg.

ARELYA MITCHELL: GROWING UP WITH THE MOVEMENT IN HOLLY SPRINGS

A cross section of the state reveals the importance of institutions of higher education such as Tougaloo College, the role of local leaders involved with the NAACP such as Aaron Henry and Vera Pigee in Clarksdale, and the audacity of young students such as Brenda Travis, who sought the support of SNCC and challenged them to bring the civil rights movement to the corners of Mississippi they called home. The students who enrolled in a Freedom School in Holly Springs, Mississippi, had already benefited from the same sources of activism as other students across the state. The history of the students in Holly Springs also illustrates how areas experienced growth in civil rights activities as a result of the confluence of the presence of the NAACP, a local college, and the infusion of SNCC activists.

Arelya Mitchell grew up in Holly Springs, the county seat of Marshall County in northern Mississippi. The town is also home to Rust College, a historically black college established in 1866, the oldest historically black college in Mississippi and the second-oldest private college in the state. Her father, Dr. W. B. Mitchell, one of the first African Americans to graduate from the University of Kansas, was a professor of business at the college and served as the chair of the department. Dr. Mitchell was also treasurer of the local NAACP and the cofounder of the Northern Mississippi Voters' League.[77]

Like Tougaloo College in Jackson, Rust College figured prominently in the development of the local movement in Holly Springs. Living near a black college afforded Arelya Mitchell and her father opportunities to observe firsthand the principles of the civil rights movement. Rust College provided a safe haven like that of Tougaloo College, which engendered an ideology that challenged segregationist policy in Mississippi. Growing up in the interracial environment facilitated by an integrated faculty, Mitchell remembered being immersed in conversations dominated by politics that introduced her to the civil rights movement. Particularly when white volunteers began to live in town during Freedom Summer, Mitchell remembered "being in the middle of [the movement]. We had a lot of political discussions about Khrushchev and all of that, communism, socialism, capitalism."[78] This intellectual environment fostered a political consciousness that characterized a freedom movement education. The environment at Rust also facilitated a strong civil rights network. Like other student activists throughout Mississippi, Mitchell met Dr. Martin Luther King Jr. on one of his several visits to the state. She also remembered meeting A. G. Gaston, a black millionaire from Birmingham, Alabama.[79] The location of her home and the position her father held at Rust College played significantly in Mitchell's eventual decision to attend a Freedom School. As she recalled, "Rust College was sort of the headquarters for the Freedom School people, and so naturally [my father] would want me involved and to go to the Freedom School."[80] As Mitchell recalled, being exposed to the movement through social and familial connections made it natural for her to attend the schools.

Holly Springs developed in ways similar to other locations across the state, with a foundation laid by the NAACP and younger activists who practiced direct-action, nonviolent protests beginning in the early 1960s. Locals established a branch of the NAACP in Holly Springs and Marshall County in 1957. Mitchell's father was very active in the NAACP, which brought her family in close contact with the aforementioned civil rights dignitaries.[81] This network of local leadership facilitated the most visible aspects of the movement, especially once SNCC activists established a more permanent presence in Holly Springs.[82] The town was galvanized around desegregating public spaces and increasing voter registration in the early 1960s when Willie Peacock, a Rust College student, organized a sit-in at the local theater. SNCC continued to organize in the area under the work and leadership of Frank Smith, a SNCC field secretary, who increased efforts to register voters. Medgar Evers established the NAACP Youth Council in 1962 and targeted youth in the growing Holly Springs movement.[83] This local movement that included NAACP organization, the intellectual freedom of a black college, and the development of direct-action protests in the early 1960s increasingly prepared the town for hosting workers and programs during the 1964 Freedom Summer campaign. In a culmination of local civil rights activities, during the summer of 1964 organizers in Holly Springs established a Freedom House at 100 Rust Avenue, directly across from campus.[84] This Freedom House served as the local headquarters of the 1964 Freedom Summer campaign.

The movement in Mississippi had stronger roots in urban or semi-urban areas. But rural areas experienced the roots of clandestine activism that laid a foundation for direct-action protest that occurred in the middle of the 1960s. Earnestine Evans and Wilbur Colom grew up deeper in the country of Mississippi, but they shared similar roots in grassroots activism. Growing up outside the town of Holly Springs, their experiences prior to enrolling in the Freedom Schools reflect how the movement unfolded in the rural areas of northern Mississippi. Evans was born on June 23, 1947, in the Martin Flat community of Benton County, about twenty miles east of Holly Springs. Her father was a member of the Citizens' League, a small clandestine group of men that attempted to register and organize black voters.[85] Wilbur Colom was born on January 8, 1950, and grew up in Ripley, which was another twenty miles east of Martin Flat. The NAACP met quietly and secretly, but you "knew who they were," Colom recalled. He remembered reading copies of the *Chicago Defender* that were passed around at church. His neighbors even read aloud some of the stories of the civil rights movement printed by the northern black press that went unpublished in the Mississippi papers. Colom remembered attending civil rights meetings as a child in Benton County with his mother: "I remember very clearly my mother taking me to meetings at St. James Church, and I would go with her as an eleven and twelve-year-old where they were talking about things like forming NAACP chapters and they talked about various things related to school desegregation."[86] Genevera Reeves, a teacher at Old Salem School in Benton County and a recognized local leader, attended meetings in Jackson and Mound Bayou. The Benton County school district did not renew her contract.[87] For Reeves and all other teachers in the age of Jim Crow, open affiliation with the NAACP and other "subversive organizations" often resulted in contract termination and unemployment. The rural areas outside of the urban areas like Jackson and even Clarksdale did not experience the Freedom Rides or the sit-ins. But the embedded political networks laid the organizational foundation needed for the Freedom Summer campaign of 1964 to be a success. Additionally, the less visible resistance to Jim Crow still instructed young people like Wilbur Colom in a form of "freedom schooling" years before the Freedom Summer campaign of 1964.

ROSCOE JONES: ORGANIZATION AND VIOLENCE IN MERIDIAN

The families of young people oftentimes provided the first exposure to the civil rights movement, particularly in areas that were not home to civil rights organization that attracted the same statewide and national attention as other parts of the state. The national media and the daily reports of activity across the country often served as a topic of profound discussion in households across Mississippi.

Roscoe Jones, a high school student in Meridian, remembers watching the CBS evening news with his family. Watching the nine African American students desegregate Little Rock High School in 1957 under the order of protection of President Dwight Eisenhower on the evening news stood out as a particularly poignant moment. He remembered that a conversation with his grandmother was instrumental in his path toward activism: "My grandmother was sitting on the porch one day and I asked my grandma: 'Why is it necessary for black kids going to a white school to have troops?' She said, 'Well you know things are not fair.' I said, 'When that comes to Meridian, I want to be a part of it. I want to be equal. I want to be just like anybody else. I am a human being.' She said, 'Yes, you are.' "[88] His grandmother's affirmation was crucial at this formative stage of Jones's young adulthood. Many parents and guardians dissuaded young people from becoming active in the movement because of the repercussions likely to be faced by young people and their families. But Jones's grandmother encouraged him to "be a part of it." His grandmother also encouraged him to join the NAACP Youth Council, which he did at the age of fourteen.

Young people in Meridian did not experience the movement like their peers in the cities. As a young man Jones felt he had to bring the movement to Meridian. But as it had in nearly all other urban or semi-urban locations across Mississippi, the NAACP already established a front. Medgar Evers and C. R. Darden established a chapter in Meridian and organized a chapter of the NAACP Youth Council. Darden served as the president of the NAACP branch in Meridian and later served as president of the state organization from 1955 to 1964. Darden remembered his years as a local leader before the movement came to Meridian as "the years of stern agony, intimidation, economic reprisals, threats of violence, personal sacrifice and anxiety. . . . Rugged years when everyone refused to accept the challenge."[89] He was an outspoken organizer. He was often in conflict with not only whites but also black leaders throughout the state, particularly when he spoke out against direct-action protest in the wake of the sit-in movement.[90] Though not as militant as young people like Jones would have preferred, the NAACP-led organization of Meridian was the foundation of a larger movement. Membership in the NAACP Youth Council, exposure to local leaders like C. R. Darden, and a supportive family facilitated a connection among young people to the more radical aspects of the movement.

Young people learned of the movement through established leadership, but younger and more militant activists often pushed those still in middle and high school to become more active, as was the case in McComb. Roscoe Jones was still in high school when he met Mickey and Rita Schwerner, who joined the CORE staff in Mississippi in January 1964. They were stationed in Meridian and served as directors of the program in that area, which was positioned to be one of the key sites for the Freedom Summer campaign of 1964. "Mickey [Schwerner] saw something in me," Jones recalled. "I used to follow Mickey around and [he] trained me to be an organizer."[91] The Schwerners also befriended James Chaney, a twenty-one-year-old born and raised in the local black Meridian community. Chaney was expelled from school for striking a teacher after a conflict that deepened when he fashioned NAACP pins at school. The Schwerners quickly established a community center in Meridian, which became a focal point for local youth.[92] This attracted Roscoe Jones and James Chaney's younger brother, Ben. "My brother got involved in the freedom rides," Chaney recalled. "I thought about being a freedom rider. Whatever my brother wanted to do or did, I wanted to do."[93]

He recalled what it was like to interact with the volunteers at the community center in Meridian: "We would sit around on the floor in a group and everybody would sing. There was always a discussion going on. Mostly adults would talk about voter registration, and what was happening. They talked about the latest attack, who got whupped recently by the racists. And we were listening."[94] Spaces where activists gathered captured the attention of young people like Roscoe Jones and Ben Chaney, and they served as crucial recruitment centers through which to facilitate their entrée into the movement. These spaces embodied the long traditions of organizing as well as the newer versions of protest that transformed the civil rights movement in the 1960s. In many instances these informal spaces were transformed into a Freedom School by the summer of 1964.

* * *

Following the history of the students before they entered the doors of the Freedom Schools reveals that the civil rights movement unfolded differently across the state based on local resources and situations and based on particular local leadership. The background of the Freedom School students also illustrates how the interplay between locally specific political networks and a growing national movement shaped the political socialization of young people. Despite the wide variance of local factors, one common trait surfaces: the Freedom School students were politicized before entering the schools during the summer of 1964. The civil rights education that young people received informally did not guarantee enrollment in the Freedom Schools or active participation in the movement, however. The students' families ultimately mediated the actual decision of whether or not young people enrolled in a Freedom School. Students like Hymethia Thompson, Hezekiah Watkins, Homer Hill, Eddie James Carthan, Brenda Travis, Arelya Mitchell, Anthony Harris, Roscoe Jones, and many others entered the movement while they were still in middle and high school. Because of their ages and legal status as minors, young people carried with them important implications for participating in the movement. Living with their parents, youth needed permission to engage in the movement. Although youthful resistance is sometimes associated with rebellion against parents, in the cases of Freedom School students, young activists acted with their parents' blessing. Hezekiah Watkins recalled:

> [My mother and I] had a discussion on my involvement. For the first time she told me that, you know, basically do what you want to do. It wasn't said in those words, but that's what she meant, and after conferring with her the last time it was more or less a boost, you know, it was like a shock, a wave going through my body, I just felt so good that I finally had my mother's blessing because during this time I began to realize what was happening to blacks in Jackson and throughout the South.[95]

As Watkins's experience indicates, parents played a particularly important role in the decision-making process to enlist young people in the civil rights movement. Parents engaged their children in discussions about the movement in their hometowns. The danger of participating was well known to all those who read newspaper accounts, listened to the radio, or watched television coverage of the movement.

The class of Freedom School students was far from homogenous, however, as indicated by a wide spectrum of socioeconomic backgrounds. As Robin Kelley found in his study of activists in Alabama, "established black leaders did not always address the issues most directly affecting working people, especially the most impoverished section of the working class."[96] Although young activists and organizations like SNCC explicitly sought to organize the poor, the unemployed and working class did not always join the front lines of the movement or agree with the movement's established principles, such as nonviolence. Many of the Freedom Schools were from the middle class or of an economic background that was not dependent upon whites for employment.[97] To a family dependent upon sharecropping, attending Freedom School during the summer meant the loss of money and security. As Wilbur Colom remembered of the Freedom School students, "The kids that attended school were mostly middle class because if you did not have to work in the fields, you could attend school since you had the time."[98] Freedom School students were never as privileged as the white volunteers who lived in Mississippi, and they were afforded none of the institutional advantages given to whites. Yet within the caste system of Jim Crow, many of the Freedom School students came from families that were able to enjoy a tenuous security defined by land or business ownership or working for sympathetic whites. Moreover, most of the Freedom School students were drawn from urban or semi-urban areas, which afforded a degree of security not typically associated with the most rural parts deep in Mississippi. Students coming of age in Jackson, Clarksdale, or Hattiesburg were more likely to be exposed to publically organized chapters of the NAACP, for instance. These were certainly not the vestiges of freedom and privilege associated with white America, and Jim Crow custom dictated that such advantages could be swiftly terminated, especially in Mississippi. Yet during the 1960s such distinctions, however minor, were enough for many black families to enroll their children into a Freedom School.

Young students across Mississippi received an informal civil rights education prior to enrolling in the Freedom Schools during the summer of 1964. They observed in person, watched on television, and in some cases directly participated in the protests that captured the national headlines in the early 1960s. They befriended the Freedom Riders who were arrested. They attended church with leaders like Medgar Evers, who paid the ultimate price for striving for freedom. They listened to their parents as they discussed the latest news of the civil rights movement in their homes and their communities. Well outside the formal boundaries of public school education provided by the state, learning the movement in marginal spaces constituted a civil rights education that taught the conceptual prerequisites needed to join the front lines of the civil rights movement. The experiences that young people brought with them to the Freedom Schools once they enrolled challenged the misconception that young people enrolled in segregated schools were uneducated. The students came of age in very rich contexts, full of movement activity, innovative organization, and inspirational local heroes. As a result, students were eager to challenge the status quo and work for substantive social and political change. Young people were ready to join the front lines of the civil rights movement. But the task of further encouraging, supporting, and organizing this youthful cohort fell upon those who organized the Freedom Summer campaign of 1964.

3

"THE STUDENT AS A FORCE FOR SOCIAL CHANGE"

The Politics and Organization of the
Mississippi Freedom Schools

The overall theme of the school would be the student as a force for social
change in Mississippi. If we are concerned with breaking the power structure, then we have to be concerned with building up our own institutions
to replace the old, unjust, decadent ones which make up the existing power
structure.

CHARLES COBB, "PROSPECTUS FOR A SUMMER FREEDOM SCHOOL PROGRAM"

A s students highlighted in this study became more and more immersed
in the growing civil rights movement on a daily basis, Freedom
Fighters from outside of their communities orchestrated the Mississippi Freedom Summer campaign. Having already been educated on the streets
in demonstrations or in homes with families sympathetic to the cause, young
people in Mississippi were eager to join the civil rights movement. As 1964
opened another year of struggle, students began to hear talk of freedom fighters
moving to Mississippi, and the rest of the country began to turn its gaze once
again upon the state and the upcoming showdown between civil rights and segregationist forces. During the winter and spring of 1964, organizers grappled
with fundamental tensions around race, class, and gender that shaped the course
of the movement and defined what form civil rights education should assume.

Although the education of young people constituted an instrumental part of the movement, the Freedom Schools began as a small idea of secondary importance. Organizers were orchestrating the largest voter registration project in the history of the United States during the presidential election year of 1964, and they were using a largely white volunteer force to do this. The national media and the American public were more interested in this development than they were in the Freedom Schools. The secondary importance of the schools granted a degree of autonomy to the education program, which, combined with the informal civil rights education that students had already acquired, facilitated the growth of revolutionary ideology and praxis in the Freedom School classroom.

Although education was the backbone of the civil rights movement, the Freedom Schools were not the major initiative during the Freedom Summer campaign of 1964. To meet the demands of the more pressing and far-reaching voter registration project, organizers conducted one of the largest recruitment efforts since Reconstruction. By the winter of 1963, civil rights organizations that had been active in Mississippi—SNCC, CORE, SCLC, and NAACP—reorganized under the umbrella organization of the Council of Federated Organizations. COFO organizers, particularly the young activists with SNCC, made plans to recruit a massive cadre of civil rights activists and volunteers in order to register as many disenfranchised African American voters as possible. As the nation began to mobilize for the presidential election, the Freedom Summer architects largely focused on organizing a grassroots alternative political party, the Mississippi Freedom Democratic Party (MFDP). Organizers trumpeted the summer campaign as the largest voter registration project and the most comprehensive assault on Jim Crow in the history of the civil rights movement. In addition to voter registration, the summer campaign included a volunteer legal corps of over 150 lawyers; the Medical Committee for Human Rights, which included more than 100 volunteer nurses and doctors; and a volunteer spiritual ministry organized by the National Council of Churches (NCC).[1] But an emphasis on voting rights particularly distanced the project from young people because the Freedom School students were still too young to vote. As the project came into fruition, however, education became intertwined with the voter registration campaign to a degree that blurred the objectives of Freedom Summer. Voting, politics, and education shared common objectives and assumptions, which suggested that any education program that grew from the movement was inherently and necessarily political.

As plans for the massive undertaking unfolded during the winter and spring of 1964, the politics of race and the prominence of whiteness belied the movement's largest frontal assault on de jure segregation and defined the course of the civil rights movement throughout the 1960s. Voluntarily leaving the comforts of the North to move to Mississippi shocked white middle-class sensibilities and deeply piqued the interest of the American public. Whites who voluntarily (and temporarily) rescinded the privileges to which they were entitled in order to work alongside African Americans made the revolution in Mississippi a newsworthy experiment in "race relations." Public intellectuals and national media outlets consequently paid significantly more attention to the large cohort of white volunteers than local blacks already enlisted in the struggle. Black organizers were well aware that whiteness was a prominent fixture in American consciousness.[2] The attention drawn to white activists during and since the summer of 1964 proved to black organizers a mixed truth about public perception of the civil rights movement. White American consciousness was more attuned to the danger, harm, or death of one of their white sons and daughters than to African Americans fighting for freedom. On the other hand, civil rights organizers reasoned, white volunteers in a black movement afforded particular advantages. Organizers could leverage the attention paid to white volunteers to secure federal protection, external funding, and political connections to high-ranking government offices.

The work of white volunteers in a black movement complicates a singular and neat understanding of the Freedom School teachers. Whites played a role in the civil rights movement not as benefactors or the change agents necessary to advance the movement but as actors constantly negotiating their place in a national movement for freedom. Yet the role of whites in the movement has whitewashed the way we remember the summer of 1964. At the pinnacle of the Mississippi civil rights movement, the historiography of the Freedom Summer campaign credits the white volunteers, teachers, and registration workers as the catalysts of change. This message is reinforced by popular and award-winning movies such as *Mississippi Burning*, in which white FBI agents heroically track down the men who murdered civil rights activists James Chaney,

Mickey Schwerner, and Andrew Goodman.[3] In an even more top-down narrative, the summers of 1964 and 1965 are often characterized as a highpoint in the movement due to civil legislation passed by Congress. To the American public, the Civil Rights Act of 1964 and the Voting Rights Act of 1965 secured political access to all citizens once and for all, marking a legislative milestone in the movement.[4] Such sentiments reinforced the marginality of the Freedom Schools and the local movements that precipitated their development. However, as the history of the Freedom Schools suggests, some of the greatest gains of the movement were not won in the halls of Congress on Capitol Hill but in the rooms of grassroots schools across Mississippi. The most inspiring change agents were not necessarily white teachers but the black students who joined the front lines of the movement.

A close analysis of the organization of the Freedom Schools illustrates the problematic discursive tensions that transformed the schoolhouse into an ideological battleground of the movement. As organizers grappled with conceptual tensions around race, class, and gender, and carried forth plans to secure the right to vote, educators quietly transformed education into one of the more revolutionary aspects of the Freedom Summer campaign. Activists called for the organization of the Freedom Schools as a statewide, grassroots, and independent school system that ran parallel to the state-supported public schools. Charlie Cobb, a field secretary for SNCC in the Mississippi Delta, formally proposed the idea of Freedom Schools in December 1963. He called for a network of Freedom Schools that would "form the basis for statewide student action such as school boycotts, based on their increased awareness."[5] Organizers adopted his proposal and fashioned the schools with educational goals directly aligned with the civil rights movement and they re-envisioned and then institutionalized pedagogy and curriculum based on the supposition that young people were key actors in the civil rights struggle. Such radical educational objectives were manifest in a curriculum conference held in New York City just months prior to the start of the summer project. Here civil rights leaders gathered to draft a Freedom School curriculum that focused on citizenship, civil rights history, and African American literature, politics, and culture. As summer campaign organizers toiled over voter registration, a small committee of activists envisioned a curriculum that adopted a very strong political extracurricular component intended to train the next generation of civil rights leaders. Those who could not yet vote, they reasoned, would carry forth the Mississippi freedom movement for generations to come, especially after the summer campaign.

Understanding how and why the Freedom Schools were organized generates a strong ideological and structural understanding of the civil rights movement. The Freedom Schools reached deep into the community by shaping the schooling of Mississippi youth and extended notions of education for liberation, a significant ideological pillar of the black freedom struggle. The Freedom Schools radicalized the larger assault on Jim Crow that summer because they developed additional modes of resistance and institution building that reached far beyond the registrar's office and the ballot box. In the process of recruiting volunteers and making innumerable logistical arrangements, the summer campaign organizers trained a corps of civil rights activists who would in turn train the next generation of activists. Though prepared in less than one year, the organization of the Freedom Schools had lasting effects as it put forth a model of education for social change that influenced reformers for the remainder of the twentieth century.

THE LOGISTICAL ROOTS OF THE MISSISSIPPI FREEDOM SCHOOLS

Charlie Cobb embodied the sense of activism that characterized the Freedom Schools and the students who enrolled in them. Cobb was from a "political family that goes all the way back to eighteenth century Mississippi." His family could boast of political activity traced to an uncle who was a union organizer; an aunt who filed civil rights cases; and his father, who was an activist-oriented minister. Still in high school, Cobb and his classmates picketed a local Woolworth at the height of the sit-in movement in 1960 and became involved at a formative age just prior to enrolling at Howard University.[6] Passing through Jackson on the way to a civil rights conference in Houston, Texas, during the summer of 1962, Lawrence Guyot, a biology student at Tougaloo College and a SNCC field organizer, challenged Cobb to stay where the "real" activity was: in Mississippi.

In less than two years, Cobb formally submitted a proposal in December 1963 to build "Freedom Schools" based on the understanding that "the overall theme of the school would be the student as a force for social change in Mississippi."[7]

Cobb's "Prospectus for a Freedom School" was timely. He submitted it a month after the Freedom Vote registration campaign that began in November 1963 and fundamentally shaped the movement in Mississippi. The Freedom Vote, the "Freedom Ballot Campaign," or the "one man, one vote" election was a statewide alternative voting project organized under the auspices of COFO. They organized a parallel political party, the MFDP, and registered African Americans whom white registrars had denied from registering to vote. Aaron Henry, president of the statewide branch of NAACP, ran as the candidate for governor, and Ed King, the well-known white activist chaplain at Tougaloo College in Jackson, campaigned for lieutenant governor. Activists organized the Freedom Vote campaign in November 1963 as a mock election in order to dramatize a very important point: contradictory to segregationists' belief, African Americans would vote if given the opportunity. To help organize the campaign and meet the goal of registering two hundred thousand voters, Bob Moses and Allard Lowenstein, a white liberal faculty member at Stanford University, recruited white activists to assist in the mock election. Together they recruited eighty volunteers to assist in the voting project. They conducted a statewide campaign in over two hundred communities in which approximately eighty thousand disenfranchised African Americans cast a vote.[8] After the success of the Freedom Vote campaign, plans were made in the winter of 1963 for a larger voter registration project, which activists dubbed the "Summer Project" (which is now popularly regarded as "Freedom Summer"). The impetus of the Freedom Summer campaign capitalized on the successful components of the voter registration drive, including raising awareness and using whites as volunteers. This time, however, the campaign attempted to register people in order to vote in the traditional Democratic Party in addition to their own grassroots political party, the MFDP. Freedom movement organizers viewed the election year as a timely opportunity for national exposure and to force Lyndon B. Johnson to commit to a proactive civil and political rights agenda. According to SNCC chairman John Lewis, Freedom Summer was "organized strictly around the issue of voting [to] force a showdown between local and federal governments in an election year."[9]

The primary focus of voter registration was never contested, which ensured the secondary status of the Freedom Schools in the summer project. But the debates over who would lead and ultimately serve as the foot soldiers of the campaign held deep implications for who would teach in the Freedom Schools. Bob Moses and Dave Dennis had to sell the idea of the Freedom Summer campaign to activists and organizers already entrenched in the Mississippi movement. It was a difficult proposition for several reasons. Recruiting one thousand college-aged whites was a major ethical responsibility because people were being killed in Mississippi for acting upon their belief in full equality and inclusion. Volunteering in Mississippi without knowing what it takes to survive in the segregated South invited immediate danger. Movement veterans were critical of the use of whites in a black civil rights movement in terms leadership development. The proposal to recruit a largely northern white volunteer corps coincided with a growing white presence in SNCC. By the fall of 1963 during the Freedom Vote campaign, one-fifth of the field staff was white. During the spring conference in 1964, one-third of the participants were white.[10] A growing white presence challenged a primary objective of SNCC, which was to organize local communities and develop a black indigenous leadership that could sustain their own struggle without external support. As Bob Moses candidly stated in a December 1963 meeting in Atlanta, "A number of problems are involved with white students this summer, including the development of Negro leadership."[11] Their philosophy maintained that the freedom movement was a grassroots movement led by and for Mississippi blacks. One thousand white volunteers moving south to assume various positions in the movement, in addition to a growing presence of whites in SNCC, would potentially disrupt the groundwork that local NAACP and SNCC organizers painstakingly cultivated. They already identified promising local leaders and those who knew young people and local communities very well.

Historically, the multitude of northerners who moved south since Reconstruction included teachers. But a presence of white teachers, among others from outside the region who worked under the banner of benevolence, religious mission, and philanthropy, prompted deep-seated questions among locals engaged in a localized movement. Though well intentioned, northerners often generated a deleterious effect on the black community because their educational endeavors in Mississippi were often incongruent with ideals of freedom and the aspirations of local black communities. Oftentimes students were educated to assimilate into society as laborers, and vocational education was the prototype used across the South. Similar expectations and philanthropic missions that existed during Reconstruction continued into the civil rights movement of the 1950s and 1960s.[12] By the winter of 1963, after the Freedom Vote campaign, it was clear to organizers that whites were not entering Mississippi with a blank slate—they were bringing different experiences, backgrounds, and racial sensibilities to the South. Northern volunteers were inexperienced and naïve in understanding the lived realities under Jim Crow and the "southern way of life." The project planned to recruit students from Yale, Stanford, Harvard, small liberal arts colleges, and larger public colleges and universities across the country. These were the ivory towers of the university system that historically denied entry to blacks. Students attending these institutions occupied privileged spaces worlds away from the experiences of the Deep South.[13] When Allard Lowenstein suggested that the white chaplain at Yale, William S. Coffin, lead the summer campaign, for instance, he awakened deeply rooted racial animosity among black veterans. Whereas SNCC and other groups sought to cultivate indigenous leadership, Lowenstein and others indicated that leadership should come from outside the movement. To black freedom movement veterans, this was tantamount to white superiority and a belief that whites were somehow more capable to assume leadership positions.[14]

In spite of vocal opposition, the decision to recruit a largely white volunteer base for the voter registration project and the Freedom Schools ultimately passed.[15] A core group of veterans, including but not limited to Bob Moses, Fannie Lou Hamer, John Lewis, Dave Dennis, Lawrence Guyot, and James Forman, strongly advocated recruiting whites. Their arguments, which ultimately rested upon the ideals of integration and goals for a "beloved community," nullified—temporarily—the arguments against using whites in the movement. Many tended to agree with Hamer when she said: "If we're trying to break down this barrier of segregation, we can't segregate ourselves."[16] Supporters argued that if whites wanted to put their lives on the line and pay for it themselves, they had a right to do so. Supporters like Moses and Dennis pointed to the lesson learned the previous fall during the Freedom Vote campaign: a group of white college students risking their lives in Mississippi was more likely to bring national visibility and, consequentially, protection. Moreover, at the very moment this discussion raged, segregationists murdered Louis Allen, a witness to the murder of Herbert Lee in 1961 who had stepped forward to speak with the Justice Department about the racially motivated crime.[17] In the wake of Allen's murder, Moses and Dennis convincingly argued that the sheer number of northern volunteers would prevent segregationists from completely stopping the movement with violence.

Organizers seriously considered the socioeconomic status of the volunteers as well. As much as class and the privilege of white volunteers inspired skepticism, the volunteers were also an economic resource. Organizers were cognizant of the fact that white volunteers came from economically affluent and politically connected families. The Freedom Summer volunteers, including the teachers, were coming from families that made, on average, $8,417 per year, nearly 50 percent higher than the national average, and nearly eight times the amount that the average family in Mississippi who hosted them made—on average, $1,200 per year.[18] The project was a massive economic undertaking, especially for the financially strapped COFO. Operating on a shoestring budget, organizers could not provide a stipend to the volunteers; indeed, organizers required them to bring $150 for living expenses during the summer in addition to covering bail of $500 in the (probable) case of arrest.[19] Such financial resources, organizers reasoned, could clearly be used in a campaign that was economically burdened with a very limited budget. Moreover, organizers used and created networks that recruited students from institutions of higher education across the nation. This meant that white volunteers would bring numbers, skills, and energy to the movement. New territories deep in Mississippi could be organized with a larger cohort of activists, making this the largest frontal assault on Jim Crow in the history of the movement.

Supporters of using whites managed to negotiate a working compromise and in January 1964 SNCC adopted the Freedom Summer plan to use white volunteers.[20] This compromise adopted by COFO was tenuous at best. Even at the meetings that adopted motions to recruit whites, black and white movement veterans "were split among themselves about the role of whites in the movement."[21] Sentiment against the use of whites always existed, and it continued to exist throughout the civil rights movement. Organizers cautiously moved forward with measures to prevent white paternalism and entitlement from influencing the project. At first, organizers placed limits on how many whites could be recruited to work in the South. It was understood that whites would have to be trained in some capacity in order to address whites' inexperience of the Deep South. Organizers at the Greenville organizational meeting decided that no white person could serve as a project director in the state, nor should white people serve in general leadership positions. White volunteers worked directly under project directors who were most often black. Organizers and civil rights leaders actively policed the meritocratic advancement of people working in the movement. Organizers also provided the option for whites to work in the "White Folks Project," an initiative of the Southern Student Organizing Committee, to recruit more southern white students into the movement.[22]

The Freedom Schools emerged in part as a viable option for occupying the majority of the white newcomers because nearly all volunteers opted not to participate in the organization of poor or middle-class white communities through the SSOC and the White Folks Project. Many organizers erroneously believed that teaching in schools was irrefutably safer than more direct-action protests, and they were less likely to attract violence. Organizers ultimately decided that the white volunteers, especially white women, would be used in what was considered less dangerous civil rights work—the Freedom Schools. Additionally, channeling the white volunteers into the Freedom Schools was an effective way to prevent whites from interfering with the process of developing black leadership in the projects that organizers considered more important.[23] Organizers were also using the Freedom Schools to facilitate other long-term plans, such as building stronger connections in the local community, creating awareness of political opportunities, and developing more permanent community outreach projects that would outlast the summer project. Not viewed as being dangerous or visible like the voter registration work, mass marches, demonstrations, or other nonviolent protests, the Freedom Schools offered a safer alternative to more conservative adults still interested in participating in the civil rights movement.[24] Southern terrorists did not make the same distinction, however. Even before the campaign began the following summer, segregationists bombed Freedom School locations as much as any other space, thereby dispelling the myth that schools were inherently safe havens.

Teaching in the Freedom Schools carried a particular type of stigma among some activists during ongoing planning for the summer project. It became very apparent at the onset of the summer project that the Freedom Schools—though a significant objective of the Freedom Summer campaign—had relatively low status among both the organizers and the volunteers. "There was a feeling in the air," Freedom School coordinator Staughton Lynd recalled, "that the voter registration folks were, so to speak, the 'elite' troops."[25] As sociologist Doug McAdam found in his exhaustive study of the summer campaign, "when compared to the voter registration workers, the Freedom School teachers were second-class citizens."[26] Education, then and now, was placed on the back burner of movement projects. Campaign organizers prioritized voter registration, and anything beyond this, including the Freedom Schools, was not afforded the same urgency or importance. Because education did not produce the direct results of the voter registration campaigns, such as registered voters, and because education was not as visible as the direct-action campaign, such as the sit-ins or voter registration attempts at the courthouse, educational programs were ascribed with a secondary importance. By comparison, the work was slow, quiet, and often hidden from the popular media that documented the more dramatic moments of the movement.

Civil rights education projects like the Freedom Schools constituted one of the most sophisticated and meaningful forms of activism that was often led by women. The women who taught in the Freedom Schools, both white and black, joined the most recent wave of women who radicalized the advancement of the civil rights movement. However, this led to an implicit though clear understanding among some organizers that teaching in the Freedom Schools was to be "women's work."[27] Volunteer teachers did not see it as such, but the premise of the Mississippi Freedom Schools harbored feminized ideas about who should teach in the schools. Women held some leadership positions within COFO, but men often decided who would teach, and teaching in the Freedom Schools fit within the politics of patriarchy that governed the behavior of women who joined the front lines of the civil rights movement.[28] As Staughton Lynd remembered, organizers operated with the mindset that voter registration was more dangerous and, hence, for men, while teaching in the schools should be reserved for female volunteers.[29] As one organizer noted, there was a recurring assumption that "the males did the voter registration and the females did the Freedom Schools. The men made the decisions and the women made the coffee."[30] As organizers sifted through applications, they more than likely selected women to teach in the Freedom Schools in a way that reflected the structural notions of gender that infused the larger society. It is important to note that men, in fact, did teach in the Freedom Schools, and both men and women in the Freedom Schools rarely, if ever, viewed their own work as "lesser" than any other project during the summer campaign. The fact remains, however, that some organizers and others since then have regarded the educational component of Freedom Summer as secondary to voter registration.

This was not the end of the debate about the role of whites or women in the civil rights movement. Indeed, the negotiations and discourse that framed the organization of the Freedom Schools were the historical continuation of ongoing debate around the role of whites in the movement. Nor did this stem the problematic assumptions that whites often brought with them to the movement. Privilege and socioeconomic influence colored the experiences of locals and volunteers. But important decisions had been made, and once the decision to move forward was reached, organizing continued in earnest with less than six months to mobilize over one thousand volunteers and projects across the state. To make matters more pressing, the larger administrative questions were not necessarily concerned with curriculum, pedagogy, or educational goals. These questions were left to a teaching force that had not yet been recruited during the winter of 1963. The Freedom Schools were on the Freedom Summer agenda, but the teachers still had to be recruited, selected, and trained.

RECEIVING THE CALL: NORTHERN FREEDOM TEACHERS AND THE DECISION TO WORK IN MISSISSIPPI

Once activists agreed to press forward with the summer campaign, the most urgent component of organizing the Freedom Schools was mobilizing and training the teaching force. Staughton Lynd, a professor of history at Spelman College in Atlanta, Georgia, accepted the invitation from John O'Neal to become the Freedom School coordinator during the summer project.[31] Lynd was a logical choice. Already active in the movement as a New Left historian, Lynd was a dynamic professor of history and adviser to the college activists, much like his colleague at Spelman, Howard Zinn. Lynd helped develop and publish the curriculum, he located spaces for schools, and he coordinated school schedules across the state. He was one of the first of the nearly 280 volunteers who worked in the Mississippi Freedom Schools.[32] Unlike Lynd, who had experience in the southern civil rights movement, the vast majority of teachers were marked outsiders with no lived experience under the oppressively segregated world of Mississippi. Over 90 percent were white and from outside the South. Their backgrounds put them at odds with their students in Mississippi, who were intimately familiar with segregation and the terror used to maintain it. They inherited a long history of white people moving south as part of larger, northern-based philanthropic endeavors undertaken to influence policy. Their presence was welcomed by most, but not all, black organizers yet condemned by all white segregationists.

The Freedom School teachers heard the call to volunteer for Freedom Summer from various sources. SNCC stressed that volunteers should be recruited from college campuses, an active source of personnel and resources since the sit-in campaigns and the Freedom Rides of 1961. Organizers used resources including organizations affiliated with SNCC such as "Friends of SNCC," campus ministries, and civil rights guest speakers across the country to recruit college students. By the eve of the Freedom Summer campaign, volunteers had come forward from 233 colleges or universities. Most of the applications, 57 percent, were from the most prestigious public and private colleges in the nation.[33] Teachers were drawn from Harvard, Yale, Stanford, Princeton, the University of California, Berkeley, and from the major institutions of the Midwest like the University of Wisconsin and the University of Michigan. Still others heard the call from smaller liberal arts colleges like Oberlin College and urban colleges like Queens College in New York.

Having been exposed to the principles of the civil rights movement through various avenues, the summer project presented an opportunity to act on their own. "I must do this for myself," twenty-two-year-old Wally Roberts wrote to Bob Moses in his application to work for the Freedom Summer campaign of 1964. "I must do something, if only to prove to myself that I am committed to something I say I believe. I am tired of hearing myself preach."[34] Roberts was an English and history teacher at a private school in Pittsfield, Massachusetts (figure 3.1). He applied to teach in the Mississippi Freedom Schools after he read the call in the *New York Times*.[35] His statement is indicative of the youthful idealism of the volunteers, suggestive of the earnest commitment to work in the civil rights movement, and demonstrative of the passion to commit themselves to the ideals that shaped white liberals during the 1960s.

FIGURE 3.1 Wally Roberts, 1964. (Photo from the Mississippi Freedom Democratic Party applications, Student Nonviolent Coordinating Committee [SNCC] Papers, Martin Luther King Jr. Library and Archives, the Martin Luther King Jr. Center for Nonviolent Social Change, Inc., Atlanta, Ga., courtesy of Cynthia Lewis and Elaine Hill)

The recruits were far from homogeneous, however. Frances O'Brien came from a small college on the West Coast and was inspired to participate in the movement through religious motivations (figure 3.2). O'Brien was born on February 10, 1943, in southern California, and at the age of twenty-one she

FIGURE 3.2 Frances O'Brien, 1964. (Photo from the Mississippi Freedom Democratic Party applications, Student Nonviolent Coordinating Committee [SNCC] Papers, Martin Luther King Jr. Library and Archives, the Martin Luther King Jr. Center for Nonviolent Social Change, Inc., Atlanta, Ga., courtesy of Wally Roberts, Cynthia Lewis, and Elaine Hill)

applied to work in the Mississippi movement. Organizers accepted her application and assigned her to work at a community center and a Freedom School in Vicksburg. She had heard about the Freedom Summer project through the United Campus Christian Fellowship at Pacific Lutheran University in Washington. A representative of the Freedom Summer campaign had spoken on campus, as representatives were doing across the country to publicize the upcoming campaign and to recruit volunteers. Her entry into the Freedom Schools suggests how volunteers harbored notions about what was "safe." As O'Brien stated, unlike the direct-action demonstrations and voter registration work that formed the more visible part of the Freedom Summer campaign, teaching in the Freedom Schools was "right up my alley."[36]

Sandy Siegel, an activist who was assigned to teach in the Mississippi Delta, also reflects the individual nuances that teachers brought to Mississippi (figure 3.3) Siegel was born on October 8, 1941, in Los Angeles, California. At the age of twenty-two, Siegel made the decision to move to Mississippi to work in the Freedom Summer campaign. He heard about the call for volunteers through friends on campus at the University of California, Davis, and others at the nearby University of California, Berkeley, who were more active in the movement. Like many of the other volunteers, Siegel had participated in some civil rights demonstrations in California before moving to Mississippi in the summer of 1964.[37]

Like many of his peers, Mark Levy, born in 1939 in New York City, similarly became more politically active while enrolled in college. Levy first enrolled at Antioch College in 1957. During his first week of college, his senior adviser informed him and his dormitory peers of an ongoing boycott of a local Yellow Springs, Ohio, barber who refused to serve African Americans. Levy's senior adviser was Stephen Schwerner, the older brother of Mickey, one of the three activists killed during the summer of 1964 in Mississippi. Upon transferring to Queens College in New York in 1960, Levy quickly became involved in campus politics and protest, which largely focused on student governance and promoting the rights of students stifled under in loco parentis policies adopted by the administration. The campus was vibrant with activism, which included organizing folk music festivals and antinuclear weapon rallies, fighting speaker ban laws, and supporting school programs in Prince Edward County, among

FIGURE 3.3 Sandy Siegel, 1964. (Photo from the Mississippi Freedom Democratic Party applications, Student Nonviolent Coordinating Committee [SNCC] Papers, Martin Luther King Jr. Library and Archives, the Martin Luther King Jr. Center for Nonviolent Social Change, Inc., Atlanta, Ga., courtesy of Cynthia Lewis, and Elaine Hill)

other demonstrations and protests. His activism earned him the title of "troublemaker," as bestowed by *Esquire* magazine in 1963. The ultimate decision to volunteer for the Freedom Summer campaign, however, was made in consultation with his wife, Betty, who had befriended Dorothy and Bob Zellner, two very active SNCC movement organizers. Given Levy's organizing experience and his wife's background in student and leftist politics, deciding to enlist in the summer campaign was "a fairly natural step" (figure 3.4).[38]

Chude Allen (Pamela Parker) joined the movement through a historically black college campus, Spelman College, where she was a white exchange student in the spring of 1964 (figure 3.5). She was not an activist when she entered Carleton College in Minnesota as a freshman in 1961. After a protest against fallout shelters that was a major "turning point," she joined the campus student group and primarily organized around changing discriminatory rules for women students. In the summer of 1963, Allen was inspired by her experience working in a black inner-city community where she lived with an African American minister's family. After leaving, she was a delegate to the National Student Association where she heard SNCC activists talk about the southern freedom movement. Returning to Carleton, Allen was accepted for the exchange program with Spelman College in Atlanta, where she was quickly exposed to realities of the Jim Crow South. When she was told it was too dangerous to visit the

FIGURE 3.4 Ronnie de Sousa, Betty (Bollinger) Levy, and Mark Levy outside the orientation sessions, Oxford, Ohio, 1964. (Mark Levy Collection, Queens College/ CUNY Rosenthal Library Civil Rights Archive, courtesy of Mark Levy)

FIGURE 3.5 Chude Allen, 1964. (Courtesy of Michael Clurman)

home of her best friend (who was black) in Montgomery, she wrote home to her parents, "I am no longer an outsider. This system has hurt me."[39] Coming from eastern Pennsylvania, twenty-year-old Allen found the experiences at Spelman to be profound. She enrolled in an American history course on nonviolence taught by Staughton Lynd, the Freedom School coordinator, and participated in direct-action protests. These experiences in the South inspired her to apply to volunteer in the Freedom Summer campaign.

Not all Freedom School teachers were white. Less than 10 percent of the volunteers were people of color. African Americans constituted the small though meaningful minority of the Freedom School teachers. Dr. Gwendolyn (Robinson) Simmons was one such volunteer. She was born and raised in Memphis,

Tennessee, and was attending school at Spelman College in Atlanta, Georgia. One of the first in a series of fortuitous events that led to serious activism was her decision to join a church. She selected a Baptist church within walking distance, the West Hunter Street Baptist Church, presided over by the Reverend Ralph Abernathy, who was a close confidante to Dr. Martin Luther King Jr. Simmons also enrolled in a course taught by Staughton Lynd, which was offered in the history department that was chaired by Howard Zinn.[40] Heeding her mother's and grandmother's warning against involvement in the movement, Simmons began volunteering at the SNCC office, which was close to the Spelman campus. Simmons initially limited herself to support work such as typing press releases and stuffing envelopes or, in other words, "work that was useful but out of the limelight and definitely away from any news cameras or police paddy wagons."[41] She eventually chose to join the front lines of the movement, was arrested, and, with the support of her new SNCC colleagues and Staughton and Alice Lynd, she volunteered against her family's will for the Freedom Summer campaign of 1964.[42]

Nor were all volunteers from a college campus; 20 percent of the summer volunteers had already graduated from college and had heard about the call for volunteers through formal connections with the movement, word of mouth, or from the printed advertisements that SNCC published in the spring of 1964. Staughton Lynd was teaching at Spelman College and was active in the Atlanta movement when a friend in SNCC called and asked for his help to coordinate the schools. His courses in American history provided a social history of the United States, which proved to be popular among students and influenced Gwendolyn Simmons and Chude Allen, among many other students, to participate in the movement.[43] Joanne Gavin, a Freedom School teacher in Tougaloo, was working with the SNCC office in Washington, D.C., when she read the call for volunteers.[44] Liz Fusco, a Freedom School teacher in Indianola, was teaching English in Evanston, Illinois, when she read the call for volunteers in the *Guardian*.[45]

Organizers also recruited teachers from the ranks of professional educators, specifically the United Federation of Teachers. The UFT, based in New York, was affiliated with the American Federation of Teachers (AFT), one of the two largest teachers' unions in the country. The AFT was increasingly supporting civil rights initiatives, not as official policy, but they supported small projects such as sending teachers to work in Prince Edward County, Virginia, whose schools had been closed since 1959 to avoid desegregation. Sandra Adickes and Norma Becker volunteered for the project in Prince Edward County, where they learned of Freedom Summer from Ivanhoe Donaldson, a Michigan State student and SNCC organizer.[46] Freedom Summer organizers viewed the UFT as an ally. Bob Moses wrote in a letter to the UFT: "We have felt that the United Federation of Teachers would be a likely sources of assistance in the implementation of [the Freedom Schools]."[47] John O'Neal, a SNCC organizer who initially led the educational component of Freedom Summer before Staughton Lynd assumed the responsibility, contacted Norma Becker of the UFT, who gained invaluable experience in Prince Edward County. O'Neal asked the New York–based union to "adopt" Freedom Schools, which carried the responsibility of funding, staffing, and providing equipment for each school it sponsored. Organizers also viewed a partnership with the UFT as a way to extend the Freedom School program beyond the summer of 1964.[48] Toward this end, Moses requested that the UFT send observers "so that the experience we gain this summer will not be lost and can perhaps be used as the basis for further planning in this area."[49]

For many of the volunteers, the call to work in the campaign was a political awakening. Gloria Xifaras Clark, a first-grade teacher in Massachusetts, had watched Bob Moses issue the call for volunteers on national television. Moses announced to a wide national audience, "We hope to send into Mississippi this summer upwards of 1,000 students from all around the country to open up Mississippi."[50] Clark felt personally called after watching Moses ask for volunteers to assist in the movement. "I felt invited," Clark recalled upon watching Moses on television. "Finally, somebody was asking me to come and help and participate."[51] Once she finished her teaching assignments in Massachusetts, Clark arranged to join the group of over twenty educators sponsored by the UFT.[52]

Thousands heard or read the call for volunteers, but it was the values and personal histories of the volunteers that led them to participate in Mississippi. Much like the students they would teach in the Freedom Schools, the volunteers had an inclination or predisposition toward struggling for full political, economic, and social equality well before they applied to work in Mississippi.

Gwendolyn Simmons's decision to volunteer for the Freedom Summer campaign was gradual, and, as noted, she had enrolled in college promising *not* to become involved. Her parents and grandparents wanted to see change, but they did not want their daughter, the first in the family to attend college, to jeopardize her future by joining the struggle. But when the call was issued, Simmons made the decision to volunteer, which was particularly difficult without family support. "Ten dollars between me and the cruel world, without the love and support of my family," Simmons recalled, "doubt assailed me from all sides."[53] Simmons's heartrending decision to disobey her parents and grandmother was rare among the volunteers, however. As Doug McAdam found in his study of the volunteers, applying to volunteer for the summer project was more often consistent with the core values the volunteers learned at home.[54] Teaching in the Mississippi Freedom Schools and participating in the movement in general was not an act of rebellion—contrary to a popular narrative often told about the activists of the 1960s. Freedom School volunteers cited their parents as a positive influence in their application process. Some applicants, in fact, viewed their participation in the Freedom Summer as an act that would please rather than antagonize their parents.[55] Many of the campaign volunteers had parents who were active in the civil right movement themselves, or at least strongly committed to social justice. Sandy Siegel remembered that his parents made him aware of the racial injustices that existed in the United States as he was growing up.[56] Betty (Bollinger) Levy was a "red diaper baby." Her mother was a union leader affiliated with the Congress of Industrial Organizations and was subpoenaed when her union was called to testify before Congress. "All my life," Levy recalled before leaving for Mississippi with her husband, Mark, "I had a feeling against social injustice. This project fits in with everything I had done before."[57] When Fran O'Brien told her parents she was going to Mississippi, they were convinced her decision was hereditary: her grandparents and great-grandparents were involved in the women's suffrage movement and the labor movement. Her great-grandfather had worked with Eugene V. Debs and published a newspaper entitled *Lucifer* (light bearer) because he wanted to enlighten people about the oppression of women and working classes.[58]

The intentions of all the volunteers were impeccable, and the risks they assumed to join the movement are noteworthy. The volunteers were of a class and generation that tends to be characterized as optimistic, idealistic, and own-ing a sense of conviction and political efficacy. As sociologists of the movement have noted, activists in the movement were "passionately committed to the full realization of the idealistic values on which they had been taught America was based."[59] The Freedom School teachers reflected this overarching commitment to moral principles. For Sandy Siegel, working in Mississippi with the convic-tion that he was doing something morally right stemmed from "the totality of the experience of being down there, we were all in it together, we were all working together, we all had a common cause."[60] For volunteer Mark Weiss, "I wasn't afraid of death, and it felt morally right, it seemed like the right thing to do."[61] This sense of morality was often grounded in religious principles, and the largest group of students expressing spiritual or religious motivations for vol-unteering held Judeo-Christian beliefs. "I was a devout Christian and believed God wanted me to go to Mississippi," Chude Allen recalled of her motivation to volunteer. "As a Christian, I believed in the concept of redemptive suffering, sacrificing oneself for something greater."[62] Liz Fusco, the coordinator for the statewide Freedom School program during the 1964/1965 school year, remem-bered that her father, a rabbi, taught her to live by the principle of "justice, jus-tice thou shall do," something she would take very seriously.[63] While tensions connected to regionalism, class, gender, and race placed the volunteers at odds with local Mississippi students and their families, their religious beliefs tilled an important common ground. The religious and spiritual convictions that spurred participation were shared between the volunteers and their students, their stu-dents' families, and the communities in which they were working. The familial connection to religion and the role of college campus ministry were important determinants in the motivational and organizational structures of freedom movement campaigns.[64]

It is easy to glorify the whites who risked their lives to work in Mississippi. Their decisions to volunteer in spite of such hostility and danger are com-mendable. But the white volunteers often harbored problematic assumptions of race that shaped preconceived notions of their students. Volunteers were from a different socioeconomic background that ensured marked differences between them and the communities they worked for.[65] "We thought we were hot shit," Liz Fusco recalled of the white teaching force. "We thought we knew everything."[66] One year prior to the release of the Moynihan Report in 1965, which enshrined a notion of cultural deficiency and deprivation theory among federal policymakers, volunteer teachers sometimes subscribed to a view that their black pupils lacked something of value. Some of the comments of Freedom School teachers reflect the sentiments behind the imperialist ideology behind the "white man's burden" to save and civilize people of color. Several volunteers carried forth the sentiment and assumed they were in Mississippi to "save" black children from a destitute existence. In the Magnolia State for less than one month, one volunteer teacher wrote that "our purpose is to expand awareness, to fortify what the student already knows—although inarticulately—that he is human being and deserving of respect." Such a mission could prevent children from becoming "that old man fading into death . . . on the shaded porch."[67] Moreover, white volunteer teachers held a nearly universal assumption about the unequivocal and necessary inferiority of black education. The NAACP propagated notions of inferiority to argue that mandated segregation was inherently unequal and therefore unconstitutional. And by 1964, the NAACP-backed argument used in *Brown* that young people were "victims" of segregated education was widely accepted, particularly among the volunteers.[68] Backed by the idea that separate was always and necessarily inferior, white volunteers were quick to chide black education in the South. "They learn nothing," a teacher in Hattiesburg wrote, "which could give them any reason to disbelieve the lies they are told about Negroes being unable to do anything worthwhile."[69] Such an uncritical assumption of inferiority overlooked the integrity of black public schools. Despite legal segregation and woeful underfunding, black educators painstakingly cultivated an alternative way of living in a segregated society by challenging it through hidden transcripts of resistance, as noted in the first chapter. Insisting upon inferiority in 1964 dismissed nearly one hundred years of organizing a separate and promising network of education throughout the South, one that pressured a democracy to live up to its ideals. The experience of teaching in the Freedom Schools challenged such assertions of inferiority. Still, such assumptions lurked and, upon reflecting on the assumptions that whites carried with them, Liz Fusco candidly noted, "Some of us did some damage."[70] White participation in the education of disenfranchised communities, in other words, was more complicated than the popular narratives portray.

IMPLEMENTING THE FREEDOM SCHOOL IDEA

Freedom Summer organizers faced the daunting challenge of developing a statewide network of Freedom Schools in less than six months. Establishing a curriculum to use in the schools was of critical importance to the organizers. The National Council of Churches funded a meeting to write a curriculum for the Freedom Schools on March 21 and 22, 1964, in New York, which Lois Chaffe, a CORE staff member, organized.[71] Although the NCC did not establish a formal headquarters in Mississippi until 1965, its leaders recognized the importance of providing as much structure, guidance, and supervision to a massive, largely untrained volunteer force. As the NCC wrote to colleges and universities across Mississippi about the upcoming summer project, "Nothing would be more harmful to the efforts of organizations trying to do constructive jobs in areas of need, and nothing would be more harmful to the states, the nation, and the students themselves, than students who simply go into an area 'to do good' without the authorization and program supervision of groups in that area."[72] Establishing a curriculum that met the needs and matched the aspirations of the local community was crucial to ensuring long-term success. The curriculum had to work outside the normative parameters of education in order to politically engage disenfranchised youth in Mississippi. Concepts like citizenship, American government, African American history, and civil rights movement philosophy therefore introduced students to solutions to segregation and unequal opportunity. Organizers reasoned that this would lead to an analysis of freedom, citizenship, and rights in Mississippi. They defined critical thinking in the Freedom Schools by asking questions fundamental to American democracy that were rarely asked within the confines of the traditional public school.

For two days, over fifty participants focused on producing a curriculum that would be used in the field in less than three months. The curriculum conference drew notable leaders of the civil rights movement: Ella Baker, an entrenched activist and founder of SNCC; Myles Horton, radical adult educator and founder of Highlander Folk School; Noel Day, the organizer behind the Boston Freedom Schools during the winter of 1963; Septima Clark, a radical educator and founder of the Citizenship Schools; Bayard Rustin, famous civil rights organizer and close associate of Dr. Martin Luther King Jr.; and Bob Moses, the informal leader of the Freedom Summer campaign.[73] The prestige, experience, and commitment of conference attendees illustrate the comprehensive nature of Freedom Summer planning, but, more importantly, it suggests the tremendous importance veteran activists attached to educating young people in the principles of freedom. As the greatest minds and theorists of the movement gathered to discuss the nature of the Freedom Schools, activists created one of the most progressive curricula in American history.

The main objective of the committee was to create a curriculum that the teachers could use in their classrooms. Some of the Freedom School teachers were trained educators, but many were not. For the volunteers without a background in education, the curriculum was a much-needed guide. Organizers presented teachers with a schedule to follow, notes on teaching, and content on the American government, the voter registration processes, and African American history. Conference attendees envisioned that one-half of each day at Freedom School would be devoted to academic development and enrichment.[74] The Freedom School curriculum served to supplement the regular education students received in the public schools. The academic component was critically important to organizers, especially to Charlie Cobb, who candidly stated in the Freedom School proposal: "It is, I think, just about universally recognized that Mississippi education, for blacks or whites, is grossly inadequate in comparison to education around the country. Negro education in Mississippi is the most inadequate and inferior in the state."[75] Yet the Freedom Schools were conceived to supplement, not replace, the regular public school curriculum. As the curriculum guide stated, the Freedom Schools served to "sharpen the students' abilities to read, write, work mathematical problems, etc. but will concentrate more on stimulating a student's interest in learning, finding his special abilities, so that when he returns to the state schools in the fall he can take maximum advantage of the public education which is offered to him."[76]

Toward this end, the curriculum committee adopted behavioral outcomes that were grounded in traditional learning objectives. For instance, each student was expected "to develop his sense of self-worth and self-confidence in his ability to learn, achieve and contribute, to improve his ability to communicate ideas, to improve his study habits and skills, to promote his sensitivity to and competence in the use of logical thinking, critical judgment and problem-solving processes [and] to develop his skills and competence in handling money and financial transaction."[77] An attendant component of the curriculum, which was ancillary to the academic objectives, focused on extracurricular, recreational, and cultural activities. Freedom School intervention sought to supplement academic work with enrichment activities based upon black culture that positively valued the contributions of local black communities.[78]

The most significant part of the curriculum focused on citizenship education and leadership development. The participatory and active sense of citizenship embedded in this portion of the curriculum and the extracurricular political activity this inspired was the hallmark of a Freedom School education. Cobb articulated the political objectives of the educational program in his original proposal, which other organizers had reinforced in earlier projects. As a Freedom School organizer in the Boston Freedom Schools, Noel Day provided continuity and learned experience to this grassroots education movement. He reiterated a crucial mission of the schools when he wrote that "one of the purposes of the Freedom School idea is to train and educate people to be active agents in bringing about social change."[79] To achieve a goal grounded in political efficacy, Freedom School teachers were given a more ideological goal of fostering critical thinking. The curriculum adopted in New York noted: "By the end of the summer, the basis will have been laid for a cadre of student leadership around the state of Mississippi committed to critical thinking and social action."[80] The teaching memo sent to the teachers prior to the summer stated that "the purpose of the Freedom School is to help them [students] begin to question [and] to provide an educational experience for students which will make it possible for them to challenge the myths of our society, to perceive more clearly its realties, and to find alternatives and, ultimately, new directions for action."[81] Additionally, the curriculum committee stressed that approximately one-half of instruction time, or twenty hours each week, was to be devoted to "field work."[82] Organizers guided "student action" toward voter registration projects in the community. "The Freedom Schools stand as an integral part of COFO's voter registration activities," a COFO Freedom Summer pamphlet stated. "They will provide politically emerging communities with new young leadership and constitute a real attack on the presently stifling system of education existing in the State."[83]

The original Freedom School proposal also called for two boarding schools to provide intensive leadership training. Although the boarding schools never materialized, it is important to note that organizers intended to provide a separate training for a select cohort of students who demonstrated leadership potential.[84] The boarding schools were to accommodate 150 to 200 students apiece and use the same curriculum and pedagogy of the day schools, meeting for one six-week session. The major difference was that the instruction would be "on a more intensive level, and with an additional goal of bringing together and training high quality student leadership."[85] The planned schedule was rigorous. Whereas the Freedom Schools were to meet forty-five hours a week, boarding school students were scheduled to meet for seventy-five hours, which meant meeting twelve hours a day during the week and fifteen hours during the weekend. Organizers also scheduled twenty-four hours a week for leadership training, more than twice the amount for the day schools. The emphasis illustrates the deep commitment organizers maintained toward identifying and training young student leaders that would lead the civil rights movement once the summer campaign concluded.

Explicitly adopting political objectives in an educational program tailored to young people is unique in the history of American education. But the intended audience of the curriculum further differentiated the Freedom Schools from any other radical educational program of the civil rights movement. Organizers targeted an overlooked yet vitally important segment of the population: young people in Mississippi still enrolled in the K–12 public school system. Students too young for college and too young to vote were not typically viewed as serious participants in the movement. But Freedom School architects thought otherwise. Activists were concerned about the number of youth leaving Mississippi in the pursuit of freedom outside the place they called home. Mississippians often protested by leaving the state on their own accord, as evidenced in the great migration of southern blacks who relocated to urban areas in the North and West. Many young African Americans did not accept intolerable living and social conditions and simply moved north, which was the traditional "promised land" that had beckoned the oppressed since the days of slavery. Between 1910 and 1970, 6.5 million African Americans left the South en masse. In Mississippi alone, 938,000 blacks migrated north to follow a promise of better jobs and social conditions.[86] Freedom School teachers and community organizers attempted to stem the flow of youth moving north in order to combat a "brain drain" effect in local communities. They planned to focus on "tenth- and eleventh-grade students, because of the need to be assured of having a workforce that remains in the state high schools putting to use what has been learned."[87] SNCC philosophy dictated that the freedom struggle was to be maintained and led by local people, and Freedom School organizers believed young people should be trained to lead the movement and remain in the state. As the volunteer teachers were instructed in their orientation before the summer campaign, the purpose of the Freedom Schools was "not to educate to move north and get a job, but to form and motivate leadership."[88]

Educator activists did not always agree with the plan to teach young people from a politically oriented curriculum. Sandra Adickes, a volunteer teacher from New York with previous experience in the Prince Edward County Freedom Schools, remembered being "unsettled by the impression received that at least some of the COFO staff regarded the schools as training grounds for activism, as subordinate to the function of canvassing for voters."[89] For the teachers exposed to the problems associated with education, or the lack of it (perceived or otherwise), emphasizing political activity instead of gaining an adequate education was antithetical to their pedagogy. Yet, espousing both political and educational goals, it becomes clear that the Freedom Schools were committed to social change. The apparently contradictory ends were reconciled for the most part because the dominant thought was that working for social and political change would itself be a transformative educational experience. While working in the middle of the Mississippi freedom movement, the goals of providing academic enrichment and opportunities for political involvement were one and the same. "Since the students' academic experiences should relate directly to their real life in Mississippi, and since learning that involved real life experiences is most meaningful," COFO organizers wrote, "we hope that the students will be involved in the political life of their communities."[90] Ideological tensions and logistical concerns aside, the committee completed the Freedom School curriculum by the end of March. The planners summarized the aims of the curriculum in a way that framed the educational program of the summer: "We have attempted to design a curriculum that begins on the level of the students' everyday lives and those things in their environment that they have either already experienced or can readily perceive, and builds up to a more realistic perception of American society, themselves, the conditions of their oppression, and alternatives offered by the Freedom Movement."[91] Freedom Summer organizers mailed several manuals to teachers prior to the start of the summer as part of the teacher–training process. "All of [the students] will have a knowledge far beyond their years," the 1964 *Freedom School Teachers Manual* stated. "This is the knowledge of how to survive in a society that is out to destroy you and the knowledge of the extent of evil in this world. Because these young people possess such knowledge, they will be ahead of you in many ways."[92] Teachers were also sent a guide entitled "Notes on Teaching in Mississippi." It included five points about teaching methods, twelve teaching hints, and fifteen points on discussion-leading techniques.[93]

Curriculum organizers determined a curricular approach that could be followed by teachers without experience, but they also accounted for autonomous decision making. As the memo sent to the teachers prior to the beginning of the summer stated, teachers were expected "to regard the curriculum material as a guide from which you should feel free to depart."[94] Organizers never intended the curricular material mailed to volunteers to dictate the exact parameters of learning that was to occur but rather to provide foundational support to those who needed it. According to Staughton Lynd, the curriculum was "like a resource, like having money in the bank that you could use if you needed to."[95] Lynd asserted that each Freedom School teacher had the flexibility and autonomy to execute lessons as he or she saw fit. As one report mailed to the volunteers stated, "The curriculum is flexible enough to provide for the use of a wide range of methods in transmitting the material," and "the development of a weekly schedule and a daily lesson plan will be left to the teachers and students of the school."[96]

A final step of implementing the Freedom School idea was to identify, locate, and secure spaces to hold classes. This was a complicated endeavor considering the degree of hostility such a massive civil rights project inspired. Freedom Summer organizers necessarily relied on networks already in place to house the Freedom Schools. As an idea too radical for white school boards across the state of Mississippi, Freedom Schools occurred in spaces well outside and alternative to the public school system. Activists established schools in recognized "safe" meeting places within the black community—churches, college campuses, storefronts, or homes used by civil rights workers—and they relied upon these places throughout the course of the summer.

One location for Freedom Schools was on a college campus at independent historically black colleges and universities. For Hymethia Thompson, attending Freedom School meant attending school outside Woodworth Chapel on the Tougaloo College campus in Jackson. Similarly, Arelya Mitchell enrolled in a Freedom School across the street from Rust College in Holly Springs. Rust College provided a safe haven in the same way that Tougaloo provided a secure place to hold a radical school. Mitchell attended class in the Freedom House, which Freedom Summer organizers rented and used as the main headquarters for civil rights operations. The dormitory at Rust College housed the volunteer teachers as well.[97]

The Freedom Schools also reflect the important role of the church in the Mississippi civil rights movement. Homer Hill attended a Freedom School in the Haven Methodist Church on Fourth Street in Clarksdale, whose organization dates back to 1880. The church congregation included Homer Hill and his family, as well as the civil rights leaders in the community. Part of the church's civil rights work included sponsoring and donating the space for a Freedom School. Under the leadership of the Reverend Theodore Trammell, the church became a regular meeting place for the civil rights movement.[98] The church, too, was critically located in a particularly activist-orientated part of Clarksdale. It was just down the street from Aaron Henry's Fourth Street drugstore and Vera Pigee's beauty shop. Similarly, students in Benton County attended Freedom School in St. James Church, which had opened up its doors to the movement (figure 3.6).[99]

In Tchula, deep in the Delta, the Freedom School location reflected the support of both local churches and members of civil rights organizations that built Freedom Homes in the local communities. Eddie James Carthan first attended Freedom School in New Jerusalem Church, which supported the civil rights movement by regularly hosting mass meetings for the community (figure 3.7). But as the movement grew in the area and began to attract white segregationist retaliation, Carthan and his peers attended class in the Freedom House that activists constructed in nearby Mileston.

FIGURE 3.6 Freedom School students outside the Benton County Freedom School at St. James Church, 1964. (Courtesy of Gloria Xifaras Clark and Larry Rubin)

The largest Freedom School in the state was in Meridian, which was held in the Meridian Baptist Seminary (figure 3.8). The seminary building was a spacious three-story brick building that had at least seven functional classrooms. Mark Levy, the Freedom School coordinator in Meridian, remembered that the seminary building "was in pretty good shape, it had been closed for a little while so we got down there and it was like a real school with blackboards and desks."[100] Compared with the porches, yards, or church sanctuaries that typically held a Freedom School, the Baptist Seminary in Meridian provided the most generous educational accouterments in the state. It was, as Staughton Lynd referred to the seminary, the "palace of the Freedom School circuit."[101]

FIGURE 3.7 Freedom School students outside New Jerusalem Church in Mileston. (Photo by Matt Henon, courtesy of Eddie James Carthan)

FIGURE 3.8 Mark and Betty Levy with Freedom School students outside the Meridian Baptist Seminary, Freedom School, 1964: Betty Bollinger Levy (*second row, far left*), Patricia Waterhouse (*third row, far left*), and Mark Levy (*standing, far right*). Also identified are Roscoe Jones (*in cap*), Richard Porter, Shirley (Porter) Patterson, and Kay Ray (*front row, center*). (Mark Levy Collection, Queens College Rosenthal Library Civil Rights Archive, courtesy of Mark Levy)

THE OXFORD CONFERENCE: TEACHING THE TEACHERS THE WAYS OF THE MOVEMENT

To minimize the danger to a large white volunteer force and to provide a smooth transition into the summer project, Freedom Summer organizers hosted an orientation that introduced the volunteers to the realities of working in the Mississippi civil rights movement. The orientation's objective was to inculcate volunteers with the goals of the summer campaign and the responsibilities of the projects to which they had been assigned. The purpose was to also introduce volunteers to the field staff, local activists and leaders, and other volunteers with whom they would be working. The orientation formally began on June 13, 1964, and consisted of two week-long training sessions at Western College for Women in Oxford, Ohio (figure 3.9). The first week was for voter registration

FIGURE 3.9 Volunteers at the Ohio training sessions, Oxford, Ohio. Pictured is Andrew Goodman (*center in dark T-shirt*), days before he was killed. (Courtesy Ted Polumbaum Photo Collection, Newseum, Washington, D.C.)

workers and the second session was for Freedom School teachers and coordinators. Organizers also hosted a second orientation in early July in Memphis to better meet the schedule of full-time professional teachers, mostly those organized through the UFT.[102] The orientation for teachers served as a crash course on how to work safely as a civil rights activist in Mississippi. Organizers provided instruction that addressed some of the privileges and naivety that volunteers unconsciously carried with them. The volunteer teachers were instructed to learn the needs of the communities they served. They were instructed to see themselves and their pupils as *people*, not as "teachers" and "students." Organizers suggested that the volunteer teachers must "learn 'un-freedom' before you can teach 'freedom.'"[103] Sessions also focused on how to teach Mississippi youth. In addition to using the curriculum guides distributed to teachers at orientation, teachers were encouraged to compile a local history of the counties they taught in and the history of the movement in their respective areas. As Mark Levy noted while attending the sessions, "everything going on in the community is a subject for discussion."[104]

The project was undertaken with great enthusiasm, confidence, and optimism from the outset. As one activist wrote of the summer, "The old institutions are crumbling and there is great reason to hope for the first time."[105] The history-making moment that they were entering was not lost on the press either. During the first week of orientation, cameras and reporters covered the event. Walter Cronkite of CBS News and *Life* covered the orientation during the first week.[106]

The violence in Mississippi and the fear it inspired was an important issue the organizers wanted to address. One of the initial concerns of Freedom Summer organizers was the fact that the volunteers were not familiar with the civil rights movement in Mississippi. Orientation leaders provided a quick though memorable tutorial in the realities of working on a civil rights project in the Magnolia State. As Doug McAdam wrote, the inexperienced volunteers were exposed to a "litany of horror" in order to demonstrate the reality of the Mississippi freedom movement. "If [the volunteers] came with stars in their eyes," Phyllis Hoyt, dean of students at Western College in Ohio, noted of the first days of the orientation, "it was only a matter of a few hours before they were dispelled."[107] One volunteer wrote home about "a quiet Negro fellow on the staff who has an ugly scar on his neck and shoulder where he stopped .45 slugs. Another fellow told us this morning how his father and later his brother had been shot to death." Not surprisingly, many expressed fear. "The reality of Mississippi grows closer to us every day," volunteer Margaret Aley wrote. "We know the blood is going to flow this summer and it's going to be our blood. I'm scared—I'm very scared."[108] In addition to discussing life in Mississippi, nonviolent strategies for survival were taught, such as how to take the physical assault common during demonstrations without fighting back. Experienced veterans of the movement led the workshops at Oxford and they passed on and taught the strategies they learned since they joined. "We were trained primarily around tactics about nonviolence," Gloria Xifaras Clark, a Freedom School teacher in Holly Springs, recalled. Clark also remembered learning "how to behave when you are arrested and what to do if you are beaten. And that kind of training and discussion about potential harm that could come to you and others."[109] Role-playing activities taught the volunteers to cover their head, hit the ground, and roll up in a knot (figure 3.10).[110] Volunteers were also given informative brochures published by the NAACP that spelled out the volunteers' constitutional rights in the case of probable arrest. Volunteers also signed over their power of attorney to the legal counsel of COFO.[111]

The organizers wanted to address issues of race as much as they wanted to address issues of violence and safety. Volunteers were given careful instructions on how to interact with their host families and all community members. Orientation organizers were candid with the white volunteers, particularly in regards to what Jane Adams, a Freedom Summer volunteer from Antioch College, called the "Race thing." Adams recalled one conversation with a SNCC organizer who informed her that, no matter the motivation to volunteer, she was "a white missionary with the missionary zeal." She went on to state that the "whole discussion upset me very much."[112] Candid discussions like this continued throughout the retreat and destabilized the entrenched belief systems of white volunteers. "I begin to mistrust my self-conception," Adams wrote in response to the ongoing conversations around race. "I guess when one's identity is threatened, it frightens him, as mine is threatened when it's put in pigeonholes that aren't quite right. And I stereotype the same way, which makes it doubly bad."[113] Intentional or not, Freedom Summer organizers sought to

FIGURE 3.10 Freedom Summer orientation in Oxford, Ohio, in which volunteers prepared for the physical brutality of challenging entrenched segregation in Mississippi. (Mark Levy Collection, Queens College Rosenthal Library Civil Rights Archive, courtesy of Mark Levy)

challenge deep-rooted beliefs among whites as much as possible before the campaign began. As Adams concluded her journal entry on June 18, the volunteers had "so much to learn."

The intensity of the orientation was intentional to inculcate the volunteers with an understanding of the real experience of the Mississippi freedom struggle and to develop a sense of trust and respect for the local staff and leaders. But the intensity was also calculated to weed out those who did not have what it took to work in Mississippi because it became painfully real during orientation that volunteering was a matter of life and death. Threats of violence turned into an act of terror during the training for the Freedom School teachers. On June 22, the first day of the second week of training, Bob Moses solemnly announced the disappearance of three civil rights workers who were reported missing the night before. The missing workers were James Chaney, a local African American

Mississippian involved with CORE; Mickey Schwerner, a white CORE staff member from New York; and Andrew Goodman, a white Freedom Summer volunteer who had been in Mississippi for just one day.[114] The Meridian-based activists had been investigating a church burning near the town of Philadelphia, Mississippi. The small congregation at the Mount Zion Methodist Church had agreed to let freedom movement workers use their church for a Freedom School during the upcoming summer.[115] Like many other churches throughout the state, the church in Philadelphia was also going to be used as a community center and the informal headquarters of a local voter registration project. The community had agreed to help despite the fact that Neshoba County, where the church was located, was long known for its terrorism inspired by local segregationists. On the evening of June 16, 1964, the Ku Klux Klan intimidated and threatened parishioners meeting there. Later that evening they burned the church to the ground—a devastating blow to the small community that had devoted their church to the freedom movement. Chaney, Schwerner, and Goodman drove to Philadelphia to investigate the church burning, to locate a new location for the Freedom School, and to support the local community after the KKK attack. On their way back to the COFO office in Meridian, the deputy sheriff arrested the Freedom Workers and threw them in jail. Police released them later that evening, but they were stopped again by the deputy and turned over to a white mob. The three were severely beaten, shot to death, and buried in an earthen dam in a remote rural location.[116]

The disappearance caused the volunteers to pause and reflect seriously upon what they were doing. It reaffirmed the message that organizers were trying to instill in the volunteers at orientation: if you struggle for freedom in Mississippi, you could lose your life. The fact that segregationist violence had targeted a church that was intended to be a Freedom School also suggested that, contrary to the organizers' assumptions, teaching could be as dangerous as voter registration in the Magnolia State. The national media closely followed the story and captivated a national audience as they speculated about the location of the victims and the identity of the aggressors still at large. The national attention fulfilled the predictions of the black organizers from the previous winter of 1963 that the media would pay more attention to the nearly all-white civil rights army moving to Mississippi. In the context of the media blitz that followed, many volunteers expressed fear and doubted whether to continue with their plans to work in Mississippi. "I honestly had to think about it real hard because I wasn't really interested in giving up my life at that point," Freedom School teacher Sandy Siegel recalled. "I felt like I had to believe in what I'm doing to not be intimidated by this kind of thing."[117]

As the volunteers prepared for the worst, white officials in Mississippi prepared for the oncoming "invasion." One of the first counteroffensives was to publicly denounce the volunteers in the local Mississippi press. Segregationists and the Mississippi press called the volunteers "race mixers," "invaders," "intruders," "left-wing agitators," "professional agitators," "carpetbaggers," "communists," "trouble makers," "do-gooders," "misled pawns," "racial zealots," "meddlers," "integrationists," "ideological manipulators," "propagandists," "CORE creeps," "weirdos," "beatnik sophomores," "immature collegians," "motley missionaries," "pseudo-religious reformers," and a "flea-bitten crowd of white screwballs."[118] "They are doing more harm than good," Governor Paul B. Johnson Jr. said. "Some of them think they are on a lark. They don't realize the seriousness of what they are doing in invading a state, [race] relations still would be good if agitators would stay out." Johnson later called the volunteers "broken-down motley first-generation aliens who have come to disrupt the peace and harmony of the state." Mayor Charles Dorrough of Ruleville said, "I could stomach them [the volunteers] if they came on a humanitarian-type mission, but they came down here to cause trouble."[119] The volunteers were not very popular with the governing white supremacists, to say the least.

Mississippi law enforcement took more direct measures and prepared for what they saw as a military invasion. Jackson mayor Allen C. Thompson outfitted city police with riot gear and a full arsenal topped off with a tank used to "defend" the city. *Newsweek* described "Thompson's Tank" as "a 13,000-pound armored battlewagon built to the mayor's specifications at roughly $1 million a pound, abristle with shotguns, tear-gas guns, and a submachine gun."[120] White legislators in the Magnolia State similarly assumed a defensive position and called for an extraordinary legislative session to pass a series of laws that could be used to punish the volunteers. The laws were also crafted to punish young offenders, which reinforced the notion that Freedom School students would suffer the same consequences as adults. Such legislation precluded any distinction of age or youth when determining legal retribution. Young people, in short, were to be tried as adults. Laws stated that the Youth Court, a court typically designated for young people under the age of twenty-one, "shall not have any jurisdiction of any child or minor, including detention for, charge or charges of, arrest for, trial of, confinement of, or conviction and punishment of minors under twenty-one years of age." The state also assumed greater responsibility in intervening in the lives of young people. If a child or minor was found guilty of civil rights violations, the state assumed the responsibility to commit the child to a more "suitable family home, or commit him to the custody of a suitable private institution or agency."[121] As much as the volunteers trained for the summer campaign, the state authorities prepared their forces as well.

* * *

With the battle lines clearly drawn, the Freedom School teachers were cognizant of the situation they would encounter. Having attended the second week of training, they were made aware of the disappearance of three of their peers and were afforded the opportunity to go home before they left for Mississippi. The volunteers who remained moved forward enthusiastically. The orientation prepared them as well as a grassroots organization could prepare inexperienced volunteers for an environment that was all but domestic warfare. It was once they crossed the state line into Mississippi, however, that their true education began.

4

"WE WILL WALK IN THE LIGHT OF FREEDOM"

Attending and Teaching in the Freedom Schools

We just couldn't get out and demonstrate, we had to first of all be taught and get involved.

HYMETHIA WASHINGTON LOFTON THOMPSON, FREEDOM SCHOOL STUDENT IN TOUGALOO, MISSISSIPPI

[Attending Freedom School] was, for me, the first time in my life that I was exposed to people that were white but were not in any manner similar to the people that we were accustomed to who happened to be white.

HOMER HILL, FREEDOM SCHOOL STUDENT IN CLARKSDALE, MISSISSIPPI

Someone has opened our eyes to freedom and we will walk in the light of freedom until we achieve the victory.

BOSSIE MAE HARRING, FREEDOM SCHOOL STUDENT IN DREW, MISSISSIPPI

The Freedom Schools began quietly in the shadows of the voter registration project but organizers, students, and teachers quickly transformed the summer's educational initiative into an unprecedented success that proffered a promising model of civil rights education for generations to follow. Statements like the ones opening this chapter are indicative of the lasting impact Freedom Schools had on those who enrolled. The experience was historically unique because learning to protest, studying a citizenship and civil rights–based curriculum, and participating in the movement were not activities typically associated with a public education in the United States, especially in Mississippi. Young people who attended the Freedom Schools experienced the movement in profound ways at a very formative age that shaped the rest of their lives and their understanding of citizenship. As Bossie Mae Herring, a Freedom School student in Drew, Mississippi, recalled, "Someone has opened our eyes to freedom and we will walk in the light of freedom."[1] Every student had a different experience in the Freedom Schools, but an important commonality emerged: the young people who studied in the schools subsequently joined and shaped the front lines of the civil rights movement.

As the national press closely followed the disappearance of Mickey Schwerner, Andrew Goodman, and James Chaney, whom movement veterans presumed to be dead, young people in elementary, middle, and high school remained undeterred and enrolled in the Freedom Schools. Well over two thousand students enrolled in forty-one Freedom Schools in a strength of numbers that far exceeded the organizers original expectations. To the Mississippi students, the violence associated with the murder of three civil rights workers was, sadly, nothing new. Students grew up learning about Emmett Till, who was ruthlessly killed at the age of fourteen. Till's murderers remained free during the summer of 1964, and these white extremists enjoyed more privileges, rights, and freedoms than the Freedom School students and their families did. Students and their families already learned firsthand that they too could suffer the consequences of challenging Jim Crow. Yet young people remained committed.

The day-to-day Freedom School experience during the summer of 1964 provides sharper insight into the legacies generated by the strategic use of civil rights education in the movement. Although disenfranchised Mississippi communities historically embraced the ideology of education for freedom, Freedom Schools implemented a new form of pedagogy and curriculum geared directly toward educating young people to be leaders in the civil rights movement. Teachers facilitated an entrée into the movement by teaching a humanities-based curriculum focused on citizenship and adopting a pedagogy that embraced dialogue, critical thinking, and hands-on activity that transformed local civil rights protests into educative spaces. In churches and homes across the state, Freedom School students studied the spirit and letter of the civil rights movement in addition to traditional academic subjects. Through a citizenship and civil rights-based curriculum, students explored ways to participate actively in the civil rights movement to acquire a goal longed for by generation upon generation of Mississippians: freedom. By attending a Freedom School, students articulated a new sense of citizenship as they and older activists dismantled Jim Crow on the front lines of the civil rights movements through protests, demonstrations, marches, youth newspapers, and canvassing for the MFDP. By the end of the summer, Freedom School students learned that they too could change the world they were about to enter as young citizens.

Closely examining the Freedom Schools corrects the whitewashed version of the Freedom Summer campaign that scholars typically recall. Interracial dialogue proved to be an unintended resource for both teachers and students as this was the first time many of the students interacted with sympathetic and friendly whites. For the white teachers who lived with black families and taught black children, this was often the first time they interacted with people victimized by the system of Jim Crow. White teachers unlearned a lot, but not all, of the assumptions they carried with them from northern privileged enclaves. The interaction between white teachers and black students facilitated interracial dialogue that modeled the ideals of social integration that voter registration and school desegregation ultimately sought. It is important to note that this experience was reciprocal. Teachers abandoned the traditional modes of instruction such as lecture and rote memorization and learned instead to embrace a radically different student-centered pedagogy. Students were encouraged to ask critical questions about the social, political, and economic context of their communities. Additionally, the teachers learned from sophisticated and organized networks of resistance that composed the larger Freedom Summer campaign. The summer project, in other words, served as a political training ground from which the volunteers learned how to organize different struggles once they returned home. The Freedom Schools disrupted traditional educational arrangements, and the teachers learned as much from the students as the students learned from them.

The Freedom Schools offered something provocatively new and, indeed, revolutionary to the field of education. Students attended Freedom School in unorthodox spaces and advanced their learning outside of the classroom by observing, participating in, and eventually leading their own protests and demonstrations. The students applied what they learned in the Freedom Schools to the front lines of the movement as they marched, protested, and demanded equal access, fair treatment, a quality education, and other goals of social and political change. The level of protest and the agency these young people demonstrated constitutes one of the most distinguishing aspects of the civil rights movement. Yet at the same time, the schools represent an ideology of education for freedom passed down through hidden transcripts of resistance since slavery. The Freedom Schools therefore represent the continuity of a revolutionary ideology long embedded in oppressed communities. The historic moment in 1964, however, presented an opportunity for young people to act in ways that diverged sharply from previous generations. As dynamic institutions that instilled radical notions of citizenship and taught the skills to achieve it, the Freedom Schools and the ideology of education for social change deepen our understanding of the revolutionary role of education in the civil rights movement.

WALKING THROUGH FREEDOM'S DOOR: THE FIRST DAY OF FREEDOM SCHOOL

School started immediately for the Freedom School teachers. Upon arrival at their assigned locations in Mississippi, the Freedom School teachers' first assignment was to recruit students for their designated schools. As Mark Levy noted in the instructions provided at the orientation in Ohio in late June, "We will start building schools from the moment we get off the bus."[2] Sometimes teachers worked with voter registration workers and canvassed local areas for students. Some made announcements at church on Sundays. Others recruited prospective students across the state at Freedom Houses, the summer campaign's local headquarters in most project sites where the volunteers lived, organized, and often held Freedom School classes. The Mississippi Student Union (MSU), a student-based civil rights organization, also assisted recruitment efforts. But students mostly heard about the school by word of mouth and from the excitement generated by Freedom

Fighters moving to their communities.[3] Recruiting students did not prove to be too difficult a task, or at least generating attention about their work did not prove to be too difficult because the volunteers held a celebrity status in the communities that housed them. Rita Walker, a student in Holly Springs, articulated young people's anticipation about meeting the volunteers: "I often heard about the freedom riders on TV and read about them in the newspapers. And I would wonder if they would ever come to Holly Springs. Then the people began to say, they will be here before long—but before long seemed like forty years."[4]

Young people like Walker ultimately met the white volunteers in the spaces that the Freedom Fighters visited, socialized, and called home while in Mississippi. Larry Martin, a Freedom School student in Meridian, recalled what it was like to live near a Freedom House:

> We lived across the street from the COFO [the umbrella civil rights organization that organized the summer project] office, right down in the heart of town. One day we saw those white guys going up those stairs. They looked different, not like the ones you'd see around here all the time. We'd go to the COFO office every day and stay until night. They let us stay and play as long as we wanted to. I wanted to be in the demonstrations. I wanted to be a part of it.[5]

Throughout the state, Freedom Houses like the office in Meridian encouraged many young people to enroll in the Freedom Schools.

After the initial period of recruitment, the Freedom Schools formally opened on July 7, 1964. Students across the state eagerly enrolled in numbers that surprised organizers. Staughton Lynd, the Freedom School coordinator, enthusiastically reported that activists opened twenty-five schools in twelve communities across the state with an estimated 1,500 students attending.[6] This surpassed original expectations of 1,000 students enrolling by the end of the summer. For organizers, this was an unexpected and unqualified success. Students already engaged in the movement boosted enrollment in cities that NAACP, CORE, SNCC, and other networks mobilized prior to Freedom Summer. In Hattiesburg, where Freedom School coordinators had previously organized a strong voter registration campaign, they expected to register 75 students. But on registration day, 600 students expressed interest in the schools. With five schools in the city for 675 students by the end of the summer, the city of Hattiesburg would become known as the "Mecca" of the Freedom Schools. Over 250 students in Meridian, whom Mickey Schwerner and his wife, Rita, organized through CORE prior to his disappearance, attended the largest single Freedom School in the state.[7] The unexpected enrollment and popularity of the schools challenged, and would continue to challenge, the relatively low social status the schools held at the onset of the summer campaign.

On the first day of Freedom School, students entered a "school" unlike the average schoolhouse. As noted in the previous chapter, students attended school in churches and other spaces that provided support for the movement, including college campuses or private homes in the local community. The typical day at a Freedom School did not follow the daily operations of an average school either. Students and teachers began each school morning by singing Freedom Songs such as "We Shall Overcome" and "Keep Your Eyes on the Prize." Instead of sitting passively in rows of desks with the teacher in the front of the room, students sat where they chose and in a way that facilitated open dialogue between teachers and students (figure 4.1). After beginning the day with movement songs, Freedom School teachers usually followed the curricular outline they received from the organizers, which generally focused on academic enrichment. This meant that formal study began in the early morning (7:00–9:00 A.M.) and emphasized individual work, such as writing or typing. Teachers usually spent the rest of the morning (9:00 A.M.–12:00 P.M.) teaching a traditional academic curriculum, which included courses in math, science, history, and English. Mark Levy, the Freedom School coordinator in Meridian, structured the school day where courses in "Freedom" and English were taught from 8:30 to 11:00 A.M. Then students were offered courses in general math, biology, chemistry, algebra, trigonometry, African American history, art, and French.[8] The academic curriculum also included extracurricular courses, including typing, dance, drama, art and music appreciation, and a host of foreign languages.

The morning academic sessions were grounded in a traditional curriculum but were steeped in the politics and culture of the civil rights movement. African American history and literature were important curricular components of the Freedom Schools (figure 4.2). As Chude Allen, a Freedom School teacher in Holly Springs, recalled about beginning each day of Freedom School, "I start

FIGURE 4.1 Gail Falk teaching Freedom School students in Meridian. (Mark Levy Collection, Queens College Rosenthal Library Civil Rights Archive, courtesy of Mark Levy)

out teaching what we call the core curriculum, which is Negro History and the History and philosophy of the Movement."[9] These subjects reinforced themes brought up in some of the segregated public schools, but not all of the students had been learning a humanities curriculum based on African American history and culture. Students studied John Brown and the abolitionists in the prelude to the Civil War. They critically studied Reconstruction and examined the speeches of Booker T. Washington.[10] "We were introduced to black authors who we didn't know anything about at the time," Thelma Eubanks, a Freedom School student in McComb, recalled. "Richard Wright and James Baldwin. I also remember *Freedom Road* by Howard Fast and *Strange Fruit* by Lillian Smith. We hadn't had any of that at school."[11] Freedom Schools deeply appreciated African American culture and proudly displayed this in the curriculum as well as the resources they provided students. "They [the Freedom School teachers] put a library in the school and many of the books were on black history," Homer Hill recalled of the Freedom School in Clarksdale. "Richard Wright,

FIGURE 4.2   A Freedom School class in Meridian. (Mark Levy Collection, Queens
College Rosenthal Library Civil Rights Archive, courtesy of Mark Levy)

Langston Hughes, Frederick Douglass's writings, a wide range of books,
plays." Roy DeBerry, a student outside of Holly Springs in Benton County,
remembered reading James Baldwin's *The Fire Next Time* alongside Richard
Wright and discussing them in great detail.[12] Because he was in and out of hospitals during his childhood, Wilbur Colom self-identified as being only func-
tionally literate at the time of enrolling in the Freedom School. He remembered
being handed one of his first books other than the Bible, *The Last of the Mohi-
cans*, while in the Freedom School in Ripley.[13] Though it did not communicate
the same messages as texts emerging from the black canon, committing oneself
to read in the context of the civil rights movement was an empowering act that
stayed with young people the rest of their lives.

Teachers and organizers also incorporated theater and drama into the classroom. Several students participated in the Free Southern Theater, a radical theater group of the civil rights movement formed by Doris Derby, John O'Neal,

and Gilbert Moses at Tougaloo College in 1963. Freedom School teachers encouraged students to write, act, and perform in plays that portrayed the brutal reality for many blacks in Mississippi. In plays like *Seeds of Freedom* and *In White America*, students reenacted and dramatized the stories of activists martyred in the movement like Herbert Lee, a civil rights supporter slain in 1961, and Medgar Evers, the NAACP field secretary killed in his driveway in 1963.[14] The dramatic act of creating and staging a play was a forceful demonstration of agency built upon students' voices. These plays incorporated the creative energy of students and presented an alternative method to communicate their understanding of how oppression operated in Mississippi. Toward the end of *Seeds of Freedom*, students took the stage one by one proclaiming the purpose of a Freedom School education and appealing to the audience:

> The reason why we are going to Freedom School is because we feel that now is the time for Negroes in Mississippi to join in the Movement. Don't you?
>
> As Freedom School students, we are helping in voter registration because we feel that the fight for Freedom in Mississippi must be fought not only by the adults, but by the teenager. And we are here to do our part.
>
> We go to Freedom School because we feel this is the era of changing conditions, and we want to participate meaningfully in that change.[15]

Theater also provided a viable cultural alternative to mainstream media that stereotyped African Americans. "The Free Southern Theater had such an impact on me," Anthony Harris, a Freedom School student in Hattiesburg, recalled. Harris's "view of black characters was in the form of Stepin Fetchit, Rochester [Eddie Anderson], Amos 'n' Andy, [and] those caricatures of stereotypes of what white people wanted black people to look like. [The Free Southern Theater] was liberating. It was freeing up my mind [because] this is different from Amos 'n' Andy." As he went on to recall, the Free Southern Theater toured with "black people who express themselves in a positive way and project a positive image. Without Free Southern Theater, I'm not sure if I would have understood that."[16] The theater production in the Freedom School was an inherently political act as students transformed theater into an avenue through which to raise awareness of injustices among their peers.

Staughton Lynd and the Freedom School organizers at the curriculum conference intended for the students' voices to be part of the curriculum and Freedom School teachers actively sought student input into what courses were taught. This maintained a degree of autonomy and independence in planning the school day. The instruction in the Meridian Freedom School illustrates how the process of democratizing the curriculum resulted in political socialization for both teachers and students. Mark Levy was initially surprised when his students in Meridian asked for a course in French, but the students instructed teachers in the deeper significance of their request. "The answer we got was really very profound," Levy recalled about learning why students wanted to learn French, "and it went on to inform the whole process of how we thought about school for the rest of the summer. The answer was simple: 'The white kids have it in the white schools. We don't have typing; we don't have French in the Negro schools. Why? What's the problem? Is there something wrong with us? Are we incapable of learning French? Do we have some intellectual or physical deficit?' "[17] Levy noted that students performed well in French, which taught the students they were indeed capable of mastering the same subjects as white students. This then led to a deeper questioning of structural inequality. As Levy recalled, "The discussion shifted from, 'is there something wrong with us that we're not getting these courses' to 'who runs the school and why would they not teach us this?' "[18] Teachers across the state incorporated student voice into school governance not only to address students' interest but also to cultivate a sense of agency, advocacy, and critical awareness among students. Students were also free to choose the classes they wanted to attend, which provided another significant point of contrast with the traditional public schools.[19]

Lessons of political efficacy and critical thinking were incorporated more directly into the courses teachers offered on citizenship. Teachers generally devoted the afternoon (2:00–4:00 P.M.) to a curriculum that focused on citizenship or government and courses that guided involvement in the local civil rights movement activity occurring outside the Freedom Schools.[20] Students moved beyond traditional academics to study seven units of analysis developed at the curriculum conference the previous spring: an examination and comparison of southern and northern culture and society; the black population in the North;

the experiences of whites; the power structure of American society; a comparison between blacks and poor whites; a critique of materialism in a unit called "material things versus soul things"; and, finally, an analysis of the ongoing civil rights movement.[21] This portion of the curriculum ultimately emphasized citizenship, an issue not explicitly taught in the public schools. "Freedom Schools focused directly toward citizenship, civil rights, politics," Eddie James Carthan recalled of attending the Mileston Freedom School. "They dealt with the basic problems of the community and especially the problem dealing with [unequal] citizenship and politics."[22] Homer Hill remembered that "human rights was a very, very common theme that [the Freedom Schools] offered us because they were working with people who were accustomed to being the underclass, and what they tried to offer us was information that would allow us to appreciate that we were free people who had the potential to be citizens and that we lived in a country that, despite local environment, embraced the idea of freedom, liberty and equality."[23] Freedom School teachers often localized the concepts to better teach students the larger meaning of the movement. One lesson executed at the Meridian Freedom School facilitated an open discussion around the difference between white music, black music, and dancing. "They feel that that the whites are tighter," one teacher lamented in his reflection.[24] Diane Pachella, a Freedom School teacher in Meridian, recorded in her notes that she examined local topics including employment, housing, schools, hospitals, and government officials in Meridian. "It is brought out that Mississippi [elected officials] say noting of improving school or anything else," Pachella noted, "because they spend so much time talking about preserving segregation."[25] By grounding concepts like de jure and institutional discrimination in their home communities, students were able to articulate a burgeoning critique of the segregated society in which they lived.

In addition to teaching content that instructed young people in the history, philosophy, and culture of the civil rights movement, Freedom School teachers created assignments in order to directly instill a social and political critique of structural discrimination in Mississippi. Rita Headrick, a teacher in the Moss Point Freedom School, developed an assignment that asked students to compare the high school they attended, the all-black Magnolia High School, to the white school, Central High. The students noted that the school buildings provided for black students were "too crowded" and "ill-equipped." The teachers were "afraid of losing their jobs," and the African American principal was "spineless" and "undedicated to his race." For Headrick, "this assignment was the most successful of the whole summer."[26] Teachers in the Meridian Freedom School asked their students to define "Freedom" and to elaborate on what this meant in their lives. Jo Lynn Polk articulated the urgency of change when she wrote, "I would like to have the chance of being treated like a human, a chance to do what I please. To have freedom of Religion, freedom of education and freedom to be free." She went on to state that "here in Mississippi and all over this country there need to be some changes."[27] Her peer, Jo Allen, reiterated a need for institutional change: "Freedom is what the Negro of America does not have, Negros have always come after the white man. It is time for the Negros of America to wake up, tell the white man we want our freedom now!"[28] Emridge Falconer began to demonstrate an awareness of the economic imperative behind freedom: "I would like to have a right to go to different places and in different stores. I would like to see colored clerks instead of janitors sweeping and mopping the floors. . . . I would like to see a colored secretary or businessman because I too would like to be a businessman myself."[29] Daisy Watson captured much of the urgency, commitment to change, and critical thinking that struck at the foundations of American democracy:

> I am an American Negro. I live in what is supposed to be a democratic free nation. If this is freedom, why can't I go and do the same as my fellow whites? Why am I turned down because my face is brown? Why are my qualifications rated lower than any other American? Why am I called second-class and not first? Why! Why! Am I not as good as any other American? If all men are created equal, then am I not as equal as you?[30]

Students also wrote poetry as part of the Freedom School experience. Submitted as an assignment, published in a Freedom School newspaper, or written for personal use, student poetry served as a way to articulate resistance to unjust policy or to provide form to a developing political consciousness. Edith Marie Moore expresses such sentiments in her poem, "Now Is the Hour," which was published in the *Freedom's Journal*, the newspaper published from the Meridian Freedom School:

Now is the hour
To stand for what is right
Together we know
We will win the fight.[31]

Assignments in the Freedom Schools provided an educational space for students to articulate the meaning of freedom and citizenship—both under the existing Jim Crow power structure and under the Constitution—and what social or political strategies could be employed to realize the promises of full citizenship in the United States. From the students' perspective, the education received at Freedom School was inherently a political education. As Anthony Harris recalled of the Freedom School he attended in Hattiesburg, "the political aspect was always present" (figure 4.3).[32]

As one of the most notable aspects of the schools, organizers planned for students to learn how to protest and to become leaders in the local movement. Students learned to critically analyze the society in which they lived and then studied the practical aspects of joining the front lines of the civil rights movement, which grounded the abstract concept of freedom in local protest. Following the guidelines established at the curriculum conference in New York, teachers embraced a "leadership development" curriculum that focused on providing students the "perspective of being in a long line of protest and pressure for social and economic justice." Teachers were encouraged to educate students in the general goals of the movement and to teach specific organizational skills, such as public speaking, public relations, organizing meetings, and canvassing.[33] As a result, students typically remember the Freedom Schools as a space where they learned to protest and join the front lines of the movement. As Wilbur Colom recalled of his experiences that summer, "The Freedom Schools were an organizing movement."[34] Looking back on the history of the Freedom Schools, Hezekiah Watkins remembered the schools as "a nonviolent course that was being taught to those who were somewhat reluctant to be arrested and they were being taught how and what to do upon your arrest."[35] For young activists

FIGURE 4.3 Anthony Harris in a Holly Springs Freedom School, 1964. (Herbert Randall Freedom Summer Photographs, McCain Library and Archives, the University of Southern Mississippi, courtesy of Herbert Randall)

interested solely in joining the movement, Freedom School was the natural fore-runner to working on the front lines. "We just couldn't get out and demonstrate; we had to first of all be taught. We would go to meetings and we would talk how to be nonviolent," Hymethia Thompson recalled about the schools. "The boys were taught how to protect the girls from being kicked in the abdomen because that would keep us from producing children."[36] The Freedom School students received invaluable lessons on how to protect their lives and health before join-ing a movement that threatened all of those who participated.

Voter registration and community canvassing were the most common forms of activism and protest learned in the Freedom Schools. Teachers first instructed their pupils on the importance of voter registration and its relation-ship to the larger movement. They then taught the practical skills of this form of community engagement. Freedom School teachers across the state distributed registration forms and instructed students how to fill them out so they could help resister their parents and other family members.[37] As the Freedom School newspaper in Greenwood reported, "[Freedom School] students are also being taught how to lay out leaflets and how to run the office machinery. [Students] work with voter registration in the distribution of leaflets throughout the community."[38] Toward the end of July, Sandy Siegel, a Freedom School teacher in Clarksdale, reported that teachers were "starting a full-scale program of getting the students active in Freedom Registration. We are having the full staff go out with the students in order to free regular voter registration workers to go out into the county."[39] Some students demanded to learn these skills while other teachers instructed students in voter registration to better meet their interests. Ultimately, however, canvassing and voter registration was a major part of the movement before Congress passed the Voting Rights Act of 1965 and Freedom School organizers envisioned voter registration and canvassing as part of movement leadership. Therefore the Freedom Schools were called upon to teach this skill set as well.

The courses and skills taught in the Freedom School differentiate the program as one of the more revolutionary aspects of the Freedom Summer campaign of 1964. But the pedagogy that underpinned it distinguishes the Freedom Schools as one of the most unique programs in the civil rights movement. The Freedom Schools explicitly taught the content and skills needed to effect political and social change among an elementary, middle, and high school population, which was practically unheard of within public education in 1964. Such unorthodox goals with such a young population necessitated a unique type of teaching. If the Freedom Schools were to be an effective catalyst for change, organizers reasoned, then education for freedom would have to be taught in a way that diverged sharply from traditional forms of teaching. The Freedom School pedagogy first and foremost rejected a traditional type of education, which encouraged rote memorization and a passive acceptance of the way things were. Liz Fusco, a Freedom School teacher who after the summer campaign served as the statewide coordinator until 1965, illustrated aspects of a traditional education that taught students "to be alert to what the authority wants, which is always a fact you can memorize. So you learn to copy, you learn not to think, you learn not to ask a question that you don't already know the answer to or that you're not sure she knows the answer to."[40] Civil rights organizers and educators across the country realized that this form of education, which relied on antiquated teaching methods, failed to meet the needs of students, and it certainly did not engage students in addressing the larger political, economic, and social issues espoused within the civil rights movement.[41]

Freedom School organizers and teachers developed a pedagogy that fully engaged students in the learning process. Discussion, debate, and critical thinking and analysis geared toward political socialization constituted the Freedom School pedagogy. As the volunteer teachers were instructed during their orientation, the "most important thing to teach is that students must think, ask questions [and] respect themselves."[42] Ultimately, discussion allowed "students to articulate the desire for change awakened by the questions they were empowered to ask."[43] For the Freedom School organizers, asking deeper questions about the society in which they lived signified that change was occurring. Teachers were therefore encouraged to ask questions to foster critical thinking and conceptualize what participation in the civil rights movement meant. For instance, teachers often asked: "Why are we [students and teachers] in Freedom Schools? What is the freedom movement? What alternatives does the freedom movement offer us?"[44] As noted, teachers selected topics of study like black history and culture, and they designed engaging assignments that analyzed resource distribution by race and examined concepts of freedom. Such strategies composed a culturally relevant, critical, and radically distinct pedagogy that facilitated a process of political socialization.

The Freedom School pedagogy also rested upon creative teaching strategies to reach young people who had been disenfranchised through an inferior education. Sandy Siegel remembered trying to keep students engaged through music (figure 4.4). "I had a guitar, so I could sing songs with them, we would sing folk songs," Siegel recalled. "We would talk about black history. I tried mostly to get them to talk about their own experiences and how they felt about their own schools and what might be wrong with their schools and things that they might be missing in their schools."[45] Steven Schraeder, a teacher in the Meridian Freedom School, held a mock panel discussion in his classroom. Students role-played the segregationist governor of Alabama, George Wallace; civil rights icons Malcolm X and Roy Wilkins; and the U.S. attorney general, Robert Kennedy.[46] In another classroom, students role-played candidates for the MFDP and the traditional Democratic Party.[47] Activists developed pragmatic

FIGURE 4.4 Clarksdale Freedom School teacher Sandy Siegel plays the guitar for young students upon a return trip during the winter break after Freedom Summer. (Courtesy of Sandy Siegel)

strategies that they felt best met the needs of each localized setting. This adaptive approach to teaching and changing the curriculum reflected the ethos of the movement and effectively met needs as they arose during the summer.

An innovative pedagogy and curriculum did not ensure a smooth or even pleasant teaching experience for all Freedom School teachers. It is easy to dismiss the level of frustration experienced by the largely northern and white teaching force when the historical record tends to focus on the liberating aspects of the Freedom Schools. Beneath the surface, though, the educator activists of 1964 experienced great difficulty in implementing the Freedom School idea. Some issues stemmed from the students' experiences attending institutions racialized by Jim Crow. Educational backgrounds, experiences in Mississippi classrooms, and lived realities under Jim Crow compounded the cultural differences between the teachers and students. The widely accepted narrative that black education was inherently inferior sometimes shaped preconceived notions of the students as victims, which generated frustration as well. Reaching the students was often a struggle as a result. Sandra Adickes commented that "the first obstacle was the lack of confidence that each student had in himself." She attributed a lack of confidence to the fact that students "learn from childhood not to be openly emotional about their plight and since they are usually not educated enough to be intellectual about it, they tend to accept it."[48] As Howard Zinn noted about his experience as a Freedom School teacher in Jackson, a major obstacle in the schools was the students' silence and submissiveness, itself a product of an oppressive and segregated society.[49] Teachers also struggled with the fact that the Freedom Schools were essentially an alternative summer school program. The students' work schedule and in many instances the ongoing public school schedule during the summer precluded regular attendance at the Freedom Schools. The attendance reports from Clarksdale are indicative of the unpredictable student turnout. In Clarksdale, average attendance for the first week of class was fifteen, the second week was eight, but at any point during the summer, a school may have had as many as thirty-five students in attendance.[50] Schools in Clarksdale reflect the fact that some public schools serving black communities were still based on an agricultural cycle. Schools were closed during the planting and harvesting seasons in order to ensure that enough labor was available. On the one hand, sparse school attendance in places like Clarksdale increased the frustrations of educators who wanted to achieve a fair amount of work in a short time. It also suggests that attending school during the summer was a privilege since most students who lived in poverty had to work instead. On the other hand, attending school during the summer when their regular public schools were still in session or when they were expected to work demonstrated a deep commitment to acquiring an education.

For the teachers who were trained in traditional teacher-education programs, the curriculum and pedagogy of the Freedom Schools was very different. "The things they talked about at the Freedom Schools were totally foreign to me as a teacher," recalled Aviva Futorian, an education major from Brandeis University. Prior to the Freedom Summer campaign, Futorian was a teacher at an all-white school in the suburbs of Chicago. "It was totally new strategies for teaching and so I certainly felt I needed it. In fact, I didn't know what in God's name was going on with the Freedom Schools and with people. I felt very much lost."[51] Even for the established veterans who had earned tenure in the public school system, the Freedom Schools presented unique dilemmas. "We find these schools challenging," Liz Fusco wrote, "because those of us who have taught school in academia find the non-graded, no-grades, no-principal, no passing-flunking-reward-punishment very exciting."[52] The volunteer teachers were also told in the Ohio orientation sessions that "instead of tests for the pupils, there should be evaluations of the teachers by the students and discussions to see if they are getting what they want because the teachers are down there to help."[53] To be evaluated by students in a new learning environment unfamiliar to nearly all teachers must have been an unnerving prospect to teachers accustomed to assessing students on their own terms in environments familiar to them.

To meet the unconventional challenges presented within the Freedom School classrooms, and to bridge the gaps created by race and class differences, teachers had to quickly learn to differentiate their teaching in a variety of settings. Many of the Freedom School teachers were used to teaching with the conveniences of traditional classrooms. Or, if they had not taught previously, they would have expected a guided curriculum and resources such as desks, typewriters, books, chalk, paper, and so on. The typical Freedom School was without such conveniences, which presented a problem. As Liz Fusco remembered, since the trained and certified teachers were used to modern resources and teaching methods, they had to unlearn what they had been doing up north and learn the Freedom School idea to be effective in Mississippi.[54] As she recalled, teaching in a Freedom School was much like "turning upside down the idea of what teaching is."[55] In many ways, the volunteers who were not trained were more apt to pick up how to be a successful Freedom School teacher than those who taught or were trained in the northern schools. As one of the teachers in Ruleville recalled, "It was fairly obvious that neither being a graduate, nor being a professional teacher had much to do with being a good Freedom School teacher."[56] The bottom line of curriculum and instruction was that the Freedom Schools were unorthodox places of learning that challenged traditional ways of teaching and learning.

The educator activists experienced frustrations as activists as well, not just as educators. As activists, the Freedom School teachers desired to dismantle the system of Jim Crow while they were in Mississippi, not unlike their colleagues in the more visible voter registration projects. Teaching in Ruleville, Wally Roberts expressed deep-seated frustration with teaching in a Freedom School. Roberts discussed the problems of teaching versus taking more direct action in a letter to Staughton Lynd:

> The kids don't see how we can help them to be free. At this point, neither do we. Slow change is unthinkable when so much change is needed, when there is so much hurt.
>
> Things are so terrible here that I want to change it all NOW. Running a freedom school is an absurd waste of time. I don't want to sit around in a classroom; I want to go out and throw a few office buildings, not to injure people but to shake them up, destroy their stolen property, convince them we mean business.[57]

Teachers like Roberts pushed the parameters of a Freedom School education to guarantee that active participation in the ongoing movement was a common goal of this civil rights educational program.

Like any classroom in the United States, the personalities of the teachers influenced whether they would be successful or effective. Good teaching was defined in part by the rapport established between the teachers and students. Strong personal connections with students characterized the teaching in the Hattiesburg Freedom Schools, which served nearly seven hundred students, about one-third of the entire Freedom School student population during the summer of 1964.[58] Carolyn and Arthur Reese, who traveled from Detroit to work in Mississippi, organized and ran the schools in Hattiesburg (figure 4.5). Arthur Reese and his wife, Carolyn, were active members of the NAACP and had served in various boycotts and marches in Michigan. The Reeses had collectively taught for sixteen years in Detroit public schools as social studies and English teachers before volunteering to teach in Mississippi. Arthur Reese was studying at the time for a master's degree in guidance and counseling. In their forties, the Reeses also brought a level of experience and maturity other volunteers in their young twenties did not.[59] Moreover, they were black educators, which afforded a racial connection with their students that the majority of white Freedom School teachers did not have.

FIGURE 4.5 Arthur Reese with students in a Hattiesburg Freedom School, 1964. (Herbert Randall Freedom Summer Photographs, McCain Library and Archives, the University of Southern Mississippi, courtesy of Herbert Randall)

The first days of Freedom School laid the foundation for full engagement with the civil rights movement, and, frustrations aside, classrooms were transformed into exhilarating places of learning. "The atmosphere in the class is unbelievable," Chude Allen recalled of her classroom in Holly Springs. "It is what every teacher dreams about—real, honest enthusiasm and desire to learning anything and everything. [The students] come to class of their own free will. . . . They are excited about learning."[60] The teaching and learning in the schools ultimately advanced the cause of the movement by connecting a form of participatory democracy learned within the classroom to actual participation in the larger movement. Learning to critique the segregated society they inhabited and then learning to protest these conditions inculcated a sense of democratic and active citizenship. Students learned that becoming a citizen in the United States translated to participating actively in the movement in ways that moved beyond voting. Once they took the opportunity to engage in the learning process by way of a student-centered pedagogy, the students were primed to engage fully with the political processes of their local community.

PUTTING THEORY INTO PRACTICE: JOINING THE FRONT LINES OF THE CIVIL RIGHTS MOVEMENT

Examining and identifying the oppressive social and political structures of Mississippi was never simply an academic exercise. Students never accepted it as such. Freedom School students demanded an education that put them squarely in the front lines of the civil rights movement. As the students in Wally Robert's class in Ruleville told him, "What we want you to do is to help us become Freedom Fighters. We want to go on picket lines and do protests. Teach us how to do that."[61] This demand resonated with young teachers firmly committed to dismantling structural inequality during their stay in Mississippi. Wally Roberts was receptive to the students' demands in the Ruleville Freedom School. Teachers across the state were similarly committed, and they too regularly integrated political activity into their curriculum. The students in Ruleville were like many students across the state who attended Freedom School for lessons on how to participate in the movement and consequently viewed the schools as a segue into joining the protests of the civil rights movement.

One visible manifestation of political socialization generated by a Freedom School education can be found in the student newspapers published from within the schools. Freedom School students across the state printed their own newspapers and used mimeograph machines to disseminate news about the movement. As William Sturkey has suggested, given the dearth of liberal and black newspapers in Mississippi, the Freedom School newspapers were the largest news source on the civil rights movement in the state during the summer of 1964.[62] Writing and publishing student newspapers was one of the most popular activities during the summer of 1964 (figure 4.6). In student-produced papers like the Meridian *Freedom Star*, the Benton County *Freedom Train*, and the McComb *Freedom's Journal*, students circulated their ideas of freedom, articulated their

FIGURE 4.6 Eddie James Carthan in the Mileston Freedom School, 1964. (Photo by Matt Herron, courtesy of Eddie James Carthan)

disdain for Jim Crow, and encouraged all readers to participate. The newspapers provided a venue through which to find a burgeoning voice for dissent. The opportunity to publish their ideas was tremendously popular. As one teacher claimed during the summer, "The idea of the student newspaper is the hottest thing going."[63]

The student newspapers constituted a form of student activism because the press presented a way to resist and openly critique the segregated world they were living in. Arelya Mitchell, a student in the Holly Springs Freedom School and later a professional journalist, published her first articles in the local *South Reporter*, and she later published her own column, "Youth Go Churchy," in the black society column of the paper. But the Freedom School newspaper in Holly Springs, the *Freedom News*, created the space to develop a strong and ongoing critique of the segregated society in which they lived. Mitchell wrote a scathing critique published in the *Freedom News* during the summer of 1964 of the Holly Springs mayor, Sam Coopwood:

[Mayor Sam Coopwood] says he's a member of the Methodist Church. I wonder if he believes all men are created equal. If he does I wonder what could be so bad about colored and white living together? I wonder if he can answer that question. As Booker T. Washington said and I quote, "You can't keep a man in the hole without being down yourself." Don't you think that kind of fits Mayor Coopwood? While he's trying to keep the Negro down he's really lowering himself and Mississippi!! (That fits a lot more Southern States too.)

Most people in Holly Springs (and other places too) aren't quite citizens— not excepting the whites. The colored people aren't quite citizens because they don't vote and some don't try to vote! The white people aren't quite citizens because if they were they'd accept the Bill of Rights.[64]

The liberation of working with a free press resonated deeply with Mitchell and other students who worked on the grassroots student presses of the civil rights movement.[65]

The student-generated newspapers provided voice to a growing student movement, but one of the most transformative elements of the curriculum was the political training and socialization embedded within the schools' community outreach programs. While the schools taught the skills, the local civil rights movement unfolding outside their homes provided the opportunity to apply the nonviolent tactics and protest strategies learned in the Freedom Schools. The ongoing civil rights movement in Mississippi, which reached a fever pitch during the Freedom Summer campaign of 1964, was the ideal laboratory in which to practice the organizational and protest skills students were learning in the schools. The students were still too young to vote, which was the main priority of the Freedom Summer campaign, but the older middle school or high school students were not too young to participate in boycotts, marches, and community organizing. Therefore, testing the Civil Rights Act of 1964 by desegregating public spaces presented an opportunity for Mississippi students to experience immediate and efficacious results from direct action nonviolent protest. One popular event occurred in Hattiesburg, the "Mecca of the Freedom Schools," where Sandra Adickes led a group of six students to get library cards at the segregated public library. The library staff refused them service, and they walked across the street to the Kress lunch counter, where she was denied service again because she sat with African American students. The police arrested Adickes for vagrancy. When students from another local Freedom School tried to desegregate the same library, Hattiesburg police arrested the students and the four teachers who led the attempt.[66] As the Freedom School students in Hattiesburg engaged in the same kind of protest as adult activists, they too endured the cost of freedom during the most dangerous moments of the movement.

For most students, however, participation in the movement occurred in the form of behind-the-scenes community organizing around voter registration. With the urgency and resources of the larger Freedom Summer project devoted to this, the Freedom Schools were an ancillary project to be called upon to support the overarching objective of registering voters. The work of Freedom School students in Cleveland, Mississippi, illustrates the level of political organizing that students engaged with. Organizers planned a "Freedom Day" in Cleveland, an event in which unregistered local African Americans marched to the courthouse to register to vote. This was the first such demonstration in Bolivar County. Local Freedom School students prepared for the demonstration in advance through learning about voter registration and, more importantly, attending nonviolence workshops where students learned what to do in case of attack or arrest. On Freedom Day, students joined the picket line and distributed leaflets near the courthouse in support of the forty African Americans who made the attempt to register to vote that day.[67] Participating in a Freedom Day voter registration drive was exceptional because it supported registration in the traditional Democratic Party. As organizing the MFDP became a major priority in the closing weeks of the summer, more Freedom School teachers helped register voters in the alternative party and occupied places in the vanguard of the largest voter registration project in the history of the civil rights movement.

Canvassing was also a very common form of political participation that occurred behind the scenes. "Canvassing," Eddie James Carthan recalled, "was tough work, we'd have certain days when we would go out and canvass all day." Carthan spoke at length about canvassing, the process by which students slowly and patiently went door-to-door to talk to neighbors about the opportunity to participate in the movement, from registering to vote to attending an upcoming mass meeting. Carthan and other students canvassed people living outside the Delta town of Mileston, on the plantations, and in the county's back hills in an attempt to register them to vote. The conditions that Carthan encountered were "some of the poorest conditions that I have ever seen in my life, people living like they were. It was quite an experience to see how my folk were living and suffering, but through it all they survived."[68] In an article for a local Freedom School paper, a young Stephanie B. described how her sister and her friends canvassed the Greenwood neighborhoods. "It was a great experience," Stephanie recalled, "because we had never been canvassing before."[69] As another student recounted in the same newspaper out of the Greenwood Freedom School:

> On July 17th, I was out canvassing with Denis Jackson, one of the teachers at Mt. Zion Freedom School. We were trying to get the people to fill out Freedom Registration forms because there was going to be a convention the following day. The people gave us a hard time but we convinced some of them to fill out the forms. One lady said she didn't believe anything was going to change in Mississippi. I was determined. I wanted that lady's eyes opened wide so that she could see all the troublesome problems confronting the Negro people in Mississippi. I wanted her eyes opened wide so that she could see the things she could do.[70]

Anthony Harris experienced canvassing in a different way. "I remember going out and having doors slammed in our faces and people being angry with us for knocking on their doors," Harris recalled, "and people were afraid. They were very much afraid to talk to us."[71] Such experiences taught the ten-year-old that a deep fear resonated throughout the older generations. The movement, the young people learned, required long, hard, patient work.

Canvassing and voter registration thus emerged as the most common political activities among students during the summer of 1964. Through canvassing and voter registration, students engaged the community through meticulous work, which led to profound observations of the towns they grew up in. Moreover, as indicated in the pages of the student-published newspapers, canvassing provided the opportunity for students to articulate what voting meant and how it related to citizenship and freedom. Though not as visible as direct action nonviolent protests, canvassing still presented a degree of imminent danger to young people. Indianola policeman W. T. Walker arrested two students, aged eight and nine, for distributing voter registration pamphlets to local community members. According to the SNCC report on the incident, Walker "made them get into his car, cursed, threatened them, and took the frightened children to the police station."[72] Mississippi law enforcement did not make the distinction between adult and child nor between violations of voter registration and segregation laws. White segregationists believed that all civil rights activists and protests threatened the Mississippi way of life.

The ongoing arrests of students and the violence that constantly threatened young people made their work even more remarkable. For white segregationists willing to resort to violence, any person regardless of age, race, or creed was subject to retaliation. Violent defenders of the status quo did not spare youth in their policing of the social mores of Mississippi, as evidenced by the slaying of Emmett Till. As noted, local police officers arrested students for attempting to desegregate public spaces and even for distributing voter registration literature throughout the summer campaign. The students engaged in political activity that put them in the same line of fire as older activists. Carthan recalled the danger associated with being seen with a white person while canvassing in the depths of the Mississippi Delta:

> I was on a team canvassing together, it was out in the hills and [the team] would get in a station wagon and get dropped off at different sections of the community to work those houses, so we were walking down a wooded area and we heard a car coming, she [a white organizer] would run and hide in the woods 'cause if that person was white and saw me and her together, we both would probably be killed.[73]

Moreover, any family with children, no matter how young, enrolled in the Freedom Schools was liable to face the consequences of joining the movement. Families connected to the schools faced the same economic reprisals, for instance, as those at the front lines of the movement. As Carthan recalled, "Everyone was scared to attend [civil rights] meetings because they would get fired. Teachers couldn't teach; they could get fired. Plantation owners putting folks off the plantations, the factory people would fire you."[74] As Carthan articulated, retaliation, violence, and proximity to death were palpable during the summer of 1964. In addition to the disappearances of Schwerner, Goodman, and Chaney, Mississippi in 1964 was experiencing an increase in racial violence. During the duration of the volunteers' stay in Mississippi, between June and August 1964, local police and segregationists murdered three freedom workers, violently assaulted over eighty activists, shot at activists or their homes over thirty-five times, arrested over one thousand workers, burned thirty-five churches, and firebombed thirty-one homes and Freedom Houses that housed the summer volunteers.[75]

One such bombing occurred at the Freedom House in McComb, which was used as the community's Freedom School. Situated in the all-black Burgland neighborhood, the Freedom House at 702 Wall Street, owned by local supporter Willie Mae Cotton, served as a very important and symbolic meeting place that attracted a lot of attention.[76] Hilda Casin, a local educator at Taggart Elementary School, remembered that heavy traffic "flooded" local streets in Burgland, which attracted an inordinate amount of attention from the police.[77] In the early morning of July 8, 1964, segregationists bombed the Freedom House. Though it housed ten COFO workers, only Curtis Hayes was injured.[78]

Freedom School students remained committed to their education and showed up the next morning for class outside the shell of the house that remained on Wall Street. They held class outside until a new space could be located, which proved to be exceedingly difficult after the bombing. Sixteen-year-old Freedom School student Joyce Brown, a mentor to the younger students and emerging community leader, wrote in a poem, "The House of Liberty":

I asked for your churches, and you turned me down,
But I'll do my work if I have to do it on the ground,
You will not speak for fear of being heard,
So you crawl in your shell and say, "Do not disturb,"
You think because you've turned me away,
You've protected yourself for another day.[79]

Students continued to attend school in the backyard until the community provided another building. In a clandestine meeting orchestrated by COFO with sympathetic blacks, the McComb community eventually donated support, funding, and community facilities to the cause. Joyce Brown and the Freedom School students galvanized support for the local movement; they formed a housing and food committee and each person contributed $50 toward the purchase of a lot to be used for a local community center.[80] The example of students organizing to find a new space for a community center provided proof of the value of a Freedom School education. As Staughton Lynd noted about the case of McComb, "The presence of a Freedom School helped to loosen the hard knot of fear and to organize the Negro community."[81]

THE EDUCATIVE ROLE OF RACE AND INTERRACIAL DIALOGUE IN THE FREEDOM SCHOOLS

Organizers and teachers purposefully implemented the revolutionary aspects of the Freedom Schools, including the political objectives, the civil rights–based curriculum and the student-centered pedagogy. The interracial dialogue between teacher and student, however, was a defining hallmark of the Freedom School legacy that proved to be an unintended consequence for many of the white volunteers working in a black movement. The curriculum of the Freedom Schools, which focused on issues of civil rights and citizenship, and the pedagogy of the Freedom Schools, which facilitated discussion and critical thinking, created an atmosphere conducive to in-depth discussions about race. This, coupled with the fact that most teachers were white, led to a dynamic dialogue between black students and white teachers. The Freedom Schools created the space where whites could openly interact with black students who typically had learned to avoid any interaction with whites. For Homer Hill, it was "the first time in my life that I was exposed to people who were white but who were not in any manner similar to the people who we were accustomed to who happened to be white. For me that experience was something that I continue to carry with me to this day because it gave me the opportunity to realize that not all white people were like the people in our community."[82] Carthan had a similar experience in Mileston: "It was the first time in my life I had seen whites and blacks associate and work together."[83] Because students had grown up in a strictly segregated and racialized society, contact with white people who treated them as equals was indeed a profound experience and one that facilitated a memorable learning experience that was not dictated by the curriculum. The experience lived up to the expectations established during the orientation sessions that "the most important experience for the students will be their relationship with their teachers."[84] What the orientation failed to note, however, was that the interracial environment was reciprocal, and the volunteers were also profoundly impacted by the experience.

Interracial dialogue aided the development of participatory citizenship as students and teachers engaged in close conversations with the racialized "other." Arelya Mitchell, who attended Freedom School in Holly Springs at the Rust College campus, "became aware, even more aware, of the color issue." She remembered actively questioning and critically examining the racialized assumptions at a larger structural level.[85] "I became aware of the interracial dynamic," Gloria Xifaras Clark recalled about teaching in Bolivar County (figure 4.7). "My own way is to try to make everything conscious rather than unconscious, to understand and to bring it to consciousness and raise it up so it's right in front of you."[86] For Clark and others, close contact with African Americans forced volunteers to contemplate race and its significance in ways that challenged preconceived notions and overarching worldviews constructed upon limited interactions with others. The racial dynamic helped actualize an essential ideal of integration that defined the freedom struggle, but it also served as a pedagogical strategy that fostered honest dialogue and further facilitated political socialization around issues of race.

Beyond the classroom, the black communities that housed the schools were at the center of the Freedom School experience. The long history of self-sustaining black communities served as an important factor in the success of the summer projects. Communities played an essential role in providing food, shelter, and protection for the summer volunteers. This type of support was imperative for activist organizations, and the very existence and strength of a program was often dependent upon the commitment and organizing strengths of the community. As one Freedom School teacher explained, regular SNCC staff made it clear that effective activism was dependent upon active engagement in the community, which meant working in the community, going to

FIGURE 4.7   Gloria Xifaras Clark with Freedom School students in Benton
County, 1964. (Courtesy of Gloria Xifaras Clark and Larry Rubin)

church, and attending meetings with community members.[87] Community support demonstrated real courage. By their very presence in black communities,
white volunteers living in the homes of local African Americans challenged the
deepest social mores of the South. This presented a grave threat to the black
families that opened their homes to white volunteers and made the situation
even more volatile and made the selflessness of those who participated all the
more poignant. Despite financial hardship and segregationist violence, communities opened their homes and welcomed the volunteers and activists who
had come to work in the state. Without the support of the community in providing homes for the workers and buildings for schools, the Freedom Schools
would have never seen the light of day.

Both interracial dialogue and the constant threat of danger quickly cemented bonds between the Freedom School teachers and the students, their families, and the communities that housed them. "In the course of the summer," Freedom School teacher Sandra Adickes noted, "the volunteers came to regard the people who sheltered and fed them as heroes, and bonds were formed between hosts and guests that lasted for lifetimes."[88] Two white volunteers lived for the duration the summer with the family of Anthony Harris. "The three months that they lived in our home provided a unique perspective for them and for my family on how persons from a different culture and a different part of the country live," Harris recalled.[89] As Harris indicates, the support of the community had a profound effect on both the local volunteers and the families that housed them. The volunteers were coming from affluent backgrounds and were living in Mississippi communities that were struggling to get by. Moreover, the volunteers were living with local black people who had long struggled for freedom, something the white volunteers did not have to fight for. Some of the local residents had been born during Reconstruction. Some told family stories that traced back to the days of slavery. All of them were personally acquainted with the reality of Jim Crow violence. "Living in [the Clarksdale] community, even though I only was there about six or seven weeks, I would say that it had a profound effect on me," Freedom School teacher Sandy Siegel recalled. "It was a privilege for me to have been there for that time and live with people who had to go through what the blacks of Mississippi had to go through. It really kind of turned my world upside down, it made me feel differently about the world that I live in and the values that I had."[90] The difference in backgrounds was the basis for some of the most profound life lessons learned during Freedom Summer.

A deeply interracial environment facilitated very intimate and sexual experiences as well, particularly given the youth of the volunteers, the absence of parents, and the intimate bonds formed between peers whose lives were constantly threatened. As much as organizers warned against sexual relationships, intimate (both platonic and sexual) bonds formed quickly between volunteers and the local community.[91] The fact that sexual relationships existed is not surprising, however. Charles Payne described the SNCC workers as sexual icons since they were "in their late teen or early twenties, were marketable items romantically. They were from out of town, they were courageous, they were intelligent, everybody in town was talking about them."[92] This is an apt description for the Freedom School volunteers, too, which situates sexuality as a prominent fixture of the Freedom Summer campaign. In addition to remaining open to forming new relationships, men and women committed themselves to experiencing equality on all fronts, which sometimes led to challenging the taboos of interracial relationships, strictly platonic or otherwise. As Chude Allen recalled:

> I'm sure I wasn't the only white woman to fall in love with a black man during that summer of 1964. There've been things written about interracial sex, but little about love. I fell in love. Oh, we kissed and held hands, but ours was an innocent romance. The night before he left for the most dangerous part of that violent, racist state, I lay on his cot with him. He held me tight, kissed my face and I wondered if I would ever see him again. I knew he might die.[93]

Allen suggests that the Freedom School teachers clearly maintained a life outside of the schoolhouse and formed meaningful and sometimes romantic relationships. Although Allen did not become sexually active that summer, the experiences of Freedom Summer helped change her mind about waiting until marriage. As she recalled, "Giving up my virginity was a big thing for me, as it was for most women I knew in 1964. That first time, if it happened before marriage, put a girl into a different category. Some men wouldn't want to marry her." But Allen met several women on the summer project who viewed sex differently. Allen remembered that "they didn't hide their relationships. What was clear to me was they weren't ashamed of being sexually active. For them sex wasn't such a big thing. That also influenced me."[94] Forming romantic relationships and engaging with larger issues of sexuality was a point of liberation for the volunteers during the summer of 1964. Forming romantic or sexual bonds with a different race was an intimate way to experience the "beloved community."[95] As many men and women volunteers learned over the course of the summer, sexuality and issues of gender equality constituted another front to be liberated and, as such, the interracial relationships of the summer campaign constituted a form of activism because it openly challenged the deepest beliefs of white purity and sanctity that the South had attempted to preserve since the Civil War.

Whether forming an intimate relationship with a partner of a different race alleviated a sense of white guilt, defined the ultimate expression of racial liberation and union, indicated a mutual and genuine admiration between two people, or some combination thereof, such relationships on the summer project were problematic, if not outwardly dangerous.[96] Freedom School teachers formed close interracial social and sexual relationships that contested miscegenation laws and social customs that legally regulated the sexual relationships between men and women in the South. Laws against miscegenation and interracial marriage in Mississippi, which were illegal in every southern state until the *Loving v. Virginia* (1967) decision, protected a white supremacist's constructed notion of "purity."[97] Any transgression translated into violence that jeopardized the entire project. Not only did it endanger the lives of volunteers, but it was also an affront to local African Americans who lived under the system of Jim Crow. Whereas white volunteers had the freedom to leave the oppressive climate whenever they wished, local African Americans were not afforded such privileges if they chose to transgress sexual mores. The sexual experiences of Freedom Summer had a destabilizing effect on both the individuals involved and the larger project. Attending a Freedom School in Hattiesburg, a young Anthony Harris was quick to note, "There was no doubt that the issues of interracial romance created noticeable tension within the leadership and the rank-and-file of the civil rights movement."[98] One memo from the summer campaign stated that the field staff was concerned with "sexual problems that racism produces."[99] A summer volunteer in McComb criticized what they viewed as "The Summer Camp Syndrome." The Freedom School report from McComb went on to explain that sexual tension is "worth mentioning because feedback from the local people indicated to us the nature of the problem." In addressing the problem, the volunteer asked if "it's wise for workers to overtly flirt with local girls. . . . How will a [Freedom School] class be affected when it is known by the student that the teacher has a favorite? Going a little further, should we exploit the movement to meet girls?"[100] Sexual and other romantic relationships during the summer illustrates that the interracial environment of 1964 made even the intensely intimate moments political.

Working and living in an intensely intimate, political, and personal interracial environment fostered a deep and lasting learning experience. Almost all oral history participants commented that their experience in Mississippi included powerful instances of seeing firsthand the living conditions and debilitating effects as well as the coping and survival methods formed under Jim Crow. As Wally Roberts remembered, "We met a lot of bright kids and met kids who had just been beat down by poverty, and I think that was the big culture shock for me in terms of seeing how bad the living conditions and the poverty were in Mississippi—it just blew me away. I had never seen it up close before, white or black or anyplace, and what we saw was just devastating, and that was a culture shock."[101] Dale Gronemeier, a Freedom School teacher in Ruleville, Mississippi, similarly reflected upon his experiences living in the black community:

> The people here have given so much. They who have nothing at all—many below subsistence income—are willing to give all and risk all for freedom. The woman I stayed with the first day lives on a $50 a month disability check of her husband, and she is a registered voter, has taken in white workers, and done other things in the movement—each of which action jeopardizes that subsistence check as well increasing the physical dangers to her. I feel humbled and inspired by their simple courage.[102]

Recollections of the teachers point toward an ideal of integration that other projects during the movement sought but never achieved.

The interracial experiences inspired a form of activism among the Freedom School teachers that included raising funds and resources for their project sites in Mississippi. As the organizers who favored using white volunteers in the summer campaign had anticipated, white volunteers were deeply moved by their experiences in the Magnolia State and used their connections back home to help support the movement. In addition to the financial backing the volunteer teachers brought with them to Mississippi, teachers were also bringing with them political, financial, and social capital that could benefit the project. The Friends of the Mississippi Summer Project in Oxford, Ohio, illustrates the rich network of connections that volunteers cultivated. After the orientation in Ohio, over sixty local community members formed the Friends of the Mississippi Summer Project to sponsor twenty-nine volunteers from the college in Oxford. They published newsletters updating subscribers of events in Mississippi, often based on the volunteers' letters, and they solicited contributions and material for the Freedom Schools. In addition to raising funds and resources, the organization also generated political support and encouraged members to place pressure on Mississippi officials. "Another way to boost morale," the newsletter from August 5, 1964, stated, "is to put pressure on local sheriffs, jailers, or other local agencies in case a sponsor is arrested. . . . This may save one from a beating or other police abuse."[103] Such connections proliferated across the country during Freedom Summer. Gronemeier, a college student from Illinois State University, regularly petitioned his institution for resources to assist the civil rights educational project he joined in Ruleville. "We have some very critical needs here, the most important is money," Gronemeier wrote to his peers and professors during the summer of 1964, "and I'd like to ask you to help us by a little effort in the University Community." He went on to write:

> I have undertaken to try to raise at least a thousand dollars from the various sources that I can tap. I think there are many people at [Illinois State University] who feel a concern about Mississippi and have the social conscience which believes in the kind of program we are working for; many of them are warm personal friends of mine. I think many of them would want to give $5–$10 to help out the summer effort. I wonder if you would contact as many people as you can to try to raise some money.[104]

Gronemeier also contacted the Unitarian Church and Representative Paul Simon of Illinois to raise funds for (and awareness of) their projects in Mississippi. Like other volunteers, Gronemeier published his reflections, observations, and descriptions of his experiences working in Mississippi in publications like the *Guardian*, *Harper's Weekly*, and *Frontier*.[105] Chude Allen's parents shared the letters she wrote home in order to garner support for the movement and to raise money, circulating them among family, friends, and the press.[106] Some volunteers brought direct connections to federal policymakers. Len Edwards, a law student at the University of Chicago and project director in Ruleville, called his father, Representative Don Edwards, when local blacks reported that segregationists plotted to bomb the Freedom House in Shaw, which served as a community center and Freedom School. The FBI responded the same night and dispatched two field agents to investigate the report.[107]

The students and the students' families taught the teachers invaluable lessons about the high cost of freedom and what it took to sustain a freedom movement. The lessons learned through integration and interracial dialogue, especially in hostile settings that further crystallized these bonds in a short period time, speak to the value attached to integration. The positive experiences of working with the racialized "other" influenced many of the teachers and students as they pursued the benefits of integration in their own organizing and political work during the fall of 1964 and, in many cases, throughout the rest of their careers.

THE END OF THE FREEDOM SUMMER: LESSONS LEARNED AND AN AGENDA ESTABLISHED

The culmination of the Freedom School program was a student-led conference on August 6–8, 1964, in Meridian. Roscoe Jones, a Freedom School student in Meridian, and Joyce Brown, the Freedom School student in McComb who penned the poem about her Freedom School that was bombed, chaired a committee of five students who organized the convention. Students were adamant about organizing their own conference on their own terms. Jones recalled the planning stages of the student conference: "This was our convention and we wanted to run it, and we did. Most people don't know that. We ran that convention."[108]

Two days before the opening of the student convention in Meridian, the FBI unearthed the bodies of the three missing activists, and funeral services were held for them. Dave Dennis, a key organizer behind the Freedom Summer campaign, gave an impassioned speech:

> What I want to talk about is the living dead that we have right in our midst, not only here in the state of Mississippi, but throughout the nation. I blame the people in Washington, D.C., and on down in the state of Mississippi for what happened just as much as I blame those who pulled the trigger. I don't grieve for James Chaney. He lived a fuller life than most of us will ever live. He's got his freedom, and we're still fighting for ours. I'm sick and tired of going to the

funerals of black men who have been murdered by white men. I've got vengeance in my heart tonight, and I ask you to feel angry with me.[109]

Dennis set the stage for intense debate among the students about how they should proceed as the summer drew to a close. After a summer of civil rights education, the Freedom School students had many questions about how to maintain the momentum of the movement. As Roscoe Jones recalled about the conference, the central question among the students at the end of the summer was, "What were the young people going to do in the state of Mississippi?"[110]

An official function of the convention was to develop a youth platform for the MFDP. But the student convention also served to coordinate long-term plans for statewide action during the upcoming year. To articulate a strategy and a plan of action to be implemented during the school year, each Freedom School was asked to send three representatives to the state convention to discuss and build upon the experiences of the Freedom Summer. For two days, more than ninety student delegates discussed issues related to jobs, schools, foreign affairs, and public accommodations in workshops. The students appointed committee chairs and delegated responsibilities following the convention's rules of standard political party protocol.[111] The convention then formally offered recommendations for the MFDP in a written declaration:

> In an age where machines are rapidly replacing manual labor, job opportunities and economic security increasingly require higher levels of education. We therefore demand:
>
> 1. Better facilities in all schools. These would include textbooks, laboratories, air conditioning, heating, recreation, and lunchrooms,
> 2. A broader curriculum including vocational subjects and foreign languages,
> 3. Low-fee adult classes for better jobs,
> 4. That the school year consist of nine (9) consecutive months,
> 5. Exchange programs and public kindergartens,
> 6. Better-qualified teachers with salaries according to qualification,
> 7. Forced retirement (women at 62, men at 65),
> 8. Special schools for mentally retarded and treatment and care of cerebral palsy victims,

9. That taxpayers' money not be used to provide private schools,
10. That all schools be integrated and equal throughout the country,
11. Academic freedom for teachers and students,
12. That teachers be able to join any political organization to fight for Civil Rights without fear of being fired,
13. That teacher brutality be eliminated.[112]

The students demonstrated a degree of political sophistication, consciousness, and an insightful understanding of human rights issues. As part of their input provided to the MFDP, the students demanded access to public accommodations, building codes for each home, integrated schools, a public works program, and the appointment of qualified blacks to state positions.[113]

The youth platform that the Freedom School students generated at the Meridian conference provide important insight into how students viewed their role as young activists in the ongoing civil rights movement. Notably, only one of the thirteen points on education demanded that schools be integrated.[114] In an era in which desegregating schools was the dominant paradigm, the Freedom School students did not make desegregation a priority. The Freedom School students sought to improve the conditions within their own schools and the boycotts that occurred the following school year reflected this desire. The conference in Meridian demonstrated to adult activists that students had internalized the commitment to enact social change and the strategies needed to do so. According to Staughton Lynd, the convention was also a turning point in the Freedom School idea. By the end of the conference, the students decided to work for change within the schools rather than creating an alternative network of Freedom Schools to replace the existing Mississippi public school structure.

* * *

The summer of 1964 was an educational success, and the Freedom Schools provide insight into the comprehensive nature of civil rights work in Mississippi. In addition to the largest voter registration project in the movement, the summer campaign also created the largest alternative civil rights educational program for young people. Freedom School students studied in schools that were very different from their regular public schools and participated in work very different from the work most students were accustomed to. Their enrollment in a summer school program was a testament to students' dual commitment to education and full participation in the movement. The Freedom School students were unafraid to challenge Jim Crow, so they constituted a new generation of civil rights activists who were directly educated in the ethos and strategies of the civil rights movement. Freedom School students knew how racial discrimination could be challenged, and they were steadfastly committed to challenging this system. The Freedom School students learned that they could challenge what many people of their parents' generation saw as unchangeable and fixed. Students ultimately learned that they did not have to accept a seemingly fixed or inherited social position; they too could challenge the structural inequities that plagued Mississippi. Hymethia Thompson recalled the abstract lessons she learned by attending a Freedom School:

> We learned that we could still make it. The Freedom Schools allowed us to believe that we could come above whatever [negative] situation, and we were inspired that we had to work harder and go extra time to try to catch up if we didn't have the supplies or the books, whatever, but that we could make it. We had to believe that we could, and we had to believe that God had given us what we needed, regardless of the color of our skin.[115]

The resolve articulated by Thompson is indicative of the intrinsic motivation that guided the civil rights generation in their work as young activists.

The Freedom Schools initially began as a project secondary to the voter registration campaign. But by the summer's end, the schools grew in importance and were largely regarded as an unprecedented success. And they were. The high point of the Freedom Schools came three weeks after their official opening. By July 27, Lynd reported that there were forty-one Freedom Schools in operation, and approximately 2,135 students were attending, more than double the organizers' expectations. There were 175 full-time teachers working in the schools, and in late July, 50 to 100 more teachers were being recruited. Lynd estimated that close to fifty schools were in operation by August.[116] Liz Fusco, who served as the Freedom School coordinator after the summer campaign, articulated the potential for collective action led by the cohort of young protestors that emerged by August 1964:

> The transformation of Mississippi is possible because the transformation of people has begun. And if it can happen in Mississippi, it can happen all over the South. The original hope of the Freedom School plan was that there would be about 1000 students in the state coming to the informal discussion groups and other sessions. It turned out that by the end of the summer the number was closer to 3000, and that the original age expectation of 16- 17- 18 year olds had to be revised to include pre-school children and all the way up to 70 year old people, all anxious about how to be Free.[117]

As the summer concluded, Freedom School teachers and students prepared to carry the struggles of the civil rights movement to their own schools. Participants possessed a strong sense of political efficacy, and they continued to organize, boycott, and protest once the volunteers began to leave the state and return home. For the young people equipped with a Freedom School education, the real movement had yet to begin.

5

"WE DO HEREBY DECLARE INDEPENDENCE"

Educational Activism and Reconceptualizing Freedom
After the Summer Campaign

We ... the Negroes of Mississippi assembled, appeal to the government of
the state, that no man is free until all men are free. We do hereby declare
independence from the unjust laws of Mississippi which conflict with the
United States Constitution.

THE FREEDOM SCHOOL STUDENTS OF ST. JOHN'S METHODIST CHURCH IN
HATTIESBURG, MISSISSIPPI, 1964

We young people had a plan. We were going to integrate everything that
was open to the public that we had to go through the back door. We were
going through the front door in movie houses, everything. We had plans
for it all. And it was not adults telling us this. It was student led.

ROSCOE JONES, FREEDOM SCHOOL STUDENT IN MERIDIAN, MISSISSIPPI,
AND MISSISSIPPI STUDENT UNION PRESIDENT

What was so beautiful was what happened with the African American people, young people and the leadership that evolved and all of these indigenous leaders. . . . The children were just brave and ready to go up against
armed guards and people with sticks and bricks just singing.

DR. GWENDOLYN (ROBINSON) SIMMONS, FREEDOM SCHOOL TEACHER IN
LAUREL, MISSISSIPPI

In the aftermath of the Freedom Summer campaign, former Freedom School students joined the front lines of the civil rights movement and sustained it after the majority of the volunteer teachers left the state and the larger movement expanded in new ideological directions. Young people envisioned a new society as they formally declared "independence from the unjust laws of Mississippi." In this historic moment, students applied the skills they cultivated, refined, and practiced during Freedom Summer under the tutelage of a corps of Freedom Fighters. Students desegregated formerly all-white public schools and other public spaces, organized school boycotts, and demanded a quality education. Young people's level of political engagement, consciousness, and commitment while still in middle and high school constituted nothing less than an educational revolution in a state that provided a notoriously poor and unequal public education. The Freedom School students implemented a new form of educational activism, and the very essence of the program prompted important questions about how quality education can be achieved as schools were desegregated for the first time in the history of Mississippi. Inspired by their summer experiences, Freedom School teachers who returned home similarly applied the skills they learned to struggles in their home communities. The rapidly changing context, which was governed by evolving movement politics, stymied the growth of the Freedom Schools by the fall of 1965. But the Freedom Schools prepared the young activists to continue the struggle for quality education and full equality within a dynamic state, local, and national context through the 1960s and, indeed, the rest of their careers. Though many teachers left the state and students left the confines of their Freedom Schools to organize their own struggles, no participant left unchanged, and in many ways the ideology of resistance and education for liberation remained entrenched in the Mississippi civil rights movement.

Freedom School students returned to schools across Mississippi as student activists trained in the philosophy and skills of the civil rights movement with a new sense of the potential of what schools could be. The Freedom School students and the nascent MSU began the 1964/1965 school year with a demonstrated public resolve to eradicate discrimination found in their own schools.[1] The determination to carry forth the struggle materialized in a year of protests that moved beyond registering voters and canvassing communities to directly address a range of issues from desegregation to fair treatment in segregated schools. Students were returning to a school system during the fall of 1964 that was undergoing a fundamental transformation. For the first time since the monumental *Brown v. Board of Education* decision, handed down ten years before the summer campaign, the federal courts ordered Mississippi to desegregate its public elementary schools, making it the last state in the country to even nominally "integrate." The prospect of desegregation reinvigorated the students' resolve to challenge discrimination on all observable fronts, and it shaped their course of action during the school year. Freedom School students joined the effort to enroll African American students in previously all-white schools. Other Freedom School students who returned to segregated public schools committed to change the quality of education they received. In these instances students began the school year voicing their opposition to institutional discrimination, organizing local chapters of the MSU, and speaking out against unfair treatment in the schools. Student protests evolved during the 1964/1965 school year, and they were more numerous, sophisticated, and far-reaching than those during the summer campaign. Working within their own schools generated a statewide movement of grassroots activism throughout the 1960s that kept the local movement alive once the volunteers returned home.

The activism of Freedom School students challenges the narrative that the civil rights movement declined, ended, or took a turn for the worse after Freedom Summer between 1965 and 1968. Conventional histories and popular understandings of the civil rights era situate the MFDP protest at the Democratic National Convention in August 1964 in Atlantic City, which was the culmination of the voter registration project of the summer campaign, as a dramatic turning point in the trajectory of the civil rights movement.[2] The larger historiography posits that civil rights organizers were battle-fatigued, exhausted, and disillusioned after the disparaging rebuffs experienced during the Atlantic City demonstration. It appeared that the Mississippi movement had lost momentum, and civil rights activists were disenchanted once again with the federal government's failure to enact substantive and equitable reform. Popular interpretation and memory of the civil rights movement marks the conclusion of the 1964 Freedom Summer campaign as the end of the "classical" nonviolent direct-action phase of the movement. As SNCC activist Cleveland Sellers, who was later wounded in the Orangeburg Massacre in 1968, commented on the experience: "Never again were we lulled into believing that our task was exposing injustices so that the 'good' people of America could eliminate them. We left Atlantic City with the knowledge that the movement had turned to something else."[3] John Lewis, a founding member and chairman of SNCC, stated in regard to the convention: "The physical and emotional toll taken by Mississippi Summer was crippling to the morale of SNCC. The disaster at Atlantic City was like a knockout punch. . . . Like soldiers who had been on the front lines too long, we were beat, burned out."[4] The experience of Dr. Gwendolyn (Robinson) Simmons, a Freedom School teacher, embodies how exhaustion, fatigue, and stress forced many veterans out of the movement. She described her departure from the movement: "I was on the verge of a nervous breakdown and I had been locked up for fifteen days in Jackson and when I came out, I didn't know how bad of shape I was in, but I had two automobile accidents back to back. And I was at fault for both and had ruined a couple of SNCC cars and then Jim [Forman] said, 'What is going on with you?' . . . I kept saying, 'I can't leave, I can't leave.' "[5] Stories of emotional frustration such as these shape a narrative of collapse and dramatic conclusion to the classical phase of the movement.

Ongoing frustrations with structural discrimination and exclusion, growing hostility over the use of whites in the movement, and mounting opposition to what looked like the failure of nonviolent protest precipitated a shift toward "black power," which is often traced to a speech Stokely Carmichael, a SNCC organizer, delivered in 1966 in Mississippi. This standard interpretation puts forth two temporally and ideology distinct movements, which suggests that the civil rights movement ended with the rise of the black power. A narrative of two distinct movements reinforces the notion that the civil rights era ended soon after Freedom Summer because the federal government extended equal protection and the right to vote once and for all with the passage of the Civil Rights Act of 1964 and the Voting Rights Act of 1965. This interpretation also posits that the black power movement grew from a spontaneous and violent break from the civil rights era and its call for integration and a "beloved community." The rise of the Black Panther Party, urban unrest in cities outside of the South such as Los Angeles, California; Detroit, Michigan; and Newark, New Jersey;

and the assassination of Dr. Martin Luther King Jr. signify the shift toward black power and the eclipse of the classic stage of nonviolence. As historian Peniel Joseph observed, this standard historiographical interpretation erroneously suggests that "Black Power simultaneously triggered the demise of civil rights and the New Left's apocalyptical descent into destructive 'revolutionary' violence."[6] This oft-referenced narrative overlooks how the Freedom Schools, a classic civil rights educational program, continued to make an impact during the era of black power. The Freedom Schools provide a lens through which to see continuity as well as a change during the movement throughout the 1960s.

Between 1964 and 1968, thousands of students joined the front lines of the movement in Mississippi and defined activism on their own terms. The grassroots activism that occurred throughout the late 1960s provides a counternarrative to the one of collapse and further defines the new struggles that grew out of the Freedom Summer campaign. Although nearly all the volunteers and organizers ultimately left or were asked to leave the state, the ideology of change, the transcripts of resistance, and the motivation to transform the closed society remained. Far from exhausted and disillusioned, Freedom School students and teachers increased their activism with vigor and in nuanced ways after the summer campaign. Moreover, though the vast majority of Freedom Schools disbanded by 1966, the Head Start program, Black Panther Liberation Schools, and other education programs of the late 1960s carried forth the ideology of education for freedom that was expressed during the summer of 1964. In spite of a narrative that suggests otherwise, the ideology and philosophy that underpinned the Freedom Schools was alive and well throughout the 1960s.

The Freedom School students and the imprint the schools left on the movement provide a lens through which to comprehend the dynamic interplay between the local movement and a rapidly changing national context during the late 1960s and 1970s. The politics and ideology surrounding the Freedom Schools illustrate an ongoing interaction with a concurrent and parallel conservative movement, which gained ground by opposing "Great Society" legislation, and the Head Start antipoverty education, which drew from the infrastructure painstakingly created by movement veterans. The activism of the Freedom School students and teachers, moreover, suggests the ongoing role of education for liberation in the movement throughout the 1960s. The work of

Freedom School teachers and students illustrate that, rather than a dramatic end to the civil right movement, the years after Freedom Summer were a dynamic moment that marked both a continuation and shift in strategies, organization, and ideology. Indeed, the civil rights movement had just begun for the Freedom School students at the conclusion of the summer of 1964. Young people fresh out of Freedom School zealously laid the groundwork of a student movement. As the Freedom Schools closed their doors, the cohort of activists that passed through them applied the skills, strategies, and knowledge on their own in a climate that remained volatile. It was a test that Freedom School students and the other activists they inspired were prepared to pass.

FREEDOM SCHOOL STUDENT ACTIVISM
AFTER THE SUMMER CAMPAIGN

Students who attended Freedom Schools reinvigorated the statewide movement in Mississippi after the defeat in Atlantic City. As campaign leadership waned and grew frustrated, Freedom School students redoubled their efforts to organize and act as they were taught during the summer. "Within the Freedom Schools," Liz Fusco wrote at the end of the summer in 1964, "[students] began to become articulate about what was wrong, and the way things should be instead: why don't they do this at our school? was the first question asked, and then there began to be answers, which led to further questions."[7] Fusco, who served as the Freedom School coordinator during the 1964/1965 school year, captured the very essence of student activism after Freedom Summer. As young people recently educated in the principles, strategies, and methods of the civil rights movement, Freedom School students critically examined the closed society and developed a plan of action to change it. The majority of the original Freedom School students did not attend a Freedom School during the 1964/1965 school year, but they maintained a level of activism by organizing on their own, aligning themselves with local projects with similar goals, and orchestrating protest through the new student organization, the MSU. As the older leadership disbanded and the Freedom Schools decreased in number, young people maintained the front lines of the civil rights movement through desegregating schools and boycotting their own schools in order to pressure the state to provide a quality education to all students.

The student-led conference in Meridian at the end of Freedom Summer was crucial in this regard. Students decided at the Freedom School conference that they would enter the new school year acting of their own accord and work *within* the schools, as opposed to abandoning the schools and enrolling full time in a local Freedom School. An understanding also emerged that students would use the MSU as a statewide student union to coordinate the impending struggles in schools. Student activists organized the MSU in January 1964 when high school students in Hattiesburg wanted to participate in the Freedom Day voter registration drive sponsored by COFO. By the end of the summer campaign, the Freedom School teachers and coordinators looked to the MSU as an avenue for continued protest and as a legitimate extension of the Freedom School idea. According to the Freedom School convention program that was held in Jackson just days after the Meridian convention in August 1964, "The latter part of the program will be devoted to the organization of the Mississippi Student Union. This will be the focal point of the convention. It is hoped a strong union will be the result of the Freedom Schools."[8] The union, in the Freedom School coordinator's words, was a student-led program whose aim was to apply "direct action to alleviate serious grievances."[9] Toward the end of the convention, student delegates elected Roscoe Jones, a Freedom School student in Meridian, as the union's first president.[10]

Former Freedom School students applied the skills they learned during the summer campaign and reentered the public schools that were being desegregated for the first time since the *Brown v. Board of Education* (1954) decision. The fifth federal circuit court, considered the most conservative court of appeals in the United States, finally ordered local schools to integrate through a "stair-step" plan in Biloxi, Clarksdale, Jackson, and Leake County beginning in the fall of 1964.[11] This was the beginning of the "freedom of choice" plans that determined the pace of gradual desegregation in Mississippi, a project not complete until 1970. White school boards and other policymakers drafted freedom of choice plans to legally delay the process of desegregation. The plans required African American parents to apply to enroll their children in all-white schools rather than drafting and enforcing comprehensive desegregation plans. The state placed the onus to desegregate squarely upon the shoulders of black families and left the actual plans of desegregation to local white school boards committed to maintaining segregation. Additionally, local newspapers often printed the names of those who applied to attend white schools, which led to violence, intimidation, and harassment.

The Freedom School teachers and students participated in the historic desegregation of Mississippi, along with the parents and church ministers of the students, by organizing the first wave of students to enter previously all-white schools. They were well trained in the organizational strategies of the movement and had been fully exposed to the intimidation tactics used by segregationists. Initially the MSU was the organizational entity through which students could join the desegregation efforts that unfolded across the state. The Jackson branch of the student union emphasized working with the desegregation process in the capital city, one of the first locations in Mississippi to desegregate. Here the union organized students to desegregate the high schools, in addition to the elementary schools the state ordered to desegregate. Plans were also made to work as tutors and "adopt" the first-grade students who desegregated the white elementary schools in September 1964.[12] The students' work complemented that of the Freedom School teachers who remained in Jackson to work closely with the registration process. During the registration of first graders, Freedom School teacher Florence Howe and her student volunteers canvassed the neighborhood to encourage parents to register their children. They talked to more than seventy families that week. The Freedom School teachers and their students could boast that they assisted eleven of the forty-three students to register in the previously all-white Jackson schools.[13] This larger campaign occurred as other groups like the Delta Ministry, the MFDP, the Mississippi Council on Human Relations, and SNCC joined in the effort to desegregate the public schools throughout the state. This was not an effort spearheaded solely by Freedom School teachers and students; rather, it was a statewide effort that demonstrates how some Freedom School students joined the larger movement toward desegregating schools once the summer campaign concluded.

The Freedom School students emerged as young trailblazers in the effort to desegregate *all* levels of public education. The federal court issued strict guidelines that only elementary grades were to be desegregated, but young activists used this as an opportunity to attempt to enroll in all-white high schools. Ben Chaney, a Freedom School student in Meridian whose brother was one of the three activists murdered at the beginning of the summer campaign, and twenty-one other students attempted to desegregate Meridian's high schools in early September. Nineteen black students attempted to register at high schools in Canton. Over twenty high school students attempted to desegregate high schools in Jackson through the MSU.[14] Segregationists effectively blocked these attempts and denied students the right to register at high schools, which were not yet under court order. These early attempts at desegregation are significant because these were the first efforts to desegregate white schools beyond the federal court order, which placed pressure on the federal courts and local school boards to desegregate at a faster pace.

Although initial attempts at desegregating high schools were blocked, it would not be long until Freedom School students joined the first waves of black students to desegregate secondary levels of education. In Jackson, civil rights workers organized a series of workshops that discussed desegregation and generated support for the movement in 1965. It was out of these meetings that Hymethia Thompson, a Freedom School student on the Tougaloo College campus, made the decision to desegregate the previously all-white Murrah High School in the fall of 1965.[15] She was one of twelve students to do so. White school boards remained lukewarm, at best, to the idea of desegregation, and African American families like Thompson's had to take the responsibility and endure the harassment if they wanted to enroll their children in white public schools. While Thompson's parents were not dependent upon whites for an income and did not have to worry about losing their jobs when their daughter enrolled at Murrah High School, others were not so fortunate, and some did face the prospect of losing their jobs.[16] Like all students of color who desegregated schools for the first time, Thompson and the other Freedom School students who desegregated the public schools paid a heavy social, emotional, and spiritual cost.[17]

Grassroots civil rights–based educational reform forced a strong white reaction that activists did not envision during the push for desegregation. Many white families reacted to the prospect of desegregation by withdrawing their support from the public schools. As plans slowly moved toward token desegregation, the Mississippi legislature passed a series of bills that authorized state-supported private schools. The state provided tuition in the form of tuition grants dispersed to individual families choosing to enroll in a private school, in addition to providing textbooks to private schools.[18] A handful of schools were therefore desegregated during the fall of 1964 at the same time that the state established private schools. The private academy system supported by the state was relatively small. In the fall of 1964, fewer than ten private schools opened. Tuition was expensive, and they were organized on short notice. By 1968, there were forty-three state-supported private academies. They were overwhelmingly located in Mississippi's urban areas and the Delta. In areas of relative wealth like the cities and in the Delta, where there were strong segregationist tendencies amid a large black population, private academies flourished.[19] Though small in number, the state-supported system of private education was dwarfed by the number of nonpublic schools supported by private means.

Young people were mindful of the stern resistance to desegregation both at the state level and within the schools they were expected to desegregate. As a result, Freedom School students embraced alternative means to achieve a quality education. The Freedom School students in Meridian at the end of Freedom Summer suggested multiple forms of activism that moved beyond desegregating schools. As Roscoe Jones recalled of his stance on desegregation: "We never asked to be integrated, we only asked for equality. I never entered the civil rights movement for integration. I entered the civil rights movement to be equal. Integration is a byproduct of equality and we ended up getting the byproduct. We never wanted integration. We wanted to be equal."[20]

The student-led conference in Meridian articulated the local and grassroots desire to reconstruct education around principles of quality, not solely desegregation. The students demanded integration but, unlike the legal organization to achieve this end, they included many aspects of reform that addressed the totality of quality education. After all, desegregating white schools was only one of the thirteen demands students articulated during the Freedom School convention in Meridian, and enrolling in all-white schools was ranked toward the bottom of the list.

Homer Hill was one of many student activists who chose not to desegregate all-white schools. Hill was a peer to Elnora Fondren, a member of the NAACP Youth Council who desegregated the all-white Clarksdale High School by herself in September 1965. Vera Mae Pigee, the local leader from Clarksdale, escorted Fondren daily and organized funds to pay for safe transportation. Hill, a contemporary of Fondren's from the all-black Higgins High School, recalled hearing the reports from his friend. "Elnora told me about the teachers forcing them to sit in the back of the classroom and she told us about being harassed," Hill recalled. "They would block seats and desks around them so they would be sort of isolated. I didn't want to leave my high school, I didn't see the advantage of going to the white high school."[21] Cognizant of the exacting cost of desegregating white schools, Hill chose not to desegregate one of the all-white schools in the Mississippi Delta. Hill's reaction to desegregating an all-white high school illustrates the critical thinking that Freedom School students exercised during the first years of desegregation. The vast majority of students like Hill and their families chose not to pay the costly emotional and psychological price of token desegregation and instead committed themselves to other forms of protest.

One method of student engagement that transpired after Freedom Summer was to test the enforcement of the Civil Rights Act of 1964 and to desegregate public spaces other than schools. In Tchula, Mississippi, Eddie James Carthan committed himself to applying methods and strategies he learned in Freedom School. At the age of fourteen, Carthan participated in the movement's first registration drive deep in the Delta. He worked alongside white volunteers to register voters, which, in 1964, directly challenged prevailing and entrenched political and social mores in Mississippi. Carthan joined his peers as they walked out of schools and boycotted unfair treatment during the fall after the Freedom Summer. But he also remembered playing a role in the movement in individualized ways as well. Carthan recalled at length what it meant to desegregate a local white barbershop in the Mississippi Delta after the Freedom Summer campaign in 1964:

There was a white barber shop and I went to integrate the barber shop and the haircuts were $1.00 and my parents gave me $1.00 and when I went to sit in the chair to get my haircut he told me it was a $1.50 and I told him to give me a $1.00 haircut and I believe he gave me a dollar haircut (*laughing*). I believe he told me a $1.50 to encourage me to leave but there were people standing observing, watching and he observed them watching and he went ahead and cut my hair, otherwise he would have took me by my seat of my pants and threw me out the door.[22]

Carthan and his peers were at the vanguard of direct-action protests throughout the Magnolia State that introduced nonviolent demonstrations to small towns that never before experienced such public modes of resistance.

Other Freedom School students were at the forefront of activism that radicalized Mississippi after the Freedom Summer campaign. After attending Freedom School during the summer and fall of 1964, Wilbur Colom committed himself to desegregating entrenched segregated businesses in the small town of Ripley, which had a population of 3,500. Colom and his peers desegregated Renfrow's Café; jumped into the all-white swimming pool downtown; organized a sit-in at the Kream Kup, a favorite local dairy stop; and desegregated the symbolically named Dixie Theater. As Colom recalled of desegregating the theater, "We went downstairs and we sat down, and white people threw popcorn and soda at us as we tried to watch the movie."[23] The students were arrested each time and spent numerous nights in jail during 1965. After generations of clandestine organizing, the students in the small town of Ripley were the first to conduct direct-action protests. Roy DeBerry, a student in the Holly Springs Freedom School, engaged in demonstrations that desegregated public spaces after Freedom Summer as well. DeBerry joined Voters League members, SNCC workers, and other local activists in desegregating the local movie theater. After local police arrested one of the protesters, they attempted to desegregate the theater again the following weekend without incident. DeBerry turned his attention to organizing a selective buying campaign, focusing on Big Start Market, a major grocery in Holly Springs.[24] Such demonstrations maintained and even generated momentum in the local parts of Mississippi after volunteers went home. But the segregated school remained one of the most significant battlegrounds of the movement after the summer campaign.

The demonstrations and boycotts that organized from segregated African American schools were the most visible forms of protest among the young activists during the 1964/1965 school year. Student activists during the fall of 1964 possessed the commitment and political efficacy to systematically address movement goals in ways that moved beyond desegregation and built upon critical thinking, analysis, and an examination of social conditions that shaped their experiences. Mississippi students actively boycotted their own schools, protested discriminatory treatment, and demanded a quality education by making explicit demands of the state of Mississippi. As noted in chapter 2, students boycotted and already viewed their own segregated schools as sites of protest in Jackson and McComb well before Freedom Summer. These walkouts were significant in galvanizing the movement but also in forming a network of activists that continued to advocate for student protests. Through these networks, Freedom School students drew upon accumulated experience and knowledge to expand their own protests.

The Freedom School delegation at the conference in Meridian at the end of the summer campaign intended to build upon this network. Students looked to the MSU to respond to discriminatory policy at the local level and organized direct-action protests to contest it. They suggested that "a committee be set up to make recommendations for school walkouts to be carried out through the Jackson school system should any student be suspended for civil rights work, the committee may recommend the student body to walk out for the length of the suspension."[25] The Natchez chapter of the MSU is indicative of how plans unfolded the fall after the Freedom Summer campaign. Students organized the Natchez chapter in early September 1964 and made plans to test public accommodations that were legally integrated by the Civil Rights Act, to picket local stores, to boycott schools to protest inadequate or nonexistent equipment, and to publish a student paper, among other considerations.[26] Student activists, in other words, quickly embraced a multifaceted agenda that moved beyond desegregating schools.

At the beginning of the 1964 academic school year, then, a cadre of student activists were committed to working on their own to secure a better education and to carry forth the momentum of the Freedom Summer campaign. Students questioned the conditions within their schools and adopted modes of critical inquiry. Students observed and called out the tangible aspects of unfulfilled promises in education and articulated a bold response. In Liberty,

Amite County, in the southwest portion of the state near McComb, students petitioned the all-white school board for an improved education and school facilities. "We, students of Central High School, Liberty, Mississippi, have met and agreed upon the following list of grievances."[27] The grievances from Central High School included addressing the quality of the curriculum used in the school, the library, the principal, teachers, courses, and physical facilities. Far from a place of complacency or passive acceptance of the remnants of Jim Crow that continued to plague the public school system, students critically observed the schools that the state provided, named the glaring shortcomings, and demanded change. At the same time, students began to take greater action. "We believe," the petitioners from Liberty continued, "there are several things which would help solve these problems." To address the issues they identified, local activists called for black citizens to be on the school board and an increased representation of students and parents in school governance.[28]

As the students in Liberty suggest, there was no shortage of issues to protest after the Freedom Summer of 1964. One major point of contention was the treatment and discipline of black students who protested. Teachers and administrators in public schools began to severely punish student protesters. One student observed in the Jackson public schools that they "wanted to protest against the bad teaching at our school—the overcrowded classes, the old books, the lousy food." More than three hundred students participated in ongoing demonstrations, "and the principal told us that those who took part wouldn't be able to graduate."[29] Another principal in Jackson expelled a student for singing a freedom song while school was in session. In Holmes County, a principal expelled two students for singing freedom songs during the lunch period. Another principal in Starkville expelled a student for distributing a MSU petition.[30] The principal at St. Mary's High School, a black private school in Holly Springs, expelled two students for taking part in the production of *Seeds of Freedom*, the play produced in Freedom Schools the previous summer.[31] The disciplinary tactics administrators employed indicated that school administrations would punish any and all civil rights activity in the schools.[32] The reaction of teachers and administrators also mark a shift from earlier in the movement. As noted in the first chapter, teachers were often at the vanguard of the movement as they demanded equal salaries. But in the politics of education after the *Brown* decision, teachers faced threats of massive unemployment, and sympathizing with student protesters would all but ensure swift termination. Across the state of Mississippi students organized in response to disciplinary actions that they deemed unfair and the institutional discrimination that supported it. As their protests grew in scope, students demanded better resources and treatment, and they forced school authorities to listen.

A burgeoning political voice among young student activists that spoke out against unfair treatment and distribution of resources persisted during the 1964/1965 school year. This led to long-term protest that directly challenged the governance of schools. As students openly questioned issues that denied a quality education, they organized boycotts and sustained protests of the schools they attended. One of the first boycotts occurred in early August 1964, setting the tone for student activity during the upcoming year. The MSU formed a partnership with community adults to form the Bolivar [County] Improvement Association. When students asked white volunteers to attend a meeting at McEvans High School, the African American principal asked them to leave if they did not have permission from the white superintendent. Students began a boycott as a result and demanded better facilities, more resources, a more diverse and academic curriculum, and more qualified teachers. Over 1,500 students walked out, and the boycotting students attended the Shaw Freedom School instead of McEvans High School, which local authorities closed and placed armed deputies to quell what they saw as a dangerous situation. The boycott lasted for nearly two months until the students decided to return to school.[33]

In December 1964, representatives of the MSU reconvened in Jackson. Roscoe Jones, the seventeen-year-old president of the organization, and other leaders called for a statewide meeting to discuss the possibility of a public school boycott against the "Super Jim Crow educational system of Mississippi." Students representing ten districts from across the state gathered and shared stories of protests from their own schools. As noted, a principal had expelled one of the attendees from Starkville for circulating an MSU petition. Another student reported his sister had been expelled for singing a freedom song. Still another had been threatened with expulsion for wearing a civil rights T-shirt to school.[34] Tensions were mounting across the state. But less than six months after Freedom Summer, students who wanted to boycott the system were still in the minority.

Delegates argued against a statewide boycott because most claimed they did not have the support of the majority of the student body. Delegates voted down the proposition. Instead they encouraged each chapter to organize locally.[35] Roscoe Jones closed the meeting by articulating the potential that all MSU members felt. "We're still trying to get on our feet," Jones conveyed to the delegates, "but you can be sure of this, if we ever do get on our feet, we're going to show Mississippi that they've got a fight on their hands."[36]

The fight resumed with larger numbers after the winter break. Members of the MSU distributed SNCC pins to wear to school in support of the movement in Sharkey and Issaquena Counties. In January 1965, over two hundred students wore pins to promote participation in the civil right movement and, when confronted by principal O. E. Jordan, they refused to take off the pins. The principal, like other administrators across the state who were under increasing pressure to curb civil rights activity, followed the instructions of an all-white school board and suspended them. After the superintendent denied the black parents' request to meet with the school board, the community decided to boycott, and over 1,300 students stayed out of school for several weeks. Nearly three hundred students remained out of school until the beginning of the next school year.[37] Shortly thereafter, forty-five students in Philadelphia demanded the right to free speech and to protest on their own terms when they fashioned SNCC "One Man, One Vote" buttons. Parents of the students who were suspended in Philadelphia for wearing the pins filed suit against the school board. They argued that being suspended or expelled for wearing political pins violated the right to free speech granted to the students by the Constitution. In the case *Burnside v. Byars* (1966) the court determined that students had the right to wear the buttons in the interest of free speech. This case became the legal precedent that the Supreme Court cited in *Tinker v. Des Moines* (1969), which stated that young people in Iowa had a First Amendment right to wear a black armband to school protesting the Vietnam War.[38]

The boycott movement continued to grow as the Issaquena-Sharkey boycott inspired further action across the state. Students attending the Indianola public schools boycotted in support of the student-led strikes across the state. An unprecedented two thousand students stayed home in Indianola. Students were committed to MSU's statement that "Negroes are fed up with inferior schools, extreme brutality by the police, and similar discrimination. We're doing something about it." The police brutality referred to the arrest of fifty-three protesters in Indianola and the police force's use of billy clubs and cattle prods to break up the demonstration.[39] Student boycotts led to other instances of school walkouts across the state and in some cases radicalized older adults to boycott the schools their children attended. The Benton County Citizens' Club, a coalition of student activists and community members, observed that across the state "at least five counties are having school boycotts."[40] This encouraged them to organize their own protest of Old Salem Attendance Center, the local segregated school that primarily served black students. The coalition drafted a petition, which over three hundred community members signed, and demanded more decision-making authority, beginning with the termination of the principal, W. B. Foster, and four teachers at Old Salem. After the Board of Education in Benton County agreed to only meet their demands if the petitioners decided *not* to desegregate white schools and businesses, the Citizens Club decided to boycott the school.[41] Students and community adults who organized around this issue wrote:

> We Negroes in Benton County have nothing EXCEPT our organized strength. With this strength we must stand together and show the nation that we refuse to cooperate with the Southern way of life, to be lied to, to be tricked, to be cheated, and to be told that we have no voice in our children's education. The only thing left for us is to keep our children out of school as a way protesting their inferior education.[42]

Local high school students established Freedom Schools during the school boycott, much like other boycotters in Mississippi. In this case, the Freedom School students worked in conjunction with Rust College students.[43] Within two months, the Benton County activists reported that the boycott was 90 percent effective and achieved a degree of success in that the district hired a "new principal who is favorable to civil rights."[44]

Students who organized boycotts across the state of Mississippi reflected the organizing ethos of the movement. In Benton County, for instance, the students worked with a countywide organization to facilitate the walkout. The students in Amite County petitioned the school board in close consultation with local parents. Freedom School students in Jackson illustrate how student-led organization spawned other local community organizing projects. Former Freedom School students and local movement staff collaborated to form the Jackson Youth Movement during the spring of 1965. By March meetings maintained an average attendance of fifty students. Young people were planning to circulate a petition against brutality in Jackson high schools. Other students were both recruiting more students to join the NAACP and protesting the "red tape" at NAACP meetings.[45] The nascent organization demonstrates the depth of organizing that former Freedom School students engaged in less than one year after the summer campaign of 1964 and the influence they had in radicalizing local movements.

The student-led protests after the summer of 1965 challenge the notion that the civil rights movement "stalled" after the Freedom Summer campaign of 1964, and they demonstrate that young people demanded equity and a distribution of power and resources that ran deeper than desegregation. Participating in boycotts challenged other students not part of the Freedom Schools to question institutional discrimination impacting their own schools. As a result, organized activism continued to grow into a statewide student movement. The boycotts generated a greater awareness and consciousness that the Freedom Schools initially intended to cultivate. While school walkouts and boycotts existed prior to the fall of 1964, most notably in McComb and Jackson, the sharp increase in size, scope, and student demands suggested a new form of protest that foreshadowed the larger walkouts of the later 1960s and early 1970s.[46] Student organization and increasing demands also provided pretext to what would be defined as the black power movement.

CARRYING FORTH THE LIGHT OF FREEDOM DURING THE ERA OF "BLACK POWER"

As Freedom School students established their own political agendas after Freedom Summer, they acted within the burgeoning "black power" movement.

Their activism disrupts the popular narrative that clearly marks the beginning of black power as the end of the civil rights movement because notions of it were already present before Freedom Summer campaign and, conversely, elements of the civil rights era were evident during the black power era. Organizers and activists began to articulate the need for an autonomous cultural, social, and political separation from a racist and unyielding white hegemony during and after the summer of 1964. Student protest after the summer of 1964 occurred on a spectrum that addressed ongoing issues such as educational inequality as well as recent developments including the Vietnam War that posed a different form of oppression of people of color in the late 1960s and 1970s. Students continued to organize nonviolent marches, but they also organized to reconstitute institutional governing structures. Freedom School protests therefore illustrate continuity and change between the classical civil rights movement and the black power movement of the late 1960s as students embraced strategies, aims, and philosophies reflective of both.[47] Some embraced black power more firmly than others, but all continued to define their own activism on their own terms, which was in and of itself an assertion of autonomy cultivated during the Freedom Schools that was also recognized as a tenet of "black power."

Freedom School students first heard the public call for black power less than two years after the Freedom Summer campaign in June 1966. James Meredith, the student who had desegregated the University of Mississippi, began the March Against Fear through Mississippi during the summer of 1966. He intended to walk from Memphis, Tennessee, to Jackson, Mississippi, but was cut down when white segregationist Aubrey James Norvell shot and wounded Meredith on the second day of his trek. Activists including Dr. Martin Luther King Jr. and Stokely Carmichael mobilized and completed the statewide march to Jackson. After being arrested in Greenwood, Carmichael addressed the marchers on June 16, 1966, and publically announced the need for "black power." SNCC organizers in Lowndes County, Alabama, were already discussing the concept, and Willie Ricks, a SNCC organizer, had used the phrase in speeches before.[48] But it was new to the crowd in Mississippi, who was overwhelmingly receptive, and black power assumed new meaning. Hymethia Thompson participated in the same march and heard the same call. She marched the last eight miles of the long journey from the Tougaloo campus to the state capital building. After nearly being arrested in the march, she recalled that it was "something I shall never forget," but it "was the last time I actively participated because I went to college in the fall."[49] Thompson illustrates how Freedom School students carried with them a penchant for protest and critical thinking as they first heard the articulation of black power in 1966. In Thompson's case, this was the last of her protests. For others, it was not.

The young men of this generation, particularly the activists committed to directly challenging entrenched social, political, and economic customs, faced the Vietnam War and the challenges it presented as a state-sanctioned form of violence. Several of the Freedom School students developed a critique of the growing conflict in Southeast Asia as they were exposed to it two years before the formal call for black power. On August 7, 1964, Staughton Lynd, the Freedom School coordinator during the summer of 1964, attended the memorial services for the three slain civil rights activists. Lynd remembered very distinctly Bob Moses's remarks connecting the deaths of these three workers to an escalating conflict in Vietnam:

> Bob Moses spoke and it was just one of the most amazing experiences of my whole life because, what did he talk about? He talked about the fact that Congress had just passed the Tonkin Bay Resolution and that until people understood that there was a connection between the killing of dark-skinned people in Vietnam and the killing of dark-skinned people in Mississippi, they didn't understand anything. I just couldn't believe it, that at that moment, which you might think was the moment of all moments, when the movement would be turned inward and thinking about the loss of these three young men, here was Bob making the connection to the war on the other side of the world, which most of us had barely heard about at that point.[50]

The prospect of enlisting or being drafted to fight in the Vietnam War presented an intimidating alternative to the young men who were educated in the principles of protest, particularly the Freedom School students.

Wilbur Colom exemplifies how black power offered a strategy to resist the war and make demands reminiscent of the earlier years of the movement. Colom moved to New York City and enrolled in Brandeis High School in 1966 where he organized and led the High School Coalition Against the War in

Vietnam. In addition to protesting the war in Vietnam, the young group organized to improve the quality of education provided in their high school, which was similar to the work his peers engaged in Mississippi immediately after the summer campaign in 1964 and 1965. Colom's group made a list of demands for the school administration that included the right to organize without interference from the administration as well as the demand for more black and Latino teachers and administrators, more black and Latin American history courses, a student committee to approve the school's curriculum, a student court to review decisions made by the administration, and, generally, more student voice in the school's decision making.[51] Colom and his peers also participated in the ongoing protests and demonstrations led by Harlem residents and black students at Columbia University. Black protesters and white allies protested Columbia University's plan to construct a gymnasium in Morningside Park, an important green space in Harlem, and the university's ties to research used by the military–industrial complex to fight the war in Vietnam. The protests grew in scope and intensity when students orchestrated the takeover of Hamilton Hall, the largest undergraduate building on campus, in 1968. Police arrested over seven hundred students and effectively shut down the university for the remainder of the semester.[52] Colom was in the midst of this protest as a high school student and, like many of his peers in Mississippi, was expelled from high school. Since he was already accepted into Howard University, he safely enrolled there.

Roy DeBerry similarly became active in the black power movement on a college campus. After graduating in the top of his class from W. T. Sims High School, DeBerry enrolled in Brandeis University in Boston, with strong encouragement and support from his Freedom School teacher, Aviva Futorian, who had graduated from Brandeis in 1959. Experiencing isolation on the predominantly white upper-class campus, DeBerry sought deeper connections with the black community of Boston and the small handful of black students on campus. After attending a black student conference at Harvard, DeBerry led the establishment of the Brandeis Afro-American Organization. After King's assassination in 1968, ongoing racist incidents on campus, and growing discontent among black students, the Brandeis Afro-American Organization occupied Ford Hall, the university's communication center, for eleven days and issued ten demands of the administration. Students demanded that the university recruit more students of color, create an African American studies program, and grant clemency for their actions, among other demands. By April 1969, faculty approved a new Department of African and Afro-American Studies, the administration doubled recruitment efforts of students of color, and they granted amnesty to the student protesters.[53]

Other students were not so fortunate. After being arrested in the Freedom Rides of 1961 at the age of thirteen, Hezekiah Watkins helped organize a high school walkout in Jackson in 1963, weeks before the assassination of Medgar Evers. Gaining notoriety among local organizers, Watkins worked with college students in Freedom Houses across Mississippi and was at times privileged with the responsibility to drive out-of-state volunteers across the state. Being arrested, working with activists traveling to Mississippi from across the country, and working in Freedom Houses where white and black activists lived together constituted a profound civil rights education, one similar to that of the Freedom Schools. Though Watkins did not enroll in a Freedom School, he was educated in similar principles of the movement and applied the same sets of skills as his peers who did. When Watkins graduated from Lanier High School in Jackson in 1965, he enrolled in nearby Unica Junior College. Soon after beginning his coursework, Watkins and his peers at Unica "started a movement" to register voters following the Voting Rights Act of 1965. However, his campus organization took an unlikely turn. Watkins recalled:

> We were trying to get in to get registered and there were some things going on on campus that we didn't like and that was the food. We were seeing hot dogs and french fries every day, but Hines Community College was right up the road and they were getting a four-course meal each day, so we set out to change that, and I was brought in to the president's office. [In the aftermath of the protest] the MPs came and brought me to Jackson at the Selected Service Bureau, swore me in, and took me from there to Louisiana, and I was in the military.[54]

By the mid-1960s, black youths like Watkins who actively worked in the movement faced consequences of not only prison but also federal coercion to enlist in the Vietnam War. Unlike Colom and DeBerry, when school authorizes expelled Watkins in 1966 he was ordered to enlist in the military.[55]

The war in Vietnam presented a clear and present danger to young men who acquired a civil rights–based education and entered the black power movement as trained activists.

As Watkins's experience suggests, young people who were educated in the Mississippi movement and were of age and had the opportunity to attend college in the late 1960s helped transform the college campus into a dynamic site of protest. The black power movement on college campuses demanded a more inclusive curriculum including Black Studies programs, more black faculty and administrators, and more support for students of color enrolled in white institutions. Black students on campus during this period engaged in more militant protest and at times took over and occupied college campus buildings that were symbols of authority, order, and institutional power. Black students formed all-black organizations and study groups, and they engaged the communities of color that lived near the college campuses they attended.[56] Demanding much more than the right to attend school, black students of the late 1960s demanded to be included in the decision-making processes that controlled institutions.

Freedom School students acting of their accord entered and shaped the volatile context of the late 1960s and black power in numerous ways. The students embraced the cultural elements of black power. They donned natural hairstyles. They fashioned African-influenced clothing. They played black music loudly and drowned out the white folk music that permeated the Freedom Summer campaign. But these cultural components constituted only a superficial engagement with black power ideology. Freedom School students engaged a spectrum of political activity in the late 1960s and 1970s that addressed deep and systemic issues of institutional discrimination. Wilbur Colom represented a more radical connection to black power through militant protest, working with black student activists at Columbia University, and articulating demands that reconstituted institutional power dynamics. Some, like Hezekiah Watkins, were sent to war and could not participate. Others, like Hymethia Thompson, were sympathetic to black power activists but focused solely on acquiring an education. From the Freedom School students' perspective, black power was a fluid movement without clearly defined boundaries that was inclusive of both the civil rights education they received in 1964 and newer ideas introduced in the late 1960s.

Black power was on the horizon for veteran organizers as well. A small group of SNCC activists including John Lewis, Fannie Lou Hamer, and Bob Moses traveled to Africa the month after the Freedom Summer campaign concluded. It was a chance for them to regroup, thanks to singer Harry Belafonte's invitation and funding. But it was ideologically significant as well. In addition to meeting Malcolm X in Kenya, the movement veterans grew dismayed by the imperial control exerted by the United States, a government they had come to deeply resent post–Atlantic City.[57] The trip to Africa foreshadowed some of the fundamental changes that were about to take place in the civil rights movement. Veteran organizers integrated themes such as black nationalism, cultural autonomy, and a strong critique of imperialism into the philosophy of the civil rights movement. When Moses returned that fall, he articulated a theory of parallel institutions that signified a move toward embracing black-controlled institutions. The larger debate of using whites in the movement, which had deep roots in the history of the movement, emerged as a divisive issue after the summer campaign of 1964. As organizers debated how to redefine the civil rights movement in the black power era, they fundamentally reframed the meaning of a Freedom School education.

SHIFTING IDEOLOGIES AND
THE TRANSFORMATION OF
THE FREEDOM SCHOOL IDEA

The Freedom School model proffered a potent example of alternative institution building during the beginning of the desegregation era, which served as a model for educational reforms at the grassroots and federal levels. During a SNCC-sponsored conference in California during the fall of 1964, Bob Moses began to articulate a separate and alternative agenda later adopted and refined within the black power movement. This agenda elaborated upon a sentiment expressed in the original Freedom School proposal the year before. As Charlie Cobb wrote, "Education in Mississippi is an institution which can be validly replaced, as much of the educational institutions in the state are not recognized around the country anyway."[58] Moses spoke more directly about expanding the role of the Freedom Schools to serve a wider purpose, which was all the more poignant after the Democratic National Convention in Atlantic City. He asked: "Why can't we set up our own schools? Because when you come right down to it, why integrate their schools? What is it that you will learn in their schools? Many of the Negroes can learn it, but what can they do with it? What they really need to learn is how to be organized to work on the society to change it."[59] Moses's statement captures veteran activists' critique of desegregation long embodied in the black freedom struggles. From this perspective, "integrating" white schools would not lead to the education that students needed in order to transform society. Moses and others developed Freedom Schools on the premise that the movement should develop their own schools that should "be organized to work on the society to change it." Although students opted to remain in the segregated public schools, grassroots civil rights activists worked to provide a network of Freedom Schools through the summer of 1965 in order to sustain a separate and parallel system of education. As black power gained momentum, the Freedom Schools proffered a model of a separate system of education that embodied a radical critique of schools supported by the state.

The vast majority of summer volunteers left Mississippi after the summer of 1964, but a critical mass remained in the state and defined on the ground what form Freedom Schools would take as prevailing ideologies shifted. In early August 1964, Staughton Lynd announced that plans were being made for the continuation of Freedom Schools. COFO made a similar announcement in the winter of 1964 and stated that "the Freedom Schools will be continued in all areas where possible, but their scope will be somewhat limited as the majority of students will be in regular school full time."[60] Liz Fusco volunteered to continue to coordinate the Freedom Schools after Lynd returned home to assume his teaching responsibilities. The schools functioned as a political supplement to the students' regular public school education. Freedom School courses were offered at night, during the weekends, and in the summer.[61] In some instances, the Freedom Schools served as the primary mode of education in instances where students refused to attend the public schools provided by the state of Mississippi.

As the new coordinator, Liz Fusco worked feverishly to maintain the Freedom Schools during the year. Activists organized approximately thirty Freedom Schools throughout the course of the 1964/1965 school year.[62] The numbers never again reached the enthusiastic pitch of the first summer, but based on the increased awareness and civil rights commitment among Mississippi students, the Freedom Schools were visible and active through the beginning of 1965. Fusco's responsibilities that year were to fundraise, train teachers, recruit students, and constantly promote the schools. Like any private educational enterprise, her primary task was to raise capital for the schools. As she remembered,

> A big part of my job in addition to traveling the state was raising money, I was always writing fund raising letters so that there would be materials and food. It was also very lonely and it was hard; it was just hard work because there were of course very few of us, and I had to deal with the teachers coming down who had not had the training in Charlie Cobb's ideals about what the Freedom Schools were. So I had to do on-the-spot teacher training and a lot of traveling and never enough money, never enough money.[63]

The COFO still financially supported the schools from its general fund, but more funding was required. Former Freedom School teachers drew upon their northern connections and maintained, for instance, the Adopt a Freedom School program sponsored by the AFT before the summer campaign. Arthur Reese returned home to Detroit and developed a Freedom School Project in conjunction with the AFT. "The major aim of the project," Reese wrote, "is to bring people together in 'in depth' living situations which commit them mutually to the task of educating people."[64] Moreover, the AFT also provided funds of $10 per week for the volunteer teachers, and they attempted to expand the union's base of operations across the South.[65] Teachers who returned home provided assistance in other ways. With assistance from the volunteers, several Freedom School students also traveled to New York to present the play *Seeds of Freedom*. Deborah Flynn, a high school English teacher from New York when she volunteered, and her students in the Holly Springs Freedom School originally wrote the play during the summer of 1964 to depict and portray the life and death of Medgar Evers. With the help of Flynn and other Freedom School teachers, including Chude Allen and Gloria Clark, students toured the play with the Free Southern Theater in New York and at other locations across the country to raise money and increase awareness about civil rights violations still occurring in Mississippi.[66] Adopt a Freedom School programs, traveling tours of Freedom School actors, and fund-raising attempts by those who volunteered in Mississippi generated a lot of publicity. Northern schools, teachers' unions, and the general public were more aware of the ongoing work in Mississippi as a result. Freedom School teachers also returned to Mississippi when they could, throughout the next year on their own time, and with their own resources. But, regardless of increased visibility, the schools struggled to function even at their reduced numbers during the 1964/1965 school year.

There was still a structure in place through which to organize new areas in Mississippi, however. Volunteers and organizers were free to build upon the Freedom School infrastructure that had been established during Freedom Summer. The events of Tippah County are a case in point. The county remained unorganized during the Freedom Summer campaign, though nearby Holly Springs, the county seat of Marshall County, was active with a Freedom House that sheltered an influx of civil rights workers, three Freedom Schools that served over 150 students, and various voter registration projects. Marshall was two counties west of Tippah County. As Freedom School student Wilbur Colom remembered, "We just knew things were going on other places and getting very close to us. We knew it had gotten to Holly Springs and it was a big kind of what's gonna go on in Holly Springs and we knew it was moving into Benton and we had heard about that. So you felt like it was closing in on you and you knew ultimately it was gonna spring here cause it was getting awful close."[67] With a safe place established on the Rust College campus to orchestrate sophisticated levels of civil rights organization, activists in Holly Springs were able to branch out into the countryside and organize nearby rural areas like Benton County. Two white volunteers, Gloria Xifaras Clark and Aviva Futorian, traveled from project centers like Holly Springs to more rural locations in the state, including Tippah County. Towns like Holly Springs served as important outposts in the Mississippi movement. Once embedded in the rural parts of Mississippi, movement workers went into the neighboring counties and organized direct-action protest there for the first time in the history of these locations.[68]

This was new territory for the Mississippi freedom struggle and presented an opportunity to grow the local movement.

The organization that occurred in Marshall County and the surrounding counties after the summer of 1964 illustrates the extent to which focused activism expanded the local movement. Volunteers planned a mass meeting at the Antioch Baptist Church in October 1964 to generate support for the MFDP in Benton County. Fannie Lou Hamer delivered an inspirational speech. This was one of the county's first attempts to organize a mass meeting, and they paid a heavy price. Local segregationists burned the church to the ground. A group of students from Oberlin College, Ohio, the "Carpenters for Christmas," organized to rebuild the church over the winter holiday and continued to send personnel and resources throughout the year. The presence of an influx of volunteers new to the area increased visibility and provided critical support to students like Colom, who had desegregated local facilities for the first time in Benton County.[69]

The Freedom Schools that remained open put forth a powerful example of what civil rights education offered to the ongoing struggle. Volunteers ensured that a Freedom School would be established to continue to educate boycotting students. During the Issaquena, Sharkey, and Benton County boycotts, students who walked out of the public schools elected to attend a Freedom School instead of state-supported public schools. Students in the Freedom Schools led discussions about national politics, they organized strategies for their respective boycotts, and they studied the conditions of blacks in Mississippi. Students who attended a Freedom School rather than the boycotted public school essentially engaged in another form of protest by creating an alternative and parallel system of education. The Freedom School classes organized by and for the boycotting students were, according to Freedom Summer volunteer Mary Aickin Rothschild, "chaos, but they represented the free expression of students that the staff had only theorized could be possible."[70] In these instances the purpose of the Freedom Schools shifted slightly to fill the void caused by school boycotts. This role restored an original vision as conceived in Chicago, New York, and Boston, where organizers established Freedom Schools during the citywide school boycotts in 1963 and 1964. The idea that Freedom Schools would educate boycotting students also met the ideals expressed in Cobb's original Freedom

School proposal. The students were questioning the political institutions of the state, organizing their own education, and committing themselves to the front lines of the civil rights movement. The Freedom Schools therefore emerged as one of the key parallel institutions that organizers could build on their own terms and for their own purposes.

Yet by the end of the summer of 1965, one year after the schools first opened their doors, the administrative structure of the Freedom Schools all but collapsed logistically due to internal ideological struggle. The summer volunteers and movement veterans asked fundamental questions that shook their beliefs and challenged prevailing understandings of what "freedom" meant. Organizers continued to discuss the problems associated with white volunteers in the movement, which ultimately challenged the pedagogical ethos of interracial dialogue that defined the Freedom Schools. In November 1964, SNCC held a weeklong retreat on the Mississippi coast in Waveland, Mississippi, at the Gulfside Methodist Church to discuss key issues affecting organizers. A contentious issue prior to the summer campaign, race came to be a defining discussion in the freedom movement during the fall of 1964. The role of whites became particularly visible when they remained in Mississippi. For instance, 85 applicants applied for full-time status within SNCC. At this point, there were 98 paid fieldworkers, most of whom were black. A staff of 104 white volunteers, most of them from the summer campaigns, augmented the permanent civil rights force in Mississippi. The administrative and logistical leadership for the Freedom Schools was drawn from a mostly white staff during the 1964/1965 school year, which exacerbated existing racial tensions. According to historian John Dittmer, "Across the state the debates over tactics, strategy, involvement of local people, and the chain of command all came down to a matter of black and white."[71] Debates over race caused disarray and disorganization in the COFO headquarters in Jackson. As one worker in the office frantically wrote in early December 1964, "Staff and volunteer discipline has broken down so far that the state headquarters had had several race riots, white workers are often subject to severe racial abuse and even violence from Negro workers. Juvenile delinquency sometimes appears to have taken over certain offices."[72] This put those who chose to remain in Mississippi to run the Freedom Schools in a precarious position. Liz Fusco, who remained with the Freedom Schools until the end of their program in 1965, recalled the shift in attitude toward white volunteers:

> Part of it was that at end of Freedom Summer there was a kind of backlash against the white people who came down because it was like, "oh yeah you can leave and go back to college and here are all these local people who stuck their necks out. And they are at risk now because you were a buffer between them and the Klan." I didn't feel that I was being productive anymore, and there was beginning to be legitimate backlash against white volunteers. Stokely [Carmichael] had talked about Black Power and people had felt betrayed, left alone, and abandoned by civil rights workers; it was time for the movement to belong to black people. It was way over time.[73]

Ongoing consternation over the use of whites intensified within the ranks of SNCC. Open questioning of—and, at times, hostility against—whites in the movement dealt a final logistical and administrative blow to the Freedom Schools, which largely relied on white volunteers. In 1966, SNCC voted to expel the remaining whites from the organization by a vote of nineteen to eighteen (and twenty-four abstaining), effectively designating the organization as exclusively African American.[74] Although whites made respected and valuable contributions to the movement and continued to work with the MFDP, the message was clear that the movement of the late 1960s would continue without them.

The Freedom School students were not privy to the dissention within the ranks around the utility of whites in the movement. Freedom School students, like the teachers, viewed the interaction with white volunteers very favorably and often recounted the experience of working with a white person who treated them with kindness and respect as one of the most memorable experiences of the movement. The teachers who remained in the state were cognizant of the debate, and white reaction varied. Some teachers accepted the reality similarly to Fusco and candidly admitted that "it was time for the movement to belong to black people."[75] Other volunteers reacted differently. "I had a right to live here, and nobody had a right to say that I shouldn't live here," Jan Hillegas, a volunteer who moved to Mississippi in August 1964, recalled of the time period.

"I was hardheaded enough to do what I thought I should do or what seemed to be the best idea I could come up with at the time and not feel like anybody should tell me what I should do or not do." [76]

Ideologically, the shift toward black power indicates how activists reconceptualized education for freedom during the latter part of the 1960s. Black power organizers in the late 1960s built upon Bob Moses's call for parallel institutions while viewing younger students as potential social change agents in the same way that Freedom School organizers did. But in the context of the black power movement, Moses's statement is indicative of an interest among organizers to create a network of schools exclusively under black control. The Organization of Afro-American Unity (OAAU), based in New York and modeled on the Organization of African Unity founded in May 1963 in Ethiopia, adopted a platform on education that echoed this ideology. To rectify the ills caused by institutional discrimination, the OAAU demanded control of the 10 percent of schools that were not included in the New York Board of Education's plan for desegregation. As the OAAU stated, "A first step in the program to end the existing system of racist education is to demand that the [schools not impacted by the plan] be turned over and run by the Afro-American community. We want Afro-American principals to head these schools. We want Afro-American teachers in these schools. We want textbooks written by Afro-Americans." The OAAU also declared that "if these proposals are not met, we will ask Afro-American parents to keep their children out of the present inferior schools they attend."[77] As organizers demanded community control of the schools in black neighborhoods in New York, a political move that laid the foundation for later strikes, such as the Ocean Hill–Brownsville strike of 1968, which pitted the black community concept of "local control" against teachers' unions, educator and teacher organizer James Campbell and Malcolm X established the country's first "Liberation School" in 1964. Mostly held on the weekend for two to four hours, students studied the biography of Fannie Lou Hamer, analyzed the foundations of racism in American history, examined Frederick Douglass's speeches, and studied the origins of liberation, abolition, and emancipation, among other topics.[78]

The Black Panther Party adopted a similar stance in their Ten Point Program in October 1966. The program called for an overhaul of public education. "We want education for our people that exposes the true nature of this decadent

American society," the educational platform called for. "We want education that teaches us our true history and our role in the present-day society."[79] By the end of the decade, Black Panther organizers had the resources to develop a similar yet distinct system of grassroots education. Lauren Watson, a Black Panther in Denver, Colorado, articulated the educational vision of the organization in 1969:

> What Black people want is freedom and the power to determine their own destiny. And black people can never realize this freedom and power by attempting to integrate themselves into a racist system. Since the start of the school integration plans, black students at every age level have been subjected to every kind of inhuman treatment by racist teachers, principals and school administrators [We] intend to survive America by any means necessary and we intend to educate black children to survive by the same means. [We will] put into practice an educational system based upon political, economical and social survival.[80]

An article in the *Black Panther*, the major organ of the Black Panther Party, stated that the Liberation Schools "will be implemented . . . to meet the needs of the people." The Panthers built this program to fully engage young people and the communities in which they live. The curriculum and pedagogy espoused at the Liberation Schools, much like the Freedom Schools, was built upon an acute understanding of structural discrimination and the need to address it. The Black Panther schools recognized "the need for all oppressed people to unite against the forces that are making our lives unbearable. Their understanding manifests itself in their definition, i.e., Revolution means Change; Revolutionaries are Changers; Liberation means Freedom."[81] Organizers of the black power movement viewed education in the same vein as the Freedom Summer organizers. Although framed in more revolutionary rhetoric and taught primarily by African Americans, the principles behind the Liberation Schools carried forth the historic notion that education was, in fact, the path to freedom.

The Black Panther Party also viewed the education of elementary, middle, and high school students as a critical part of their organizing. The organization first organized Liberation Schools in Berkeley, California, in June 1969, five years after the Freedom Summer campaign. The program grew in the Bay Area and included schools in Oakland and San Francisco. Organizers also founded schools in Chicago. The schools were founded with the objectives to transmit a culture, education, and ideology independent of and autonomous from the white dominant culture.[82] The Liberation Schools reflected trends in the Black Studies movement in institutions of higher education as organizers implemented a curriculum focused on black history and culture and employed an all-black teaching staff. The earliest manifestations of the program cultivated a revolutionary pedagogy that embraced politics, ethos, and strategies aimed at sustaining a separate black community.[83] The Black Panther Party developed and maintained an educational program that was philosophically similar to the Freedom Schools in that both were manifestations of education for freedom connected to community organizing. While the Freedom Schools did not survive in the era of black power, the much older notion of education for liberation thrived and, once again, continued to be a cornerstone of grassroots organizing in the late 1960s and 1970s.

Issues of gender ideologically fragmented the remaining network of activists as well, which further depleted the ranks of teachers who taught in the Freedom Schools during the 1964/1965 school year. Two SNCC workers in the freedom movement, Mary King and Casey Hayden, submitted a memo for consideration at the Waveland retreat in November 1964. King and Hayden's statement challenged the gendered assumptions and practices of sexual discrimination that were embedded within the freedom movement. The memo correctly charged: "Women who are competent, qualified, and experienced are automatically assigned to the 'female' kinds of jobs such as typing, desk work, telephone work, filing. Women are the crucial factor that keeps the movement running on a day-to-day basis. Yet they are not given equal say-so when it comes to day-to-day decision making."[84] In the publication that stemmed from the memo, they wrote: "There seem to be many parallels that can be drawn between treatment of Negroes and treatment of women in our society as a whole. But in particular, women we've talked to who work in the movement seem to be caught up in a common-law caste system that operates, sometimes subtly, forcing them to work around or outside hierarchical structures of power which may exclude them."[85] Hayden and King began to articulate gender discrimination issues that regularly surfaced in the freedom movement. The patriarchal assumptions (and statements) of movement leaders like King and Carmichael structured the movement. The fact that women were more than likely disciplined for risqué behavior on the project rather than men signifies misogynistic assumption as well.[86] In spite or even because of this, the movement's ideals inspired important work in feminist thought and organization. Women involved in the Freedom Schools experienced the sexual double standard of this movement, especially as they volunteered for teaching positions that assumed gendered stereotypes. While this did not have a direct impact on the women who remained to teach in Mississippi, the questions of gender and sexuality further fractured the administrative structure that organized the Freedom Schools during the 1964/1965 school year and illustrates another factor by which the Freedom Schools were marginalized.

THE FREEDOM SCHOOL TEACHERS DURING THE FIRST YEAR AFTER FREEDOM SUMMER

The ideology of the movement assumed new forms as Freedom School teachers left Mississippi and applied skills learned during the movement in new venues. The experience in Mississippi changed the worldviews of the Freedom School teachers, and their work after the summer campaign shaped a changing national context throughout the 1960s in profound ways. The Freedom Summer campaign inadvertently trained a cadre of activists to begin organizing in their home communities around issues that were just beginning to emerge as key political and social issues during the late 1960s and 1970s. One of the best-known instances of volunteer activism after the summer campaign is the case of Mario Savio, a philosophy student at the University of California, Berkeley, and voter registration worker in McComb. Savio returned to Berkeley in the fall of 1964 and spoke against the injustices in Mississippi and the Jim Crow system still in place in McComb. When the Berkeley administration systematically shut down public demonstrations and arrested students for distributing movement literature, Savio led students in a series of events that culminated in the takeover of the Sproul Hall administration building. As a leader of the free speech movement, Savio illustrates how Freedom Summer activists left the state and organized movements that addressed new issues with new strategies.[87] Similarly influenced by the profound experience in Mississippi, the Freedom School teachers remained committed to the struggle and extended their activism to their own networks. "The Freedom Schools shaped my teaching throughout the rest of my life," Mark Levy, the Freedom School coordinator in Meridian reflected, "and I continue to look to those experiences for inspiration and ideas."[88] As Levy indicates, the experiences garnered in Mississippi significantly shaped teachers' activism, and they embarked in new struggles. Upon their arrival home, some Freedom School teachers who returned to teaching in a classroom focused on quality education while others turned their attention to issues that addressed women's rights or the antiwar movement.

The classroom became a logical site of activism for many of the Freedom School teachers once they returned home. After serving as a Freedom School coordinator, Levy accepted a teaching position at a junior high school in West Harlem, New York. He applied the skills he had learned that summer in his classroom, particularly the cultivation of critical thinking and political efficacy. Levy asked guided questions of his eighth-grade students to generate discussions about the students' identity and the history of their neighborhood, which developed in them an acute understanding of the world in which they lived. Questions closely mirrored those posed during the Freedom School sessions, such as "What do you like about your neighborhood? What don't you like? What would you like to preserve? What would you like to change? How can we go about doing that?"[89] This facilitated student-led activism just as it had in the Freedom Schools. Levy observed that students led yearlong community-based projects in Harlem connected to issues such as neighborhood housing, the provision of utility services, the quality of recreational facilities, and access to government services.[90] For Levy and other professional teachers who volunteered in Mississippi, the Freedom Schools provided informal lessons in teacher education, and these lessons shaped the pedagogy of many teachers as they returned to their classrooms.

The activism of former Freedom School teachers was not limited to the classroom. Chude Allen returned home to complete her degree at Carleton

College in Minnesota. After a saddening departure with her parents at the beginning of the summer, her parents, like all of the parents of the summer volunteers, eagerly awaited her return. "They looked forward to my coming home," Allen later recalled. "Yet when I did come home, I couldn't adjust. I was distant and uncommunicative." Her mother struggled with her daughter's dramatic shift in demeanor. She wrote (though never delivered) a letter to Carolyn Goodman, the mother of Andrew Goodman, one of the three civil rights workers killed during the summer campaign. "You lost a son," she wrote, "but I lost a daughter."[91] Living on the other end of the Mississippi River in Minnesota, Allen threw herself into supporting the civil rights movement. With two other women who had also returned from Mississippi, she organized support for SNCC at Carleton College by speaking, raising money, and collecting clothing, curtains, and bedspreads to donate to her friends in Mississippi. With a couple of African American students, she organized a student support group for African American and international students. For Allen, the public speaking was significant because, as she noted, "women didn't do much public speaking. The three of us who came back to Carleton were female; I am quite sure if one of the men had returned rather than graduated, he would have done the major public speaking."[92] This experience was influential in Allen's later work as an organizer in the women's liberation movement.

As the Freedom School teachers changed as activists and educators, so did their politics and activism. Sandy Siegel returned to his studies at the University of California, Davis, and looked back upon the Freedom Schools experience as one of politicization. "[Freedom Summer] politicized me, and it made me more of an activist, and it made me feel that if we could do it for desegregation and civil rights, we should be able to do it to stop the war," Siegel recalled. "It was a very direct connection, and we saw the war as really being part of the same [movement]."[93] For Siegel and many of the other volunteers, protesting the Vietnam War was a likely path to follow after working in the Mississippi civil rights movement. Siegel and other teachers faced expulsion. "The head of the education department who notified me that I was being kicked out told me that the civil rights work was okay," Siegel recalled, "but they did not sanction and approve our protests of the Vietnam War."[94] Activists faced a difficult conundrum with the Vietnam War because protests often led to a criminal record and probable time in jail. As the ongoing war in Southeast Asia continued to rage and as the federal government devoted more resources to fight that war, serving in active combat in the military and facing the chances of being killed was a haunting prospect for many former Freedom School teachers and students alike in the aftermath of the Freedom Summer campaign.

Those who were teachers before and after Freedom Summer committed themselves to the antiwar movement immediately upon their return as well. This often jeopardized their careers. Norma Becker, a Freedom School teacher in Greenville, and Sandra Adickes, who had taught in Hattiesburg, returned to New York and participated in the first stages of the antiwar movement. Together they cofounded the Teachers Committee for Peace in Vietnam. In May 1965, the organization published a statement against the war, "To Our President, a Former Teacher," in the *New York Times*, which stated, "We are horrified by the slaughter of innocents, by the tragic waste of American and Vietnamese lives. . . . For the sake of humanity, we implore you to stop the bombings immediately and initiate a peaceful settlement in Vietnam." The ad was supported with 2,700 signatures, including fellow Freedom School teachers Betty and Mark Levy.[95] The statement demonstrates the commitment of professional teachers, not just students, to the peace movement at a time when organized dissent against the war in Vietnam was rare. Such organization provided the foundation for the antiwar movement of the late 1960s and early 1970s.

The activism of the former Freedom School teachers further challenges the popular narrative that ends the movement after the Freedom Summer campaign. Many of the teachers recommitted themselves to the movement in robust ways upon their arrival home. They applied the knowledge and skills acquired in Mississippi to new fronts that shaped the nature of protest in the United States during the late 1960s and 1970s. In the process they redefined the movement and made it more inclusive of other struggles. Moreover, their activism post-Mississippi illustrates a dynamic interplay between the local and national context. Even as the schools disbanded throughout 1964 and 1965, the ideology and training acquired through a Freedom School education continued to serve as a foundation that influenced programs at the national level, including those funded by the ambitious "War on Poverty."

HEAD START AND THE APPROPRIATION
OF THE FREEDOM SCHOOL IDEA

The dynamic interplay between the local and national context shaped the implementation of federal programs during the era of desegregation, especially those that aimed to construct Lyndon B. Johnson's "Great Society." The local infrastructure painstakingly laid by movement organizers enabled the growth of federal education programs that reached into the same communities as the Freedom Schools. The momentum generated at the grassroots level around the Freedom School concept intersected with a federal movement that activists at first glance disparaged. As organizers struggled to move forward ideologically, particularly around race and gender issues, the federal government extensively grew its commitment to public education and other educational programs that targeted poverty. Congress had already passed the Civil Rights Act during the summer of 1964 and, after the Selma to Montgomery march that illustrated the need for tougher voter rights protection, Congress introduced legislation that led to the Voting Rights Act of 1965. The federal government became involved in other ways that shaped the contours of the local civil rights movement in Mississippi, specifically in regard to education. By the spring of 1965 President Lyndon B. Johnson had signed the Elementary and Secondary Education Act (ESEA), the most comprehensive and far-reaching educational policy passed in the history of American education.[96] The act introduced categorical federal support to all levels of public education and targeted high-poverty school districts with extra federal support. Johnson touted education as the means to alleviate poverty once and for all in the United States, making it an important piece of his domestic War on Poverty legislation. As part of this campaign, the Johnson administration orchestrated the largest early childhood educational program in the history of the United States: Head Start, a federally funded program to provide education, nourishing meals, medical services, and a positive social environment for children about to enter the first grade.

Organizers already mobilized the ideological and logistical infrastructure of the Freedom Schools, which raised consciousness around the liberating effect of civil rights education. Therefore, an early childhood program like Head Start that sought to educate disenfranchised youth gained immediate support at the local grassroots level. "[The Freedom Schools] brought about the Head Start for the black children," Ida Ruth Griffin, a Freedom School student from Carthage, Mississippi, recalled. "Most of the people that were Freedom Riders," she remembered, "were the ones who originated Head Start."[97] Others in the movement articulated similar connections between the Freedom Schools and Head Start. "They [Head Start and the freedom movement] had to come together at some point in time," remembered Owen Brooks, an activist enmeshed in Mississippi politics, including Head Start, "because they were the same people. The same people were involved in the counties and communities, so what was in place for political action also was in place to assist Head Start."[98] At first glance, the connection between the Freedom Schools, a grassroots and radical educational project, and Head Start, a massive federally funded early childhood education project, is unlikely. Yet for Griffin, Brooks, and others closely involved in the Mississippi movement, Head Start was a logical next step after the Freedom Summer campaign. Since Head Start embodied the same ideologies, pedagogy, and grassroots organization of the Freedom Schools, the federally funded early childhood education program placed civil rights movement education in the national spotlight and in the center of national discourse. Tracing the development of Head Start in Mississippi, which developed less than one year after the Freedom Schools, illustrates the rhetoric of the New Right that helps explain the trajectory and apparent dissolution of Freedom School ideology.

Head Start teachers and organizers were not unlike their Freedom School predecessors. The two educational programs were strikingly similar. Head Start organizers were entrenched in the civil rights movement, and they were influenced by the movement's principles. The organizers who implemented Head Start and the teachers who taught in the programs were already active in grassroots or otherwise political organization. One movement fed into the other. Laura Johnson, a Head Start teacher in Greenville, Mississippi, was a registered voter since 1958 and worked with the NAACP, the Delta Ministry (the National Council of Churches organization formed to work specifically in the Mississippi Delta), and other civil rights groups in Mississippi when she heard about the call for Head Start.[99] "I was out of high school," Hattye Gaston, a Head Start teacher in Durant, Mississippi, recalled. "I was watching the television and seeing how people were being treated in Alabama and I was working at a private home during the time and would turn on the TV and I just couldn't wait to get involved. And at that time, they was called 'freedom riders.' And that's what I said I want to be: a freedom rider."[100] Dr. W. B. Mitchell, the chair of the business department at Rust College and the father of Arelya Mitchell, who had enrolled in the Holly Springs Freedom School, began a Head Start program in northern Mississippi with Bernice Totten. Helen Anderson, a Citizenship School teacher trained by Victoria Gray in Hattiesburg, who worked closely with the Freedom Summer project, became a director of the Head Start center in Hattiesburg.[101] Head Start volunteers were freedom movement activists, and it was through these connections that Head Start teachers and organizers learned about the educational program that was being funded from Washington.

Activists organized Head Start programs following the same grassroots strategies that the Freedom Summer organizers had used the previous summer for voter registration. This time, however, the focus of organizers was solely on providing a quality education to young children not yet in school. Laura Johnson recalled, "The first thing we had to do for Head Start was we had to canvass the neighborhoods to see how many children there were in Greenville and Washington County that were eligible for Head Start."[102] Johnson and others already working in the movement were familiar with civil rights organizations centered upon mobilizing resources and people around issues of social change. They were therefore familiar with work such as canvassing communities to generate support and locate buildings that were safe places to meet and organize various initiatives. The first stage of any Head Start program consisted of canvassing the neighborhood to enroll students. Canvassing, the slow and grinding work of walking door-to-door and talking to neighbors about the movement, had been the foundation of freedom movement work in Mississippi.[103] These networks, built over generations of civil rights organizing, were instrumental in locating the space for running Head Start programs, which in the mid-1960s was still largely equated with civil rights work and was therefore a target of segregationists. White school boards were unwilling to rent out schools, white grocers were unwilling to extend credit, and bus contractors were unwilling to lease transportation rights.[104] Therefore, by the time Head Start organizers opened the first programs in local churches or community centers in July

1965, Mississippians were organized to undertake a massive mobilization of people, resources, and time—the invaluable soft donations that were required to make such a large-scale educational campaign a success. By the time Head Start opened in the summer of 1965, the state had just gone through an organized campaign that had primed the state of Mississippi more than any other state to organize at such a sophisticated level.

The motivations and the organizational methods behind the Head Start campaign were the same used during the organization phase of the Freedom Schools. Federal funding provided new opportunities that the financially strapped Freedom Schools (and an ideologically divided grassroots administration) could not. In addition to the educational component, Head Start provided physical, health, and medical attention for each child, including delivering hot meals to children twice a day and arranging medical examinations and follow-up treatment to those who needed it.[105] "We went out in the schools of rural areas of Hinds County and examined the children at the school and there was hearing and vision screening done by other groups during the day, but most of the examination were at night or on Saturdays or Sundays," Dr. Jim Hendrick remembered about working with the program. "It was a big affair. Everybody came."[106] For those involved with the program, Head Start provided services to communities impoverished by the exploitative system of Jim Crow. As the Reverend James F. McRee of the Delta remembered, "Head Start had something that we needed. Because what you had here were malnourished kids. Some kids were eating but one meal per day, and some were getting a meal whenever they could."[107]

One major difference between the Freedom Schools and Head Start was that the fact that the federal government paid substantial salaries to Head Start teachers during the first summer of implementation. Therefore, the federal government offered something to the black staff who ran Head Start centers that grassroots organizations such as SNCC could not: opportunity for employment at substantial salaries. Head Start was a significant component of the larger War on Poverty, which in part sought to provide jobs to the unemployed. As such, federal paychecks provided a massive economic stimulus package to the state of Mississippi. At a time when farm labor paid $15 per week, Head Start employees were given $50 to $60 per week, and the coveted teachers' positions paid $75 per week.[108]

With federal funding, educators, community members, and activists involved with Head Start were able to realize fully the ideas that were associated with the Freedom Schools. One key distinction was that Head Start funded an early childhood program, whereas the Freedom Schools focused on middle and high schools. The level of political socialization, however, remained high in the Head Start program. Like the Freedom Schools, Head Start was also a benefit to the parent and adult volunteers, teachers, and employees who worked with the program. Their experiences politicized the participants, as evident in their control of the program, their demands to keep the programs open, their decisions to enroll in recently desegregated colleges, and the decisions they made on how to implement the program. Not as radically politicized as the Freedom Summer volunteers, these volunteers did become politically active in subtle yet profound ways. Federal guidelines supported and funded a decision-making framework with "maximum feasible participation," which involved parents in the educational process. Local Head Start volunteers lived out the highest feasible level of participation by visiting their students' homes to work with the parents in ensuring the best development of children. Connecting to a grassroots movement history in Mississippi, these teachers sought to engage the children in as many ways as they could, which included visiting students' homes and working with parents and involving them in the education of their children. Parent involvement, long recognized as an instrumental component in any child's education, was a very important part of Head Start from its inception, and the program continues to value its importance today.[109]

In this way Head Start, like the Freedom Schools that came before it, used education as an organizing tool, and it was immensely popular among grassroots organizers. The scale of the Head Start program in Mississippi dwarfed the reach of the Freedom Schools, which were already struggling financially and politically. Less than one year after the first Freedom Schools opened their doors to two thousand student activists, over twenty-five thousand young children were enrolled in Head Start centers across the state. Once teachers and community members became involved in the program, they organized and worked for change within their communities. They articulated a collective voice and used it to petition the government to continue the Head Start program. Using the same resources of community donations, networks of safe meeting places, and ideologies that focused on providing a quality education, the Head Start program in Mississippi in many ways subsumed the trajectory of the Freedom Schools. Another distinguishing feature of Head Start that explains its national significance in 1965 (as opposed to the Freedom Schools) is that the program was funded federally and provided a national framework from which to operate. The program offered resources to volunteers that grassroots and financially strapped civil rights organizations in Mississippi could not.

The initial stages of Head Start were a phenomenal success that was largely enabled by the local Freedom School infrastructure already in place. The fact that over twenty-five thousand children received an education and medical and health services, volunteers were reimbursed for their services, and participants were able to foster the goals of the civil rights movement illustrates the ongoing work of civil rights education. The victory was short lived, however. Because Head Start was tantamount to a civil rights organization, staunch opposition from white segregationists soon followed federal investment in civil rights–based forms of education like Head Start. Because significant federal funding was attached to the program, the Head Start initiative in Mississippi inspired a national controversy that influenced the rhetoric of the New Right.

Barry Goldwater, the staunchly conservative Republican candidate for president, decisively carried the state of Mississippi with 87 percent of the vote during the fall of 1964. Goldwater also won majorities in Alabama, Georgia, Louisiana, and South Carolina, the first time since Reconstruction that the Deep South had voted for a Republican candidate.[110] As Sunbelt scholars have noted, this political swing was the beginning of a movement that housed much of the race-neutral rhetoric and the defense of individual values.[111] The events of 1964 and 1965 marked important milestones of the civil rights movement, but it also demarcates the rise of neoconservative policies and rhetoric that sought to mitigate such victories. As Joseph Crespino has suggested, "Whites in Mississippi rearticulated their resentment of the liberal social policies that allowed for black advancement in ways that would come to resonate with white Americans far outside of the Deep South. They conceived of their struggle against civil rights activists and federal officials not merely as a regional fight to preserve white supremacy but as a national battle to preserve fundamental American freedoms."[112] Thus, when local civil rights activists organized for federal funding for their Head Start programs, they entered a larger national context, and on this stage they were opposed by other grass-roots organizers, "cold warriors concerned about an expansive federal state [and] parents opposed to federal school desegregation efforts, who wanted to determine where and with whom their children would attend."[113] Head Start generated extensive public discourse around the topic of civil rights education that questioned the role, depth, and duration of the federal government in supporting grassroots educational programs. Because Head Start drew from the same ideological and organizational base as the Freedom Schools, the controversy that surrounded Head Start suggests a deep level of national opposition to such any education program with even mild connections to the civil rights movement.[114]

Mississippi legislators, elected officials, and other conservative politicians attacked and framed Head Start as a welfare-based program that carried a burden of responsibility outside the jurisdiction of federal purview. Head Start was also attacked because it hired local African Americans as teachers, teacher aides, and program assistants and paid them wages much higher than local standards. The injection of wealth into impoverished black communities radically upset the economic and class standings throughout Mississippi. In their attack on the system, Mississippi legislators generated restrictive guidelines that nullified the potential of incorporating the value of civil rights education projects into the national discourse. Senator John Stennis of Mississippi, a vocal segregationist, adopted race-neutral rhetoric on a national stage and attacked the Head Start program in his home state. He charged the program with mismanaging funds and using federal money to subsidize civil rights demonstrations, including the payment of fines and bail.[115] Conservative charges from powerful leaders like Stennis prompted the Johnson administration to moderate its policies and publicly distance itself from any connection to the civil rights movement like the operation of Head Start in Mississippi. The Office of Economic Opportunity renewed Head Start funding through 1966 and 1967, but the office steered federal funding away from civil rights organizations, namely the Children's Development Group of Mississippi (CDGM), which was by this time chastised as a radical civil rights program.[116] The government responded by sending auditors and investigators to formally evaluate the Head Start headquarters at Mt. Beulah center in Edwards, Mississippi.[117] Moreover, the federal government encouraged Mississippians to appoint biracial and moderate boards to run Head Start programs through alternative community action programs such as the Mississippi Action for Progress.[118] Federal money was now going to moderate and traditional groups, rather than civil rights groups. National evaluations conducted by outsiders and social scientific "experts," such as the influential Westinghouse Report, found no substantial gains in the cognitive or affective gains of Head Start students and generated anti–Head Start sentiment at a national level.[119] Behind the cries of financial mismanagement and ineffective programs was a forceful rejection of the empowerment of local Mississippians through the Head Start program at the federal level. Although the federal government did not abandon the project altogether, the administration wrested control of the program from the local level and dictated how the program should be run and by whom. Federal oversight ensured that the federal government and the American public would not support the civil rights framework of Head Start and the ideological expressions of the Freedom Schools.

To SNCC, CORE, and the more radical elements of the movement including Freedom School organizers, especially after the Atlantic City Democratic National Convention of 1964, Head Start was doomed to fail solely because of its association with the federal government. SNCC and other movement leaders loudly criticized any federal intervention at the state and local level, including Head Start. Stakeholders in the movement were highly skeptical of federal money, paternalistic sentiments, and the prevalence of middle-class values associated with Head Start. The money invested in the program was interpreted as "buying out" activists who would otherwise be committed to the more radical elements of the civil rights movement. For those who orchestrated the Freedom Summer campaign, joining the program was tantamount to selling out "by a few middle-class bourgeoisie and some of the Uncle Toms who couldn't care less."[120] Already skeptical of federal intervention after losing their challenge in Atlantic City, SNCC was "too politicized and too committed to alternative institutions to support" federally funded organizations like Head Start.[121] Discriminatory oversight and the federal push toward biracial moderate Head Start governing boards validated their suspicions. Moreover, federal intervention carried with it paternalistic and problematic assumptions. At the federal level, Head Start was very much composed of federal policymakers and "experts" in the field of education with racist assumptions of the black family, which was evident in their analysis of poverty. In light of the Moynihan Report, which was released to the Johnson administration during the summer of 1965, an influential faction of federal policymakers traced the origins of poverty to the "pathology" of black homes, which, according to experts, needed to be corrected by middle-class (i.e., white) values.[122] The African American home, they concluded, was culturally deprived of values that would lead to educationally, socially, and economically successful lives.

SNCC members and other activists who opposed Head Start and federal intervention were correct in that the government pacified or mitigated the direct-action component of the movement. Head Start did not train students or its teachers to protest and become key stakeholders in the ongoing struggle as the Freedom Schools did. Segregationist policymakers influenced the direction of Head Start by implementing moderate biracial governing boards that explicitly denounced full-time activity in the civil rights movement and the burgeoning influence of black power. Whether they intended to or not, however, the structures that SNCC, the NAACP, and other organizations established in Mississippi were open to local Mississippians to use and create schools in their own way.

The grassroots organization that defined the Freedom Schools and CDGM-styled Head Start and the democratic curriculum and pedagogy that stemmed from this would not incorporate itself into national discourse around the merits of educational reform in the desegregation era. The architects of desegregation in Mississippi—the white governor, the white school boards, and the white state legislature—paid little attention to the progressive education swelling within local communities. The controversy over Head Start foreshadowed the civil rights generation's struggle to provide a quality education and to gain a voice in a changing national context. The reaction at the federal level further marginalized the Freedom School idea within national discourse and historical memory.

* * *

The Freedom Schools left an indelible mark on the civil rights movement. The Freedom School students and their student activist contemporaries occupied an important place in the civil rights movement, especially between 1964 and 1970, when the larger national movement was beginning to experience profound ideological changes. The schools trained a youthful activist base that sustained and even expanded the movement in Mississippi as students continued to register voters, desegregate public spaces, and join, if not radicalize, local movements in their home communities. They also shaped educational reform efforts as the Magnolia State began to desegregate its schools for the first time since the historic *Brown v. Board of Education* decision. Students organized boycotts, protests, and demonstrations with the objective to acquire a quality education, whereas desegregating schools remained the major priority of older activists. Moreover, the students were active at a time when movement veterans questioned the essential ideological foundations of the movement. Students participated in a multifaceted movement that organized for a quality education, equitable treatment under the law (including educational policy), and a fairer distribution of resources. The Freedom Schools also occupied a temporal space in the movement during a time in which popular interpretations suggest that the civil rights movement ended as the black power movement rose in prominence. The Freedom School students maintained essential components of the civil rights era as they adopted new modes of protest and goals as veteran organizers began to call for black power. At the same time, the local ideological and logistical infrastructure of the Freedom Schools enabled the growth of federal programs like Head Start and the attendant resources this brought to the state. The same infrastructure invited national oversight and ultimate rejection of civil rights–based education programs. The reactionary response shaped the articulation of policies associated with the New Right and neoconservatism that framed educational policy for decades. The Freedom Schools were shaped— and were shaped by—a rapidly changing context during the late 1960s and 1970s, but their ongoing influence despite dwindling numbers indicate that the ideology of education for liberation was a powerful and enduring concept. The ideology, pedagogy, and notions of activism espoused in the Freedom Schools would continue to leave individual and institutional imprints on reform efforts well into the twenty-first century.

6

CARRYING FORTH THE STRUGGLE

Freedom Schools and Contemporary Educational Policy

Attending Freedom School was like shining a very bright light into a very dark place for a time, and it just changed my perception about many things for the rest of my life. It wasn't until much later that I appreciated how important those schools were. I carry that experience to this very day.

HOMER HILL, FREEDOM SCHOOL STUDENT IN CLARKSDALE, MISSISSIPPI

[Freedom Summer] was the most profound experience of my life. . . . It solidified the attitudes and beliefs that I had and crystallized them and just really put into me the realization that I would not be able to live my life any other way outside of this.

WALLY ROGERS, FREEDOM SCHOOL COORDINATOR IN
RULEVILLE, MISSISSIPPI

As former Freedom School student Homer Hill articulated nearly fifty years after the historic summer of 1964, attending a Freedom School during the civil rights movement had a profound and lasting influence on his life. The Freedom School model of education offered a "bright light" in the darkness created by inequitable segregated public schools in Mississippi and an entrenched system of de jure segregation that the state was slow to dismantle. The immediate influence of the Freedom Schools is evident in the personal lives and professional careers of those involved in the civil rights educational project. Students and educators continued to apply the lessons they learned in the colleges they attended, in the classes they returned home to teach, and in the professions they pursued after working in the Freedom Schools in 1964. The Freedom Schools as a distinct network of grassroots schools, however, ceased to exist by 1966. After the dissolution of the Freedom Schools, the expansive Elementary and Secondary Education Act and federally funded programs like Head Start appropriated the Freedom Schools' ideology and infrastructure. Grassroots organizers focused on the Mississippi Freedom Democratic Party, especially after the Voting Rights Act of 1965, and teaching the art and philosophy of resistance to young people faded from the agendas of activists who remained in Mississippi. Although the participants readily recall the Freedom Schools' influence, it appears that federal legislation, alternative political parties, and popular discourse extinguished the bright light of a Freedom School education from our collective imagination and memory.

The Freedom School idea remained alight at the margins of educational discourse, however, and it burned deeply at the center of the students' and teachers' lives as well as various educational programs that carry the same name. The ongoing legacy was most evident in how the students and teachers chose to live their lives after their experiences in Mississippi. Freedom School students selected career paths that included teaching, journalism, law, entrepreneurship, and political office. Their work uniformly embodied notions of community activism that the Freedom Schools ultimately desired to teach. The volunteer teachers were similarly motivated in profound ways and embarked upon long and notable careers. Former Freedom School teachers returned home reinvigorated and deeply committed to the principles of freedom and continued the legacy in a diverse array of fields and professions that included education, but in many instances their activism moved beyond the classroom. Those who taught in the Freedom Schools continued to act upon the lessons they learned well after the Freedom Summer of 1964, much like the students they taught. This individualized interpretation of success of the Freedom Schools is not limited to those who participated, however. The impact of the Freedom Schools can still be observed at a philosophical level and an institutional level. Indeed, many of the philosophical and pedagogical tenets embedded in the Freedom Schools influenced a notion of "critical peda-gogy" that influenced educators who sought to transform society through educa-tion. The name, ideology, and concepts behind the Freedom Schools continue to inspire subsequent institutional reform efforts as well. Today, scores of schools, programs, and reform initiatives across the country refer to or cite the Freedom Schools in their mission statements. The Freedom Schools are alive and well in various manifestations across the United States, which provides irrefutable testi-mony to the legacy of this form of civil rights education.

The Freedom Schools must be evaluated and interpreted by different crite-ria. More than fifty years after the summer of 1964, more contemporary notions of academic success rely on positivist-oriented measurement such as quantifi-able and value-added test scores, measurable student enrollment, and standards-based assessment. Such evaluative measures suggest that the Freedom Schools were unsuccessful or were at best a program of a bygone era disconnected from our contemporary systems of education. This prevailing logic has diluted our understanding of how the Freedom School model continues to influence con-temporary educational policy, pedagogy, and curricula. The late social historian Howard Zinn, who himself taught in the Freedom Schools in Jackson, claimed just months after the end of the summer campaign of 1964 that the Freedom Schools were "an experiment that cannot be assessed in the usual terms of 'suc-cess' and 'failure,' and it would be wrong to hail it with an enthusiasm which would then lead it to be judged by traditional criteria. But that venture of last summer in Mississippi deserves close attention by Americans interested in the relationship between education and social change."[1]

Indeed, the Freedom Schools enjoy a legacy in that they transformed the lives of countless individuals. Those who passed through the doors of the Freedom Schools selected to commit their lives, careers, and livelihood to inspiring social change. The ideology embedded in the Freedom Schools also inspired institutional reform that sought to transform a system of education to better meet the needs of all children. Any notion of "success" that the Freedom School students and teachers experienced after the summer of 1964 is therefore qualitatively and markedly different from higher test scores and other tradi-tional forms of quantifiable evaluation. Instead, political consciousness, suc-cessful grassroots organization that centered upon community engagement, and ongoing commitment to the principles of the civil rights movement are criteria that can be used to examine the success of the Freedom School model. Using a different set a criteria to examine the legacy of the Freedom Schools during the "post–civil rights era" illustrates how a cohort of activists carried forth the legacy in diffuse venues that continue to challenge the nation to live up to its democratic ideals.

FREEDOM SCHOOL STUDENTS AFTER THE CIVIL RIGHTS MOVEMENT

Violence continued to threaten former Freedom School students who remained to toil in the Mississippi freedom struggle after the summer of 1964. Even those who focused their struggles on the perennial and seemingly "safe" quest for a quality education faced a palpable danger throughout the late 1960s and 1970s. Freedom School students could enroll in the same institutions of higher learning that had previously barred their parents and older generations from attending. Enrolling in higher education became an active extension of their civil rights work. But these institutions of higher education, whether predominantly black or white, were still unsafe for people of color. One such instance of state-supported violence occurred in May 1970, which communicated yet another warning to young people. Jackson State College students were in the midst of ongoing demonstrations against the war in Vietnam and continued civil rights violations occurring in the capital city. The campus experienced a heightened anxiety particularly because of the shootings at Kent State University, which claimed the lives of four students just a few days earlier. On the night of May 14, 1970, Jackson police responded to a fire with unknown causes that burned brightly on Lynch Street. Police approached campus with "Thompson's Tank," the armored vehicle police outfitted for the Freedom Summer campaign in 1964. As law enforcement officers arrived on campus, police barraged Alexander Hall, an all-women's dormitory on campus, and fatally shot two students, Phillip Lafayette Gibbs, a prelaw student at Jackson State, and James Earl Green, a senior at the local Jim Hill High School. Nine others were wounded.[2]

Approximately one year later on, May 25, 1971, Wesley Parks, a twenty-five-year-old white man of Drew, Mississippi, fired a single bullet into a small group of black teenagers walking through the black section of town. The bullet struck and killed Jo Etha Collier, an eighteen-year-old student who had graduated that same evening with honors from Drew High School. The school was in the midst of controversy as it had recently been desegregated, one of the many schools forced to desegregate after the *Alexander v. Holmes County Board of Education* (1969) decision. Mississippi officials framed the incident as one without apparent motivation and a random act of violence attributed to drunkenness.[3] But to civil rights leaders Aaron Henry, Ralph Abernathy, and Fannie Lou Hamer, and to the thousands of mourners who gathered in this small Delta town to mourn the death of this teenage girl, it was an act of terrorism connected to a long history of violence and white resistance to the Mississippi civil rights movement. These acts of terrorism served as a stark reminder to the Freedom School students that freedom at any level of education still exacted a heavy toll.

The career of Hymethia Washington Lofton Thompson, who attended the Freedom School at Tougaloo College, illustrates how activism took shape after receiving a Freedom School education during the civil rights movement. At the age of sixteen, Thompson served as a mentor and teacher to the younger Freedom School students, which placed her in the role of educator at a very early age. After she graduated from Rosa Scott Parks High School in 1966, she recalled that participating in the march after a segregationist shot James Meredith "was the last time I actively participated [in the movement]."[4] Thompson indicates that this "last" individual act of protest coincided with college enrollment. Her ongoing commitment to education, however, is indicative of a historic tradition within the civil rights movement of establishing, building, and teaching in schools. It was through pursuing a degree in education that Thompson embodied and continued to carry with her the potential and promises of a Freedom School education. "I acquainted the lessons we learned from being involved in those Freedom Schools," Thompson recalled, "so I look back. I never let it go."[5] Elaborating upon what this meant to her, Thompson stated that "being the first *means* something." She was the first to desegregate Murrah High School in Jackson in 1965. After receiving her education degree from Jackson State University (she also earned a doctorate in religious education), she went on to complete forty-two years of service as an English teacher, first in Jackson, Mississippi, and later in Racine, Wisconsin, where she was the first African American speech teacher at Park High School in Racine and the only black resident in her neighborhood. She drew on the lessons of the past and instilled in her students what she herself had learned in attending the Freedom Schools and becoming a student activist in the movement.[6]

Anthony Harris, who attended a Freedom School in Hattiesburg, followed a similar path in earning an advanced degree and working in the field of higher education. His work also illustrates how Freedom School students continued to commit themselves to the betterment of their home communities. Harris remained in Hattiesburg after attending an all-white high school and earned a bachelor's degree from the University of Southern Mississippi. He earned a doctoral degree in counseling with an emphasis in higher education from East Texas State University in 1982. He held faculty and administrative positions at the University of Southern Mississippi, East Texas State University (Texas A&M University-Commerce), and Mercer University. As a former Freedom School student, Harris remained committed to the community in which he lived. He was elected to the school board in Commerce, Texas; he served with distinction as a recipient of the W. K. Kellogg Foundation's National Fellowship, through which he traveled extensively throughout Africa; and he founded a mentorship program, Project Keep Hope Alive, which focused on improving the academic achievement of black male students.[7]

Freedom School students also had opportunities to apply the lessons they learned not only in the field of education or in the demonstrations of the civil rights movement but also in the career paths they chose once they graduated from high school in Mississippi. Eddie James Carthan embarked upon an ambitious career in local politics that took advantage of opportunities not afforded in Mississippi since Reconstruction. In the wake of statewide voter registration and the Voting Rights Act of 1965, Carthan organized political campaigns using the same canvassing and voter registration strategies he practiced as a Freedom School student. Black voters first elected Carthan to the school board in 1977, when he was twenty-six years old. Four years later, the same voters elected him mayor—the first black mayor of Tchula, which was over 80 percent African American. He applied for federal grants in order to enact local economic development. He also advocated for community improvement and cultivated black leadership in his struggling Delta town.

As an elected politician, he embodied the political lessons and virtues of citizenship enshrined in the Freedom Schools. It was through this line of work, however, that Carthan became implicated in the "Tchula Seven" incident. Local white officials fabricated charges of murder conspiracy against Carthan and arrested him in 1981. Carthan was eventually released from prison after a protracted legal battle that flared racial tensions in the early 1980s (figure 6.1).[8] The incident illustrated the depths of racism and fear that still gripped Mississippi.

Is This Mayor a Murderer? A Jury Says No

Wearing her sentiments, a well-wisher applauds former Tchula, Miss., mayor Eddie Carthan as he enters the county courthouse on the first day of his murder trial. Carthan, 33, was accused of hiring two men to kill a black Tchula alderman, an ally of Carthan's white political opponents. The case attracted national attention when liberal church groups and prominent black leaders such as Congressman Ron Dellums and actor-director Ossie Davis raised money for Carthan's defense, contending

that the charges against the pattern of harassment of bla Although Tchula, a small to Delta, is 85 percent black, it black mayor until 1977 whe in. The two-and-a-half-week an all-black jury, after delibe found the defendant not guil did not emerge a free man—h separate three-year sentenc bank fraud, convictions that

FIGURE 6.1   Eddie James Carthan outside the courthouse after his trial, 1981. (Courtesy of Eddie James Carthan)

Carthan continues to serve his small Delta town as a pastor and youth organizer. He speaks proudly of his father, his grandfather, and older generations that long struggled for equality and dignity in the face of state-sanctioned segregation. His career and continued work carries forth the trajectory of this long line of resistance, which the Freedom Schools helped cultivate. As Carthan reflected upon his work in the Mississippi freedom movement and his work since then, he stated, "If I had to attribute anything to my community involvement, I would attribute it to my attending the Freedom School."[9]

Arelya Mitchell wrote inflammatory articles as a Freedom School student in Holly Springs that reported on the operations of local white officials during the summer of 1964. Mitchell and other Freedom School students published these articles in student newspapers across the state. For Mitchell, however, the vocation of journalism was historic. "Newspaper was in my bloodline," she recalled. In 1913, her great-great uncle founded the *St. Louis Argus*, which was one of the oldest black newspapers in the country. Just over fifty years later, she was the editor of the Freedom School newsletter, "and it was something to fight for."[10] This experience was tremendously influential to the young Arelya Mitchell as it reaffirmed her commitment to journalism and provided invaluable experience. Mitchell followed in the footsteps of other Freedom School students, but she also followed in the path of her family, which was imbued with a deep commitment to postsecondary education. Her siblings graduated from the University of Kansas, Purdue University, the University of Iowa, and Lincoln University. Mitchell was one of five black students to desegregate the dormitories at Mississippi University for Women, where she earned her bachelor's degree in journalism and political science. She earned a master's degree in political science from the University of Memphis, specializing in international relations, political analysis, and comparative politics.

Mitchell's activism in the field of journalism continued throughout her career, and she remained committed to covering local, state, and national politics (figure 6.2). She has interviewed national and international luminaries, including President Bill Clinton, Senator Hillary Clinton, the Reverend Jesse Jackson, attorney Johnnie Cochran, Supreme Court Justice Clarence Thomas, and minister Louis Farrakhan. She founded the *Mid-South Tribune* in Memphis, Tennessee, and has worked for numerous years in radio, television, newspaper,

FIGURE 6.2   Arelya Mitchell, seated directly across from President George H. W. Bush
and next to Robert Gates, then director of the CIA, was one of twelve African American
journalists invited to a special luncheon in the White House shortly before the first Desert
Storm operation. (Photo by Glen Yaun, courtesy of Arelya Mitchell)

and public relations and advertising. She received a Southern Educational
Communications Association Award while working in public broadcasting,
including journalism for PBS and NPR. *Memphis Magazine* named her the first
African American journalist/editor to be one of "Most Influential in Memphis,"
an honor that stemmed from her coverage of the first black mayor elected in
Memphis, Willie Herenton, in 1991. She also covered the historic election of
President Barack Obama during the presidential campaign of 2008.[11] Mitchell, and all of the people who helped register black voters during the campaign,
saw this election as a realization of full political rights that their parents, grandparents, and generations of disenfranchised voters had long struggled for. Her
column continues to remind readers of the ongoing struggle of the civil rights
movement, particularly in the wake of the case of Trayvon Martin, a young
black male shot and killed in suspect circumstances. The shooter, George Zimmerman, was tried but not convicted based on the controversial "stand your

ground" laws in Florida. As a Mississippian raised in the aftermath of the brutal murder of Emmett Till, Mitchell insightfully pointed out the connection between past discrimination and ongoing violence. "Typifying the men who brutalized Till," Mitchell wrote, "Zimmerman regarded Trayvon Martin as no more than a good kill when he engaged and shot to death a young African American male who was carrying only Skittles and a can of tea." She went on to write that "where there is progress, there is also regression. Where there is outrage, there is also acceptance."[12]

Freedom School students were committed to movement principles throughout their careers, but their activism did not always follow conventional paths established by the movement. "I learned to be a good organizer," Wilbur Colom recalled about his Freedom School experience. The ability to organize around a particular goal or issue was "one of the things the movement taught me." Colom's career demonstrates the legacy of organizing among former Freedom Schools and the controversy this sometimes inspired. In addition to organizing protests against the Vietnam War, which led to his expulsion from high school, Colom organized protests for the SCLC, the National Tenants Association, the National Welfare Rights Organization, and the AFL-CIO at the 1972 Democratic and Republican National Conventions, both of which were held in Miami, Florida. After completing his undergraduate studies at Howard University, Colom attended the Antioch School of Law in Washington, D.C., which focused on issues of public advocacy. Colom interned in the office of Chief Justice Warren Burger, who told Colom that he should be proud to have some (but not all) of the charges in his criminal record revealed. Colom later argued *Mississippi University for Women v. Hogan* (1982) in front of the Supreme Court, which included his mentor, Chief Justice Burger, and Thurgood Marshall. He argued that the Mississippi University of Women violated the equal protection clause when it denied Joe Hogan admission because of his gender. Colom argued in the case that "the assertion that women should be isolated in a single-sex environment because they are unable to compete with men is reminiscent of a similar argument concerning racially segregated education." Some members of the black community rebuked him for making the argument because they thought the issue of racial equality was more salient than that of gender equality.[13] Colom won the case, and Hogan was admitted into a previously female-only state institution.[14] Colom invited more controversy when he represented a white family that sued black administrators over their treatment of their child in a predominantly black school. When the court ruled in favor of the white family and found that black administrators violated the white student's rights, he earned the scorn of parts of the black community.[15]

The demonstrated record of Freedom School students like Hymethia Thompson, Anthony Harris, Eddie James Carthan, Arelya Mitchell, and Wilbur Colom indicate that the Freedom School model of education was profoundly instrumental in influencing a life of civic engagement based upon a critical examination of social, political, and economic inequality. Indeed, the Freedom Schools directly educated for this form of political socialization. The pedagogy, expectations, curriculum, interracial dialogue, and the unorthodox educational experiences constituted a form of education markedly different from the average school experience in the 1960s. As Hymethia Thompson recalled, "The Freedom Schools instilled in us some things that we didn't get in the regular classroom. The Freedom Schools allowed us to believe that we could rise above any situation, and that we could make it."[16] The students who attended Freedom Schools received something extra, something that those who did not attend did not receive. Yet the Freedom Schools only reached a very small part of the school-age population in Mississippi, less than 1 percent, and not all young people benefited from the tutelage of a Freedom School education.[17] This is not to suggest, however, that the influence of the Freedom Schools was limited to the students who attended.

Hezekiah Watkins, a high school activist in Jackson, Mississippi, acquired a civil rights education by participating in all aspects of it. He survived his experiences in the U.S. military in the mid-1960s after being expelled from Unica Junior College for organizing a protest. More than fifty years later, Watkins looked back upon his activism during the movement (figure 6.3). He spoke from the small grocery store he owned in the city of Jackson, a city whose predominantly black neighborhoods are still de facto segregated and subject to a failing public school system, high unemployment, and drug use:

> You look at Martin Luther King, you look at Medgar Evers and others who gave their life . . . it could have been me, hell I could have gotten killed and

FIGURE 6.3   Hezekiah Watkins. (Courtesy of Eric Etheridge)

you say, "why was he killed?" If someone came down here, closed their eyes and started talking about Medgar Evers and talking about Martin Luther King, how great those people were, you know they're gonna sit back and laugh at you and say, "hell no, they couldn't have been that great, they didn't do shit, look at this situation." So apparently Martin Luther King failed. Medgar Evers failed. And all the others out there who gave the ultimate price, they failed. I failed. We all failed. We were out there marching, getting our ass whooped. We failed, you know?

Watkins exemplifies the legacy of the civil rights generation because he stayed in Mississippi after the activists left, like most of the young people educated in the movement. He also illustrates the fact that the Freedom School generation remains critical of the progress of the movement. For many of these activists, the promises of equality and opportunity remain elusive and unrealized.

THE FREEDOM SCHOOL TEACHERS AFTER
THE CIVIL RIGHTS MOVEMENT

The Freedom School experience was reciprocal, and the experience of teaching in a Freedom School had a profound impact on the teachers as well. The Freedom School experience exposed teachers to the debilitating effect of Jim Crow but at the same time introduced them to effective means to challenge it. "There were very few of us northern white volunteers who went through that summer who weren't deeply affected by it," recalled Freedom School teacher Wally Roberts. "A lot of us were very affected by it, and it changed the rest of our lives."[18] He elaborated on what was a very common experience of working with the Freedom Schools in 1964:

> [The Freedom Summer experience] was key, it was the deciding event, and it was the most profound experience of my life. It solidified the attitudes and beliefs that I had and crystallized them and just really put into me the realization that I would not be able to live my life any other way outside of this. When you are part of a group where three people get murdered, it makes a big impression because it could have been me. Like any traumatic experience, it leaves a big impact.[19]

When the volunteer teachers returned home or moved to different locations across the country after the Freedom Summer campaign of 1964, they—like the students they had taught during the summer of 1964—remained committed to the movement in myriad ways. Some teachers remained in the field of education, which was a logical extension of Freedom School teaching, but many did not. Some left the field of education because they felt they could not teach in a traditional classroom after the Freedom School experience. Others embarked upon careers in journalism, community organizing, and labor organizing. Regardless of the career path selected, the Freedom School experience deeply shaped the lives of the teachers.

After remaining in Mississippi as a Freedom School coordinator until the spring of 1966, Liz Fusco returned to the Northeast to teach in the public school system. "The Freedom Schools and the civil rights movement influenced everything I did after," Fusco recalled, looking back upon her career as a lifelong organizer and educator.[20] Her first work as an educator after Freedom Summer was in Manhattan as a substitute teacher. Working in a predominantly Latino and African American public school, she quickly assessed her school environment as "another situation where the kids needed Freedom School." Fusco immediately employed the culturally relevant strategies she learned as a Freedom School teacher. She infused rock 'n' roll lyrics to teach her students poetry, much to the chagrin of the principal and chair of the English department. She also applied the grassroots organizing strategies that pervaded the Freedom Summer campaign, in addition to embodying the idea that young people still in middle and high school were, in fact, social change agents. Fusco was summarily dismissed less than two months after leaving Mississippi.[21] Soon after she fought the teachers' union in New York during the grand experiment in "community control" that was central to the Ocean Hill–Brownsville strike in 1968 and volunteered as a "scab" teaching first grade.[22]

Fusco earned a doctorate in education at the age of fifty and resumed her work as a teacher educator at Central Connecticut State University for more than twenty years. She remained committed to alleviating social ills, especially in Connecticut, which she saw clearly as an "apartheid state."[23] As an educator, Fusco organized opportunities for cross-district dialogue between white students attending suburban schools and students who attended predominantly black high schools in Hartford. Inspired by the interracial experiences of the Freedom Summer campaign, she organized discussions between socially segregated black and white young people. "We brought them over for a movie series together with students from a couple of other towns and the students from Hartford, who said they had never sat next to a white person before," Fusco recalled. The fact that black students in the Northeast could legitimately claim they had never interacted closely with whites resembled her experiences in Mississippi. From her perspective, racial animosity is still prevalent among the sons and daughters of the civil rights generation. "We all inhaled the smog and the poison of racism in this country," Fusco stated, "and that can still be felt at this point."[24]

Frances O'Brien worked as a Freedom School teacher in Vicksburg, Mississippi. The experiences of Freedom Summer influenced her work deeply, which was immediately evident upon her return to Pacific Lutheran University in Washington State. As the only student from her campus to take part in the Freedom Summer campaign, she was invited to speak across campus and the town of Forest Grove. She also became more involved in a student antidiscrimination league at her university. O'Brien earned her bachelor's degree in sociology and proceeded to earn her teaching certificate in California in elementary and special education. She taught for thirty-four years in Bakersfield, California, before retiring.[25] Her experiences as a Freedom School taught her several important lessons that were unlikely to be learned in special education programs at the time. Mrs. Garrett, a Vicksburg, Mississippi resident and local teacher, housed O'Brien during her for the duration of the summer campaign. O'Brien recalled that "Mrs. Garrett was actually more helpful than more modern instructors would have been."[26] Her hostess often wrote down the stories she heard from her students who had trouble reading and writing. Once the students learned the idea that reading is speech written down, many students were able to grasp the concept of reading and writing. In teaching special education students, O'Brien found this strategy particularly helpful with students who had dyslexia. The Freedom School curriculum shaped O'Brien's work too: "[The experience] changed the way I taught, especially American history, which at that time did not include African Americans." As O'Brien went on to explain, teaching in the Freedom Schools introduced her to historical figures such as Frederick Douglass and Harriet Tubman and other subjects not often taught to white students prior to the civil rights movement.[27] O'Brien made a concerted effort to integrate black history into her teaching and curriculum after her Freedom School experience.

O'Brien used the time after Freedom Summer to apply the skills she acquired, but she also used the time to heal. Four white men attacked and assaulted O'Brien one evening in Vicksburg as she was waiting for a ride. She remembered the men saying, "We're going to make you sorry you ever came to Mississippi, and we're going to make you say you're sorry." She survived the assault but was emotionally scarred. "I kept quiet for twenty-five years," she recalled.[28] O'Brien felt that as a professional she could not share this and other profound experiences with her colleagues since her work environment was largely white and conservative. However, there were moments when she felt compelled to speak directly about her involvement with the civil rights movement. Upon hearing several students comment in the wake of the assassination of Martin Luther King Jr. (whom she had personally met in Vicksburg), saying he was a Communist, O'Brien "shut the door" and informed her students about the work of King and the Freedom Summer campaign of 1964.[29] For O'Brien and many other volunteers, moving forward after Freedom Summer rarely followed a linear or neat path.

According to Liz Fusco, teaching in a Freedom School translated into the profoundly transformative act of "rethinking what teaching is." She explained that the "idea was to have all teachers question America and use what they know from the immediate reality of their own lives to see the larger picture."[30] As the experiences of O'Brien and Fusco indicate, the Freedom School curriculum and the pedagogical methods of dialogue, discussion, and the use of experience-based problems were influential to those who returned to classrooms after the summer campaign of 1964.[31] Indeed, the Freedom School experience was in some ways tantamount to professional development and an intensive teacher-education program. One of the Freedom School legacies, therefore, is the pedagogy and curriculum that educators embraced and introduced to their colleagues, however indirectly, in the schools to which they returned to after the summer campaign of 1964. The Freedom Schools' emphasis on the importance of students' race, culture, and socioeconomic background constituted a very early form of "multicultural education" and "culturally relevant teaching," which are late-twentieth-century pedagogical interventions to address the educational realities of resegregation, high drop-out rates among students of color, academic performance disparity between white students and students of color, and ongoing public disapproval of public education.[32] As such, the Freedom Schools were one of the first historical instances of "critical pedagogy," a theory of education based on resistance and education for social change that still resonates through the contemporary period. Beginning with the publication of Paulo Freire's *Pedagogy of the Oppressed* in 1968, radical educators sought methods to fundamentally restructure society through education.[33] The theory of "critical pedagogy" influenced a generation of educational scholars and practitioners who sought to transform society by adopting a radical pedagogy that put revolutionary theory into practice through education, or praxis. Critical pedagogy incorporates the ideas of collapsing the student/teacher dichotomy, instilling a sense of agency among students, educating students to identify matrices of oppression, and developing and implementing the strategies to overcome institutional barriers to equity.[34] Within this theory of radical education, much like that espoused in the Freedom School model, students and teachers are the agents of social change.

Some of the Freedom Schools maintained a commitment to the field of education but devoted their time away from school to other issues, particularly Vietnam. The Freedom School teachers were part of the first wave of activists to publically speak out against the war in Vietnam. As noted in chapter 5, Norma Becker, a Freedom School teacher from Greenville, cofounded the Teachers Committee for Peace in Vietnam with fellow Freedom School teacher Sandra Adickes in the spring of 1965. Becker remained a public school teacher in New York for over thirty years and emerged as a leader of the antiwar movement. Later in 1965, she founded the Fifth Avenue Peace Parade Committee and led the organization of one of the nation's first antiwar rallies. On October 16, 1965, more than ten thousand people gathered in New York and marched to protest the war in Southeast Asia.[35] After the war ended, Becker chaired the War Resisters League from 1977 to 1982. She also founded Mobilization for Survival, which organized over one hundred thousand people at Central Park on June 12, 1982, to demand an end to the nuclear arms race.[36] Becker illustrated how the Freedom School teachers devoted themselves to providing a quality education as well as addressing larger social and political grievances outside the classroom.

A segment of the Freedom School teachers returned to the classroom after Freedom Summer but ultimately left the classroom to commit themselves to organizing in other ways. Mark Levy taught middle school in Harlem for two years after the Freedom Summer campaign but chose to leave the classroom and commit himself to union organizing for over thirty years. "My understanding of the world was that it was important to build working-class and multiracial organizations that could engage in struggles so that the leaders could be local leaders instead of outside organizers," Levy recalled, "and that led me to the labor movement."[37] Indeed, Levy worked in an ongoing labor movement for the majority of his career. This work centered upon forming and leading unions, which included organizing for the United Electrical, Radio and Machine Workers of America;

the Drug, Hospital, and Health Care Employees Union–Local 1199 (now the National Health Care Workers' Union); and the Service Employees International Union, among other unions.[38] Levy practiced an understanding that local leaders, not outside or external help, must compose the leadership ranks. A theory of local leadership and multiracial organization is directly attributable to his experiences in the civil rights movement. Today Levy works extensively with social studies teachers and students in diversifying their curriculum and teaching methods to better meet the needs of all students through a civil rights–based education. For Levy and other organizers, activism began in the civil rights movement but soon translated into other fields of protest and organizing.

Gloria Xifaras Clark, a Freedom School teacher in Holly Springs, similarly chose to leave the traditional classroom as the result of her experiences in Mississippi. "I could never teach in a regular classroom again after [Freedom Summer]," Clark recalled, "because of what I felt were restrictions."[39] Clark remained committed to providing a quality education, but her experience in Mississippi pushed her to toward unorthodox if not radical means to achieve it. Upon her return, Clark assisted with the Friends of SNCC chapter in Cambridge, Massachusetts, and she established a NAACP Youth Council chapter in New Bedford. She served as a Head Start director, and her activism included working with other programs funded by the War on Poverty. Clark worked with the Job Corps, an Office of Economic Opportunity program that supported Lyndon B. Johnson's Great Society. The Job Corps targeted young people between the ages of sixteen and twenty-one who had dropped out of high school and suffered from other social and economic disadvantages, providing them with intensive job training, education, and mentorship.[40] Working with the "poorest of the poor" was difficult work, but her training in Mississippi had prepared Clark. "I got along great because of my background with Mississippi," she remembered. "It was a perfect job for me."[41] In the process, Clark aligned her work with the Black Panther Party and the Students for a Democratic Society. When she enrolled in the education program at Harvard to study under John Holt, a radical critic of public education, she participated in the student takeover of University Hall, the Harvard administration building in 1969.[42] Later in her career, Clark worked with the new careers program at Bristol Community College to enroll welfare recipients and other disenfranchised communities. She was also instrumental in the founding of the Free University of New Bedford. Later in her career, Clark labored in children's advocacy and continued to serve the field of education as a grant writer for early childhood education programs through the 1980s.[43]

Wally Roberts, who served as a Freedom School teacher and coordinator in Ruleville, Mississippi, further illustrates how the political work associated with the Freedom Schools translated into other manifestations of activism. Despite his work with the Freedom Schools in 1964, Roberts did not pursue a career in the field of education. "The experience in Mississippi convinced me that the overriding issue was what I could do to help bring about greater social and economic justice," Roberts recalled. He was slated to attend graduate school at Brown University to study European history, but after working in the trenches of the civil rights movement as a Freedom School teacher and coordinator in the Mississippi Delta, examining the history of Europe seemed irrelevant, so he looked for other work that extended his activism in the movement. The wages of organizers would not cover the expenses of raising a family of three, so Roberts looked into the field of journalism, which was, in his words "the next best thing."[44]

Roberts made a career in journalism, starting out in a professional context that parallels the work of Arelya Mitchell. Roberts's first published article was about his Freedom School experiences in a successful Freedom Vote drive in Cleveland, Mississippi. Roberts oversaw the Freedom School where local high school students discussed the meaning of "Freedom Day" (the day designated for voter registration). Teachers set up a mock picket line to "prepare for any eventuality," which meant preparing for heckling, arrest, and other violent reprisals. Police arrested over one hundred demonstrators in a similar Greenwood campaign, but the sheriff in Cleveland allowed forty people to attempt to register. Writing back home to a northern audience in Pittsfield, Massachusetts, through the *Berkshire Eagle*, Roberts reported on the events surrounding Freedom Day to a captive audience. Roberts's observation and participation in the event afforded him a unique perspective valued by the northeastern press.[45] But it also taught Roberts and others how to use the media to affect social change. Freelance investigative journalism and grassroots politics required using applied research methods for a particular cause. As Roberts noted, "to deal with the power structure, you have to do investigative work."[46] SNCC practiced the idea that acquiring knowledge through applied research was needed to confront and effectively challenge the structures that maintained oppressive conditions, and they employed Jack Minnis as a researcher to explore various positions and actions the organization could take.[47] This approach had a lasting effect on Roberts's career in journalism. Roberts continued to write articles critical of unfair or undemocratic practices in the American economy. He wrote for the *Providence Journal*, *Saturday Review*, *Citizen Advocate*, and *American Prospect*, among other newspapers and journals. Through investigative journalism, he published critiques of the privatization of utilities in Massachusetts and further connected the criminal economic activity at Enron with the deregulation of gas and electric companies.[48]

Teachers also joined the women's liberation movement and similarly applied the skills they learned during the Freedom Summer project. Chude Allen began organizing the women's liberation movement after returning north and acted with a similar conviction to eradicate sexism and continue the work of gender and sexual equality that was noted at the Waveland retreat and in Mary King and Casey Hayden's article "Sex and Caste," a seminal feminist document. "I was committed to building a multi-racial women's liberation movement," she remembered, "and understood that required white women addressing racism in themselves and the society."[49] Allen worked diligently around issues of gender equality and feminism after her experiences as a Freedom School teacher. She organized numerous women's liberation groups, including New York Radical Women, before she moved to San Francisco, where she founded Sudsofloppen, the city's first consciousness-raising feminist group. Allen was also instrumental in founding Breakaway, a women's liberation school that focused on educating women about equality outside of patriarchal and traditional educational structures. As an extension of her work around gender and sexual equality, she wrote and published *Free Space: A Perspective on the Small Group in Women's Liberation*, in which she outlined the steps to identify a collective free space in order to cultivate autonomous thinking and action among women. While in the Bay Area, she also joined the Union Women's Alliance to Gain Equality (Union WAGE) and became editor of the paper *Union WAGE*.[50] Allen also maintained deep interracial relationships. She married Robert Allen, a Morehouse College graduate, sociologist, and a writer for the *Guardian*, in 1967, when the state of Mississippi and most other southern states deemed such marriages illegal.[51]

Dr. Gwendolyn (Robinson) Simmons embarked on an illustrious career that built upon her experiences as a Freedom School teacher and as a southerner who came of age under Jim Crow. As a black woman on the Freedom Summer project, her experiences were different from white women who volunteered in Mississippi. Simmons attended the Waveland retreat in which King and Hayden released "Sex and Caste." She also noted that it was mostly white women who attended the groundbreaking event. For Simmons, organizing black women in local communities required a different approach. In 1968, after her work with SNCC, she worked for the National Council of Negro Women as the Midwest field director for "Project WomenPower." She then worked for American Friends Service Committee, the Quaker peace and justice organization, traveling to countries torn asunder by war, including Vietnam and Laos; organizing around civil rights issues; and exposing the illegal practices of U.S. intelligence agencies.[52] Like many participants in the Freedom Schools, Simmons also pursued an advanced degree that developed from her interest and experience in the civil rights movement. She earned her bachelor's degree from Antioch University and her doctorate in religion. As she wrote in her dissertation, "The Islamic Law of Personal Status and Its Contemporary Impact on Women in Jordan":

> My own thinking and research has been conditioned by the fact that I am an African American who grew up in the "Jim Crow" South and that I spent years in the organized struggle against legalized racism and oppression. Simultaneously, I have been engaged in a thirty-year deconditioning and reconditioning process related to overcoming the harmful psychological effects of living in a racist society—exorcising the internalized demons of racism. This process has greatly affected my worldview.[53]

Simmons's experience as a Freedom School teacher and her subsequent struggles led her to extensive work in the international community. This included attending a United Nations conference on women in Beijing, China, in 1995 as well as conducting research in residence in Jordan, Egypt, Palestine, and Syria, where she extensively researched the impact of Islamic law on the role of women after earning the prestigious Fulbright Pre-Doctoral Fellowship and a NERMTA Fellowship from 1996 to 1998.[54] Today, Simmons is a professor of religion at the University of Florida.

Although the Mississippi Freedom Schools only ran for approximately two years, the education they provided shaped numerous lives and careers. The Freedom School participants were and still are committed to principles of equality, freedom, and community involvement. Students attending the Freedom Schools were provided additional opportunities during the 1960s. In addition to the skills learned in schools and the opportunities afforded to participate in the movement, Freedom School students learned to create for themselves a more equitable position previously denied by Jim Crow. Both students and teachers were unafraid to commit themselves to realizing the opportunities they helped create for their generation and reform policy in the interest of the public good.

THE INSTITUTIONAL LEGACY OF THE FREEDOM SCHOOLS AND CONTEMPORARY EDUCATIONAL POLICY

The Freedom Schools as an institution are an important lens through which to evaluate the transformative context of educational policy of the late 1960s, the beginning of the 1970s, and the "end" of the civil rights movement. The dynamic interplay between the local movement in Mississippi, which by 1965 included the advent of Head Start programs, and the federal context mediated how young activists continued the ongoing movement once the volunteers returned home. Federal educational policy dramatically expanded as it ordered once and for all the total desegregation of public schools by the early 1970s. The Civil Rights Act of 1964 contained a provision that denied federal funding to institutions that maintained de jure segregation. This provision extended to the public school systems when Congress passed ESEA in 1965. The act was an integral part of Lyndon B. Johnson's Great Society agenda and appropriated federal support for schools serving communities with a high percentage of poor and working-class families.[55] Under ESEA, public schools that received federal support, which

included all public schools in the southern United States, had to maintain desegregated schools in order to retain funding from the federal government. The
Supreme Court rendered decisions that further accelerated the pace of desegregation. The *Green v. County School Board of New Kent County* (1968) and *Alexander v. Holmes County Board of Education* (1969) decisions effectively ended the
"all deliberate speed" standard embedded in federal enforcement procedures
since the *Brown v. Board of Education* (1954) decision. In Mississippi, thirty-three
schools districts were ordered to desegregate by 1970.[56]

The final and complete termination of de jure segregation did not ensure
the quality education that Freedom School students, their families, and the civil
rights generation ultimately sought. Nor did it quell popular white resistance to
desegregated schools, which was evident in the brutal murder of Jo Etha Collier. Northern states and policymakers remained recalcitrant. They balked at the
notion of desegregating northern schools, as demonstrated when Senator John
Stennis of Mississippi introduced an amendment to a federal education bill that
aimed to enforce desegregation in highly segregated schools in the North.[57] The
development of conservative and neoconservative politics shrouded national
discourse in race-neutral and colorblind rhetoric. Desegregation, especially
when connected to busing, was viewed as an attack on white individuals' rights,
and a conservative though "silent" majority embraced privatization, school
"choice" plans, and a gradual abandonment of public education. In early 1970,
John Bell Williams, the governor of Mississippi, and Senator Stennis endorsed
the statewide organization Freedom of Choice in the United States (FOCUS),
which the former mayor of Jackson, Allen Thompson, founded in 1970 to maintain public and legal support for freedom of choice plans.[58] The move toward
privatization in Mississippi and across the country continued. Between 1965 and
1970, the number of private schools in Mississippi nearly doubled, and the number of white students who enrolled in private schools tripled.[59]

Prevailing educational policy discourse, which was more and more shaped
by growing white sentiment against school desegregation, summarily dismissed
the Freedom School example, which sought ways to effectively teach historically disenfranchised students, to inspire critical thinking, and to see students as
change agents and educate them in the principles of the civil rights movement.
The idea that young people could and should radically reconstruct political,

social, and economic structures challenged fundamental conservative values that shaped national discourse. Such questions, educational aims, and otherwise radical propositions inherent in the Freedom School idea were rejected or at best marginalized within dominant discourse and were consequently excluded from discourse that shaped the local, state, and federal levels.

The marginality of the Freedom Schools during the growth of federal involvement in educational policy since ESEA did not, however, preclude a generative or productive influence. As noted, much of the revolutionary pedagogy and goals of the Freedom Schools are embraced by "critical pedagogy" advocates. Moreover, various educational policies or school programs throughout the country trace their origins to the Freedom Schools. Since the Freedom Schools first opened in 1964, several scholars and educators often have looked to them for ideas on educational reform.[60] Marian Wright Edelman, civil rights activist and the first African American admitted to the Mississippi State Bar in 1963, illustrates the most direct connection to the Freedom School idea within a contemporary context. Edelman established the Children's Defense Fund (CDF) in 1973, which years later organized a Freedom School after-school and summer enrichment program across the country. Since 1995, the CDF Freedom Schools have reached more than 70,000 students and their families in sixty-one cities in twenty-four states. More than 7,000 college students, 2,000 high school students, and 1,500 adult site coordinators and project directors have been trained to work in Freedom School programs. Freedom School teachers, much like those who volunteered during the 1964 Freedom Summer, go through a rigorous training program that instructs teachers in the principles of freedom. To develop teaching skills in the Freedom School idea, CDF Freedom School teachers participate in the Ella Baker Child Policy Training Institute, a national training workshop at the historic CDF Haley Farm in Clinton, Tennessee, and at the University of Tennessee.[61] The opportunities for student engagement have been institutionalized to some degree on a national level in the CDF Freedom School program, which means that student-centered curriculum and instruction focus on issues relevant to their communities, much like the Freedom Schools of 1964.

Other school districts across the country have adopted the name and ideas behind the Freedom Schools as well. These schools and school programs attempt to engage students in a learning process that ensures the academic success of all students. Programs such as the Philadelphia Freedom Schools offer on-site tutoring and mentoring programs distinct from the CDF but still indicative of the Freedom School legacy. School districts across the country also use the term "Freedom School": the Philadelphia Freedom Schools; the Chicago Freedom Schools; Paulo Freire Freedom School in Tucson, Arizona; Saint Paul Freedom School in St. Paul, Minnesota; and in Michigan, the Black Radical Congress in Detroit decided to launch a campaign to create a model based on the Freedom Schools. These are contemporary examples of schools that have cited the influence of the 1964 Freedom Schools in their mission statements. The Freedom Schools today address citizenship, civil rights, and political education much like the schools of 1964. Current Freedom Schools and Freedom School programs are mindful of the need for the rebuilding of a democratic society. These programs actively seek to incorporate the role of students, their families, and their communities in the schooling process.

Perhaps the greatest legacy of the Freedom Schools is the structural questions this civil rights–based program still inspires. Those who led the organization of Freedom Summer prioritized voter registration to open the closed society and to make America aware of the injustices endemic to Mississippi. However, over fifty years after the Voting Rights Act of 1965 and recognizing the fact that Mississippi has more elected black officials than any other state, the original goals of the civil rights movement remain unfulfilled. Bob Moses and Dave Dennis, the civil rights activists who co-organized the Freedom Summer campaign of 1964, view education as an organizing tool for a quality education. Moses and Dennis see the necessity of organizing students, parents, their communities, and educators much like the Freedom Schools during the summer of 1964. Their work and current organizing illustrates a shift from prioritizing voter registration in the 1960s to implementing a quality education for students failed by the public school system.

For a small though vocal number of the Freedom Summer organizers, education is not only a political act; it is a contemporary civil rights struggle and a defining issue of the twenty-first century. Bob Moses created the Algebra Project in the 1990s based on the idea that mathematical literacy was crucial for economic, political, and social success in the twenty-first century. Denying this literacy, as is common practice in underfunded and still segregated schools, violates the civil rights of all students and denies the path to citizenship. As Moses explains: "The most urgent social issue affecting poor people and people of color is economic access. In today's world, economic access and full citizenship depend crucially on math and science literacy. I believe that the absence of math literacy in urban and rural communities throughout this country is an issue as urgent as the lack of registered Black voters in Mississippi was in 1961."[62]

Like the organizational predecessors before it, the Algebra Project uses education as an organizing tool at the community level from the "bottom up." Algebra is the point of entry into a larger struggle that not only advocates for mathematical literacy in a culturally responsive way at all levels of school but one that also advocates equitable resource distribution, fairer treatment of all students, and constitutional provisions that guarantee a quality public school education for all students. The Algebra Project and its attendant organization, the Young People's Project, harness the grassroots organization legacy of the Freedom Schools and embody the radical, transformative goals of education that the Freedom Schools embodied. Like the Freedom School predecessors of 1964, the meaning behind student activists organizing for social change are more profound than their modest numbers suggest. Two contemporary examples are instructive of the program's significance in perpetuating the gains made in the civil rights movement.

The organization of young people continues to reflect the ideology and community-organizing model manifest in the Freedom Schools of 1964. In McComb, Mississippi, a small group of students from McComb High School organized a commemoration of the fiftieth anniversary of the Burgland High School walkout of 1961, an anniversary that would have gone unnoticed until young people spoke up. The students organized a chapter of the Young People's Project to develop a commemoration service, a community engagement project, and a documentary of the 1961 high school walkout (which they traveled to Washington, D.C., to present). They are connecting with local teachers in the area through developing a "Local Cultures" course in the public school curriculum, which they developed in response to Mississippi House Bill 2718—a bill passed in 2008 that permits the incorporation of civil rights movement history into the social studies curriculum. The students also articulated an agenda for educational reform that promotes stronger parenting strategies among young parents and sex education in schools to combat the rise of pregnancy and sexually transmitted infections.[63]

The Baltimore, Maryland, branch of the Algebra Project in particular resonates with the grassroots organizing, nonviolent ethos, and political consciousness of the civil rights movement (figure 6.4). The Baltimore branch illustrates the more radical forms of activism that young people engage with to inspire institutional change. Young students under the age of twenty-three run the

FIGURE 6.4 For all the ancestors who gave their lives so that we could have education. (Courtesy of Baltimore Algebra Project)

Algebra Project. They have participated in nonviolent protests, marches, and demonstrations aimed at raising money and resources for failing public schools. They have disrupted the state of Maryland's plans to build a juvenile detention center, which the state designed to house minors charged as adults, by occupying the site in protest. They have also attempted to make a citizen's arrest of the state school superintendent. Police arrested several students as they, too, occupy the front lines of grassroots protests.[64]

* * *

The work of organizers and activists in addressing contemporary issues provides testimony to the legacy of education for social change and the idea that young people are agents for such change. Their commitment to acquiring an education to address social, political, and economic injustice constitutes an unquantifiable notion of success. The success of adopting the Freedom School idea does not necessarily translate into popular indicators of achievement such as higher test scores or data-driven teaching strategies. Nor does a grassroots Freedom School model claim to meet such contemporary notions of academic success. Critical thinking, community engagement, and a commitment to the public good, among other radical goals of education, defy such narrow definitions of academic success. The ongoing struggle of young people working in the Freedom School tradition remind us that the promises of a quality education outlined in the *Brown v. Board of Education* decision are still unfulfilled. More importantly, their work suggests the means by which to make this a reality.

EPILOGUE

Remembering the Freedom Schools Fifty Years Later

No education, no what?
No education, no life!

YOUNG PEOPLE OF THE MISSISSIPPI FREEDOM SUMMER
FIFTIETH ANNIVERSARY CONFERENCE, TOUGALOO COL-
LEGE, JACKSON, MISSISSIPPI, JUNE 2014

During the summer of 2014, community organizers, activists, and scholars gathered across the country to commemorate the fiftieth anniversary of the Freedom Summer campaign. Veterans of the movement gathered at the institutions that provided safe places to meet during the summer of 1964. Two notable institutions hosted conferences that helped shape how the nation remembered the summer of 1964: Tougaloo College, the historically black college in Jackson, Mississippi, that provided a safe space for activists throughout the civil rights movement; and Miami University of Ohio, the institution in Oxford, Ohio, that absorbed the Western College for Women, which had hosted the orientation for volunteers before they left for Mississippi. The conferences provided a space for volunteers to reunite and share their memories of their work in the movement fifty years ago. As the summer of 1964 is now enshrined in American history, the volunteers carried themselves with an air of gravitas, and those who organized the original Freedom Summer commanded the respect of those who came to pay homage, to speak their mind, or, like over fifty years ago, to see the "Freedom Fighters" in person.

These conferences hosted the veterans of the nation's greatest social and political movement in American history who carry with them the scars of warfare. But, unlike the veterans of wars formally sanctioned by the government, these heroes go unrecognized, without medals of honor. Most of the activists have not retired either. In true activist fashion, conference organizers used the opportunity to build upon social and political networks already in place to address ongoing civil and human rights violations. The discussions about how to carry the movement forward to address issues of civil rights constituted a modern Freedom School education.

Harassed, jailed, and assaulted over fifty years ago, the volunteers and activists of the Freedom Summer campaign were now welcomed with open arms. Those who organized the Freedom Summer project—Bob Moses, Dave Dennis, Charlie Cobb, Charles McDew, Julian Bond, and others—gave keynote speeches. Representative Bennie Thompson of Mississippi; historian Taylor Branch; Marian Wright Edelman, director of the CDF; and Derrick Johnson, president of the Mississippi branch of the NAACP, among other civil rights dignitaries, sat on panels and led workshops. Numerous civil rights organizations were in attendance. The Young People's Project, the Algebra Project, the Dream Defenders, the NAACP Youth and College Division, One Voice, and other groups gathered for the largest meeting of civil rights activists since the historic summer of 1964. The American public, prompted by the release of Stanley Nelson's film *Freedom Summer*, viewed the fiftieth anniversary events as a time to reflect upon the gains made as a result of a corps of courageous Freedom Fighters.[1] It was also a time to pay collective and national respect to those who gave their lives and livelihood for the struggle. Organizers, however, did not memorialize the struggle as such because the movement—or, rather, the need for a movement—is not over. The conferences were a time to work, organize, and demand that the American public and its elected officials finally act upon the promises made over fifty years ago. For several days and on two different occasions, organizers gathered to meet other organizers, network, and identify next steps in the ongoing struggle. The level of discourse, the content of the presentations and discussions, and the ideas shared over the course of the conferences inculcated a very important message to young and old: the civil rights movement was alive and well, and everyone was called upon to join the struggle.

Freedom School was literally in session. Much like the typical day at Freedom School over fifty years ago, organizers (this time from the CDF) opened the conference in Mississippi each day with *harambee*, a stirring session of Freedom Songs (both old and new) to liven up students. Throughout the day, students from across the country, mostly in high school and college, attended sessions organized specifically for young people that ran concurrently with other sessions for the older veterans. Young people who enrolled in the Freedom School sessions learned about issues connected to immigration, voting rights, quality education, workers' rights, health, and environmental justice. Also like their historic predecessors, students engaged one another through discussion, debate, and open dialogue. They discussed strategies and shared stories of where they came from. They networked, exchanged contact information, and put forth ideas on how to move forward. At the end of each day, "youth congress" was held in order to identify strategies to plan for action. Young people discussed the most progressive and, indeed, radical ideas about improving the system of education. They petitioned for signatures to pass a ballot initiative that would require the state of Mississippi to fund a truly adequate education promised by the state constitution. Students also gathered signatures for a "Students' Bill of Rights" as a way to achieve a quality education. Following the ongoing work of Bob Moses and Dave Dennis, young people continued to articulate a demand for a quality education and to put forth the provocative suggestion that the U.S. Constitution should recognize and protect the right to a quality education as a civil and human right.

The work of the Freedom School initiatives during the fiftieth anniversary conferences reveals an important truth about the status of education. Education, then and now, remains a major civil rights issue and is arguably one of the defining civil rights issues of the twenty-first century. The work of the freedom movement is unfinished. Indeed, when one conceives of the freedom movement as an ongoing struggle with roots during the era of slavery, the demand for freedom still exists alongside the notion that an education for social change, as embodied in the Freedom School model, is a viable and necessary path to achieve it. Especially in this era of "school choice," privatization, standardized test–focused assessment found under No Child Left Behind and the Common Core, frustrated educators, policymakers, parents, and scholars have looked to the democratic idealism expressed in educational programs such as the Mississippi Freedom Schools. The history of the Freedom Schools provides historical lessons for addressing contemporary educational problems adversely impacting public education, including but not limited to racial tracking; privatization, a move toward charter schools; the "achievement gap"; a majority-white teaching force in minority-serving schools; and resegregation.[2] Such indicators of tragic failure within the public school system warrant further critical examination of educational reform in the post-*Brown* era, revising how we understand the complexities and lessons of the civil rights movement. A Freedom School education posits how we can address such issues that continue to plague our system.

The Freedom School sessions at the commemorative conferences also illustrate how young people are not being taught about the influential role youth played in the civil rights movement. As Julian Bond, former SNCC activist and chairman of the NAACP, stated in a study published by the Southern Poverty Law Center on the status of civil rights education, students learn "sanitized versions" of Martin Luther King Jr. and Rosa Parks, "but the stories of bravery and sacrifice in the movement for civil rights were absent from their memories and their high school curricula."[3] As a result of this sanitized version, students and the American public in general are far less familiar with the Freedom School students, young people closer to the age of the students that many educators seek to inspire. The fact that their story is relatively absent from popular narratives limits our understanding of the civil rights movement.[4] The role of young people and the inherently political nature of education, as evident in the history of the Mississippi Freedom Schools, challenge this popular narrative and places young people at the center of the struggle. Young people still in middle and high school have the ability, if not the responsibility, to become social change agents in the ongoing movement for full inclusion and equity.

The commemoration of the Freedom Summer campaign also reveals that the Freedom School model and theory of education remains marginalized from mainstream and popular discourse. Those who are denied a quality public education and continue to face other realities precipitated by social, political, and economic injustice use a Freedom School theory of education to address such issues. As evidenced in the commemorative events, young people and veteran organizers alike established Freedom Schools to engage the stakeholders of social, economic, and political reform. The theory maintains that participants study and learn about contemporary injustices through engagement, discussion, and participation. Freedom School theory, then, maintains that students become active and work toward identifying solutions to such injustices. The idea is embraced fully by activists, which includes some educators and administrators, but the formal bureaucracy that governs public education dismisses the Freedom School idea. The Freedom School idea remains, yet its inherently radical provocation necessitates that it remains at the margins of educational reform. Yet, much like Frederick Douglass over 150 years prior to this moment, the pathway to freedom is clear to those who demand structural reform.

The Freedom School idea is marginalized within the contemporary context, but the flame burns brightly where the light of freedom is sparked. At Tougaloo College during the Freedom Summer conference in June 2014, conference organizers concluded sessions with a "veterans' roll call," in which the volunteers were called by name in recognition for their contribution to Freedom Summer. During one such roll call, young people stirred restlessly in the back of the gymnasium at Tougaloo College. "No education, no what?" one group of young people called; "No education, no life!" another responded. Another group of young people spoke up, "Fight, Fight, Fight! Education is a human right!"

Less than one year later and over seven hundred miles distant, concerned community members gathered on the steps of the North Charleston City Hall in South Carolina in April 2015 in the wake of the death of Walter Scott, yet another unarmed black man gunned down by a white police officer, this time caught on film. Muhiyidin d'Baha of #BlackLivesMatter in Charleston encouraged growing crowds to attend a Freedom School. The Freedom School that evening taught protesters how to use the nonviolent strategies that were going to be employed in protest. Those who attended the informal Freedom School also learned their constitutional rights in case of arrest and debated the next steps protesters should take. Just over two months later, the Charleston community would grieve again after a white gunman shot and killed nine victims gathered for Bible study on June 17, 2015, in the basement of the Emmanuel AME Church. The church was steeped in a liberation theology that often linked education with politics for social change.[5] The crowds that gathered were large and earnestly committed to finding the means to demand justice, eradicating all forms of institutional racism including quality education, not only the removal of the Confederate flag and the public memorials of defenders of slavery and oppression. D'Baha and others, including Daron Calhoun of the historic Avery Research Center for African American History and Culture, called for Liberation Schools and teach-ins as part of the strategy to address discrimination in the economy, education, housing, and policing strategies.[6] The actions of youths in these instances, which is replicated in local settings across the country, serves as an affirmation of youth and the role of young people in the ongoing movement. To those involved, this is what democracy looks like, and education promised a role in its actualization.

The Mississippi Freedom Schools offer powerful lessons from the history of the civil rights movement that can still inform the struggle to complete the unfinished educational legacy of the freedom movement. The students of freedom who made their voice heard in Jackson, Mississippi, and those who organized schools for liberation in Charleston, South Carolina, occupy the new front lines of the long and ongoing civil rights movement. They are demanding the torch be passed from the older activists who have carried it for over fifty years. For those who move beyond commemoration and are called to work in the ongoing movement, a collective responsibility emerges to guarantee that the torch of freedom is passed to young people as they build upon decades of work to dismantle institutional discrimination. The history of the Freedom Schools provides a way to keep the torch of Freedom alight.

NOTES

INTRODUCTION

1. James D. Anderson, *The Education of Blacks in the South, 1860–1935* (Chapel Hill: University of North Carolina Press, 1988), 1.

2. For an excellent discussion of the role of youth in the civil rights movement, see Rebecca de Schweinitz, *If We Could Change the World: Young People and America's Long Struggle for Racial Equality* (Chapel Hill: University of North Carolina Press, 2011); Jennifer Lynn Ritterhouse, *Growing Up Jim Crow: How Black and White Children Learned Race* (Chapel Hill: University of North Carolina Press, 2006); Gael Graham, *Young Activists: American High School Students in the Age of Protest* (DeKalb: Northern Illinois University Press, 2006); and Ellen Levine, *Freedom's Children: Young Civil Rights Activists Tell Their Own Stories* (New York: Puffin, 2000).

3. For a larger historiography on the construction of youth, see de Schweinitz, *If We Could Change the World*; Steven Mintz, *Huck's Raft: A History of American Childhood* (Cambridge, Mass.: Harvard University Press, 2004), 234–36; Edward A. Krug, *The Shaping of the American High School*, vol. 2, *1920–1941* (Madison: University of Wisconsin Press, 1972), 301–14, esp. 307; Wilma King, *African American Childhoods: Historical Perspectives from Slavery to Civil Rights* (New York: Palgrave Macmillan, 2005); Ritterhouse, *Growing Up Jim Crow*; Kristie Lindenmeyer, *The Right to Childhood: The U.S. Children's Bureau and Child Welfare, 1912–1946* (Urbana: University of Illinois Press, 1997); and Viviana A. Zelizer, *Pricing the Priceless Child: The Changing Social Value of Children* (New York: Basic Books, 1985). For a seminal text that promoted a distinct categorization of youth, see G. Stanley Hall, *Adolescence* (New York: Appleton, 1904).

4. A larger body of literature has examined the role of the college in both the civil rights and black power movements; representative works include Martha Biondi, *The Black*

Revolution on Campus (Berkeley: University of California Press, 2012); Jeffrey A. Turner, *Sitting In and Speaking Out: Student Movement in the American South, 1960–1970* (Athens: University of Georgia Press, 2010); Stefan M. Bradley, *Harlem vs. Columbia University: Black Student Power in the Late 1960s* (Urbana: University of Illinois Press, 2009); Ibram H. Rogers, *The Black Campus Movement: Black Students and the Racial Reconstitution of Higher Education, 1965–1972* (New York: Palgrave Macmillan, 2012); and Robert Cohen and David J. Snyder, eds., *Rebellion in Black and White: Southern Student Activism in the 1960s* (Baltimore: Johns Hopkins University Press, 2013). Some of the literature focuses specifically on the role of collegiate student activism in Mississippi during the civil rights movement. For instance, see Joy Ann Williamson, "'This Has Been Quite a Year for Heads Falling': Institutional Autonomy in the Civil Rights Era," *History of Education Quarterly* 44 (2004): 559–60; Joy Ann Williamson, *Radicalizing the Ebony Tower: Black Colleges and the Black Freedom Struggle in Mississippi* (New York: Teachers College Press, 2008), 64–68; and Clarice T. Campbell and Oscar Allan Rogers, *Mississippi: The View from Tougaloo* (Jackson: University Press of Mississippi, 1979). A number of works reinforce the notion that college students served as the primary change agents in the civil rights movement. They include John Dittmer, *Local People: The Struggle for Civil Rights in Mississippi* (Urbana: University of Illinois Press, 1994), 143–55; Aldon D. Morris, *The Origins of the Civil Rights Movement: Black Communities Organizing for Change* (New York: Free Press, 1984), 195–228; Charles Payne, *I've Got the Light of Freedom: The Organizing Tradition and the Mississippi Freedom Struggle* (Berkeley: University of California Press, 1996), 210–20; Howard Zinn, *SNCC: The New Abolitionists* (Boston: Beacon Press, 1965); and Bruce Watson, *Freedom Summer: The Savage Season That Made Mississippi Burn and Made America a Democracy* (New York: Viking, 2010).

5. Mamie Till-Mobley and Christopher Benson, *Death of Innocence: The Story of the Hate Crime That Changed America* (New York: Random House, 2003); Stephen J. Whitfield, *A Death in the Delta: The Story of Emmett Till* (Baltimore: Johns Hopkins University Press, 1991); J. Todd Moye, *Let the People Decide: Black Freedom and White Resistance Movements in Sunflower County, Mississippi, 1945–1986* (Chapel Hill: University of North Carolina Press, 2004), 82–84; Dittmer, *Local People*, 56–58. The fullest account of Emmett Till may be found in Till-Mobley and Benson, *Death of Innocence*.

6. John Lewis, with Michael D'Orso, *Walking with the Wind: A Memoir of the Movement* (New York: Simon & Schuster, 1998), 57.

7. Howard Zinn, "Schools in Context: The Mississippi Idea," *Nation*, November 23, 1964, 10; Liz Fusco, "Deeper Than Politics: The Mississippi Freedom Schools," *Liberation* 9 (1964); Sally Belfrage, *Freedom Summer* (New York: Viking, 1965); Florence Howe, "Mississippi's Freedom Schools: The Politics of Education," *Harvard Educational Review* 35 (1965): 144–60; Staughton Lynd, "The Freedom Schools," *Freedomways* 5, no. 2 (1965): 305; Mary Lucille Gillard, "The Concept of the Mississippi Freedom School and Its Implementation in Gulfport, Mississippi" (master's thesis, Kearn University, 1965).

8. James W. Silver, *Mississippi: The Closed Society* (New York: Harcourt, Brace & World, 1964); Payne, *I've Got the Light of Freedom*; Neil R. McMillen, *Dark Journey: Black Mississippians in the Age of Jim Crow* (Urbana: University of Illinois Press, 1990); Dittmer, *Local People*; Clayborne Carson, *In Struggle: SNCC and the Black Awakening of the 1960s* (Cambridge, Mass.: Harvard University Press, 1995).

9. François N. Hamlin, *Crossroads at Clarksdale: The Black Freedom Struggle in the Mississippi Delta After World War II* (Chapel Hill: University of North Carolina Press, 2012); Emilye Crosby, *A Little Taste of Freedom: The Black Freedom Struggle in Claiborne County, Mississippi* (Chapel Hill: University of North Carolina Press, 2005); Chris Myers Asch, *The Senator and the Sharecropper: The Freedom Struggles of James O. Eastland and Fannie Lou Hamer* (New York: New Press, 2008); and Constance Curry, *Silver Rights* (Chapel Hill: Algonquin Books of Chapel Hill, 2014).

10. Doug McAdam, *Freedom Summer* (New York: Oxford University Press, 1988); Watson, *Freedom Summer*; Belfrage, *Freedom Summer*; Roberto M. Fernandez and Doug McAdam, "Social Networks and Social Movements: Multiorganizational Fields and Recruitment to Mississippi Freedom Summer," *Sociological Forum* 3 (1988): 378–82; Mary Aickin Rothschild, *A Case of Black and White: Northern Volunteers and the Southern Freedom Summers, 1964–1965* (Westport, Conn.: Greenwood Press, 1982), 33–35, 44; Mary Aickin Rothschild, "The Volunteers and the Freedom Schools: Education for Social Change in Mississippi," *History of Education Quarterly* 22 (1982): 401–20; Elizabeth Sutherland, ed., *Letters from Mississippi: Reports from Civil Rights Volunteers and Poetry from the 1964 Civil Rights Summer* (New York: McGraw-Hill, 1965); Carson, *In Struggle*; Payne, *I've Got the Light of Freedom*; McMillen, *Dark Journey*; Dittmer, *Local People*; Silver, *Mississippi*.

11. Daniel Perlstein, "Teaching Freedom: SNCC and the Creation of the Mississippi Freedom Schools," *History of Education Quarterly* 30 (1990): 297–324.

12. Charles M. Payne, "More Than a Symbol of Freedom: Education for Liberation and Democracy," *Phi Delta Kappan* 85 (2003): 22–28; Charles M. Payne, "Education for Activism: Mississippi's Freedom Schools in the 1960s" (paper presented at the American Educational Research Association annual conference, March 24–28, 1997); George Chilcoat and Jerry A. Ligon, "Discussion as a Means for Transformative Change: Social Studies Lessons from the Mississippi Freedom Schools," *Social Studies* 92 (2001): 213; George Chilcoat and Jerry A. Ligon, " 'We Talk Here. This Is a School for Talking.' Participatory Democracy from the Classroom out into the Community: How Discussion Was Used in the Mississippi Freedom Schools," *Curriculum Inquiry* 28 (1998): 165–93; George Chilcoat and Jerry A. Ligon, "Theatre as an Emancipatory Tool: Classroom Drama in the Mississippi Freedom Schools," *Journal of Curriculum Studies* 29 (1998): 515–43; George Chilcoat and Jerry A. Ligon, "Helping to Make Democracy a Living Reality," *Journal of Curriculum and Supervision* 15 (1999): 43–68; Sandra Adickes, *Legacy of a Freedom School* (New York: Palgrave Macmillan, 2005); William Sturkey, " 'I Want to Become a Part of History': Freedom Summer, Freedom Schools, and the Freedom News," *Journal of African American History* 95 (2010):

348–68; William Sturkey and Jon N. Hale, eds., *To Write in the Light of Freedom: The Newspapers of the 1964 Mississippi Freedom Schools* (Jackson: University Press of Mississippi, 2015); Kristal Moore Clemons, "I've Got to Do Something for My People: Black Women Teachers of the 1964 Mississippi Freedom Schools," *Western Journal of Black Studies* 38, no. 3 (2014): 141–54; LaKersha L. Smith, "Telling Their Side of the Story: Mississippi Freedom Schools, African Centered Schools and the Educational Development of Black Students" (Ph.D. diss., City University of New York, 2007); John Rachal, "We'll Never Turn Back: Adult Education and the Struggle for Citizenship in Mississippi's Freedom Summer," *American Educational Research Journal* 35 (1998): 167–98; Judith Collins Hudson, "Freedom Teachers: Northern White Women Teaching in Southern Black Communities, 1860s and 1960s" (Ph.D. diss., University of Massachusetts Amherst, 2001); Harold F. Smith " 'The Thoughts of Being Free Has Entered Many Minds': The Student Nonviolent Coordinating Committee and the Process of Community Education, 1960–1966" (Ph.D. diss., Harvard University, 2000); Peatchola Jones-Cole, "Mississippi Freedom Schools: A Response Strategy to the Civil Rights Movement in Mississippi" (Ph.D. diss., University of Memphis, 2007); Daniel Peter Hinman-Smith, " 'Does the Word Freedom Have a Meaning?' The Mississippi Freedom Schools, the Berkeley Free Speech Movement, and the Search for Freedom Through Education" (Ph.D. diss., University of North Carolina at Chapel Hill, 1993); Mark Levy, "What Did You Learn in School Today," *Association of Teachers of Social Studies Journal (ATSS/UFT)* 52, no. 1 (2015) (copy in possession of the author, courtesy of Mark Levy); Mark Levy, "I'm Still Arguing with My Mother," *Queens College Journal of Jewish Studies*, Spring 2014, 111–18. Finally, the website Education and Democracy (http://www.educationanddemocracy.org/), maintained by Kathy Emery, has collected and made available many of the original documents, essays, and articles related to the Freedom Schools.

1. "THE PATHWAY FROM SLAVERY TO FREEDOM"

1. A major theme of the civil rights movement has been the long and fruitful history of the African American search for liberation through educational advancement. Historians have covered this quest in great detail. See James D. Anderson, *The Education of Blacks in the South, 1860–1935* (Chapel Hill: University of North Carolina Press, 1988); Heather A. Williams, *Self-Taught: African American Education in Slavery and Freedom* (Chapel Hill: University of North Carolina Press, 2005); Christopher M. Span, *From Cotton Field to Schoolhouse: African American Education in Mississippi, 1862–1875* (Chapel Hill: University of North Carolina Press, 2009); and Eric Foner, *Reconstruction: America's Unfinished Revolution, 1863–1877* (New York: Harper & Row, 1988), 96–99. On the discussion of education for liberation as found in the slave narratives, see William L. Andrews and Henry Louis Gates, eds., *Slave Narratives* (New York: Library of America, 2000).

1. "The Pathway from Slavery to Freedom"

2. Wayne J. Urban and Jennings Wagoner, *American Education: A History*, 5th ed. (New York: Routledge-McGraw Hill, 2014).

3. Williams, *Self-Taught*, 12–14; Peter Wood, *Black Majority: Negroes in Colonial South Carolina from 1670 Through the Stono Rebellion* (New York: Norton, 1974), 324–25; Jack Shuler, *Calling out Liberty: The Stono Slave Rebellion and the Universal Struggle for Human Rights* (Jackson: University Press of Mississippi, 2009), 101–3.

4. Frederick Douglass, *Narrative of the Life of Frederick Douglass, an American Slave, Written by Himself* (1845; repr., New York: Norton, 1997), 29–30.

5. Ibid., 32. See also Williams, *Self-Taught*, 22–23.

6. Williams, *Self-Taught*, 19–27; Span, *From Cotton Field to Schoolhouse*, 33–34; Henry Allen Bullock, *A History of Negro Education in the South: From 1619 to the Present* (Cambridge, Mass.: Harvard University Press, 1967), 14–15. Anderson estimates that 5 percent of all slaves were literate in 1860, in *Education of Blacks in the South*, 16. See also John Blassingame, *The Slave Community: Plantation Life in the Antebellum South* (New York: Oxford University Press, 1979).

7. Span, *From Cotton Field to Schoolhouse*, chap. 1; Anderson, *Education of Blacks in the South*, 6–7.

8. As John Roy Lynch noted, the system of education established was a "creditable monument" to the Reconstruction government of Mississippi (*The Facts of Reconstruction* [New York: Neale, 1913], 34). Mississippi voters ratified the new state constitution in December 1869. H. R. Pease, a superintendent of freedmen's education, reported that the state opened more than three thousand schools the first year, with over sixty-six thousand students attending. See Bullock, *History of Negro Education in the South*, 117–52; Charles C. Bolton, *The Hardest Deal of All: The Battle over School Integration in Mississippi, 1870–1980* (Jackson: University Press of Mississippi, 2005), 6–8; and W. E. B. Du Bois, *Black Reconstruction, 1860–1880* (1935; repr., New York: Free Press, 1998), 437–43.

9. Du Bois, *Black Reconstruction in America*, 638.

10. Neil R. McMillen, *Dark Journey: Black Mississippians in the Age of Jim Crow* (Urbana: University of Illinois Press, 1990), 78.

11. Anderson, *Education of Blacks in the South*, 156; McMillen, *Dark Journey*, 78–79.

12. Span, *From Cotton Field to Schoolhouse*, 172–76; Bullock, *History of Negro Education in the South*, 74–81. For an overview of the implementation of the Black Codes in Mississippi, see McMillen, *Dark Journey*, 38–44; William C. Harris, "The Reconstruction of the Commonwealth, 1865–1870," in *A History of Mississippi*, ed. Richard McLemore (Hattiesburg: University and College Press of Mississippi, 1973), 1:542–70; Vernon Lane Wharton, *The Negro in Mississippi, 1865–1890* (Chapel Hill: University of North Carolina Press, 1947), 80–96; and Bernard E. Powers, *Black Charlestonians: A Social History* (Fayetteville: University of Arkansas Press, 1999), 263. After the new Mississippi constitution was adopted in 1890, blacks were disenfranchised further. According to the new constitution, blacks in Mississippi would be subject to a two-year residency requirement, a two-dollar poll tax, and an "understanding clause" that

stated potential voters must be able to read and understand arbitrary sections of the state constitution, all in order to vote. On this, see John Dittmer, *Local People: The Struggle for Civil Rights in Mississippi* (Urbana: University of Illinois Press, 1994), 6, 12–13; McMillen, *Dark Journey*, 39–41; and Williams, *Self-Taught*, 194.

13. Dittmer, *Local People*, 6, 12–13; McMillen, *Dark Journey*, 14, 39–41; Williams, *Self-Taught*, 194; Foner, *Reconstruction*, 553–54; Bolton, *Hardest Deal of All*, 10–13.

14. The Slaughter-House Cases of 1873 and the Civil Rights Cases in 1883 were instrumental in weakening protecting afforded to formerly enslaved communities. On this, see Bullock, *History of Negro Education in the South*, 66–68; and Foner, *Reconstruction*, chap. 11.

15. Quoted in McMillen, *Dark Journey*, 72.

16. W. E. B. Du Bois, "The Talented Tenth," in *The Negro Problem: A Series of Articles by Representative Negroes of To-day* (1903; repr., Miami: Mnemosyne, 1969). See also Joe M. Richardson and Maxine D. Jones, *Education for Liberation: The American Missionary and African Americans, 1890 to the Civil Rights Movement* (Tuscaloosa: University of Alabama Press, 2009), 120.

17. Bolton, *Hardest Deal of All*, 35–36. Coahoma Agricultural High School, established in Clarksdale in 1924 for the education of African Americans, reflects the vocational emphasis. On this, see *The Coahoman* (Clarksdale: Coahoma Junior College and Agricultural High School yearbook, 1982), Mississippi Department of Archives and History, Jackson (hereafter, MDAH). See also "Coahoma County Agricultural High School" (vertical file), MDAH; and Homer Hill, interview with the author, September 25, 2011. For an outstanding description of the ideologically rich debates that move far beyond the DuBois–Washington dichotomy, see Derrick P. Alridge, *The Educational Thought of W. E. B. Du Bois: An Intellectual History* (New York: Teachers College Press, 2008), chap. 6.

18. The history of self-determination and agency in black education is well known and has been established with great detail and eloquence. See Anderson, *Education of Blacks in the South*; Vanessa Siddle Walker, *Their Highest Potential: An African American School Community in the Segregated South* (Chapel Hill: University of North Carolina Press, 1996); Christopher M. Span, "Alternative Pedagogy: The Rise of the Private Black Academy in Early Postbellum Mississippi, 1862–1870," in *Chartered Schools: Two Hundred Years of Independent Academies in the United States, 1727–1925*, ed. Nancy Beadie and Kim Tolley (New York: RoutledgeFalmer, 2002), 211–27; Christopher M. Span, "I Must Learn Now or Not at All: Social and Cultural Capital in the Educational Initiatives of Formerly Enslaved African Americans in Mississippi, 1862–1869," *Journal of African American History* 87 (2002): 196–205; Span, *From Cotton Field to Schoolhouse*; Williams, *Self-Taught*; and Constance Curry, *Silver Rights* (Chapel Hill: Algonquin Books of Chapel Hill, 2014).

19. Vanessa Siddle Walker, *Hello Professor: A Black Principal and Professional Leadership in the Segregated South* (Chapel Hill: University of North Carolina Press, 2009); Walker, *Their Highest Potential*; William Chafe, *Civilities and Civil Rights: Greensboro, North*

Carolina, and the Black Struggle for Equality (New York: Oxford University Press, 1980); David S. Cecelski, *Along Freedom Road: Hyde County, North Carolina, and the Fate of Black Schools in the South* (Chapel Hill: University of North Carolina Press, 1994); R. Scott Baker, *Paradoxes of Desegregation: African American Struggles for Educational Equity in Charleston, South Carolina, 1926–1972* (Columbia: University of South Carolina Press, 2006); R. Scott Baker, "Pedagogies of Protest: African American Teachers and the History of the Civil Rights Movement, 1940–1963," *Teachers College Record* 113 (2011): 2777–803.

20. C. J. Cunningham, "Meaning of Education," in Charles J. Cunningham Papers, Box 1, Folder 4, "Compositions, 1932–1933; n.d.," MDAH. See also C. J. Cunningham, "Education for a Changing Civilization," "Mankind at the Cross-roads," and "Meaning of a Liberal Education," in Charles J. Cunningham Papers, Box 1, Folder 3, "class papers/ notes 1933, n.d.," MDAH. For a brief introduction to the history of Progressive education, specifically the theorists whom Cunningham studied in school, see John Dewey, *Democracy and Education: An Introduction to the Philosophy of Education* (New York: Macmillan, 1916); George Counts, *Dare the Schools Build a New Social Order?* (New York: Day, 1932); Lawrence A. Cremin, *The Transformation of the School: Progressivism in American Education, 1876–1957* (New York: Vintage, 1962); and Gerald L. Gutek, *The Educational Theory of George S. Counts* (Columbus: Ohio State University Press, 1971).

21. Richard Kluger, *Simple Justice: The History of Brown v. Board of Education and Black American's Struggle for Equality*, 2nd ed. (New York: Vintage, 2004), 214–15; Mark Tushnet, *The NAACP's Legal Strategy Against Segregated Education*, 2nd ed. (Chapel Hill: University of North Carolina Press, 2004), chap. 5.

22. Gladys Noel Bates, interview with Catherine Jannik, December 23, 1996, University of Southern Mississippi Center for Oral History and Cultural Heritage; Bolton, *Hardest Deal of All*, 45–60; Edward S. Bishop Sr., interview with Charles Bolton, February 27, 1991, Corinth, Mississippi, University of Southern Mississippi Digital Collection; "Community in Which I Live," in Gladys Noel Bates Papers, Box 3, "Speeches and Papers, 1948, 1968, 1991–1992," MDAH; "Address Delivered at the Black Women's Political Action Forum, February 1, 1991, Jackson, MS," in Gladys Noel Bates Papers, Box 3, "Speeches and Papers, 1948, 1968, 1991–1992," MDAH; Gladys Noel Bates, "The Gladys Noel Bates Teacher-Equalization Pay Suit, May 16, 1992," in Box 3, "Speeches and Papers, 1948, 1968, 1991–1992," MDAH; Robert L. Carter to A. L. Johnson, April 19, 1949, in Gladys Noel Bates Papers, Box 2, "Scrapbook, 1948–1960," MDAH; Cleopatra D. Thompson, *The History of the Mississippi Teachers Association* (Washington, D.C.: NEA Teachers Rights, 1973), 15–18.

23. Kluger, *Simple Justice*, 187–94, 201–3, 346–67. On the politics of equalization in Mississippi, see Bolton, *Hardest Deal of All*, 37–46; Michael J. Klarman, *Brown v. Board of Education and the Civil Rights Movement* (Oxford: Oxford University Press, 2007), 41–46; Tushnet, *NAACP's Legal Strategy*, chap. 5; James Patterson, *Brown v. Board of Education: A Civil Rights Milestone and Its Troubled Legacy* (New York: Oxford University Press, 2001), 15–20; Peter Irons, *Jim Crow's Children: The Broken Promise of the Brown*

Decision (New York: Penguin, 2002), 55–61; and Patricia Sullivan, *Lift Every Voice: The NAACP and the Making of the Civil Rights Movement* (New York: New Press, 2009), 231–33, 247–49, 380–82. On the role of federal judges, see Jack Bass, *Unlikely Heroes* (1981; repr., Tuscaloosa: University of Alabama Press, 2006).

24. The five court cases that comprised the *Brown v. Board of Education* decision originated in Kansas, Delaware, Virginia, South Carolina, and the District of Columbia. Cases were organized at the grassroots level, targeted the K–12 system, and often began with the request for equal resources for black schools. For a complete history of the Brown decision, see Kluger, *Simple Justice*; Klarman, *Brown v. Board of Education*; and Tushnet, *NAACP's Legal Strategy*.

25. "Press Release—Youth Division, November 16, 1953," NAACP Papers, Series 19, Part C, Reel 10, Thomas Cooper Library, University of South Carolina, Columbia; Adam Fairclough, *A Class of Their Own: Black Teachers in the Segregated South* (Cambridge, Mass.: Harvard University Press, 2006), 385–86; Dittmer, *Local People*, 75.

26. Marjorie Murphy, *Blackboard Unions: The AFT and the NEA, 1900–1980* (Ithaca, N.Y.: Cornell University Press, 1990), 203–6.

27. Fairclough, *Class of Their Own*, 357.

28. Dittmer, *Local People*, 75. See also Fairclough, *Class of Their Own*, 381–82.

29. Kluger, *Simple Justice*, 25.

30. Patterson, *Brown v. Board of Education*, xxvii.

31. Jack M. Balkin, "*Brown v. Board of Education*: A Critical Introduction," in *What Brown v. Board of Education Should Have Said: The Nation's Top Legal Experts Rewrite America's Landmark Civil Rights Decision*, ed. Jack M. Balkin (New York: New York University Press, 2001), 4.

32. Quoted in "Private School System Setup Is Considered" *Vicksburg Evening Post*, December 9, 1953, in "Education 1950–1956" Subject File, MDAH.

33. Bolton, *Hardest Deal of All*, chap. 2; Neil R. McMillen, "Development of Civil Rights, 1956–1970," in *History of Mississippi*, ed. Richard Aubrey McLemore (Hattiesburg: University and College Press of Mississippi, 1973), 2:154–57; "Amendment Gains Nod of Approval in Tuesday's Vote; Pearl Rive County Votes Against Proposal," *Weekly Democrat* (Natchez, Miss.), December 23, 1954, in "Education 1950–1956" Subject File, MDAH; "Private School System Setup Is Considered," *Vicksburg Evening Post*, December 9, 1953, in "Education 1950–1956" Subject File, MDAH.

34. McMillen, "Development of Civil Rights," 155; "Education Board Moves to Carry on Segregation," *Clarion-Ledger* (Jackson, Miss.), June 9, 1954, MDAH.

35. Bolton, *Hardest Deal of All*, 67–72; McMillen, "Development of Civil Rights," 154–57; "'Go Slow' Attitude Urged by Governor in Court Decision," *Clarion-Ledger*, May 18, 1854, MDAH; "White Delays Statement, Says Court Ruling Is Disappointing," *Clarksdale Press Register*, May 17, 1954, MDAH.

36. Bolton, *Hardest Deal of All*, chap. 2; McMillen, "Development of Civil Rights," 154–57; "Amendment Gains Nod of Approval in Tuesday's Vote; Pearl Rive County Votes Against Proposal," *Weekly Democrat*, December 23, 1954, MDAH; "Private

School System Setup Is Considered," *Vicksburg Evening Post*, December 9, 1953, in "Education 1950–1956" subject file, MDAH; Laws of the State of Mississippi: Appropriations, General Legislation and Resolutions (Jackson: Legislature of Mississippi, 1964), 5, 58–60, MDAH; "Committee to Request State Scholarship Plan," *Clarion-Ledger*, June 18, 1964; "Tuition Grant Approved by Senate," *Clarion-Ledger*, July 7, 1964. For a comprehensive examination of the evasive politics of the Mississippi legislature, see Bolton, *Hardest Deal of All*, chap. 3. When Mississippi was ordered to begin token integration in 1964, the Citizens' Council members were some of the first to open a private academy in Jackson. On this, see Michael W. Fuquay, "Civil Rights and the Private School Movement in Mississippi, 1964–1971," *History of Education Quarterly* 42 (2002): 159–80.

37. Mississippi Statistical Abstract, 1971 (Division of Research, College of Business and Industry, Mississippi State University, 1971), 184–85, MDAH.

38. McMillen, *Dark Journey*, 73.

39. Division of Administration and Finance, *Biennial Report and Recommendations of the State Superintendent of Public Education, Scholastic Years 1953–1954 and 1954–1955* (Jackson: Legislature of Mississippi), 130, MDAH.

40. Len Holt, *The Summer That Didn't End* (New York: Morrow, 1965), 102.

41. David F. Labaree, *How to Succeed in School Without Really Learning: The Credentials Race in American Education* (New Haven, Conn.: Yale University Press, 1998); David B. Tyack, *Seeking Common Ground: Public Schools in a Diverse Society* (Cambridge, Mass.: Harvard University Press, 2003); W. Norton Grubb and Marvin Lazerson, *The Education Gospel: The Economic Power of Schooling* (Cambridge, Mass.: Harvard University Press, 2007), esp. chap. 6.

42. Neil R. McMillen, *Citizens' Council: Organized Resistance to the Second Reconstruction, 1954–64* (Urbana: University of Illinois Press, 1994), 11–16; John White, "The White Citizens Council of Orangeburg County," in *Toward the Meeting of the Waters: Currents in the Civil Rights Movement of South Carolina During the Twentieth Century*, ed. W. B. Moore Jr. and Vernon Burton (Columbia: University of South Carolina Press, 2008), 261–73; Bolton, *Hardest Deal of All*, 74–75, 174–77; Dittmer, *Local People*, 45–48.

43. Although the charges were dropped, no desegregation suits were filed until after the 1955 implementation decision. See Dittmer, *Local People*, 46.

44. Bolton, *Hardest Deal of All*, 66–67, 73–75; Dittmer, *Local People*, 49–51.

45. Fairclough, *Class of Their Own*, 344–346. On Septima Clark and South Carolina, see Katherine Mellen Charron, *Freedom's Teacher: The Life of Septima Clark* (Chapel Hill: University of North Carolina Press, 2009), 242–47; and John F. Potts, *A History of the Palmetto Education Association* (Washington, D.C.: National Education Association, 1978), 66–67. The reaction of white educational policymakers contributes to the prevailing belief that black teachers were not active in the civil rights movement.

46. Robert L. Carter to A. L. Johnson, April 19, 1949, in Gladys Noel Bates Papers, Box 2, "Scrapbook, 1948–1960," MDAH; Potts, *History of the Palmetto Education Association*, 66–67; Fairclough, *Class of Their Own*, 345–49; Charron, *Freedom's Teacher*, 242–47; Jerome A. Gray, Joe L. Reed, and Norman W. Walton, *History of the Alabama State*

Teachers Association (Washington, D.C.: National Education Association, 1987), 151–54. Black college presidents were often in a precarious role as well, and often harshly penalized civil rights activity. On this, see Jeffrey A. Turner, *Sitting In and Speaking Out: Student Movement in the American South, 1960–1970* (Athens: University of Georgia Press, 2010), 23–24, 167–69; and Joy Ann Williamson, " 'This Has Been Quite a Year for Heads Falling': Institutional Autonomy in the Civil Rights Era," *History of Education Quarterly* 44 (2004), 554–76.

47. For an introduction to the number of displaced and dismissed teachers in the wake of *Brown*, see James Anderson, " 'A Tale of Two Browns': Constitutional Equality and Unequal Education," in *With More Deliberate Speed: Achieving Equity and Excellence in Education—Realizing the Full Potential of Brown v. Board of Education*, NSSE Yearbook, part 2, ed. Arnetha F. Ball (Malden, Mass.: Blackwell, 2006), 30–32. See also Michael Fultz, "The Displacement of Black Educators Post-Brown: An Overview and Analysis," *History of Education Quarterly* 44 (2006): 11–45. These scholars also note that over twenty-one thousand black teachers lost their jobs between 1984 and 1989. Also see Fairclough, *Class of Their Own*, 406–408.

48. Fairclough, *Class of Their Own*, 357–61.

49. Hill, interview.

50. Aaron Henry with Constance Curry, *Aaron Henry: The Fire Ever Burning* (Jackson: University Press of Mississippi, 2000), 73; François N. Hamlin, *Crossroads at Clarksdale: The Black Freedom Struggle in the Mississippi Delta After World War II* (Chapel Hill: University of North Carolina Press, 2012), 27–28, 172.

51. Ineva May-Pittman, interview with the author, July 26, 2013.

52. Mississippi Sovereignty Commission Files, SCR ID nos. 2-7-0-29-1-1-1; and 9-15-0-4-1-1-1. W. A. Higgins is listed as a known informant on Mississippi Sovereignty Commission Files, SCR ID no. 2-62-1-14-1-1-1, MDAH, http://mdah.state.ms.us/arrec/digital_archives/sovcom/.

53. Williamson, "This Has Been Quite a Year for Heads Falling," 558–51, Turner, *Sitting In and Speaking Out*, 167–171; Fairclough, *Class of Their Own*, 383–84.

54. Carter G. Woodson, *The Mis-Education of the Negro* (1933; repr., New York: AMS Press, 1977).

55. For a history of the influence of Highlander Folk School on the Freedom Schools, see Jon Hale, "Early Pedagogical Influences on the Mississippi Freedom Schools: Myles Horton and Critical Education in the Deep South," *American Educational History Journal* 34 (2007): 315–30. For a comprehensive history of Highlander Folk School, see Myles Horton, Judith Kohl, and Herbert Kohl, eds., *The Long Haul: An Autobiography* (New York: Doubleday, 1990); John Glen, *Highlander: No Ordinary School* (Knoxville: University of Tennessee Press, 1996); Frank Adams, *Unearthing Seeds of Fire: The Idea of Highlander* (Winston-Salem, N.C.: Blair, 1975); and Charron, *Freedom's Teacher*, chap. 7. Although the Citizenship Schools originated in the back of a grocery store in the rural low country of South Carolina, the network had grown to include nearly nine hundred schools and 1,600 volunteer teachers who registered over 50,000 voters within a decade.

On this, see Charron, *Freedom's Teacher*; Septima Clark, Poinsette Brown, and Cynthia Stokes Brown, *Ready from Within: Septima Clark and the Civil Rights Movement* (Navarro, Calif.: Wild Tree Press, 1986); and David P. Levine, "The Birth of the Citizenship Schools: Entwining the Struggles for Literacy and Freedom," *History of Education Quarterly* 44 (2004): 388–414.

56. The school was disbanded by 1962. See Dittmer, *Local People*, 112–14; Charles Payne, *I've Got the Light of Freedom: The Organizing Tradition and the Mississippi Freedom Struggle* (Berkeley: University of California Press, 1996), 125; Charles McDew, interview with Katherine Shannon, August 24, 1967, Civil Rights Documentation Project, Moorland Spingarn Research Center, Howard University (transcript in possession of author, courtesy of Joellen ElBashir), 93–100; and Curtis Muhammad, interview with Benjamin Hedin and Sam Pollard, conducted for the documentary *Blues House*, June 18, 2014 (transcript and audio in the author's possession).

57. Sandra Adickes, *The Legacy of a Freedom School* (New York: Palgrave Macmillan, 2005), 28–32. For a larger history of the Prince Edward County school closures, see Jill Ogline Titus, *Brown's Battleground: Students, Segregationists, and the Struggle for Justice in Prince Edward County, Virginia* (Chapel Hill: University of North Carolina Press, 2011); Bob Smith, *They Closed Their Schools: Prince Edward County, Virginia, 1951–1964* (1965; repr., Farmville, Va.: Martha E. Forrester, Council of Women, 1996); and Christopher Bonastia, *Southern Stalemate: Five Years Without Public Education in Prince Edward County, Virginia* (Chicago: University of Chicago Press, 2012).

58. Dionne Danns, "Chicago High School Students' Movement for Quality Public Education, 1966–1971," *Journal of African American History* 88 (2003): 139; Alan B. Anderson and George W. Pickering, *Confronting the Color Line: The Broken Promise of the Civil Rights Movement in Chicago* (Athens: University of Georgia Press, 1986), 116–20. For a comprehensive history of movement for quality education in Chicago, see Dionne Danns, *Something Better for Our Children: Black Organizing in Chicago Public Schools, 1963–1971* (New York: Routledge, 2003); John Rury, "Race, Space, and the Politics of Chicago's Public Schools: Benjamin Willis and the Tragedy of Urban Education," *History of Education Quarterly* 39 (1999): 132; "Attendance Falls off at Freedom Schools," *New York Times*, March 17, 1964; and "Harlem Organizes 'Freedom Schools,'" *New York Times*, October 13, 1963.

59. The Boston Freedom Schools, organized during the winter of 1963 after local activists boycotted public schools in the city, were a significant model of civil rights education that helped lay the curricular foundation of the Mississippi Freedom Schools. See Mississippi Freedom Democratic Party (MFDP) Papers, Box 14, Folder 6, "Boston Freedom Schools," King Center Library and Archives, Atlanta, Ga. (hereafter, KCLA); Jeanee F. Theoharis, "'I'd Rather Go to School in the South': How Boston's School Desegregation Complicates the Civil Rights Paradigm," in *Freedom North: Black Freedom Struggles Outside the South, 1940–1980*, ed. Jeanne F. Theoharis and Komozi Woodard (New York: Palgrave Macmillan, 2003), 130–33; and James Breeden and Jeanne Breeden, interview with Tess Bundy, October 22, 2012, Leyden, Mass. (transcript in the author's

and interviewer's possession). For excellent analysis of the Boston movement, see Tess Bundy, "'I Realized It Was More Than Myself': The Birth of a Mass Movement for Educational Liberation, 1959–1965" (Ph.D. diss., University of Maryland, 2014), chap. 2; and Peter Cummings, "Boston Groups Plan School Boycott Despite Attorney General's Warning," *Harvard Crimson*, February 12, 1964.

2. "THERE WAS SOMETHING HAPPENING"

1. For extensive histories of resistance in Mississippi, see Charles Payne, *I've Got the Light of Freedom: The Organizing Tradition and the Mississippi Freedom Struggle* (Berkeley: University of California Press, 1996); Neil R. McMillen, *Dark Journey: Black Mississippians in the Age of Jim Crow* (Urbana: University of Illinois Press, 1990); and John Dittmer, *Local People: The Struggle for Civil Rights in Mississippi* (Urbana: University of Illinois Press, 1994). For extensive histories of the Freedom Summer campaign of 1964, see Doug McAdam, *Freedom Summer* (New York: Oxford University Press, 1988); and Bruce Watson, *Freedom Summer: The Savage Season That Made Mississippi Burn and Made America a Democracy* (New York: Viking, 2010).
2. Hymethia Washington Lofton Thompson, interview with the author, August 26, 2008.
3. Aldon D. Morris, *The Origins of the Civil Rights Movement: Black Communities Organizing for Change* (New York: Free Press, 1984), 40–41. See also Maria Lowe, "Sowing the Seeds of Discontent: Tougaloo College's Social Science Forums as a Prefigurative Movement Free Space, 1952–1964," *Journal of Black Studies* 39 (2009): 865–87.
4. Joy Ann Williamson, "'This Has Been Quite a Year for Heads Falling': Institutional Autonomy in the Civil Rights Era," *History of Education Quarterly* 44 (2004): 554.
5. "Jackson Reaches Turning Point," *Southern Patriot*, May 1961; John R. Salter Jr., *Jackson, Mississippi: An American Chronicle of Struggle and Schism*, 2nd ed. (Lincoln: University of Nebraska Press, 2011), 7–8; "Tougaloo Nine Honored Here and In North," *Tougazette*, May 17, 1961, L. Zenobia Coleman Library, Tougaloo College (hereafter, Tougaloo College).
6. Joyce Ladner, "A Cause for Concern," in *Voice of the Movement*, January 13, 1963, Ed King Papers, Box 2, Folder 80, Tougaloo College.
7. "Mississippi Council on Human Relations Constitution," Ed King Papers, Box 2, Folder 53, Tougaloo College; Tim Spofford, *Lynch Street: The May 1970 Slayings at Jackson State College* (Kent, Ohio: Kent State University Press, 1988), 1–12; Williamson, "This Has Been Quite a Year," 563. The Sovereignty Commission turned to Rust College—another college whose experiences demonstrates similar results in the relationship between higher education and the local movement. See Williamson, "This Has Been Quite a Year," 573; and Jelani Manu-Gowon Favors, "Shelter in a Time of Storm: Black Colleges and the Rise of Student Activism in Jackson, Mississippi" (Ph.D. diss., Ohio State University, 2006), 143–96.

8. Williamson, "This Has Been Quite a Year," 559–60; Maria Lowe, "An Unseen Hand: The Role of Sociology Professor Ernst Borinski in Mississippi's Struggle for Racial Integration in the 1950s and 1960s," *Leadership* 4 (2008): 27; Clarence T. Campbell and Oscar Allan Rogers, *Mississippi: The View from Tougaloo* (Jackson: University Press of Mississippi, 1979).

9. Spofford, *Lynch Street*, 1–17.

10. In 1963, Millsaps College opened its doors to black ticket holders for various cultural events on campus. Although they were arrested, this gesture toward integration proved symbolic in the strictly segregated capital. See "Busy Fall," *Voice of the Movement*, November 15, 1963, Ed King Papers, Box 2, Folder 80, Tougaloo College.

11. Michael Vinson Williams, *Medgar Evers: Mississippi Martyr* (Fayetteville: University of Arkansas Press, 2011), 73–83; Medgar Evers, *The Autobiography of Medgar Evers: A Hero's Life and Legacy Revealed Through His Writings, Letters, and Speeches*, ed. Myrlie Evers-Williams and Manning Marable (New York: Basic Books, 2005), 13–22.

12. Payne, *I've Got the Light of Freedom*, 47–56, 288–90; Dittmer, *Local People*, 166–69. See also Jennie Brown, *Medgar Evers* (Los Angeles: Melrose Square, 1994). By 1954, there were seventeen NAACP branches in the state with a membership of 2,700. By 1959, under Evers's leadership, the NAACP could boast a membership of 15,000. On this, see Dittmer, *Local People*, 25–34; and Payne, *I've Got the Light of Freedom*, 27, 60, 85.

13. Medgar Evers, "1956 Annual Report," Medgar and Mylie Evers Papers, Box 2, Folder 39, "Annual Reports NAACP–Mississippi Field Secretary, 1955–1957," MDAH; Medgar Evers, "Annual Report, 1957, Mississippi State Office, NAACP," in Evers, *Autobiography of Medgar Evers*, 82–84.

14. The NAACP organized Youth Councils extensively across the United States. By 1940, the NAACP organized branches in 32 states and 132 cities. See "Resources in Negro Youth," p. 8, in NAACP Papers, Part 19, Series C, Reel 9, Frames 782–801, Thomas Cooper Library, University of South Carolina, Columbia; Rebecca de Schweinitz, *If We Could Change the World: Young People and America's Long Struggle for Racial Equality* (Chapel Hill: University of North Carolina Press, 2011), 163–73; Minnie Finch, *The NAACP: Its Fight for Justice* (Metuchen, N.J.: Scarecrow Press, 1981); Thomas L. Bynum, *NAACP Youth and the Fight for Black Freedom, 1936–1965* (Knoxville: University of Tennessee Press, 2013); and Kenneth Robert Janken, *White: The Biography of Walter White, Mr. NAACP* (New York: New Press, 2003).

15. Williams, *Medgar Evers*, 178–80. While Evers was instrumental in bringing in youth, we must also recognize tireless efforts of Vera Mae Pigee, *The Struggle of Struggles*, Part 1 (Detroit: Harlo Press, 1975), 26–30. Pigee in Clarksdale and other women across the state were crucial to recruiting youth, building a movement, and generating political networks at the local level. On some of the more involved female activists, see Françoise N. Hamlin, *Crossroads at Clarksdale: The Black Freedom Struggle in the Mississippi Delta After World War II* (Chapel Hill: University of North Carolina Press, 2012), chap. 2; and Françoise N. Hamlin, "Vera Mae Pigee (1925–): Mothering the Movement," in

Mississippi Women: Their Histories, Their Lives, ed. Martha H. Swain, Elizabeth A. Payne, and Marjorie J. Spruill (Athens: University of Georgia Press, 2003), 281–98.

16. Thompson, interview; Dittmer, *Local People*, 166–69; Payne, *I've Got the Light of Freedom*, 47–56, 288–90.

17. For a stirring account of the Alabama incident, see John Lewis, with Michael D'Orso, *Walking with the Wind: A Memoir of the Movement* (New York: Simon & Schuster, 1998), 150–75; and Emily Stoper, *The Student Nonviolent Coordinating Committee: The Growth of Radicalism in a Civil Rights Organization* (Brooklyn, N.Y.: Carlson, 1989), 7.

18. "27 Mixers Jailed on Arrival Here," *Clarion-Ledger* (Jackson, Miss.), May 25, 1961.

19. "Five Riders Post Bond, 22 Others Still in Jail," *Clarion-Ledger*, May 28, 1961; "This Gets Monotonous; 17 'Riders' Jailed for Peace Breach," *Clarion-Ledger*, May 28, 1961; "Eight More 'Riders' Given $200 Fines in Court Here," *Clarion-Ledger*, May 31, 1961. The "Nashville Group" included John Lewis, Diane Nash, and James Bevel, who would become instrumental during the first years of SNCC. See Lewis, *Walking with the Wind*.

20. "Plan Orderly Trial for 'Riders' Today," *Clarion-Ledger*, May 26, 1961; "27 'Riders' Convicted; Choose Jail at Present," *Clarion-Ledger*, May 27, 1961.

21. "Racial Scene Is Quiet Once More in Jackson," *Clarion-Ledger*, May 26, 1961; "Bike Riders Surprised at Calm in Jackson," *Clarion-Ledger*, May 28, 1961.

22. Hezekiah Watkins, interview with the author, August 26 and 27, 2008, and October 11, 2011.

23. Ibid.

24. For a harrowing collection of the Freedom Rider photographs, see Eric Etheridge, *Breach of Peace: Portraits of the 1961 Freedom Riders* (New York: Athens, 2008).

25. Watkins, interview, August 26 and 27, 2008.

26. Thompson, interview.

27. Ibid.; Watkins, interview, August 27, 2008; Dr. Gene Young, interview with the author, August 7, 2008; "Agitators Seek Troops, Mayor Thompson Says," *Clarion-Ledger*, May 31, 1963; "Racial Agitator Leads as Children Go to Jail," *Clarion-Ledger*, June 1, 1963.

28. Neil R. McMillen, *Citizens' Council: Organized Resistance to the Second Reconstruction, 1954–64* (Urbana: University of Illinois Press, 1994), 11–16; Homer Hill, interview with the author, June 24, 2008; Hamlin, *Crossroads at Clarksdale*, 215.

29. Homer Hill, interview with the author, September 25, 2011. Hill's mother worked in Chicago and sent money home to help raise Hill and his sister. For a history of the great migration, see Isabel Wilkerson, *The Warmth of Other Suns: The Epic Story of America's Great Migration* (New York: Random House, 2010); Ira Berlin, *The Making of African America: The Four Great Migrations* (New York: Penguin, 2010); and Nicholas Lemann, *The Promised Land: The Great Black Migration and How It Changed America* (New York: Knopf, 1991).

30. Hill, interview, June 24, 2008.

31. U.S. Bureau of the Census, *U.S. Census of Population: 1960 Mississippi*, vol. 1, *Characteristics of the Population, Mississippi* (Washington, D.C.: Government Printing Office,

1963), 26. For an eloquent and rigorous history of the civil rights movement in Clarksdale, Mississippi, see Hamlin, *Crossroads at Clarksdale*. Hamlin's work illustrates the progression of the civil rights movement to include and even place an emphasis on local history and the centralization of the voices and perspectives of local participants. A work in this vein is Linton Weeks, *Clarksdale & Coahoma County: A History* (Clarksdale, Miss.: Carnegie Public Library, 1982).

32. Bob Boyd and Evans Harrington, "Conversation with Aaron Henry," *Per/Se*, Summer 1967, 52, "Aaron Henry" subject file, Carnegie Public Library, Clarksdale, Miss. For a complete autobiography by Aaron Henry, see Aaron Henry, with Constance Curry, *Aaron Henry: The Fire Ever Burning* (Jackson: University Press of Mississippi, 2000).

33. In regard to this organization, Hamlin also cited Henry's objective to create organizations other than the NAACP with the purpose of incorporating teachers into civil rights organization (*Crossroads at Clarksdale*, 92). See also Henry, *Aaron Henry*, 101; and Dittmer, *Local People*, 118–19.

34. Dittmer, *Local People*, 118–19; Dave Dennis, interview with the author, October 25, 2011.

35. Hamlin, *Crossroads at Clarksdale*, 5–6, chap. 2, esp., 42–48; Pigee, *Struggle of Struggles*, 26–30; Hill, interview, June 24, 2008; Hamlin, "Vera Mae Pigee (1925–)."

36. Hamlin, *Crossroads at Clarksdale*, 106; Dittmer, *Local People*. This also included visits from Dr. Martin Luther King Jr.—less than one month before his assassination—while he supported the sanitation workers' strike in nearby Memphis, Tennessee.

37. Hill, interview, June 24, 2008.

38. For a stirring description of the atmosphere of such meeting places in Clarksdale, see Hamlin, *Clarksdale at the Crossroads*, 65–70.

39. Hill, interview, June 24, 2008.

40. Hamlin, *Crossroads at Clarksdale*, 127; "Haven United Methodist Church: Centennial Celebration," "Churches—Coahoma County—Methodist" subject file, Carnegie Public Library, Clarksdale, Miss.

41. Pigee, *Struggle of Struggles*, 25–27.

42. Hill, interview, June 24, 2008.

43. "Negroes Try for Service at Downtown Lunch Counter," *Clarksdale Press Register*, August 3, 1963; "Negro Protest Activities Ebb: Kneel-In Attempted at Church," *Clarksdale Press Register*, August 3, 1963; "Youthful Negro Paraders Sent to City Court," *Clarksdale Press Register*, August 14, 1963; Hamlin, *Crossroads at Clarksdale*, 118–28.

44. Hill, interview, June 24, 2008.

45. Bureau of the Census, *U.S. Census of Population: 1960 Mississippi*, 1:12.

46. Eddie James Carthan, interview with the author, September 5, 2008.

47. McMillen, *Dark Journey*, 112–13.

48. Jess Gilbert and Spencer E. Wood, "Experiments in Land Reform and Racial Justice: The New Deal State and Local African-Americans Remake Civil Society in the Rural South, 1935–2004" (paper presented at the Rural Sociological Society Annual

Meeting, August 2004, Sacramento, Calif., and at the Association of Public Policy and Management Annual Meeting, November 2003, Washington, D.C.), 6–18; Eddie James Carthan, interviews with the author, September 4, 2008; October 16, 2011; and July 7, 2012.

49. Carthan, interview, September 4, 2008.

50. "History of McComb Schools," and "Educational McComb," "McComb, Miss—Schools—History" subject file, McComb Public Library, McComb, Miss. Schools in this era were part of the state's plan to equalize education to preemptively avoid desegregation. See Charles C. Bolton, *The Hardest Deal of All: The Battle over School Integration in Mississippi, 1870–1980* (Jackson: University Press of Mississippi, 2005), chap. 2, p. 33–61.

51. C. C. Bryant was also active in the area with Webb Owens and E. W. Steptoe. See Dittmer, *Local People*, 101–2; and Payne, *I've Got the Light of Freedom*, 113–16.

52. Quoted in "Making Amends, Standing up for Equality, Honoring Heroes," *Enterprise-Journal* (McComb, Miss.), June 23, 2006. See also Brenda Travis, interview with Alex F. et al., May 6 and 7, 2010, McComb, Miss., McComb Legacies Oral History Project. Earlier organization and resistance is remembered in local history as well. Local teacher Hilda Casin remembered S. Bernard O'Neal, a local deacon, who traveled to Jackson to protest discriminatory poll taxes enforced by Theodore Bilbo; Hilda Casin, interview with the author, July 2, 2012.

53. Howard Zinn, *SNCC: The New Abolitionists* (Boston: Beacon Press, 1964), 62–64; Payne, *I've Got the Light of Freedom*, 104–6; Dittmer, *Local People*, 101–3.

54. Taylor Branch, *Pillar of Fire: America in the King Years, 1963–65* (New York: Simon & Schuster, 1998), 492–96; Payne, *I've Got the Light of Freedom*, 115–17.

55. Travis, interview.

56. "Two Summit Negroes Jailed After Sit-Ins," *Enterprise-Journal*, August 21, 1961; "Sit-In Youths Tried, Given Maximum Fine," *Enterprise-Journal*, August 31 1961; "Negro Trio Convicted in Sit-Ins," *Enterprise-Journal*, August 31, 1961; Dittmer, *Local People*, 107–15; Payne, *I've Got the Light of Freedom*, 118–28.

57. No doubt this was a difficult decision for C. D. Higgins, the principal at Burgland High School, who committed himself tirelessly to improving the educational opportunities for African Americans in McComb. See "Commodore Dewey Higgins: Dedication," Black History Gallery, McComb, Miss.; and Casin, interview.

58. Travis, interview; Joe Lewis, interview with Taylor G., Shuntell S., Sabrena M., Dominic C., Vo'neicechsi W., Alyssa M., Hannah G., Mai Li I., Jacob R., and Wilson K., with Deborah Dent-Samake, Vickie Malone, and Howard Levin, March 26, 2011, McComb, Miss., McComb Legacies Oral History Project; Dittmer, *Local People*, 107–15; Payne, *I've Got the Light of Freedom*, 118–28; Curtis Muhammad, interview with Benjamin Hedin and Sam Pollard, conducted for the documentary *Blues House*, June 18, 2014 (transcript and audio in the author's possession).

59. Travis, interview.

60. Quoted in "Making Amends, Standing up for Equality, Honoring Heroes."

61. Bob Zellner, *The Wrong Side of Murder Creek: A White Southerner in the Freedom Movement* (Montgomery, Ala.: NewSouth Books, 2008), 157. Zellner, the only white in the march from the Masonic Temple, was beaten almost to the point of death.

62. Travis, interview; "Striking Students Face Ouster for School Year," *Enterprise-Journal*, October 15, 1961; "Girl Committed as Delinquent," *Commercial Appeal* (Memphis, Tenn.), October 10, 1961; "19 of 119 Marchers Will be Tried Today," *Enterprise-Journal*, October 4, 1961; "Reign of Terror Draws Denial," *Enterprise-Journal*, October 5, 1961; "Fifteen Demonstrators Are Fined, Draw Sentences," *Enterprise-Journal*, October 31, 1961; Mississippi Sovereignty Commission Files, SCR ID no. 2-36-1-43-1-1-1, MDAH, http://mdah.state.ms.us/arrec/digital_archives/sovcom/; Dittmer, *Local People*, 107–15; Payne, *I've Got the Light of Freedom*, 118–28. The McComb school board, prompted by concerned local community members and activists, conferred honorary degrees on Brenda Travis and other students who had been expelled for their participation in the sit-in and formally recognized them forty-five years after the initial sit-in. See "Making Amends, Standing up for Equality, Honoring Heroes."

63. Charles McDew, interview with Katherine Shannon, August 24, 1967, Civil Rights Documentation Project, Moorland Spingarn Research Center, Howard University, Washington, D.C. (transcript in the author's possession, courtesy of Joellen ElBashir), 93.

64. Ibid., 100.

65. Payne, *I've Got the Light of Freedom*, 125; Taylor Branch, *Parting the Waters: America in the King Years, 1954–63* (New York: Simon & Schuster, 1988), 119–20.

66. McDew, interview, 97–98.

67. Dittmer, *Local People*, 101–6.

68. Zellner, *Wrong Side of Murder Creek*, 157.

69. McDew, interview, 76. See also Dittmer, *Local People*, 110; and Dennis, interview.

70. McDew, interview, 100.

71. Anthony Harris, interview with the author, October 14, 2014. See also Anthony J. Harris, *Ain't Gonna Let Nobody Turn Me 'Round: A Coming-of-Age Story and Personal Account of the Civil Rights Movement in Hattiesburg, Mississippi* (Privately published, 2013), 24–25.

72. Dittmer, *Local People*, 79–84; Payne, *I've Got the Light of Freedom*, 55; Harris, *Ain't Gonna Let Nobody Turn Me 'Round*, 138–42; Harris, interview; Sandra Adickes, *The Legacy of a Freedom School* (New York: Palgrave Macmillan, 2005), 10–12.

73. Harris, *Ain't Gonna Let Nobody Turn Me 'Round*, xi; Harris, interview.

74. Payne, *I've Got the Light of Freedom*, 128–29; Dittmer, *Local People*, 179–80; "Oral History with Ellie Dahmer, 1974," interview with Orley Caudill, University of Southern Mississippi, Center for Oral History and Cultural Heritage Digital Collections, http://digilib.usm.edu/cdm/ref/collection/coh/id/15828.

75. Victoria Gray Adams, "Mississippi, the Closed Society: Turning Points in the Life of a Christian Activist," in *Freedom Is a Constant Struggle: An Anthology of the Mississippi Civil Rights Movement*, ed. Susie Erenrich (Montgomery, Ala.: Black Belt Press, 1999), 73–75. One such application to be rejected by Staughton Lynd was that of David E. Robertson, a

local biology teacher awarded with a National Science Foundation scholarship for a year of study at Cornell University. See Dittmer, *Local People*, 179–84; Payne, *I've Got the Light of Freedom*, 128–129; Adickes, *Legacy of a Freedom School*, chap. 1; and James Marshall, *Student Activism and Civil Rights in Mississippi: Protest Politics and the Struggle for Racial Justice, 1960–1965* (Baton Rouge: Louisiana State University Press, 2013), 73–74. It should be noted that Lynd—the Freedom School coordinator during the summer of 1964—is not a relation of Theron, which he makes very clear. On this, see Marshall, *Student Activism*, xvii.

76. Harris, "Freedom Day," in *Ain't Gonna Let Nobody Turn Me 'Round*, 37–42; Mark Newman, *Divine Agitators: The Delta Ministry and Civil Rights in Mississippi* (Athens: University of Georgia Press, 2004), 46–51; Dittmer, *Local People*, 219–21; Adickes, *Legacy of a Freedom School*, 19–21.

77. Dr. W. B. Mitchell was instrumental in building the department and supplying crucial support and personnel to many local black businesses in Holly Springs. See Arelya Mitchell, interview with the author, September 2, 2008; Arelya Mitchell, correspondence with the author, February 20, 2015; and Gertrude R. Anderson, *Holly Springs, Mississippi: African Americans of the Past & Present*, Leontyne Price Library Archives, Rust College, Holly Springs, Miss. (copy in the author's possession, courtesy of Anita Moore).

78. Mitchell, interview.

79. Ibid., Carol Jenkins and Elizabeth Gardner Hines, *Black Titan: A. G. Gaston and the Making of a Black American Millionaire* (New York: Random House, 2006); "Remembering Arthur G. Gaston," *Black Enterprise*, February 1, 2004, 102–6.

80. Mitchell, interview.

81. Sylvester W. Oliver Jr., *Civil Rights History in Marshall County, Mississippi from 1957 to 1989* (Holly Springs, Miss.: Rust College, 2003), 3–6; Mitchell, interview.

82. Oliver, *Civil Rights History in Marshall County, Mississippi*, 4; Payne, *I've Got the Light of Freedom*, 244–46; Dittmer, *Local People*, 225; Zinn, *SNCC*, 87. The NAACP Youth Council branch was established in Holly Springs in 1962. This level of organization in Holly Springs laid the groundwork for the 1964 Freedom Summer campaign, which was symbolized by the Freedom House at 100 Rust Avenue. This became a central meeting place for movement workers in Holly Springs and Marshall County. See "Partial Chronology," in *Holly Springs Civil Rights Celebration*, North Mississippi Oral Archives Project, Box S–Z, "2003 Civil Rights Reunion Booklet," Leontyne Price Library Archives, Rust College, Holly Springs, Miss.

83. Oliver, *Civil Rights History in Marshall County, Mississippi*, 4; Payne, *I've Got the Light of Freedom*, 244–46; Dittmer, *Local People*, 225; Zinn, *SNCC*, 87.

84. Oliver, *Civil Rights History in Marshall County*, 3–5; "Partial Chronology," in *Holly Springs Civil Rights Celebration*.

85. Payne, *I've Got the Light of Freedom*, 157; Earnestine Evans Scott, interview with the author, July 10, 2012.

86. Wilbur Colom, interview with Gloria Clark, December 12, 1995, North Mississippi Oral Archives Project, Box A–J, Transcripts, "Wilbur Colom," 5–6, Leontyne Price Library

Archives, Rust College, Holly Springs, Miss.; Scott, interview; Wilbur Colom, interview with the author, March 9, 2015.

87. Ginevera Reeves, interview with Aviva Futorian, December 11, 1995, North Mississippi Oral Archives Project, Box 2, Transcript, "Ginevera Reeves," 2–3, Leontyne Price Library Archives, Rust College, Holly Springs, Miss.; Gloria Clark, interview with Wilbur Colom, December 12, 1995, North Mississippi Oral Archives Project, Box 1, Transcript, "Gloria Clark," 23, Leontyne Price Library Archives, Rust College, Holly Springs, Miss.; Bolton, *Hardest Deal of All*, 145–47.

88. Roscoe Jones, interview with the author, March 18, 2014.

89. Quoted in Payne, *I've Got the Light of Freedom*, 356.

90. Payne, *I've Got the Light of Freedom*, 355–56; Dittmer, *Local People*, 42, 85–86; Jones, interview.

91. Jones, interview.

92. Seth Cagin and Philip Dray, *We Are Not Afraid: The Story of Goodman, Schwerner, and Chaney and the Civil Rights Campaign for Mississippi* (New York: Nation Books, 2006), 166–68, 261–63; Dittmer, *Local People*, 246.

93. Quoted in Ellen Levine, *Freedom's Children: Young Civil Rights Activists Tell Their Own Stories* (New York: Puffin, 2000), 102.

94. Quoted in ibid., 101.

95. Watkins, interview, August 26 and 27, 2008.

96. Robin Kelley, *Race Rebels: Culture, Politics, and the Black Working Class* (New York: Free Press, 1996), 78.

97. For a discussion on the politics of class, poverty, and economic security in the movement, see Gordon Mantler, *Power to the Poor: Black-Brown Coalition and the Fight for Economic Justice, 1960–1974* (Chapel Hill: University of North Carolina Press, 2013), chap. 1; and Kelley, *Race Rebels*, chap. 4. Robert Allen, writing in the context of the black power movement, suggested that the NAACP, SCLC, and other nationally recognized civil rights organization were "representatives of the privileged black bourgeoisie," which easily maintain control over "organizations dedicated to militant reform" (*Black Awakening in Capitalist America: An Analytic History* [Garden City, N.Y.: Doubleday, 1969], 120). This analysis illustrates a critique of class consciousness within the black freedom struggle.

98. Wilbur Colom, interview with the author, March 9, 2015.

3. "THE STUDENT AS A FORCE FOR SOCIAL CHANGE"

1. COFO Program (Winter 1964–Spring 1965), Box 2, Folder 7, "Freedom Summer—COFO Program," Civil Rights Archive, Mark Levy Collection, Benjamin Rosenthal Library, Queens College, New York (hereafter, Levy Collection, QC); James Marshall, *Student Activism and Civil Rights in Mississippi: Protest Politics and the Struggle for Racial Justice, 1960–1965* (Baton Rouge: Louisiana State University Press, 2013), 120–27; Doug McAdam, *Freedom Summer* (New York: Oxford University Press, 1988), 154–57; James

3. "The Student as a Force for Social Change"

Findlay, *Church People in the Struggle: The National Council of Churches and the Black Freedom Movement, 1950–1970* (New York: Oxford University Press, 1993), chap. 4, 111–39. For a detailed history on the Medical Committee for Human Rights and the larger movement for health care, see John Dittmer, *The Good Doctors: The Medical Committee for Human Rights and the Struggle for Social Justice in Health Care* (New York: Bloomsbury Press, 2009).

2. The role of whites in the Freedom Summer campaign contributes to how we understand the function of "whiteness" during the larger freedom movement. For the larger theoretical considerations surrounding "whiteness studies," see Theodore Allen, *The Invention of the White Race: Racial Oppression and Social Contract*, vol. 1 (London: Verso, 1994); Theodore Allen, *The Invention of the White Race: The Origins of Racial Oppression in Anglo-America* (London: Verso, 1997); Eric Arnenson, "Whiteness and the Historian's Imagination," *International Labor and Working Class History* 60 (2001): 3–32; Peter Kolchin, "Whiteness Studies: The New History of Race in America," *Journal of American History* 89 (2002): 154–73; Richard Dryer, *White: Essays on Race and Culture* (New York: Routledge, 2007); Grace Hale, *Making Whiteness: The Culture of Segregation in the South, 1890–1940* (New York: Vintage, 1999); Andrew Hartman, "The Rise and Fall of Whiteness Studies," *Race and Class* 46 (2004): 22–38; Mike Hill, *After Whiteness: Unmaking an American Majority* (New York: New York University Press, 2004); and David Roediger, *The Wages of Whiteness: Race and the Making of the American Working Class* (London: Verso, 1991). The last study focuses on the relationship between whites and African Americans in Mississippi, but more recent scholarship advances and complicates such a binary. For a brief introduction to the emerging historiography through scholarship on Asian, South Asian, and Latina/o communities, see Stanley Thangaraj, *Brown Out, Man Up! Basketball, Leisure, and Making South Asian American Masculinity* (New York: New York University Press, 2015); Stanley Thangaraj, "Playing Through Difference: The Black-White Racial Logic and Interrogating South Asian American Identity," *Journal of Ethnic and Racial Studies* 35 (2012): 988–1006; Vivek Bald, *Bengali Harlem and the Lost Histories of South Asian America* (Cambridge, Mass.: Harvard University Press, 2013); Ronald Takaki, *Strangers from a Different Shore: A History of Asian Americans* (New York: Little, Brown, 1998); Jeffrey Ogbar, "Rainbow Radicalism: The Rise of Radical Ethnic Nationalism," in *The Black Power Movement: Rethinking the Civil Rights-Black Power Era*, ed. Peniel E. Joseph (New York: Routledge Press, 2006), 193–228 ; Sonia Song-Ha Lee, *Building a Latino Civil Rights Movement: Puerto Ricans, African Americans, and the Pursuit of Racial Justice in New York City* (Chapel Hill: University of North Carolina Press, 2014); Mario Garcia, ed., *The Chicano Movement: Perspectives from the Twenty-First Century* (New York: Routledge, 2014); Guadalupe San Miguel Jr., *Chicana/o Struggles for Education: Activism in the Community* (Houston: University of Houston Press, 2013); and Paul Chaat Smith and Robert Allen Warrior, *Like a Hurricane: The Indian Movement from Alcatraz to Wounded Knee* (New York: New Press, 1997).

3. McAdam, *Freedom Summer*; Bruce Watson, *Freedom Summer: The Savage Season That Made Mississippi Burn and Made America a Democracy* (New York: Viking, 2010); Sally

Belfrage, *Freedom Summer* (New York: Viking, 1965); Elizabeth [Sutherland] Martínez, ed., *Letters From Mississippi: Reports from Civil Rights Volunteers and Poetry of the 1964 Freedom Summer* (1965; repr., Brookline, Mass.: Zephyr Press, 2007); Roberto M. Fernandez and Doug McAdam, "Social Networks and Social Movements: Multiorganizational Fields and Recruitment to Mississippi Freedom Summer," *Sociological Forum* 3 (1988): 378–82; Mary Aickin Rothschild, *A Case of Black and White: Northern Volunteers and the Southern Freedom Summers, 1964–1965* (Westport, Conn.: Greenwood Press, 1982), 33–35, 44; Mary Aickin Rothschild, "The Volunteers and the Freedom Schools: Education for Social Change in Mississippi," *History of Education Quarterly* 22 (1982): 401–20; Martínez, *Letters from Mississippi*, 8.

4. Jacquelyn Dowd Hall, "The Long Civil Rights Movement and the Political Uses of the Past," *Journal of American History* 91 (2005): 1234–35. Hall also cites Bayard Rustin as someone who describes a "classical" phase of the civil rights movement, which has since become entrenched in our understanding of the movement. See Bayard Rustin, *Down the Line: The Collected Writings of Bayard Rustin* (Chicago: Quadrangle Books, 1971), 111–22.

5. Charles Cobb, "Prospectus for a Summer Freedom School Program," *Radical Teacher* 40 (1991).

6. John Rachal, interview with Charles Cobb, October 21, 1996, in *Mississippi Oral History Program: North Mississippi Oral History and Archives Program*, vol. 751 (Hattiesburg: Center for Oral History and Cultural Heritage, 2001); Charles Payne, *I've Got the Light of Freedom: The Organizing Tradition and the Mississippi Freedom Struggle* (Berkeley: University of California Press, 1996), 107. See also Charles E. Cobb Jr., *On the Road to Freedom: A Guided Tour of the Civil Rights Trail* (Chapel Hill, N.C.: Algonquin Books of Chapel Hill, 2008).

7. Cobb, "Prospectus for a Summer Freedom School Program."

8. Sandra Adickes, *The Legacy of a Freedom School* (New York: Palgrave Macmillan, 2005), 18; Clayborne Carson, ed., "Over 70,000 Cast Freedom Ballots," *Student Voice*, November 11, 1964; Clayborne Carson, *In Struggle: SNCC and the Black Awakening of the 1960s* (Cambridge, Mass.: Harvard University Press, 1995), 103–4; Rothschild, *Case of Black and White*, 19–21.

9. Quoted in "Executive and Central Committees, 1961–1967," SNCC Papers, Subgroup A, Series II, Reel 3, File 326, University of Illinois at Urbana-Champaign Archives (hereafter, UIUC).

10. Carson, *In Struggle*, 99–101.

11. Quoted in "Executive and Central Committees, 1961–1967," SNCC Papers, Subgroup A, Series II, Reel 3, File 326, UIUC.

12. James D. Anderson, *The Education of Blacks in the South, 1860–1935* (Chapel Hill: University of North Carolina Press, 1988); Christopher M. Span, *From Cotton Field to Schoolhouse: African American Education in Mississippi, 1862–1875* (Chapel Hill: University of North Carolina Press, 2009); Joe M. Richardson and Maxine D. Jones, *Education for Liberation: The American Missionary Association and African Americans, 1890 to the*

Civil Rights Movement (Tuscaloosa: University of Alabama Press, 2009). For an excellent historical analysis of the educators who taught the freedmen during Reconstruction, see Ronald Butchart, *Schooling the Freed People: Teaching, Learning, and the Struggle for Black Freedom, 1861–1876* (Chapel Hill: University of North Carolina Press, 2010).

13. Carson, *In Struggle*, 99–102; Howard Zinn, *SNCC: The New Abolitionists* (Boston: Beacon Press, 1965), 185–88.

14. John Dittmer, *Local People: The Struggle for Civil Rights in Mississippi* (Urbana: University of Illinois Press, 1994), 234.

15. "Executive and Central Committees, 1961–1967," SNCC Papers, Subgroup A, Series II, Reel 3, File 326, UIUC; Zinn, *SNCC*, 187; Carson, *In Struggle*, 88–101.

16. Quoted in Zinn, *SNCC*, 188.

17. Dittmer, *Local People*, 215; Payne, *I've Got the Light of Freedom*, 199–200.

18. McAdam, *Freedom Summer*, 41.

19. MFDP Papers, Applications for the Mississippi Summer Project 1964, Accepted (Boxes 27–55), KCLA; McAdam, *Freedom Summer*, 40; Rothschild, *Case of Black and White*, 35.

20. Carson, *In Struggle*, 99–101; Dittmer, *Local People*, 209–11; Rothschild, *Case of Black and White*, 25; Zinn, *SNCC*, 180–88.

21. Zinn, *SNCC*, 188.

22. Organizers also provided the option to work in the "White Folks Project," an initiative of the SSOC, to recruit more southern white students into the movement. See Gregg L. Michel, *Struggle for a Better South: The Southern Student Organizing Committee, 1964–1969* (New York: Palgrave Macmillan, 2004), 64–74; Carson, *In Struggle*, 102; Bruce Maxwell, "We Must be Allies . . . Race Has Led Us Both to Poverty," Box 2, Folder 26, "Freedom Summer—Whites Folks Program, Bruce Maxwell," Levy Collection, QC.

23. Charlie Cobb, presentation at the University of Illinois Urbana-Champaign, and conversation with the author, October 6, 2008.

24. McAdam, *Freedom Summer*, 41, 109–111; Payne, *I've Got the Light of Freedom*, 305.

25. Staughton Lynd, interview with the author, August 28, 2006.

26. McAdam, *Freedom Summer*, 110. As Kenneth Andrews reiterates in his study of the Mississippi movement, "Schools were less central than political and economic objectives throughout the period" (*Freedom Is a Constant Struggle: The Mississippi Civil Rights Movement and Its Legacy* [Chicago: University of Chicago Press, 2004], 155).

27. On the role of women and the operation of gender in the civil rights movement, see Françoise N. Hamlin, *Crossroads at Clarksdale: The Black Freedom Struggle in the Mississippi Delta After World War II* (Chapel Hill: University of North Carolina Press, 2012); Katherine Mellen Charron, *Freedom's Teacher: The Life of Septima Clark* (Chapel Hill: University of North Carolina Press, 2009); Dayo F. Gore, *Radicalism at the Crossroads: African American Women Activists in the Cold War* (New York: New York University Press, 2011); Faith S. Holsaert, Martha Prescod Norman Noonan, Judy Richardson, Betty Garman Robinson, Jean Smith Young, and Dorothy M. Zellner, eds., *Hands on the Freedom Plow: Personal Accounts by Women in SNCC* (Urbana: University of Illinois Press, 2010); Barbara Ransby, *Ella Baker and the Black Freedom Movement: A Radical*

Democratic Vision (Chapel Hill: University of North Carolina Press 2003); Chana Kai Lei, "Anger, Memory, and Personal Power: Fannie Lou Hamer and Civil Rights Leadership," in *Sisters in the Struggle: African American Women in the Civil Rights-Black Power Movement*, ed. Bettye Collier Thomas and V. P. Franklin (New York: New York University Press, 2001), 139–70; Kay Mills, *This Little Light of Mine: The Life of Fannie Lou Hamer* (New York: Dutton, 1993); Tiyi Morris, "Local Women and the Civil Rights Movement in Mississippi: Re-visioning Womanpower Unlimited," in *Groundwork: Local Black Freedom Movements in America*, ed. Jeanne Theoharis and Komozi Woodard (New York: New York University Press, 2005), 193–214; and Ruth Feldstein, "The World Was on Fire: Black Women Entertainers and Transnational Activism in the 1950s," *OAH Magazine of History* 26 (2012): 25–29. On the unique place that women maintained in the movement because of gendered stereotypes, see Belinda Robnett, "African-American Women in the Civil Rights Movement, 1954–1965: Gender, Leadership, and Micromobilization," *American Journal of Sociology* 101 (1996): 1661–93. For the seminal critique of sexism and gendered assumptions in the movement, see Casey Hayden and Mary King, "Sex and Caste: A Kind of Memo," *Liberation* 10 (1966). For a larger discussion involving conceptions of masculinity and their impact on the civil rights movement, see Steve Estes, *I am a Man! Race, Manhood, and the Civil Rights Movement* (Chapel Hill: University of North Carolina Press, 2005).

28. Marisa Chappell, Jenny Nutchinson, and Brian Ward, "'Dress Modestly, Neatly . . . As If You Were Going to Church': Respectability, Class and Gender in the Montgomery Bus Boycott and the Early Civil Rights Movement," in *Gender and the Civil Rights Movement*, ed. Peter J. Ling and Sharon Menteith (New Brunswick, N.J.: Rutgers University Press, 2004), 69–99 ; Gwendolyn Audrey Foster, *Troping the Body: Gender, Etiquette, and Performance* (Carbondale: Southern Illinois University Press, 2000). For a discussion of respectability and SNCC women, see Tanisha C. Ford, "SNCC Women, Denim, and the Politics of Dress," *Journal of Southern History* 3 (2013): 625–58, esp. notes 6 and 7.

29. Lynd, interview.

30. Lois Chaffe, interview with the author, June 21, 2008.

31. Lynd attempted to find a black coordinator. He noted:

> I made an effort to find an African American co-director because it seemed to me even in those days a little odd that a white person would coordinate a project for black teenagers, so I approached . . . a graduate student in sociology named Harold Bardonille, who had been involved in the sit-in movement in Orangeburg, South Carolina, and had become a graduate student in sociology in Atlanta University. I asked Harold how he would like to be co-director of the Freedom Schools, and he said he would go to Mississippi and check it out. He took a bus there and came back and told me that we were all out of our minds, that people were going to be killed there in the summer, and that's how I became the sole director or sole coordinator of the Freedom Schools. (Lynd, interview)

For a larger biography on Lynd, see Alice Lynd and Staughton Lynd, *Stepping Stones: Memoir of a Life Together* (Lanham, Md.: Rowman & Littlefield, 2009); and Carl Mirra, *The Admirable Radical: Staughton Lynd and Cold War Dissent, 1945–1970* (Kent, Ohio: Kent State University Press, 2010).

32. McAdam, *Freedom Summer*, 4; Rothschild, *Case of Black and White*, 98; Watson, *Freedom Summer*, 18. Rothschild cites 750 volunteers as working in Mississippi, in *Case of Black and White*, 31; and Dittmer, *Local People*, 243.

33. McAdam, *Freedom Summer*, 42–43.

34. Wally Roberts, interview with the author, June 23, 2008; Wally Roberts Application, MFDP Papers, Applications for the Mississippi Summer Project 1964, Accepted, Box 48, "Roberts, Wallace," KCLA; MFDP Papers, Applications for the Mississippi Summer Project 1964, Accepted (Boxes 27–55), KCLA

35. Roberts, interview.

36. Frances O'Brien, interview with the author, June 5, 2008; Frances O'Brien Application, MFDP Papers, Applications for the Mississippi Summer Project 1964, Accepted, Box 45, "O'Brien, Fran," KCLA; Watson, *Freedom Summer*, 131–33.

37. Sanford Siegel, interview with the author, June 16, 2008; Sandy Siegel Application, MFDP Papers, Applications for the Mississippi Summer Project 1964, Accepted, Box 48, "Siegel, Sanford," KCLA.

38. Mark Levy, interview with the author, November 24, 2014. See also Ben Somoroff, "Troublemakers," *Esquire: The Magazine for Men*, Month 1963, 78–99. For a fuller account on the Zellners' activism, see Bob Zellner, *The Wrong Side of Murder Creek: A White Southerner in the Freedom Movement* (Montgomery, Ala.: NewSouth Books, 2008); and Dorothy Zellner, "My Real Vacation," in *Hands on the Freedom Plow*, ed. Holsaert et al., 311–25. For a full account of the Prince Edward County School history, see Christopher Bonastia, *Southern Stalemate: Five Years Without Public Education in Prince Edward County, Virginia* (Chicago: University of Chicago Press, 2012); Jill Ogline Titus, *Brown's Battleground: Students, Segregationists, and the Struggle for Justice in Prince Edward County, Virginia* (Chapel Hill: University of North Carolina Press, 2011); and Bob Smith, *They Closed Their Schools: Prince Edward County, Virginia, 1951–1964* (1965; repr., Farmville, Va.: Martha E. Forrester, Council of Women, 1996).

39. Chude Pam (Parker) Allen, interview with the author, October 22, 2014; Chude Allen, "My Parents Said Yes!," in *Finding Freedom: Memorializing the Voices of Freedom Summer*, ed. Jacqueline Johnson (Oxford, Ohio: Miami University Press, 2013), 25–27.

40. For an overview on the role of Howard Zinn and Staughton Lynd during Freedom Summer, see Zinn, *SNCC*; Howard Zinn, *You Can't Be Neutral on a Moving Train: A Personal History of Our Times* (Boston: Beacon Press, 2004); Lynd and Lynd, *Stepping Stones*; and Mirra, *Admirable Radical*.

41. Gwendolyn Zoharah Simmons, "From Little Memphis Girl to Mississippi Amazon," in *Hands on the Freedom Plow*, ed. Holsaert et al., 16.

42. Dr. Gwendolyn Simmons, interview with the author, October 21, 2014. For a fuller account of Simmons's participation, see Simmons, "From Little Memphis Girl." For an insightful account of three black female Freedom School teachers, see Kristal T. Moore Clemons, "'She Who Learns, Teaches': Black Women Teachers of the 1964 Mississippi Freedom Schools" (Ph.D. diss., University of North Carolina, 2009); and Kristal Moore Clemons, "I've Got to Do Something for My People: Black Women Teachers of the 1964 Mississippi Freedom Schools," *Western Journal of Black Studies* 38, no. 3 (2014): 141–54.

43. Lynd, interview; Allen, interview; Allen, "My Parents Said Yes!"

44. Joanne Gavin, "Joanne Gavin's Answers to Jon Hale's Freedom School Questionnaire" (copy in the author's possession).

45. Liz Fusco, interview with the author, July 2, 2008.

46. Marjorie Murphy, "Civil Rights: The Contest for Leadership," in *Blackboard Unions: The AFT and the NEA, 1900–1980* (Ithaca, N.Y.: Cornell University Press, 1990), 196–208; Jonna Perillo, *Uncivil Rights: Teachers, Unions, and Race in the Battle of School Equity* (Chicago: University of Chicago Press, 2012), 130–32; Adickes, *Legacy of a Freedom School*, 32–33.

47. Bob Moses to Ted Bleeker, March 10, 1964; Charles Cogen, president of UFT, to colleagues, April 4, 1964, both in Norma Becker Papers, 1961–1975, Micro 817, Reel 1, Wisconsin Historical Society Archives, Madison (hereafter, WHSA). These and other collections associated with the Freedom Summer project held at the Wisconsin Historical Society have been recently digitized and are available at http://search.library.wisc.edu/catalog/ocn879205899.

48. John O'Neal to Norma Becker, March 6, 1964, Norma Becker Papers, 1961–1975, Micro 817, Reel 1, WHSA.

49. Bob Moses to Ted Bleeker, March 10, 1964, Norma Becker Papers, 1961–1975, Micro 817, Reel 1, WHSA.

50. Robert Moses, Freedom Summer press conference with James Forman, 1964, NBC News clip (stock footage shared with author, courtesy of Benjamin Hedin, coproducer, *The Blues House*). See also Benjamin Hedin, *In Search of the Movement: The Struggle for Civil Rights Then and Now* (San Francisco: City Lights Books, 2015).

51. Gloria Xifaras Clark, interview with the author, October 21, 2014.

52. Ibid.; Arnold Lubasch, "22 Leave New York to Teach in Mississippi Freedom Schools," *New York Times*, July 5, 1964, 37; Jerald Podair, *The Strike That Changed New York: Blacks, Whites, and the Ocean Hill–Brownsville Crisis* (New Haven, Conn.: Yale University Press, 2012), 40. For the ongoing connection between the AFT and the Freedom Schools, see Arthur Reese, "Freedom School Program," American Federation of Teachers (AFT) Collection, PE 012, "American Federation of Teachers, Freedom School Project" folder, Tamiment Library, New York University. Perillo observed that the UFT recruited thirty-six teachers (*Uncivil Rights*, 130).

53. Simmons, "From Little Memphis Girl," 25; Simmons, interview. See also Clemons, "'She Who Learns, Teaches.'"

54. McAdam, *Freedom Summer*, 49.

55. Ibid., 49.

56. Siegel, interview.

57. Ted Knap, "Rights Worker Talks: 'I Felt I Was Needed,' " *New York World Telegram and Sun*, June 30, 1964 (copy in the author's possession, courtesy of Mark Levy).

58. O'Brien, interview.

59. Quoted in McAdam *Freedom Summer*, 5, 44–53. See also Rothschild, *Case of Black and White*, 31–47.

60. Siegel, interview.

61. Mark Weiss, interview with the author, June 16, 2008.

62. Allen, interview; Allen, "My Parents Said Yes!," 25–27.

63. Fusco, interview.

64. Rothschild, *Case of Black and White*, 43–44; McAdam, *Freedom Summer*, 48.

65. MFDP Papers, Applications for Mississippi Summer Project 1964, Accepted (Boxes 27–55), KCLA; McAdam, *Freedom Summer*, 40; Rothschild, *Case of Black and White*, 35.

66. Fusco, interview.

67. Martínez, *Letters from Mississippi*, 103–4.

68. Perillo, *Uncivil Rights*, 100–102; Rebecca de Schweinitz, *If We Could Change the World: Young People and America's Long Struggle for Racial Equality* (Chapel Hill: University of North Carolina Press, 2011), 69; Lani Guiner, "From Racial Liberalism to Radical Literacy: *Brown v. Board of Education* and the Interest-Divergence Dilemma," *Journal of American History* 9 (2004): 92–118; Kenneth Clark, *Prejudice and Your Child* (Boston: Beacon Press, 1963).

69. Quoted in Martínez, *Letters from Mississippi*, 106.

70. Fusco, interview.

71. On the role of the NCC in planning Freedom Summer, see Findlay, *Church People in the Struggle*, 86. It is important to note that movement participants recall additional curriculum planning conferences. Indeed, Mark Levy recalled a conference in Boston (interview with the author, March 3, 2015). Chaffe recalled another conference in Mississippi (interview). SNCC records thoroughly document the New York conference, and it appears to have had the most illustrious leaders, too. This is not to suggest that other conferences were not held in relation to planning the curriculum, but this research corroborates the fact that the New York conference was the most significant of the planning meetings.

72. "National Council of Churches Letter to Presidents, Deans and Religious Advisers of Colleges, Universities and Seminaries," Ed King Papers, Box 2, Folder 54, MDAH.

73. Introduction to *To Write in the Light of Freedom: The Newspapers of the 1964 Mississippi Freedom Schools*, ed. William Sturkey and Jon N. Hale (Jackson: University Press of Mississippi, 2015), 22–25; Adickes, *Legacy of a Freedom School*, 34–37; Ransby, *Ella Baker*, 326–328; Lynd, interview; Chaffe, interview; "Curriculum Conference, New York, 1964," SNCC Papers, Auburn Avenue Research Library, Atlanta, Ga. (hereafter, AARL).

74. "Curriculum Conference, New York, 1964," SNCC Papers, AARL.

75. Cobb, "Prospectus for a Summer Freedom School Program," 36.

76. "Freedom Schools, Curriculum, general," SNCC Papers, Subgroup D, Appendix A, Reel 67.340.864, UIUC.

77. "Freedom Schools, Curriculum, general," SNCC papers, Subgroup D, Appendix A, Reel 67.340.1022, UIUC.

78. "Overview of the Freedom Schools," SNCC Papers, Subgroup D, Appendix A, Reel 67.340.864, UIUC. The Freedom School educational model embraced a culturally responsive pedagogy and incorporated affirmative cultural values in the curriculum. Incorporating marginalized cultural values into the learning process was a distinguishing form of alternative education programs during the movement, most notably Highlander Folk School. See Jon Hale, "Early Pedagogical Influences on the Mississippi Freedom Schools: Myles Horton and Critical Education in the Deep South," *American Educational History Journal* 34 (2007): 315–30.

79. Noel Day, "Freedom Schools 1964," MFSP Papers, Box 15, Folder 3, "F. S. Noel Day," KCLA. Day's work with boycotting the public schools in Boston provided important context for student protest and boycotts after Freedom Summer during the fall of 1964. For more information on this, see James Breeden and Jeanne Breeden, interview with Tess Bundy, October 22, 2012, Leyden, Mass. (transcript in the author's and interviewer's possession). For an excellent analysis of the Boston movement, see Tess Bundy, "'I Realized It Was More Than Myself': The Birth of a Mass Movement for Educational Liberation, 1959–1965" (Ph.D. diss., University of Maryland, 2014), chap. 2.

80. "Freedom Schools, Curriculum, general," SNCC Papers, Subgroup D, Appendix A, Reel 67.340.994, UIUC.

81. "Freedom Schools, Curriculum, general," SNCC Papers, Subgroup D, Appendix A, Reel 67.340.1032 and 1114. UIUC.

82. "Curriculum Conference, New York, 1964," SNCC Papers, AARL.

83. Ibid.

84. Charles Cobb, "Prospectus for a Summer Freedom School Program," SNCC Papers, Subgroup D, Appendix A, Reel 64, File 71, UIUC.

85. "Proposed Schedule for the Freedom Schools," SNCC Papers, Subgroup D, Appendix A, Reel 64, File 90, UIUC.

86. McMillen, *Dark Journey*, 262; Lemann, *Promised Land*, 6. The idea or promise or freedom in the North was almost always ideological; rarely was its actuality realized. Once people arrived in cities like Chicago, St. Louis, Detroit, and Milwaukee, their lots were often just as difficult as they had been in the South. Blacks left the de jure segregation of Mississippi only to encounter a more visceral and insidious de facto segregation in the North. The North as the Promised Land continued to be an operating mythology that would call many students away from Mississippi during the freedom struggle of the 1960s. For an eloquent analysis of the subject, see Wilkenson, *Warmth of Other Suns*; and Thomas J. Sugrue, *Sweet Land of Liberty: The Forgotten Struggle for Civil Rights in the North* (New York: Random House, 2008).

87. Cobb, "Prospectus for a Summer Freedom School Program," *Radical Teacher*.

88. Mark Levy, "Abstracts from Mark Levy's Notes on Freedom School Teaching Oxford, OH, Orientation, June 1964" (copy in the author's possession, courtesy of Mark Levy), also available in the Levy Collection, QC.

89. Adickes, *Legacy of a Freedom School*, 37.

90. "Mississippi, MSP, miscellaneous," SNCC Papers, Subgroup D, Appendix A, Reel 39.166, UIUC; "Freedom Schools, Curriculum, general," SNCC Papers, Subgroup D, Appendix A, Reel 67.340.1183, UIUC.

91. "Citizenship Curriculum," SNCC Papers, Subgroup D, Appendix A, Reel 67.340,834, UIUC.

92. "Freedom Schools—Teaching Manual," MFDP Papers, Box 15, Folder 13, "Freedom Schools Curriculum & Teaching Manual," KCLA.

93. "Overview of the Freedom Schools," SNCC Papers, Subgroup D, Appendix A, Reel 39.166,148, UIUC; "Notes on Teaching in Mississippi," SNCC Papers, Subgroup D, Appendix A, Reel 67.340.1005, UIUC.

94. Quoted in "Freedom Schools, Chaffe, Lois, general," SNCC Papers, Subgroup D, Appendix A, Reel 67.328. See also "Freedom Schools, Curriculum, general," SNCC Papers, Subgroup D, Appendix A, Reel 67.340.1189, UIUC; and "Freedom Schools, Lynd, Staughton," SNCC Papers, Subgroup D, Appendix A, Reel 68.356.451, UIUC.

95. "Freedom Schools, Lynd, Staughton," SNCC Papers, Subgroup D, Appendix A, Reel 68.356.451, UIUC.

96. SNCC, "Summary of Freedom School Curriculum," SNCC Papers, Subgroup A, Series IX, Box 87, Folder 12, KCLA.

97. Arelya Mitchell, interview with the author, September 2, 2008; Arelya Mitchell, e-mail correspondence with the author, July 5, 2012.

98. "History of Haven United Methodist Church," *Clarksdale Press Register*, January 9, 1988; "Haven United Methodist Church: Centennial Celebration," "Churches—Coahoma County—Methodist" subject file, Carnegie Public Library, Clarksdale, Miss.; Hamlin, *Crossroads at Clarksdale*, 57, 127.

99. Gloria Clark, interview with Wilbur Colom, December 12, 1995, North Mississippi Oral Archives Project, Box A–J, Transcripts, "Gloria Clark," 9, Leontyne Price Library Archives, Rust College, Holly Springs, Miss.; Clark, interview with the author.

100. Levy, interview, November 24, 2014. See also Roscoe Jones, interview with the author, March 18, 2014; and "Freedom School class schedule," Box 3, Folder 3, "Freedom School: Classroom Duty Assignments," Levy Collection, QC.

101. Staughton Lynd, "The Freedom Schools," *Freedomways* 5, no. 2 (1965): 305. See also Mark Levy, interview with the author, November 24, 2014.

102. Gavin, "Joanne Gavin's Answers to Jon Hale's Freedom School Questionnaire"; Clark, interview with Colom; Adickes, *Legacy of a Freedom School*, 50–51; Lubasch, "22 Leave New York," 37. The original orientation was supposed to be held at Berea College in Kentucky. The president of Berea at the time, Frances Hutchins, withdrew support after a prominent alumnus from Mississippi voiced opposition to the plan. See "Freedom Summer at Berea College," Box 1, Folder 1, "Berea College and the Training of the Civil Rights Workers," Mississippi Freedom Summer 1964 Collection, Western College Memorial Archives, Miami University, Oxford, Ohio (hereafter, WCMU).

103. Levy, "Abstracts from Mark Levy's Notes on Freedom School Teaching," Levy Collection, QC.

104. Ibid.

105. Jane Stembridge, "Notes on Teaching in Mississippi," SNCC Papers, Subgroup D, Appendix A, Reel 67.340.1005, UIUC.

106. Adickes, *Legacy of a Freedom School*, 41; Belfrage, *Freedom Summer*, 4–27; McAdam, *Freedom Summer*, 66–77; Rothschild, *Case of Black and White*, 53; Rothschild, "Volunteers and the Freedom Schools," 404–5; "Freedom Schools, Lois Chaffee, general," SNCC Papers, Subgroup D, Appendix A, Reel 67.328, UIUC.

107. "Thoughts on Civil Rights Orientation, June 26, 1964, Oxford, Ohio," Box 1, Folder 3, "Western After the Conference, June 26–July 22, 1964," Mississippi Freedom Summer 1964 Collection, WCMU.

108. Quoted in McAdam, *Freedom Summer*, 69–71.

109. Clark, interview with Colom, 9.

110. Belfrage, *Freedom Summer*, 5; McAdam, *Freedom Summer*, 69.

111. "If You Are Arrested in Mississippi," and "Power of Attorney for Selection of Legal Counsel," both in Box 2, Folder 1, "Articles, Papers, Correspondence, ca. 1964," Mississippi Freedom Summer 1964 Collection, WCMU.

112. Jane Adams, June 18, 1964, "Notes from Freedom Summer Training, Oxford, Ohio, June 17–26, 1964," Box 1, Folder 15, "Notes from Freedom Summer Training," WCMU; Renee C. Romano, *Race Mixing: Black-White Marriage in Postwar America* (Cambridge, Mass.: Harvard University Press, 2003), 175–85.

113. Adams, "Notes from Freedom Summer Training, Oxford, Ohio, June 17–26, 1964," Box 1, Folder 15, "Notes from Freedom Summer Training," WCMU.

114. Rothschild, *Case of Black and White*, 97; Seth Cagin and Philip Dray, *We Are Not Afraid: The Story of Goodman, Schwerner, and Chaney and the Civil Rights Campaign for Mississippi* (New York: Nation Books, 2006), 319–21.

115. Cagin and Dray, *We Are Not Afraid*; Dittmer, *Local People*, 246–52; Ellen Levine, *Freedom's Children: Young Civil Rights Activists Tell Their Own Stories* (New York: Puffin, 2000), 92–115; Watson, *Freedom Summer*, 77–104.

116. Dittmer, *Local People*, 246–52; Levine, *Freedom's Children*, 92–115.

117. Siegel, interview.

118. John Rachal, "'The Long, Hot Summer': The Mississippi Response to Freedom Summer," *Journal of Negro History* 84 (1999): 316.

119. "Mayors Consider Caravan to Protest CR Workers," *Clarion-Ledger* (Jackson, Miss.), June 30, 1964; "CR Recruiting for State Closed; Area Restricted," *Clarion-Ledger*, July 1, 1964; "School Mixing Local Affair—Governor," *Clarion-Ledger*, August 11, 1964; "Johnson Signs CR Bill in Historic Ceremony" *Clarion-Ledger*, July 3, 1964.

120. "Mississippi: Allen's Army," *Newsweek*, February 24, 1964.

121. *Laws of the State of Mississippi: Appropriations, General Legislation and Resolutions* (Published by Authority, 1964), 487–88, 507–11, 543. New laws permitted the names of such offenders to be published.

4. "WE WILL WALK IN THE LIGHT OF FREEDOM"

1. Bossie Mae Harring, "The Fight for Freedom," *Drew Freedom Fighter* (July 1964), in *To Write in the Light of Freedom: The Newspapers of the 1964 Mississippi Freedom Schools*, ed. William Sturkey and Jon N. Hale (Jackson: University Press of Mississippi, 2015), 58.

2. Mark Levy, "Abstracts from Mark Levy's Notes on Freedom School Teaching Oxford, OH, Orientation, June 1964" (copy in the author's possession, courtesy of Mark Levy), also available in the Levy Collection, QC.

3. Sandy Siegel, interview with the author, June 16, 2008; "Freedom Schools, correspondence," Subgroup D, Appendix A, Reel 67.335,595, SNCC Papers, UIUC; "Freedom Schools, Curriculum, general," Subgroup D, Appendix A, Reel 67.340.755, SNCC Papers, UIUC.

4. Rita Walker, "Meeting the Freedom Workers," in Robert Feinglass Papers, Folder 1, WHSA.

5. Quoted in Ellen Levine, *Freedom's Children: Young Civil Rights Activists Tell Their Own Stories* (New York: Puffin, 2000), 96–101.

6. The numbers that are generally cited today emerged as forty-one schools across twenty communities with over two thousand students. See "Freedom School Data," Box 4, Folder 13, Staughton Lynd Papers, WHSA; Sandra Adickes, *Legacy of a Freedom School* (New York: Palgrave Macmillan, 2005), 103; "Freedom Schools, general," Subgroup D, Appendix A, reel 68.347.393, SNCC Papers, UIUC; "Freedom Schools, Historical Data," Subgroup D, Appendix A, Reel 68.352.0429, SNCC Papers, UIUC; "Mississippi, Freedom Schools, Retrospect and Prospect," Subgroup A, Series XV, Reel 38.112.338, SNCC Papers, UIUC.

7. The largest Freedom School was in Meridian, which, based on documents and reports of Mark Levy and Gail Falk, reported 250 to 300 students who attended classes in the brick building that formerly housed a Baptist seminary. The next largest Freedom School district was in rural Madison County, where there were five schools and 225 students. According to conversations with Staughton Lynd, the "official" numbers reported above do not encompass all the Freedom Schools in Mississippi. For instance, these figures do not include the city of Jackson, which in fact held several Freedom Schools. Florence Howe, Howard Zinn, and Joanne Gavin remembered and discussed at length their experiences teaching in Jackson Freedom Schools. The numbers reported reflect the numbers that teachers reported in early July 1964. Staughton Lynd, conversation with the author, July 6, 2012; Mark Levy, interview with the author, December 15, 2014; Levy, "Abstracts from Mark Levy's Notes on Freedom School Teaching," Levy Collection, QC; "School for Freedom," in *Letters from Mississippi*, ed. Elizabeth Sutherland (New York: McGraw-Hill, 1965), 107; Florence Howe, "Mississippi's Freedom Schools: The Politics of Education" *Harvard Educational Review* 35 (1965): 144–60; Joanne Gavin, "Joanne Gavin's Answers to Jon Hale's Freedom School Questionnaire" (copy in the author's possession); Howard Zinn, interview with the author, September 25, 2006.

Evidence suggests that the oft-cited number of forty-one is too low. At the very least, simply including the Jackson Freedom Schools would increase the number to something between forty-five and fifty.

8. "Meridian Classroom Assignments," Box 3, Folder 3, "Freedom School: Classroom Duty Assignments," Levy Collection, QC. The autonomy granted to teachers permitted volunteers to draw from their respective backgrounds, which did not always translate into issues directly relevant to the movement. One Freedom School teacher in Meridian taught a class on reproduction and human anatomy. He also "discussed masturbation, homosexuality, and the psychology of love and sex," among other topics ("L. Kabat," Box 3, Folder 4, "Freedom School: Classroom Summaries," Levy Collection, QC). This particular class was anomalous to the Freedom School teacher corps, who largely focused on political issues. Considering the morally conservative and traditionally religious nature of even the most politically liberal black families, a lesson like this from a white northern volunteer was out of place, to be sure. Yet it illustrates the degree to which Freedom School teachers designed lessons, for better or worse, based on their own backgrounds and also reflected the cultural milieu that young white college liberals existed within during the 1960s.

9. "Pam Parker—Freedom School Report, 18 July 1964," MFDP, Box 17, Folder 6, "Holly Springs," KCLA.

10. "Tina Dungan, July 20, 1964," Box 3, Folder 4, "Freedom School: Classroom Summaries," Levy Collection, QC.

11. Quoted in Levine, *Freedom's Children*, 94.

12. Homer Hill, interview with the author, June 24, 2008; Roy DeBerry Jr., interview with Aviva Futorian, December 10, 1995, 15–18, North Mississippi Oral Archives Project, Leontyne Price Library Archives, Rust College, Holly Springs, Miss. For a complete list of the readings assigned in many of the Freedom Schools, see MFDP Papers, Box 14, Folder 5, "Freedom Schools—Bibliography," KCLA.

13. Wilbur Colom, interview with the author, March 9, 2015.

14. George Chilcoat and Jerry A. Ligon, "Theatre as an Emancipatory Tool: Classroom Drama in the Mississippi Freedom Schools," *Journal of Curriculum Studies* 29 (1998): 515–43; "Seeds of Freedom," and "In White America" (summaries), MFDP Papers, Box 17, Folder 6, "F. S. Holly Springs," KCLA; Adickes, *Legacy of a Freedom School*, 126; Earnestine Evans Scott, interview with the author, July 10, 2012. See also Liz Fusco, "Issaquena Freedom: A Play Written in Jail in Mississippi," Liz Fusco Papers, Folder 1, WHSA; Anthony J. Harris, *Ain't Gonna Let Nobody Turn Me 'Round : A Coming-of-Age Story and Personal Account of the Civil Rights Movement in Hattiesburg, Mississippi* (Privately published, 2013), 53–55; and John Dittmer, *Local People: The Struggle for Civil Rights in Mississippi* (Urbana: University of Illinois Press, 1994), 261. For a larger history of the Free Southern Theater, see James Harding and Cindy Rosenthal, *Restaging the Sixties: Radical Theaters and Their Legacies* (Ann Arbor: University of Michigan Press, 2006), 263–67.

15. "*Seeds of Freedom*: A Play Based on the Life and Death of Medgar Evers, by Deborah Flynn and Students of the 1964 Freedom School in Holly Springs" (transcript in the author's possession, courtesy of Chude Allen).

16. Anthony Harris, interview with the author, October 21, 2014; Harris, *Ain't Gonna Let Nobody Turn Me 'Round*, 53–55; Harding and Rosenthal, *Restaging the Sixties*, 263–67.

17. Mark Levy, interview with the author, December 15, 2014.

18. Ibid.

19. "Asbury School, July 6, 1964," Subgroup D, Appendix A, MFDP Papers, Freedom School, Reel 67, File 325, UIUC); "Freedom School Report," MFDP Papers, Box 7, Folder 10, "F. S. McComb," KCLA.

20. "Overview of the Freedom Schools," SNCC Papers, Subgroup D, Appendix A, Reel 39.166,148, UIUC; "Prospectus for the Freedom School Program in Mississippi," SNCC Papers, Subgroup A, Series 15, Box 101, Folder "MSP—Freedom Schools, Mar. 1964," KCLA. Organizers also reserved Freedom Schools for evening instruction with adults and continued voter registration and other community organizing.

21. "Summary of Freedom School Curriculum," SNCC Papers, KCLA.

22. Eddie James Carthan, interview with the author, September 5, 2008.

23. Hill, interview.

24. "Last Week English, Steve Schraeder," Box 3, Folder 4, "Freedom School: Classroom Summaries," Levy Collection, QC.

25. "Diane Pachella, Freedom and the Negro in America, Class Record July 6–10 and July 13–17," Box 3, Folder 4, "Freedom School: Classroom Summaries," Levy Collection, QC.

26. "Magnolia High School," Rita Headrick Papers, Folder 1, WHSA.

27. Jo Lynn Polk, "Freedom, July 7, 1964," Box 4, Folder 8, "Student Essays," Levy Collection, QC.

28. Jo Allen, "What Freedom Means to Me," Box 4, Folder 8, "Student Essays," Levy Collection, QC.

29. Emridge Falconer, Box 4, Folder 8, "Student Essays," Levy Collection, QC.

30. Daisy Watson, "What Freedom Means to Me," Box 4, Folder 8, "Student Essays," Levy Collection, QC.

31. Edith Marie Moore, "Now Is the Hour," *Freedom's Journal* (McComb, Miss., July 24, 1964), in *To Write in the Light of Freedom*, ed. Sturkey and Hale, 145–46; "Report on the Pilgrims Rest Freedom School, July 31, 1964," SNCC Papers, Subgroup D, Series A, Reel 68.363.546, UIUC. For further discussion on how poetry played a role of resistance in the Freedom Schools, see Vonzell Agosto, "Intratexturealities: The Poetics of the Freedom Schools," *Journal of Negro Education* 77 (2008): 168–79.

32. Harris, interview.

33. "Curriculum Needs for the Freedom Schools: Leadership Development," SNCC Papers, Subgroup D, Appendix A, Reel 64, File 90, UIUC.

34. Colom, interview. See also Tim Spofford, *Lynch Street: The May 1970 Slaying at Jackson State College* (Kent, Ohio: Kent State University Press, 1988), 102–4.

35. Hezekiah Watkins, interview with the author, August 26 and 27, 2008.

36. Hymethia Washington Lofton Thompson, interview with the author, August 26, 2008. For an analysis of the role of nonviolence tactics in the movement, see Dennis Chong, *Collective Action and the Civil Rights Movement* (Chicago: University of Chicago Press, 1991); and Joseph E. Luders, *The Civil Rights Movement and the Logic of Social Change* (New York: Cambridge University Press, 2010).

37. "Freedom Schools," Subgroup D, Appendix A, Reel 67, File 325, SNCC Papers, AARL; MFDP, "Freedom Schools," SNCC Papers Subgroup D, Appendix A, Reel 67, File 325, AARL.

38. "Freedom School Opens," *Freedom Carrier* (Greenwood, Miss.), July 16, 1964.

39. SNCC, "Freedom Schools, Clarksdale," SNCC Papers, Subgroup D, Appendix A, Reel 67, File 329, Reel 371, AARL.

40. Quoted in George Chilcoat and Jerry A. Ligon, "Discussion as a Means for Transformative Change Social Studies Lessons from the Mississippi Freedom Schools," *Social Studies* 92 (2001): 214. See also Liz Fusco, "Deeper Than Politics: The Mississippi Freedom Schools," *Liberation* 9 (1964). This form of traditional pedagogy found in the majority of schools at this period would best be described as a "banking" form of education, as defined in Paulo Freire, *Pedagogy of the Oppressed* (New York: Herder and Herder, 1970).

41. Larry Cuban, *How Teachers Taught: Constancy and Change in America's Classrooms, 1890–1990*, 2nd ed. (New York: Teachers College Press, 1993); Barry M. Franklin, *Building the American Community: The School Curriculum and the Search for Social Control* (London: Falmer Press, 1986); John Holt, *How Children Fail* (New York: Pitman, 1964); Jonathan Kozol, *Death at an Early Age: The Destruction of the Hearts and Minds of Negro Children in the Public Schools* (New York: Bantam Books, 1968); Joel Spring, *The Sorting Machine Revisited: National Educational Policy Since 1945*, 2nd ed. (New York: Longman, 1988). See also V. P. Franklin and Ronald Batchelor, "Freedom Schooling: A New Approach to Federal-Local Cooperation in Public Education," *Teachers College Record* 80 (1978): 225–48.

42. Levy, "Abstracts from Mark Levy's Notes on Freedom School Teaching," Levy Collection, QC.

43. Chilcoat and Ligon, "Discussion as a Means for Transformative Change," 215.

44. "Basic Set of Questions, Citizenship Curriculum," Subgroup D, Appendix A, Reel 67.340,834, SNCC Papers, UIUC; Levy, "Abstracts from Mark Levy's Notes on Freedom School Teaching," Levy Collection, QC.

45. Siegel, interview.

46. "Last Week English, Steve Schraeder," Box 3, Folder 4, "Freedom School: Classroom Summaries," Levy Collection, QC.

47. "Diane Pachella, Freedom and the Negro in America, Class Record July 6–10 and July 13–17," Box 3, Folder 4, "Freedom School: Classroom Summaries," Levy Collection, QC.

48. "Holly Springs, Mississippi Reports, July 8–August 1964," SNCC Papers, KCLA.

49. Zinn, interview.

50. "Freedom Schools, Clarksdale," Subgroup D, Appendix A, Reel 67.371.329, SNCC Papers, UIUC.

51. Aviva Futorian, interview by Roy DeBerry Jr., December 10, 1995, in *Mississippi Oral History Program: North Mississippi Oral History and Archives Program*, vol. 751 (Hattiesburg: Center for Oral History and Cultural Heritage, 2001), 7.

52. Liz Fusco to Mr. Kenneth C. Frederick, October 10, 1964, MDFP papers, Box 14, Folder 15, "F. S., Contributions of Books and Materials," KCLA.

53. Levy, "Abstracts from Mark Levy's Notes on Freedom School Teaching," Levy Collection, QC.

54. Liz Fusco, interview with the author, July 2, 2008.

55. "Freedom Schools, Fusco, Liz," SNCC Papers, Subgroup D, Appendix A, Reel 68.346.0138, UIUC.

56. "Freedom Schools, Ruleville," SNCC Papers, Subgroup D, Appendix A, Reel 68.367.587, UIUC.

57. Quoted in Charles Payne, *I've Got the Light of Freedom: The Organizing Tradition and the Mississippi Freedom Struggle* (Berkeley: University of California Press, 1996), 305.

58. "Freedom School Data," Box 4, Folder 13, Staughton Lynd Papers, WHSA; Adickes, *Legacy of a Freedom School*, 103; "Freedom Schools, general," Subgroup D, Appendix A, Reel 68.347.393, SNCC Papers, UIUC; "Freedom Schools, Historical Data," Subgroup D, Appendix A, Reel 68.352.0429, SNCC Papers, UIUC; "Mississippi, Freedom Schools, Retrospect and Prospect," Subgroup A, Series XV, Reel 38.112.338, SNCC Papers, UIUC.

59. Arthur and Carolyn Reese Applications, MFDP Papers, Applications for the Mississippi Summer Project 1964, Accepted, Box 46, "Reese, Arthur L.," and "Reese, Carolyn," KCLA; Staughton Lynd, interview with the author, August 28, 2006.

60. "Pam Parker, Freedom School Report 15 July 64," Subgroup D, Appendix A, Reel 68.353.432, SNCC Papers, UIUC.

61. Wally Roberts, interview with the author, June 23, 2008.

62. William Sturkey, "'I Want to Become a Part of History': Freedom Summer, Freedom Schools, and the Freedom News," *Journal of African American History* 95 (2010): 358–63; "Freedom Schools, Fusco, Liz," Subgroup D, Appendix A, Reel 68.346.0045, SNCC Papers, UIUC; Sturkey and Hale, eds., *To Write in the Light of Freedom*.

63. "Freedom Schools, Fusco, Liz," Subgroup D, Appendix A, Reel 68.346.0045, SNCC Papers, UIUC.

64. Arelya Mitchell, *Freedom News* (Palmer's Crossing, Miss., July 14, 1964), in *To Write in the Light of Freedom*, ed. Sturkey and Hale, 111–12.

65. Arelya Mitchell, interview with the author, September 2, 2008; Arelya Mitchell, correspondence with the author, February 20, 2015.

66. Dittmer, *Local People*, 333; Adickes, *Legacy of a Freedom School*, 89–93; "City Library Open to Card Holders," *Hattiesburg American*, September 9, 1964; "Public Library Will Reopen Here Wednesday," *Hattiesburg American*, September 8, 1964; Harris, *Ain't Gonna Let Nobody Turn Me 'Round*, 51–52.

67. In this particular instance, no students were arrested. See Roberts, interview; and Wally Roberts, "Freedom Day in Cleveland, Miss.," *Berkshire Eagle* (Pittsfield, Mass.), July 25, 1964.

68. Carthan, interview. See also Payne, *I've Got the Light of Freedom*, 255–56.

69. Stephanie B., "Our Day Canvassing," *Freedom Carrier*, July 16, 1964.

70. "When the Wall Falls," *Freedom Carrier*, July 16, 1964.

71. Harris, interview.

72. "Sunflower County Harassment," Linda M. Seese Papers, folder 1, WHSA.

73. Carthan, interview.

74. Ibid.

75. Neil R. McMillen, "Development of Civil Rights, 1956–1970," in *A History of Mississippi*, ed. Richard Aubrey McLemore (Hattiesburg: University and College Press of Mississippi, 1973), 2:168; Len Holt, *The Summer That Didn't End* (New York: Morrow, 1965), 207–52; Doug McAdam, *Freedom Summer* (New York: Oxford University Press, 1988); "Schwerner, Chaney, and Goodman File," Freedom Information Service Library, Jackson, Miss. (hereafter, FIS). John Dittmer also documented that a crowd of segregationists shot at a group of Ruleville students who attempted to integrate a local restaurant there (*Local People*, 333).

76. Dittmer, *Local People*, 267; "Freedom Schools, McComb," Subgroup D, Appendix A, Reel 67.779.340, 68.0308.347, 68.0093, SNCC Papers, UIUC.

77. Hilda Casin, interview with the author, July 2, 2012.

78. "Blast Rips Quarters of Mixed COFO Group," *Enterprise-Journal* (McComb, Miss.), July 8, 1964; SNCC, "Running Summary of Incidents," University of Southern Mississippi, Digital Collections, http://digilib.usm.edu/index.php; Dittmer, *Local People*, 267–69; "N.Y. Solon Sees Negroes in Area," *Enterprise-Journal*, July 8, 1964.

79. Joyce Brown, "Houses of Liberty," *Freedom Star* (Meridian, Miss., July 30, 1964), in *To Write in the Light of Freedom*, ed. Sturkey and Hale, 164–65; Dittmer, *Local People*, 268; "Houses of Liberty," Subgroup D, Appendix A, Reel 68.0093, SNCC Papers, UIUC.

80. Dittmer, *Local People*, 268–69. According to Dittmer, the Martin Luther King Memorial Center in McComb is the result of that initial meeting.

81. Quoted in "Freedom School Data," MFDP Papers, Box 14, Folder 4, "Freedom School: Background Data," KCLA.

82. Hill, interview.

83. Carthan, interview.

84. Levy, "Abstracts from Mark Levy's Notes on Freedom School Teaching," Levy Collection, QC.

85. Mitchell, interview.

86. Gloria Clark, interview with Wilbur Colom, December 12, 1995, North Mississippi Oral Archives Project, Box A–J Transcripts, "Gloria Clark," Leontyne Price Library Archives, Rust College, Holly Springs, Mississippi, p. 13.

87. Adickes, *Legacy of a Freedom School*, 56; Mary Aickin Rothschild, "The Volunteers and the Freedom Schools: Education for Social Change in Mississippi," *History of Education*

Quarterly 22 (1982): 403; Mary Aickin Rothschild, *A Case of Black and White: Northern Volunteers and the Southern Freedom Summers, 1964–1965* (Westport, Conn.: Greenwood Press, 1982), 12, 19.

88. Quoted in Rothschild, *Case of Black and White*, 70–71.

89. Harris, *Ain't Gonna Let Nobody Turn Me 'Round*, 48.

90. Siegel, interview.

91. Harris, *Ain't Gonna Let Nobody Turn Me 'Round*, 61; Renee C. Romano, *Race Mixing: Black-White Marriage in Postwar America* (Cambridge, Mass.: Harvard University Press, 2003), 175–85.

92. Payne, *I've Got the Light of Freedom*, 251.

93. Chude Allen, "Thank You (Ralph Featherstone, 1939–1970)," Civil Rights Movement Veterans, http://www.crmvet.org/mem/feather.htm; Chude Allen, "Would You Marry One?" Civil Rights Movement Veterans, http://www.crmvet.org/info/marry-one.htm. For a larger discussion on interracial sexuality during Freedom Summer, see McAdam, *Freedom Summer*, 93–96, 143–45; and Wesley C. Hogan, *Many Minds, One Heart: SNCC's Dream for a New America* (Chapel Hill: University of North Carolina Press, 2007), 173–76.

94. Allen, "Would You Marry One?"; Chude Allen, interview with the author, October 22, 2014; Chude Allen, correspondence with the author, March 2–4, 2015. Allen went on to state:

> I don't think this change had anything to do with interracial relationships as such, although the possibility of people dying did. That is, if you loved someone, whether he was black or white, and he might be killed by the racist whites, well loving him seemed a whole lot more important than waiting until marriage. Those were my thoughts about sex when I left Mississippi, although I hadn't acted on them. However, the issue I was wrestling with was interracial marriage. That, not sex, was the big question for me. (correspondence with the author, March 18, 2015)

95. For a thorough analysis of white women during Freedom Summer, see Mary Aiken Rothschild, "White Women Volunteers in the Freedom Summers: Their Life and Work in a Movement for Social Change," *Feminist Studies* 5, no. 3 (1979): 466–95.

96. McAdam, *Freedom Summer*, 106–8; Rothschild, "White Women Volunteers and the Freedom Summers," 481–83.

97. For insights on the relationship between miscegenation and the construction of race and sexuality in American history, see Peggy Pascoe, *What Comes Naturally: Miscegenation Law and the Making of Race in America* (New York: Oxford University Press, 2009); and Romano, *Race Mixing*. For an outstanding historiographical overview of women's and gender history that examines the intersectionality of race, class, gender, and sexuality in American history, see Cornelia H. Dayton and Lisa Levenstein, "The Big Tent of U.S. Women's and Gender History: A State of the Field," *Journal of American History* 99 (2012): 793–817; and Crystal N. Feimster, "The Impact of Racial and Sexual Politics on Women's History," *Journal of American History* 99, no. 3 (2012): 822–26.

98. Harris, *Ain't Gonna Let Nobody Turn Me 'Round*, 61.

99. "Some Aspects of Black-White Problems," Fox 2, Folder 21, "Freedom Summer: Orientation (Oxford, Ohio)," WCMU.

100. "Freedom School Report," MFDP Papers, Box 7, Folder 10, "F. S. McComb," KCLA.

101. Roberts, interview.

102. Dale Gronemeir to Art White (undated), Dale Gronemeier Papers, Folder 1, WHSA.

103. "Friends of the Mississippi Summer Project" Newsletter, Folder 2, "Articles and Papers, ca 1964," Mississippi Freedom Summer 1964 Collection, WCMU; "Friends of the Mississippi Summer Project" Newsletters, Folder "Friends of the Mississippi Summer Project Newsletters—Donated by Jane Stripple, June 28, 1964–January 25, 1965," Mississippi Freedom Summer 1964 Collection, WCMU.

104. Gronemeir to White, Dale Gronemeier Papers, Folder 1, WHSA.

105. Ibid.; Dale Gronemeir to Senator Paul Simon, July 7, 1964, Dale Gronemeier Papers, Folder 1, WHSA.

106. Chude Allen, "My Parents Said Yes!," in *Finding Freedom: Memorializing the Voices of Freedom Summer*, ed. Jacqueline Johnson (Oxford, Ohio: Miami University Press, 2013), 27.

107. "Jackson's Decision to Integrate Breaks Mississippi's Solid Front," *New York Times*, July 13, 1964; Wallace Roberts, article, July 13, 1964 (in the author's possession). The promptness of the FBI illustrates the utility of politically connected whites working during the Freedom Summer campaign. The FBI rarely responded to even serious threats and violations of the law, including murder, filed by African Americans in Mississippi.

108. Roscoe Jones, interview with the author, March 18, 2014.

109. Quoted in Dittmer, *Local People*, 284.

110. Jones, interview.

111. Mark Levy, "1964 Statewide FS Convention Delegates" (in the author's possession, courtesy of Mark Levy); "Meridian to Host Freedom School Convention," *Freedom Star* (Meridian, Miss., July 23, 1964), in *To Write in the Light of Freedom*, ed. Sturkey and Hale, 155–56; "1964 Platform of the Mississippi Freedom School Convention," MFDP Papers, Box 14, Folder 16, "F. S. Convention," KCLA.

112. "Public Accommodations," SNCC Papers, Subgroup A, Series 15, Box 101, Folder, "MSP—Freedom Schools, Curriculum Materials," KCLA.

113. "1964 Platform of the Mississippi Freedom School Convention," MFDP Papers, Box 14, Folder 16, "F. S. Convention," KCLA; Adickes, *Legacy of a Freedom School*, 86–87; Sally Belfrage, *Freedom Summer* (New York: Viking, 1965), 91–92; "Public Accommodations," SNCC Papers, Subgroup A, Series 15, Box 101, Folder, "MSP—Freedom Schools, Curriculum Materials," KCLA.

114. "1964 Platform of the Mississippi Freedom School Convention," MFDP Papers, Box 14, Folder 16, "F. S. Convention," KCLA.

115. Hymethia Washington Lofton Thompson, interview with the author, August 26, 2008.

116. "Freedom School Data," Box 4, Folder 13, Staughton Lynd Papers, WHSA; Adickes, *Legacy of a Freedom School*, 103; "Freedom Schools, general," Subgroup D, Appendix A, Reel 68.347.393, SNCC Papers, UIUC; "Freedom Schools, Historical Data," Subgroup

D, Appendix A, Reel 68.352.0429, SNCC Papers, UIUC; "Mississippi, Freedom Schools, Retrospect and Prospect," Subgroup A, Series XV, Reel 38.112.338, SNCC Papers, UIUC. The schools that developed later in the summer include a school in Issaquena County, the site of an important protest the following school year, as noted in Bruce Watson, *Freedom Summer: The Savage Season That Made Mississippi Burn and Made American a Democracy* (New York: Viking, 2010), 180.

117. Liz Fusco, "Freedom Schools in Mississippi, 1964," SNCC Papers, Subgroup A, Series 15, Box 101, Folder, "MSP—Freedom Schools, Curriculum Materials," KCLA.

5. "WE DO HEREBY DECLARE INDEPENDENCE"

1. "1964 Platform of the Mississippi Freedom School Convention," MFDP Papers, Box 14, Folder 16, "F. S. Convention," KCLA; Sandra Adickes, *Legacy of a Freedom School* (New York: Palgrave Macmillan, 2005), 86–87; Sally Belfrage, *Freedom Summer* (New York: Viking, 1965), 91–92.

2. The main objective of the Freedom Summer campaign was to seat MFDP delegates at the Democratic National Convention, and, as previously noted, much of the Freedom School activity was geared toward registering voters for the party. African Americans who registered for the MFDP voted in a "freedom election" that elected an alternative delegation of sixty-four blacks and four whites. Activists challenged the Democratic nominee, Lyndon B. Johnson, and other national leaders to seat their delegates over the traditional party from Mississippi because black voters had been excluded from the process. If white politicians were going to exclude blacks from the official electoral process, so the reasoning went, the MFDP was going to send an alternative delegation. This alternative process was seen to be more in line with the Constitution because it did not exclude any person from voting and featured organizers followed the precise electoral rules of the Democratic Party. See Clayborne Carson, *In Struggle: SNCC and the Black Awakening of the 1960s* (Cambridge, Mass.: Harvard University Press, 1995), 111–54; John Dittmer, *Local People: The Struggle for Civil Rights in Mississippi* (Urbana: University of Illinois Press, 1994), 272–337; and Doug McAdam, *Freedom Summer* (New York: Oxford University Press, 1988), 77–83.

3. Quoted in Dittmer, *Local People*, 302.

4. John Lewis, with Michael D'Orso, *Walking with the Wind: A Memoir of the Movement* (New York: Simon & Schuster, 1998), 284.

5. Quoted in Kristal T. Moore Clemons, "'She Who Learns, Teaches': Black Women Teachers of the 1964 Mississippi Freedom Schools" (Ph.D. diss., University of North Carolina, 2009), 104–5.

6. Peniel E. Joseph, "Introduction: Toward a Historiography of the Black Power Movement," in *The Black Power Movement: Rethinking the Civil Rights-Black Power Era*, ed. Peniel E. Joseph (New York: Routledge, 2006), 3. For an excellent historiographical interpretation of civil rights history and the rise of a traditional paradigm, see Peniel E.

Joseph, "The Black Power Movement: A State of the Field," *Journal of American History* 96 (2009): 751–66. Another theme in the literature is that there exists a popular understanding that casts black power as a negative legacy of the civil rights movement. Works that deal with this explicitly include David Garrow, *Bearing the Cross: Martin Luther King, Jr., and the Southern Christian Leadership Conference* (New York: Vintage, 1986); Allen Matusow, *The Unraveling of America: A History of Liberalism in the 1960s* (Athens: University of Georgia Press, 2009); Gilbert Jonas, *Freedom's Sword: The NAACP and the Struggle Against Racism in America, 1909–1969* (New York: Routledge, 2005); and Adam Fairclough, *To Redeem the Soul of America: The Southern Christian Leadership Conference and Martin Luther King Jr.* (Athens: University of Georgia Press, 2001).

7. Liz Fusco, "Freedom Schools in Mississippi, 1964," SNCC Papers, Subgroup A, Series 15, Box 101, Folder "MSP—Freedom Schools, Curriculum Materials," KCLA.

8. "Freedom Schools, Jackson," SNCC Papers, Subgroup D, Appendix A, Reel 68.355, 344–445, UIUC; "Freedom Schools, Jackson," MFDP Papers, Box 17, Folder 8, KCLA.

9. Liz Fusco, "Freedom Schools in Mississippi, 1964," SNCC Papers, Subgroup A, Series 15, Box 101, Folder, "MSP—Freedom Schools, Curriculum Materials," KCLA.

10. Roscoe Jones, interview with the author, March 18, 2014.

11. "Johnson May Speak Today," *Clarion-Ledger* (Jackson, Miss.), June 6, 1964; "Legislature Coming Back," *Clarion-Ledger*, June 7, 1964; "Lawmakers Head Home; Will Return on June 17," *Clarion-Ledger*, June 8, 1964; "Appeal in School Case Won't Stop Integration," *Clarion-Ledger*, July 8, 1964; "Biloxi to Join Court Appeal," *Clarion-Ledger*, July 9, 1964; *Laws of the State of Mississippi: Appropriations, General Legislation and Resolutions* (Published by Authority, 1964), 5. For a full account of desegregation in Mississippi, see Charles C. Bolton, *The Hardest Deal of All: The Battle over School Integration in Mississippi, 1870–1980* (Jackson: University Press of Mississippi, 2005), chap. 5.

12. "Jackson Project Plans—Week of Aug 30th," MFDP Papers, Box 17, Folder 8, "Freedom Schools, Jackson," KCLA.

13. Florence Howe, "Mississippi's Freedom Schools: The Politics of Education," *Harvard Educational Review* 35 (1965): 155–56.

14. "19 Negroes Apply at Canton High," *Clarion-Ledger*, September 4, 1964; "18 Negroes Seeking Transfer to Canton," *Hattiesburg American*, September 3, 1964; "Meridian Leaders Take Legal Action," *Hattiesburg American*, September 4, 1964; "Integration Sought by Meridian Group," *Clarion-Ledger*, September 5, 1964; "Canton, Summit Integration Attempts Are Turned Back," *Clarion-Ledger*, September 9, 1964; "Canton School Turns Back Negro Pupils," *Clarksdale Press Register*, September 8, 1964; "High Schools in Jackson Bar Negroes," *Clarksdale Press Register*, September 10, 1964; Bolton, *Hardest Deal of All*, 111–12.

15. Bolton, *Hardest Deal of All*, 149; Hymethia Washington Lofton Thompson, interview with the author, July 4, 2012.

16. Bolton, *Hardest Deal of All*, 141–42. For extensive oral histories of the desegregation of Murrah High School in the 1969/1970 school year, see "Murrah High School Oral History Project," Mississippi Department of Archives and History, Jackson.

17. For historical documentation of students' experiences in desegregating an all-white school, see Millicent Brown, "Somebody Had to Do It," Lowcountry Digital History Initiative, http://ldhi.library.cofc.edu/exhibits/show/somebody_had_to_do_it. The oral history project is a multidisciplinary study to identify, locate, and acknowledge African American "First Children" who desegregated America's schools. The project seeks to create a database of those First Children whose narratives are needed to adequately and accurately interpret the issues and results associated with *Brown vs. Board of Education* (1954) and Title VI of the Civil Rights Act (1964).

18. State plans endorsed a scholarship grant at $165 per year that limited aid to those attending nonsectarian schools, and it also required that local districts provide a supplemental $35 stipend. U.S. District Judge Oren R. Lewis refused to stop grant payment for private schools, despite NAACP challenges. See *Laws of the State of Mississippi, 1964*, 5; "Committee to Request State Scholarship Plan," *Clarion-Ledger*, June 18, 1964; "Tuition Grant Approved by Senate," *Clarion-Ledger*, July 7, 1964; and "Judge Refuses to Break Up Alleged Segregation Plans," *Clarion-Ledger*, July 10, 1964.

19. Michael W. Fuquay, "Civil Rights and the Private School Movement in Mississippi, 1964–1971," *History of Education Quarterly*, 42 (2002): 168–172.

20. Jones, interview.

21. Homer Hill, interview with the author, September 25, 2011. See also Françoise N. Hamlin, *Crossroads at Clarksdale: The Black Freedom Struggle in the Mississippi Delta After World War II* (Chapel Hill: University of North Carolina Press, 2012), 169–71.

22. Eddie James Carthan, interview with the author, October 16, 2011.

23. Quoted in Tim Spofford, *Lynch Street: The May 1970 Slayings at Jackson State College* (Kent, Ohio: Kent State University Press, 1988), 103; Wilbur Colom, interview with the author, March 9, 2015. Phillip Gibbs, one of the students slain in the 1970 shooting at Jackson State College, was a peer of Wilber Colom and was active in the Ripley sit-in movement.

24. J. Anthony Lukas, *Don't Shoot—We Are Your Children!* (New York: Random House, 1971), 88–91.

25. "Freedom Schools, Jackson," SNCC Papers, Subgroup D, Appendix A, Reel 68.355, 344–445, UIUC; "Freedom Schools, Jackson," MFDP Papers, Box 17, Folder 8, KCLA.

26. "Freedom Schools, Natchez," SNCC Papers, Subgroup D, Appendix A, Reel 68.361.541, UIUC; "Freedom Schools, reports, July 10–Dec. 27, 1964," SNCC Papers, Subgroup D, Appendix A, Reel 68.366,566- 567.366, UIUC; "The Mississippi Student Union Convention—December 1964," Mississippi Student Union (MSU) Folder, FIS.

27. "Amite County List of Grievances: Introduction," SNCC Papers, Subgroup A, Series 15, Box 101, Folder "MSP—Freedom Schools, Curriculum Materials," KCLA.

28. Ibid.

29. Quoted in "Massive School Boycott in Indianola," press release, February 22, 1965, Freedom Schools, miscellaneous folder, FIS. See also "The Mississippi Student Union Convention—December 1964," MSU Folder, FIS; and "Freedom Fighter: Issaquena MSU," MSU Folder, FIS.

30. "Massive School Boycott in Indianola, Press Release 22 February 1965," FIS; "Freedom Fighter: Issaquena MSU," MSU Folder, FIS.

31. Lukas, *Don't Shoot*, 91.

32. Gael Graham, *Young Activists: American High School Students in the Age of Protest* (DeKalb: Northern Illinois University Press, 2006), 45–63.

33. "Issaquena M.S.U. Freedom Fighter, August, 1965," MSU Folder, FIS; Bolton, *Hardest Deal of All*, 111; *Freedom Star* (Meridian, Miss.), in *To Write in the Light of Freedom: The Newspapers of the 1964 Mississippi Freedom Schools*, ed. William Sturkey and Jon N. Hale (Jackson: University Press of Mississippi, 2015), 162–66; Mary Aickin Rothschild, *A Case of Black and White: Northern Volunteers and the Southern Freedom Summers, 1964–1965* (Westport, Conn.: Greenwood Press, 1982), 110–15; Kenneth Andrews, *Freedom Is a Constant Struggle: The Mississippi Civil Rights Movement and Its Legacy* (Chicago: University of Chicago Press, 2004), 158–60.

34. "The Mississippi Student Union Convention—December 1964," MSU Folder, FIS.

35. Ibid.

36. Ibid.; Jones, interview.

37. "Issaquena M.S.U. Freedom Fighter, August, 1965," MSU Folder, FIS; Rothschild, *Case of Black and White*, 110–15; Bolton, *Hardest Deal of All*, 143–45. Some of the leaders in the boycott movement did not return to school. The leaders of the Issaquena boycott took paying jobs with the Delta Ministry, a civil rights organization based in the Mississippi Delta. One of its leaders became the first to integrate the all-white Issaquena-Sharkey public school. On this, see Rothschild, *Case of Black and White*, 115.

38. *Burnside v. Byars*, 363 F.2d n. 22681 (5th Cir. 1966); *Tinker v. Des Moines*, 393 U.S. 503; 89 S. Ct (1969); Staughton Lynd, interview with the author, August 28, 2006.

39. "Massive School Boycott in Indianola, COFO news release, Freedom Schools," miscellaneous folder, FIS; "Youth Court Eyeing School Attendance," *Enterprise-Tocsin* (Indianola, Miss.), February 25, 1965. Ironically enough, the town of Indianola required black students to attend public schools, although six months earlier the town had provided a charter for a private white segregationist academy. See "Local Group Given Charter to Operate Private School," *Enterprise-Tocsin*, August 13, 1964.

40. "Let's Keep Our Children out of School," 2, Aviva Futorian Papers, Folder 1, WHSA.

41. Ibid., 1.

42. Ibid., 2.

43. "Dear Fellow Members of the Great Society," March 15, 1965, Aviva Futorian Papers, Folder 1, WHSA.

44. "Dear——," May 7, 1965, Aviva Futorian Papers, Folder 1, WHSA; Bolton, *Hardest Deal of All*, 145–47.

45. "Jackson Project Report, March 7, 1965," miscellaneous folder, FIS.

46. For a larger discussion of a student rights movement of the late 1960s and 1970s, see Graham, *Young Activists*; Gael Graham, "Flaunting the Freak Flag: *Karr v. Schmidt* and the Great Hair Debate in American High Schools, 1965–1975," *Journal of American History* 91 (2004): 522–43; Jeremi Suri, *Power and Protest: Global Revolution and the Rise*

of Détente (Cambridge, Mass.: Harvard University Press, 2005); Roger Snajek, *The Future of Us All: Race and Neighborhood Politics in New York City* (Ithaca, N.Y.: Cornell University Press, 1988); Parker Frisbie, "Militancy Among Mexican American High School Students," *Social Science Quarterly* 53 (1973): 865–83; Dionne Danns, "Black Student Empowerment and Chicago School Reform Efforts in 1968," *Urban Education* 37 (2002): 631–55; and Vincent D. Willis, "Rhetoric, Realism, and Response: *Brown*, White Opposition, and Black Youth Activism, 1954–1972" (Ph.D. diss., Emory University, 2013).

47. For a larger historiography on black power and the work of challenging popular narrative of black power and reframing this history, see Joseph, *Black Power Movement*; Jeanne F. Theoharis and Komozi Woodard, eds., *Freedom North: Black Freedom Struggles Outside the South, 1940–1980* (New York: Palgrave Macmillan, 2003); Jeanne F. Theoharis and Komozi Woodard, eds., *Groundwork: Local Black Freedom Movements in America* (New York: New York University Press, 2005); Komozi Woodard, *A Nation Within a Nation: Amiri Baraka (LeRoi Jones) and Black Power Politics* (Chapel Hill: University of North Carolina Press, 1999); Timothy B. Tyson, *Radio Free Dixie: Robert F. Williams and the Roots of Black Power* (Chapel Hill: University of North Carolina Press, 2001); Jeffrey Ogbar, *Black Power: Radical Politics and African American Identity* (Baltimore: Johns Hopkins University Press, 2004); Yohuru Williams and Jama Lazerow eds., *Liberated Territory: Untold Perspectives on the Black Panther Party* (Durham, N.C.: Duke University Press, 2008); Hassan Jeffries, *Bloody Lowndes: Civil Rights and Black Power in Alabama's Black Belt* (New York: New York University Press, 2009); Jeffrey Ogbar, "Rainbow Radicalism: The Rise of Radical Ethnic Nationalism," in *The Black Power Movement: Rethinking the Civil Rights-Black Power Era*, ed. Peniel E. Joseph (New York: Routledge, 2006), 193–228; and Sundiata Keita Cha-Jua and Clarence Lang, "The 'Long Movement' as Vampire: Temporal and Spatial Fallacies in Recent Black Freedom Studies," *Journal of African American History* 92 (2007): 265–88.

48. Jeffries, *Bloody Lowndes*, 180–89; Dittmer, *Local People*, 389–407; Charles Payne, *I've Got the Light of Freedom: The Organizing Tradition and the Mississippi Freedom Struggle* (Berkeley: University of California Press, 1996), 374–82.

49. Hymethia Washington Lofton Thompson, interview with the author, August 26, 2008, and July, 4, 2012.

50. Lynd, interview.

51. C. Gerald Fraser, "School Confers with Protesters," *New York Times*, June 7, 1968; "Faculty's Effort Fails to Resolve Columbia Dispute," *New York Times*, April 27, 1968; Wilbur Colom, interview with the author, March 10, 2015.

52. Fraser, "School Confers with Protesters"; "Faculty's Effort Fails to Resolve Columbia Dispute." For an excellent history of the strikes at Columbia University in the 1960s, see Stefan M. Bradley, *Harlem vs. Columbia University: Black Student Power in the Late 1960s* (Urbana: University of Illinois Press, 2009).

53. Lukas, *Don't Shoot*, 104–13.

54. Hezekiah Watkins, interview with the author, October 1, 2011, and October 16, 2011.

55. Ibid. By 1966, at the end of the Freedom Summer campaign, SNCC was actively against the war. See Payne, *I've Got the Light of Freedom*, 375–76; and Lynd, interview.

56. On the role of black students during the black power movement, see Martha Biondi, *The Black Revolution on Campus* (Berkeley: University of California Press, 2012); Jeffrey A. Turner, *Sitting In and Speaking Out: Student Movement in the American South, 1960–1970* (Athens: University of Georgia Press, 2010); Bradley, *Harlem vs. Columbia University*; Ibram H. Rogers, *The Black Campus Movement: Black Students and the Racial Reconstitution of Higher Education, 1965–1972* (New York: Palgrave Macmillan, 2012); Robert Cohen and David J. Snyder, eds., *Rebellion in Black and White: Southern Student Activism in the 1960s* (Baltimore: Johns Hopkins University Press, 2013); Joy Ann Williamson, *Radicalizing the Ebony Tower: Black Colleges and the Black Freedom Struggle in Mississippi* (New York: Teachers College Press, 2008); Donna Murch, *Living for the City: Migration, Education, and the Rise of the Black Panther Party in Oakland, California* (Chapel Hill: University of North Carolina Press, 2010); and Gordon Mantler, *Power to the Poor: Black-Brown Coalition and the Fight for Economic Justice, 1960–1974* (Chapel Hill: University of North Carolina Press, 2013).

57. Lewis, *Walking with the Wind*, 287–88; Carson, *In Struggle*, 134–36.

58. Charles Cobb, "Prospectus for a Summer Freedom School Program," *Radical Teacher* 40 (1991): 36–37. See also Charles Cobb, "Freedom Schools, Curriculum, general," SNCC Papers, Subgroup D, Appendix A, Reel 67.340, UIUC; and Charles Cobb, "Freedom Schools, Day, Noel, 1964," SNCC Papers, Subgroup D, Appendix A, Reel 67, File 342, Slide 342, AARL.

59. Quoted in Dittmer, *Local People*, 326. The statements of Moses on the value of maintaining segregated schools, like the black power proclamation of Carmichael, was not necessarily a new idea. W. E. B. DuBois had penned "Does the Negro Need Separate Schools?" *Journal of Negro Education* 4 (1935): 328–35. His article suggested that he was not in favor of separate schooling but that, in the racialized climate of Jim Crow, desegregated schools would only hurt the students who had to attend. DuBois wrote, among other things, about the emotional and physical toll taken on black students integrating all-white schools. Moses's statement in many ways anticipated the development of the latter Black Panther Liberation Schools of the late 1960s. See Daniel Perlstein, "Minds Stayed on Freedom: Politics and Pedagogy in the African-American Freedom Struggle," *American Educational Research Journal* 39 (2002): 249–77; and Joy Ann Williamson, "Community Control with a Black Nationalist Twist: The Black Panther Party's Educational Programs," in *Black Protest Thought and Education*, ed. William Watkins (New York: Lang, 2005), 137–58.

60. "COFO Program," Robert Reingrass Papers, Folder 1, WHS.

61. "Freedom Schools, correspondence," SNCC Papers, Subgroup D, Appendix A, Reel 67.335.540, UIUC.

62. As of September 2, 1964, Liz Fusco, in a letter to Myles Horton, reported that there were twenty-eight active Freedom Schools across the state, down from the summer high of forty-one. She also reported that there were plans for three to four more schools in

the immediate future. On September 10, civil rights worker Lois Chaffe reported that there were thirty Freedom Schools in operation throughout Mississippi. On October 22, Fusco wrote that there were thirty-one schools in operation. On November 6, she reported that there were thirty-five Freedom Centers across the state. See "Freedom Schools, Convention," SNCC Papers, Subgroup D, Appendix A, Reel 67.334.465, UIUC; and "Freedom Schools, correspondence," SNCC Papers, Subgroup D, Appendix A, Reel 67, 335.492, 540, 548, UIUC. It is difficult to measure the exact number during the 1964/1965 school year. But it does appear certain that there were at least thirty Freedom Schools still in operation.

63. Liz Fusco, interview with the author, July 2, 2008.

64. Arthur Reese, "Freedom School Program," American Federation of Teachers (AFT) Collection, PE 012, "American Federation of Teachers, Freedom School Project" folder, Tamiment Library, New York University.

65. Ibid.

66. George Chilcoat and Jerry A. Ligon, "Theatre as an Emancipatory Tool: Classroom Drama in the Mississippi Freedom Schools," *Journal of Curriculum Studies* 29 (1998): 522–24; "*Seeds of Freedom*: A Play Based on the Life and Death of Medgar Evers, by Deborah Flynn and Students of the 1964 Freedom School in Holly Springs" (transcript in the author's possession, courtesy of Chude Allen); Chude Allen, correspondence with the author, March 2–4, 2015. Earnestine Evans traveled with a group from Mississippi to perform *Seeds of Freedom* in New York City. See Gloria Xifaras Clark, interview with the author, October 21, 2014; and Anthony J. Harris, *Ain't Gonna Let Nobody Turn Me 'Round: A Coming-of-Age Story and Personal Account of the Civil Rights Movement in Hattiesburg, Mississippi* (Privately published, 2013), 53–55.

67. Wilbur Colom, interview with Gloria Clark, December 12, 1995, in *Mississippi Oral History Program: North Mississippi Oral History and Archives Program*, vol. 751 (Hattiesburg: Center for Oral History and Cultural Heritage, 2001), 34–37.

68. Gloria Clark, interview with Wilbur Colom, December 12, 1995, 9–12, North Mississippi Oral Archives Project, Box A–J, Transcripts, "Gloria Clark," 9, Leontyne Price Library Archives, Rust College, Holly Springs, Miss.; Aviva Futorian, interview with Roy DeBerry Jr., December 10, 1995, 7, North Mississippi Oral Archives Project, Box A–J, Transcripts, "Aviva Futorian," Leontyne Price Library Archives, Rust College, Holly Springs, Miss.

69. Gloria Clark and Ginevera Reaves, interviewers, *Mississippi Oral History Program: North Mississippi Oral History and Archives Program*, vol. 751; Wilbur Colom, interview with the author, March 10, 2015.

70. Rothschild, *Case of Black and White*, 115.

71. Dittmer, *Local People*, 328.

72. Quoted in ibid., 330.

73. Liz Fusco, interview with the author, November 18, 2013.

74. Carson, *In Struggle*, 237–43; Dittmer, *Local People*, 408; Wesley C. Hogan, *Many Minds, One Heart: SNCC's Dream for a New America* (Chapel Hill: University of North Carolina

Press, 2007), 202–7. For a Latina perspective on the black/white divide, see Elizabeth (Betita) Sutherland Martinez, "Neither Black nor White in a Black-White World," in *Hands on the Freedom Plow: Personal Accounts by Women in SNCC*, ed. Faith S. Holsaert, Martha Prescod Norman Noonan, Judy Richardson, Betty Garman Robinson, Jean Smith Young, and Dorothy M. Zellner (Urbana: University of Illinois Press, 2010), 531–39.

75. Fusco, interview, November 18, 2013.

76. Jan Hillegas remains in Mississippi (interview with the author, June 14, 2008).

77. "Statement from the Organization of Afro-American Unity," Box 1, Folder 25, "OAAU Liberation School, 1964–1965," James E. Campbell Collection, Avery Research Center for African American History and Culture, Charleston, S.C.

78. "December 12, 1964, notes," "February 6, 1965 notes," "February 20, 1965, notes," "Liberation School—Certificate of Completion," Box 1, Folder 25, "OAAU Liberation School, 1964–1965," James E. Campbell Collection, Avery Research Center for African American History and Culture, Charleston, S.C.

79. Black Panther Party, "Ten Point Program," quoted in Murch, *Living for the City*, 178–79.

80. Lauren Watson, "Denver Panthers Determined: Community Control of Schools," *Black Panther*, June 7, 1969, http://www.itsabouttimebpp.com/BPP_Newspapers/bpp_newspapers_index.html.

81. "Liberation Schools," *Black Panther*, July 5, 1969, in *The Black Panthers Speak*, ed. Philip Foner (Cambridge, Mass.: Da Capo Press, 1970), 170–71.

82. For more on the Black Panther Liberation Schools, see Perlstein, "Minds Stayed on Freedom," 249–77. Perlstein found that "whereas SNCC had once embraced a pedagogy of open-ended inquiry, the Panthers applauded explicit, direct instruction in revolutionary analysis" (262).

83. Murch, *Living for the City*, 178–82; Perlstein, "Minds Stayed on Freedom," 260–64; "Liberation Schools," 170–71. See also Williamson, "Community Control with a Black Nationalist Twist," 137–58.

84. Casey Hayden and Mary King, "Sex and Caste: A Kind of Memo," *Liberation* 10 (1966). See also Casey Hayden, "In the Attics of My Mind," in *Hands on the Freedom Plow*, ed. Holsaert et al., 381–88; Dittmer, *Local People*, 331–32.

85. Hayden and King, "Sex and Caste."

86. Jane Adams, June 18, 1964, "Notes from Freedom Summer Training, Oxford, Ohio, June 17–26, 1964," Box 1, Folder 19, "Notes from Freedom Summer Training," Miami University, Oxford, Ohio; Renee C. Romano, *Race Mixing: Black-White Marriage in Postwar America* (Cambridge, Mass.: Harvard University Press, 2003), 175–85.

87. Robert Cohen, *Freedom's Orator: Mario Savio and the Radical Legacy of the 1960s* (New York: Oxford University Press, 2009); McAdam, *Freedom Summer*, 163–68; Taylor Branch, *Pillar of Fire: America in the King Years, 1963–65* (New York: Simon & Schuster, 1998), 493–95; Dittmer, *Local People*, 270–71; Bruce Watson, *Freedom Summer: The Savage Season That Made Mississippi Burn and Made America a Democracy* (New York: Viking, 2010); Eric Pace, "Mario Savio, Protest Leader Who Set a Style, Dies at 53," *New York Times*, November 8, 1996.

88. Mark Levy, "What Did You Learn in School Today? Mississippi Freedom Summer's Challenge for Teaching Now," *Association of Teachers of Social Studies Journal* 52, no. 1 (2015); Mark Levy, interview with the author, December 15, 2014.

89. Levy, "What Did You Learn in School Today?"; Levy, interview.

90. Mark Levy, "I'm Still Arguing with My Mother," *Queens College Journal of Jewish Studies*, Spring 2014, 111–18; Levy, "What Did You Learn in School Today"; Levy, interview.

91. Chude Allen, "My Parents Said Yes!," in *Finding Freedom: Memorializing the Voices of Freedom Summer*, ed. Jacqueline Johnson (Oxford: Miami University Press, 2013), 27.

92. Chude Allen, interview with the author, October 22, 2014; Allen, correspondence.

93. Sandy Siegel, interview with the author, June 28, 2008.

94. Ibid.

95. "To Our President, a Former Teacher," *New York Times*, May 30, 1965, E12; Adickes, *Legacy of a Freedom School*, 137–38; McAdam, *Freedom Summer*, 174–75. Mark Levy taught in the same school as Norma Becker (interview).

96. Hugh Davis Graham, *The Uncertain Triumph: Federal Education Policy in the Kennedy and Johnson Years* (Chapel Hill: University of North Carolina Press, 1984); Adam R. Nelson, "The Federal Role in American Education: A Historiographical Essay," in *Rethinking the History of American Education*, ed. William J. Reese and John L. Rury (New York: Palgrave Macmillan, 2008), 261–80; Stephen Bailey and Edith Mosler, *ESEA: The Office of Education Administers a Law* (Syracuse, N.Y.: Syracuse University Press, 1968); Julie Roy Jeffrey, *Education for Children of the Poor: A Study of the Origins and Implementation of the Elementary and Secondary Education Act of 1964* (Columbus: Ohio State University Press, 1978). More nuanced and comprehensive policy analysis place the origins of Head Start in and the "rediscovery" of poverty during the Kennedy administration, which was in part triggered by mainstream accounts of poverty, such as Michael Harrington's *The Other America: Poverty in the United States* (New York: Macmillan, 1962), that conveyed to the American public the existence of poverty in the land of prosperity. See also Michael Gillette, *Launching the War on Poverty: An Oral History* (Oxford: Oxford University Press, 2010), 6–12; Maris Vinovskis, *The Birth of Head Start: Preschool Education Policies in the Kennedy and Johnson Administrations* (Chicago: University of Chicago Press, 2005), 2–34; and Philip Meranto, *The Politics of Federal Aid to Education in 1965: A Study in Political Innovation* (Syracuse, N.Y.: Syracuse University Press, 1967), 16–20. For a history of the Head Start program in Mississippi and its relationship to the Freedom Schools, see Jon Hale, "The Struggle Begins Early: Head Start and the Mississippi Freedom Movement," *History of Education Quarterly* 52 (2012): 506–34; Crystal Sanders, "To Be Free of Fear: Black Women's Fight for Freedom Through the Child Development Group of Mississippi" (Ph.D. diss., Northwestern University, 2011); and Crystal Sanders, *Preschool Politics: Mississippi's Black Freedom Struggle and a Radical Head Start* (forthcoming).

97. Ida Ruth Griffin O'Leary, interview with the author, September 4, 2008.

98. Owen Brooks, interview with the author, July 1, 2010.

99. Laura Johnson, interview with the author, June 25, 2010.

100. Hattye Gatson, interview with Harriet Tanzman, January 16, 2000, in *Mississippi Oral History Program: North Mississippi Oral History and Archives Program*, vol. 751.

101. Adickes, *Legacy of a Freedom School*, 16, 151–55. Totten was later elected as the first black district superintendent of Marshall County. Her car was bombed shortly thereafter, and her sons adopted a policy of armed self-defense to protect her. Arelya Mitchell, conversation with the author, February 20, 2015.

102. Johnson, interview.

103. Payne, *I've Got the Light of Freedom*, 255–56. See also Dittmer, *Local People*, 103–15; Payne, *I've Got the Light of Freedom*, 111–31; and Hogan, *Many Minds, One Heart*, 59–61.

104. Andrew Kopkind, "Bureaucracy's Long Arm," *New Republic* 153 (1965): 19–22.

105. Johnson, interview; Floree Smith, interview with the author, June 24, 2010; Edward Zigler, Sally Styfco, and Bonnie Gordic, "What Is the Goal of Head Start? Four Decades of Confusion and Debate," *NHSA Dialog* 10, no. 2 (2007): 85–86; Polly Greenberg, *The Devil Has Slippery Shoes: A Biased Biography of the Child Development Group of Mississippi (CDGM): A Story of Maximum Feasible Poor Parent Participation* (New York: Macmillan, 1969), 181–208. For a full description of CDGM goals, see "Proposal for Structure of Child Development Project for Mississippi Communities—Summer 1965," Tom Levin Papers, Series 1, Box 3, "Grant Applications," KCLA.

106. Dr. Jim Hendrick, interviewed by Lavaree Jones, May 10, 1989, Head Start Oral History Interviews, Margaret Walker Alexander National Research Center, Jackson State University, Jackson, Miss.

107. Reverend James F. McRee interview transcript, 44–45, Head Start Oral History Interviews, Margaret Walker Alexander National Research Center, Jackson State University, Jackson, Miss.

108. Dittmer, *Local People*, 368–73; Payne, *I've Got the Light of Freedom*, 329; Rothschild, *Case of Black and White*, 117; James McRee Papers, Volume 2, Box 3, "Teacher Development and Program for Children," MDAH; Johnson, interview; Smith, interview; Joe Morse, interview with the author, June 10, 2010.

109. Hilda Wilson Papers, Box 4, Folder 30 "Press Releases," MDAH.

110. Joseph Crespino, *In Search of Another Country: Mississippi and the Conservative Counterrevolution* (Princeton, N.J.: Princeton University Press, 2007), 1; James C. Cobb, *The South and America Since World War II* (Oxford: Oxford University Press, 2011), 121–22.

111. Matthew D. Lassiter, *The Silent Majority: Suburban Politics in the Sunbelt South* (Princeton, N.J.: Princeton University Press, 2005), 132–47; Lisa McGirr, *Suburban Warriors: The Origins of the New American Right* (Princeton, N.J.: Princeton University Press, 2001), 239–40; Bruce J. Schulman, *The Seventies: The Great Shift in American Culture, Society, and Politics* (New York: Free Press, 2001), 56–58.

112. Crespino, *In Search of Another Country*, 4.

113. Ibid.

114. Matthew D. Lassiter and Joseph Crespino, eds., *The Myth of Southern Exceptionalism* (Oxford: Oxford University Press, 2010); Kevin M. Kruse, *White Flight: Atlanta and*

the *Making of Modern Conservatism* (Princeton, N.J.: Princeton University Press, 2007); McGirr, *Suburban Warriors*; Lassiter, *Silent Majority*; Schulman, *Seventies*.

115. "OEO Is Readying Head Start Report," *Clarion-Ledger*, August 3, 1965; "Head Start Payment for Fines Revealed," *Clarion-Ledger*, September 11, 1965; "Stennis Asks Probe of Report," *Clarion-Ledger*, August 14, 1965; Vinovskis, *Birth of Head Start*, 97–98; Dittmer, *Local People*, 371–73; Adickes, *Legacy of a Freedom School*, 151–52.

116. Hilda Wilson Papers, Box 4, Folder 12 "History of FCM," MDAH; Dittmer, *Local People*, 373–84, 635–56.

117. Although mismanagement and less-than-perfect budgetary restraint were found, it problem was not to the degree that Stennis charged. Moreover, the OEO forced the resignation of Tom Levin, the founder of CDGM, and pressured them to move its headquarters from Mt. Beulah, which had become known as a civil rights headquarters. See "Shriver Denies U.S. Funds Used to Bail CR Agitators," *Clarion-Ledger*, August 22, 1965; and Greenberg, *Devil Has Slippery Shoes*, 259–79.

118. Dittmer, *Local People*, 375–83; Payne, *I've Got the Light of Freedom*, 329, 343; "Well, Mt. Beulah Is Closed," *Jackson Daily News*, October 15, 1965; "12 Man Board Replaces CDGM," *Jackson Daily News*, September 30, 1966; "Bi-Racial Group Is Reported Slated for CDGM Takeover," *Clarion-Ledger*, October 1, 1966.

119. Marshall Smith and Joan Bissell, "The Impact of Head Start: The Westinghouse-Ohio Head Start Evaluation," *Harvard Educational Review* 40 (1970): 51–104.

120. Fannie Lou Hamer, quoted in Dittmer, *Local People*, 378.

121. Rothschild, *Case of Black and White*, 118. For the radicalization of SNCC, see Carson, *In Struggle*, 133–211; and Hogan, *Many Minds, One Heart*, 197–225.

122. For a discussion of the Moynihan Report and its origins, influence, and implications within the Johnson administration, see David Carter, *The Music Has Gone Out of the Movement: Civil Rights and the Johnson Administration, 1965–1968* (Chapel Hill: University of North Carolina Press, 2009); 51–74. For an extensive discussion on the culture of poverty, see Oscar Lewis, *La Vida: A Puerto Rican Family in the Culture of Poverty* (New York: Random House, 1966); and Oscar Lewis, *Five Families: Mexican Case Studies in the Culture of Poverty* (New York: Random House, 1959).

6. CARRYING FORTH THE STRUGGLE

1. Howard Zinn, "Schools in Context: The Mississippi Idea," *Nation*, November 23, 1964, 3.

2. Tim Spofford, *Lynch Street: The May 1970 Slayings at Jackson State College* (Kent, Ohio: Kent State University Press, 1988), 62–69. Compared with the killings at Kent State, the shootings at Jackson State receive scant historical attention. A lawsuit brought by the families of the victims was initially dismissed after the judge found it "unclear" who killed the victims. For a full account of the Jackson State shootings, see Spofford, *Lynch Street*; "The Shootings at Jackson State University: Thirty Years Later," *Journal of*

Blacks in Higher Education 28 (2000): 42–43; and Victoria Sherwood, "Phillip Lafayette Gibbs & James Earl Green," *Jackson Free Press*, October 19, 2012.

3. Mississippi Sovereignty Commission Files, SCR ID nos. 1-118-0-16-1-1-1; 8-20-2-82-1-1-1; and 8-20-2-82-2-1-1, MDAH, http://mdah.state.ms.us/arrec/digital_archives /sovcom/; "Shooting Case Appeal Fails," *Times-Picayune* (New Orleans, La.), April 24, 1973; M. Susan Orr-Klopfer, *Where Rebels Roost: Mississippi Civil Rights Revisited* (M. Susan Orr-Klopfer, 2005), 561–90.

4. Hymethia Washington Lofton Thompson, interviews with the author, August 26, 2008, and July 4, 2012. See also John Dittmer, *Local People: The Struggle for Civil Rights in Mississippi* (Urbana: University of Illinois Press, 1994), 389–407; and Charles Payne, *I've Got the Light of Freedom: The Organizing Tradition and the Mississippi Freedom Struggle* (Berkeley: University of California Press, 1996), 374–82.

5. Thompson, interviews.

6. Thompson desegregated Murrah High School but graduated from the all-black Rosa Scott High School due to the pressures of desegregation and other personal issues. The toll of desegregation was exacting on the young people called on to desegregate white schools. For a moving narrative, see Melba Pattillo Beals, *Warriors Don't Cry: A Searing Memoir of the Battle to Integrate Little Rock's Central High* (New York: Pocket Books, 1994); and Thompson, interviews.

7. Anthony J. Harris, "Farewell Mississippi; Hello Texas," and "Farewell Texas; Hello Mississippi," both in *Ain't Gonna Let Nobody Turn Me 'Round: A Coming-of-Age Story and Personal Account of the Civil Rights Movement in Hattiesburg, Mississippi* (Privately published, 2013), 209–63; Anthony Harris, interview with the author, October 21, 2014.

8. Eddie James Carthan, interviews with the author, September 5, 2008; October 16, 2011; and July 7, 2012; "FBI Joins Tchula Murder Investigation," *Jackson Daily News*, July 13, 1981; "'Tchula 7' Juror Recants Verdict," *Jackson Daily News*, July 26, 1982; "Black Mayor Politically Assassinated," *Tchula Times*, May 30, 1981; "Ex-Mayor Ends Defense Against Murder Charge," *New York Times*, November 4, 1982. For a complete follow-up of the case in federal court, see George A. Sewell and Margaret L. Dwight, *Mississippi Black History Makers* (Jackson: University Press of Mississippi, 1984), 69–71.

9. Carthan, interview, September 5, 2008.

10. Arelya Mitchell, interview with the author, September 2, 2008. As a young child, Mitchell regularly corresponded with Donald Klopfer, a founder of Random House, and submitted her poetry for him to read. Klopfer encouraged her to keep writing. Arelya Mitchell, correspondence with the author, February 20, 2015.

11. Mitchell, interview; and Arelya Mitchell, correspondence with the author, November 14–17, 2013, and February 20, 2015.

12. Arelya J. Mitchell, "Killing of Trayvon Martin Highlights Open Season on Black Boys," *Black Information Highway* (blog), March 23, 2012, https://blackinformationhighway .wordpress.com/2012/03/23/killing-of-trayvon-martin-highlights-open-season-on -black-boys/.

13. Wilbur Colom, interview with the author, March 10, 2015. See also Mona Vance, "Fighting the Wave of Change: Cultural Transformation and Coeducation at Mississippi University for Women, 1884 to 1982" (master's thesis, University of North Carolina–Wilmington, 2008), 76.

14. *Mississippi University for Women v. Hogan*, 458 U.S. 718 (1982); Wilbur O. Colom, "The Trials of a Mississippi Lawyer," *New York Times*, May 15, 1983; Colom, interview.

15. Colom, "Trials of a Mississippi Lawyer"; Colom, interview.

16. Thompson, interview, August 26, 2008.

17. Based on an extrapolation of numbers presented in Neil R. McMillen, *Dark Journey: Black Mississippians in the Age of Jim Crow* (Urbana: University of Illinois Press, 1990), 88.

18. Wally Roberts, interview with the author, June 23, 2008. Sandra Adickes also reports a strong commitment of Freedom School educators after the summer campaign of 1964 in "Freedom Summer as a Life-Shaping Event," in *The Legacy of a Freedom School* (New York: Palgrave Macmillan, 2005), 155–82.

19. Roberts, interview.

20. Liz Fusco, interview with the author, November 18, 2013.

21. Ibid.

22. Mark and Betty Levy, Freedom School teachers in Meridian, also determined that the teacher union's stance against the community control model put forth by the local black community was inherently racist, and they worked against the union during the strike as well. See Mark Levy, interview with the author, December 15, 2014. The "strike that changed New York" illustrates the tensions between white liberals and black activists who demanded that they control the provision of public education, much to the dismay of whites who had been long sympathetic to the movement. For an eloquent and insightfully analytical account of the strike, see Joseph Podair, *The Strike That Changed New York: Blacks, Whites, and the Ocean Hill–Brownsville Crisis* (New Haven, Conn.: Yale University Press, 2002). See also Fusco, interview.

23. Fusco, interview.

24. Liz Fusco, interview with the author, July 2, 2008.

25. Frances O'Brien, interview with the author, November 18, 2013.

26. Ibid.

27. Ibid.

28. Frances O'Brien, "Journey into Light," in *Freedom Is a Constant Struggle: An Anthology of the Mississippi Civil Rights Movement*, ed. Susie Erenrich (Montgomery, Ala.: Black Belt Press, 1999), 285–89; Watson, *Freedom Summer*, 232–35, 264.

29. Frances O'Brien, interviews with the author, June 5, 2008, and November 18, 2013.

30. Fusco, interview, November 18, 2013.

31. Mississippi directly influenced the practice of teachers in terms of their perception of black students and their parents, the curriculum they taught, and their method of teaching in the classroom, according to Judith Collings Hudson, "Freedom Teachers: Northern White Women Teaching in Southern Black Communities" (Ph.D. diss., University of Massachusetts Amherst, 2001), vi, 219.

32. Such training is imperative for white educators, as over 85 percent of teachers are white, but minorities are quickly becoming the majority of the student population within public schools. This is discussed in Beverly E. Cross, "New Racism, Reformed Teacher Education, and the Same Ole' Oppression," *Educational Studies* 38 (2005): 263–74. For a brief introduction to multicultural education and culturally relevant teaching, see James A. Banks, *An Introduction to Multicultural Education* (Boston: Allyn and Bacon, 2002); Gloria Ladson-Billings, *Dreamkeepers: Successful Teachers of African American Children* (San Francisco: Jossey-Bass, 1994); and Sonia Nieto, *Affirming Diversity: The Sociopolitical Context of Multicultural Education* (Boston: Pearson/Allyn and Bacon, 2004).

33. Paulo Freire, *Pedagogy of the Oppressed* (New York: Herder and Herder, 1970).

34. For further reading on critical pedagogy and its major tenets, see Antonia Darder, Marta Baltodano, and Rodolfo D. Torres, eds., *Critical Pedagogy Reader* (New York: RoutledgeFalmer, 2003); Henry A. Giroux, *Theory and Resistance in Education: Towards a Pedagogy for the Opposition* (Westport, Conn.: Bergin & Garvey, 2001); Henry Giroux, "Critical Theory and Educational Practice," in *Critical Pedagogy Reader*, ed. Darder, Baltodano, and Torres, 27–56; Michael W. Apple, *Education and Power* (Boston: Routledge, 1982), 27–56; and Peter McLaren, "Critical Pedagogy: A Look at the Major Concepts," in *Critical Pedagogy Reader*, ed. Darder, Baltodano, and Torres, 69–96. For a historic look at critical pedagogy in the civil rights movement through the life of Ella Baker, see Barbara Ransby, "A Freirian Teacher: A Gramscian Intellectual, and a Radical Humanist," in *Ella Baker and the Black Freedom Movement: A Radical Democratic Vision* (Chapel Hill: University of North Carolina Press, 2003), 357–74.

35. Douglas Robinson, "Vietnam Protest Called a Success," *New York Times*, October 18, 1965.

36. Dennis Hevesi, "Norma Becker, 76, Organizer of Opposition to the Vietnam War, Is Dead," *New York Times*, June 27, 2006; Judith Mahoney Pasternak, "Norma Becker, 76, Fought for Peace and Civil Rights," *Villager*, July 5–11, 2006; Adickes, *Legacy of A Freedom School*, 137–38.

37. Levy, interview.

38. Ibid.; Adickes, *Legacy of a Freedom School*, 159.

39. Gloria Xifaras Clark, interview with the author, October 21, 2014.

40. Ibid.; Jama Lazerow, "The Black Panthers at the Water's Edge: Oakland, Boston, and the New Bedford 'Riots' of 1970," in *Liberated Territory: Untold Local Perspectives on the Black Panther Party*, ed. Yohuru Williams and Jama Lazerow (Durham, N.C.: Duke University Press, 2008), 88–92; Michael L. Gillete, *Launching the War on Poverty: An Oral History* (Oxford: Oxford University Press, 2010), 212–34.

41. Clark, interview; Gloria Xifaras Clark, correspondence with the author, March 4, 2015.

42. Robert Reinhold, "Harvard Ousts 75 in Black Protest," *New York Times*, December 12, 1969; Robert Reinhold, "Harvard Ousts 16 for Protest Role," *New York Times*, December 16, 1969; Robert Reinhold, "Harvard's Faculty Assails Protesters and University: Faculty at Harvard Is Critical of Both Sides," *New York Times*, April 12, 1969; and Robert Reinhold, "Harvard Office Invaded In Protest on Expansion," *New York Times*,

April 26, 1969. On John Holt's critical examination of public education and the origins of the "unschooling" movement, see John Holt, *How Children Fail* (New York: Pitman, 1964); John Holt, *How Children Learn* (New York: Pitman, 1967); Clark, interview; Clark, correspondence.

43. Clark, interview; Clark, correspondence; Gloria J. Clark, résumé (in the author's possession, courtesy of Gloria Xifaras Clark).

44. Wally Roberts, interview with the author, December 4, 2013.

45. Wally Roberts, "Freedom Day in Cleveland, Miss.," *Berkshire Eagle* (Pittsfield, Mass.), July 25, 1964.

46. Roberts, interview, December 4, 2013.

47. Jack Minnis notably uncovered a law in Lowndes County, Alabama, that allowed for a countywide political party that eventually became the Lowndes County Freedom Organization, which adopted the Black Panther as the political logo. See Clayborne Carson, *In Struggle: SNCC and the Black Awakening of the 1960s* (Cambridge, Mass.: Harvard University Press, 1995), 164–66.

48. Wally Roberts, "Samuel Insull, Where Are You?" *Boston Sunday Globe*, February 14, 1999; Wallace Roberts, "Enron's Schemes 'The Very Nature of Profit-Based, Market Capitalism,'" *Common Dreams*, May 26, 2006. Roberts's work later in life also extended into gubernatorial politics in Vermont, where he served as a campaign manager and press secretary for candidates representing progressive agendas and nonprofit agencies. See Roberts, interview, December 4, 2013.

49. Chude Allen, interview with the author, October 22, 2014; Chude Allen, correspondence with the author, March 2–4, 2015.

50. Allen, interview; Allen, correspondence; Kieran Taylor, "Turn to the Working Class: The New Left, Black Liberation, and the U.S. Labor Movement (1967–1981)" (Ph.D. diss., University of North Carolina, 2007), 188–94; Ginette Castro, *American Feminism: A Contemporary History* (New York: New York University Press, 1990), 245–46; Kathryn T. Flannery, *Feminist Literacies, 1968–75* (Urbana: University of Illinois Press, 2005), 169–76; Pamela Allen, *Free Space, A Perspective on the Small Group in Women's Liberation* (New York: Times Change Press, 1970). Allen also coauthored a book on radicals in American history: Robert Allen, with Pamela Allen, *Reluctant Reformers: Racism and Social Reform Movements in the United States* (Washington, D.C.: Howard University Press, 1983). See also Robert Allen, *Black Awakening in Capitalist American: An Analytic History* (Garden City, N.Y.: Doubleday, 1969).

51. Chude Allen, "Would You Marry One?" Civil Rights Movement Veterans, http://www.crmvet.org/info/marryone.htm; Allen, correspondence; Chude Allen, "Meeting Bob" (essay in the author's possession, courtesy of Chude Allen).

52. Gwendolyn (Robinson) Simmons, interview with the author, October 12, 2014; Kristal T. Moore Clemons, "'She Who Learns, Teaches': Black Women Teachers of the 1964 Mississippi Freedom Schools" (Ph.D. diss., University of North Carolina at Chapel Hill, 2009), 105; Gwendolyn Zoharah Simmons, "From Little Memphis Girl to Mississippi Amazon," in *Hands on the Freedom Plow: Personal Accounts by Women in SNCC*, ed.

Faith S. Holsaert, Martha Prescod Norman Noonan, Judy Richardson, Betty Garman Robinson, Jean Smith Young, and Dorothy M. Zellner (Urbana: University of Illinois Press, 2010), 32; and Kristal Moore Clemons, "I've Got to Do Something for My People: Black Women Teachers of the 1964 Mississippi Freedom Schools," *Western Journal of Black Studies* 38, no 3 (2014): 148–52. For an insightful and excellent discussion on black women in the Freedom Summer campaign and the development of black feminist thought and ideology, see Clemons, " 'She Who Learns, Teaches,' " 106–16.

53. Gwendolyn Simmons, "The Islamic Law of Personal Status and Its Contemporary Impact on Women in Jordan" (Ph.D. diss., Temple University, 2002), 31.

54. Ibid., 39–42; Simmons, interview.

55. Patrick J. McGuinn, *No Child Left Behind and the Transformation of Federal Educational Policy, 1965–2005* (Lawrence: University Press of Kansas, 2006), 31–39. "Title I" funding, as labeled under ESEA, is the major source of federal support for public education, so how this money is distributed remains a controversial issue.

56. Charles C. Bolton, *The Hardest Deal of All: The Battle over School Integration in Mississippi, 1870–1980* (Jackson: University Press of Mississippi, 2005), 167–92; Gareth Davies, *See Government Grow: Education Politics from Johnson to Reagan* (Lawrence: University of Kansas Press 2007), 122–26; Joseph Crespino, *In Search of Another Country: Mississippi and the Conservative Counterrevolution* (Princeton, N.J.: Princeton University Press, 2007), 173–76.

57. For a brilliant analysis of the Stennis Amendment and its implications in American politics and history, see Crespino, *In Search of Another Country*, 167–92; and Warren Weaver Jr., "Stennis Amendment Seems Sure to Haunt Liberals, Despite Doubts on Effect," *New York Times*, February 21, 1970.

58. The rally in support of FOCUS drew over four thousand people. See Bolton, *Hardest Deal of All*, 171; and Crespino, *In Search of Another Country*, 190.

59. In his impressively thorough historical examination of desegregation in Mississippi, Bolton found that the number of private schools rose from 121 to 236 (*Hardest Deal of All*, 173). For an examination of the desegregation of private academies in the South, which broadens our view of private school education during desegregation, see Michelle Purdy, "Blurring Public and Private: The Pragmatic Desegregation Politics of an Elite Private School in Atlanta," *History of Education Quarterly* 56 (2016): 61–89; and Michelle Purdy, "Southern and Independent: Public Mandates, Private Schools, and Black Students, 1951–1970" (Ph.D. diss., Emory University, 2011).

60. Scholars V. P. Franklin and Ronald Batchelor and former Freedom School teacher Howard Zinn have contemplated the use of Freedom Schooling to improve American education for all students. See V. P. Franklin and Ronald Batchelor, "Freedom Schooling: A New Approach to Federal-Local Cooperation in Public Education," *Teachers College Record* 80 (1978): 225–48; Zinn, "Schools in Context"; Robert Moses, "An Earned Insurgency: Quality Education as a Constitutional Right," *Harvard Educational Review* 79 (2009): 370–81; Bob Moses and Charles Cobb, *Radical Equations: Math Literacy and Civil Rights* (Boston: Beacon Press, 2001); Leslie Etienne, "A Different Type of Summer

Camp: SNCC, Freedom Summer, Freedom Schools, and the Development of African American Males in Mississippi," *Peabody Journal of Education* 88 (2013): 449–63; and Tambra O. Jackson and Gloria S. Boutte, "Liberation Literature: Positive Cultural Messages in Children's and Young Adult Literature at Freedom Schools," *Language Arts* 87, no. 2 (2009): 108–16.

61. Kamu Aysola, "2008 CDF Freedom Schools Fact Sheet" (Washington, D.C.: Children's Defense Fund, 2008). See also "CDF Freedom Schools Program," Children's Defense Fund, http://www.childrensdefense.org/programs/freedomschools/.

62. Moses and Cobb, *Radical Equations*, 5.

63. Lisa Deer Brown and the McComb Young People's Project, conversations with the author, July 2, 2012. Howard Zinn, popular activist and historian, was a Freedom School teacher in Jackson briefly during the summer of 1964. See Zinn, "Schools in Context"; Howard Zinn, *You Can't be Neutral on a Moving Train: A Personal History of Our Times* (Boston: Beacon Press, 2004); and Howard Zinn, interview with the author, September 25, 2006. The Howard Zinn Education Project was founded to honor his legacy and to continue the struggle to honor and learn from the perspectives of those who have historically struggled for equity. The group in McComb received funding from the Howard Zinn Education Project and a Teaching for Change grant. Vickie Malone's "Local Cultures" course at McComb High School in Mississippi is an invaluable example of incorporating local civil rights history into the high school curriculum.

64. Brown and the McComb Young People's Project, conversations; Umar Farooq, "Baltimore Algebra Project Stops Juvenile Detention Center," *Nation*, January 24, 2012; Erin Sullivan, "Algebra Project Mobilizes Students to Protest in Honor of National Day of Action to Defend Education," *Nation*, March 4, 2010; Donn Worgs, "Public Engagement and the Coproduction of Public Education," in *Public Engagement for Public Education: Joining Forces to Revitalize Democracy and Equalize Schools*, ed. Marion Orr and John Rogers (Stanford, Calif.: Stanford University Press, 2011), 92.

EPILOGUE

1. *Freedom Summer*, directed by Stanley Nelson (Austin: Firelight Films, 2014), DVD.

2. For a critical introduction to contemporary issues impacting public education in the United States, see Gary Orfield and Chungmei Lee, "Historic Reversals, Accelerating Resegregation, and the Need for New Integration Strategies," Civil Rights Project/ Proyecto Derechos Civiles, University of California, Los Angeles, August 29, 2007, http://civilrightsproject.ucla.edu/research/k-12-education/integration-and-diversity /historic-reversals-accelerating-resegregation-and-the-need-for-new-integration -strategies-1/orfield-historic-reversals-accelerating.pdf; Gloria Ladson-Billings, "Pushing Past the Achievement Gap: An Essay on the Language of Deficit," *Journal of Negro Education* 76, no. 3 (2007): 316–23; Prudence L. Carter and Kevin G. Welner, eds., *Closing the Opportunity Gap: What America Must Do to Give Every Child an Even Chance*

(New York: Oxford University Press, 2013); Linda Darling-Hammond, "Evaluating 'No Child Left Behind': The Problems and Promises of Bush's Educational Policy," *Nation*, May 21, 2007; Diane Ravitch, *The Death and Life of the Great American School System: How Testing and Choice Are Undermining Education* (New York: Basic Books, 2010); Gloria Ladson-Billings, Deborah Meier, and George Woods eds., *Many Children Left Behind: How the No Child Left Behind Act Is Damaging Our Children and Our Schools* (Boston: Beacon Press, 2004); Michael Fabricant and Michelle Fine, *Charter Schools and the Corporate Makeover of Public Education: What's at Stake?* (New York: Teachers College Press, 2012); Jonathan Kozol, *Shame of the Nation: The Restoration of Apartheid Schooling in America* (New York: Random House, 2005); Daniel J. Losen and Jonathan Gillespie, "Opportunities Suspended: The Disparate Impact of Disciplinary Exclusion from School," Civil Rights Project/Proyecto Derechos Civiles, University of California, Los Angeles, August 12, 2012, http://civilrightsproject.ucla.edu/resources/projects/center-for-civil-rights-remedies/school-to-prison-folder/federal-reports/upcoming-ccrr-research; and "The School to Prison Pipeline," special issue, *Teaching Tolerance* 43 (2013), http://www.tolerance.org/magazine/number-43-spring-2013/school-to-prison.

3. Julian Bond, *Teaching the Movement: The State of Civil Rights Education in the United States 2011* (Montgomery, Ala.: Southern Poverty Law Center, 2011), 5, http://www.tolerance.org/sites/default/files/general/Teaching_the_Movement.pdf.

4. The story of Claudette Colvin, the high school student who was the first to resist bus segregation in Montgomery, Alabama, reflects the same pattern of failing to educate our youth about the role of young people in the movement. Colvin, a fifteen-year-old student at Booker T. Washington High School in Montgomery, Alabama, refused to move from her bus seat on March 2, 1955, nine months before Rosa Parks did. Police arrested, harassed, and jailed Colvin, who clearly and publically violated city segregation ordinances. This started a series of events that led to the Montgomery Bus Boycott, yet her role is largely overlooked. On Colvin, see Claudette Colvin, "The Other Rosa Parks," interview with Amy Goodman and Juan Gonzalez, *Democracy Now!*, National Public Radio, March 29, 2013; Philip Hoose, *Claudette Colvin: Twice Toward Justice* (New York: Farrar, Straus and Giroux, 2009); Clayborne Carson, "To Walk in Dignity: The Montgomery Bus Boycott," *OAH Magazine of History* 19 (2005): 14; and Jeanne Theoharis, *The Rebellious Life of Rosa Parks* (Boston: Beacon Press, 2013).

5. Richard S. Newman, *Freedom's Prophet: Bishop Richard Allen, the AME Church, and the Black Founding Fathers* (New York: New York University Press, 2008); Edward A. Pearson, ed., *Designs Against Charleston: The Trial Record of the Denmark Vesey Slave Conspiracy of 1822* (Chapel Hill: University of North Carolina Press, 1999); David Robertson, *Denmark Vesey* (New York: Vintage, 1999).

6. Edmund L. Drago, *Initiative, Paternalism, and Race Relations: Charleston's Avery Normal Institute* (Athens: University of Georgia Press, 1990). See also Avery Research Center, College of Charleston, http://avery.cofc.edu.

INDEX

Numbers in italics refer to pages on which illustrations appear.

Abernathy, Ralph, 87, 200
abolitionist movement, 21, 114. *See also* slavery
academic freedom, 146
academic success, 198, 211, 223, 226
achievement gap, 227
Adams, Jane, 103–4
Adickes, Sandra: antiwar activity of, 185, 212; background of, 88; Freedom School experience of, 9, 11, 96, 125, 131–32, 139
Adopt a Freedom School (program), 88, 174–75
AFL-CIO (American Federation of Labor and Congress of Industrial Organizations), 205
Alexander v. Holmes County Board of Education (1969), 200, 218
Aley, Margaret, 103
Algebra Project, 16, 220–23, *222*, 225
Allen, Chude (Pamela Parker), *86*; background of, 85–87, 90; career of, 282n.50; Freedom School experience of, 113–14, 128, 143, 175, 183–84; on interracial relationships, 140, 266n.94; women's liberation movement activity of, 215–16
Allen, Jo, 119
Allen, Robert, 215, 249n.97, 282n.50

Alston, Melvin, 26
Alston v. City School Board of City of Norfolk (1940), 27
American Federation of Teachers (AFT), 87–88, 174, 255n.52
American Friends Service Committee, 216
American Prospect (magazine), 215
Amite County, Mississippi, 162, 166
Anderson, Eddie, 116
Anderson, Helen, 188
Anderson, James D., 3
Andrews, Kenneth, 252n.26
Anniston, Alabama, 43
antiliteracy laws, 21
Antioch Baptist Church, burning of, 176
Antioch College (Ohio), 83, 103
antiwar movement, 9, 15, 183, 185, 205, 212. *See also* Vietnam War
arrest and incarceration of youth, 44, 46, 53, 57, 131–34, 165, 223. *See also* student activism
Asch, Chris Myers, 10

Baker, Ella, 52, 92
Baldwin, James, 114–15
Balkin, Jack, 29

Bardonille, Harold, 253n.31
Bates, Gladys Noel, 27, 31–32
beauty parlors and barber shops, 48–49, 98. *See also* employment; safe meeting places
Becker, Norma, 88, 185, 212
Beittel, Adam, 41
Belafonte, Harry, 172
Belfrage, Sally, 9
Benton County, Mississippi, school boycott in, 61–62, 165–66, 176
Benton County Citizens' Club, 165
Berea College (Kentucky), 258n.102
Berkeley Free Speech Movement, 182–83
Bilbo, Theodore, 246n.52
Black, Aline, 26
black brain drain, 95–96. *See also* Great Migration
black cooperatives, 2, 51. *See also* black land ownership
black cultural autonomy, 172
black education: accomplishments of, 91; funding of and legislation on, in Mississippi, 3, 19, 23–25, 27, 30, 91; and history of self-determination, 236n.18; purpose and scope of, 25–26, 146, 273n.59; vocational v. liberal arts debate about, 25, 75, 145, 236n.17. *See also* education; Freedom Schools; historically black colleges and universities; schools, desegregation of
black educators: education of, for freedom concept, 32; firings and unemployment of, 31–32, 62, 163, 240n.47; pay equalization for, 27, 30, 162–63; and pedagogies of protest, 26, 181; role of, in civil rights movement, 28, 33, 239n.45
black elected officials, 23
black history, 14, 92–93, 113–14, 123, 181, 210, 227
black journalism, 203–5
black land ownership, 2–3, 50–51, 66
black literature and culture, 71, 94, 113–17
#BlackLivesMatter, 228
black nationalism, 172. *See also* black power movement
Black Panther (newspaper), 180

Black Panther Liberation Schools, 15, 153, 179–81, 273n.59, 275n.82
Black Panther Party, 152–53, 179–80, 213
black power movement: and black students, 9, 273n.56; and civil rights movement, 249n.97, 268n.6; historiography of, 153, 268n.6, 272n.47; political development of, 166–73; and SNCC, 152–53; views of, on education, 179–80, 273n.59
black press, 62
Black Studies, 169–71, 181
Bolivar Improvement Association, 163
Bond, Julian, 225, 227
Borinski, Ernst, 41
Boston, school boycott in, 257n.79
Boston Freedom Schools, 35, 92, 94, 176, 241n.59
boycotts: of black businesses, 31; and desegregation of public spaces, 83; and Freedom School students, 2, 5, 71, 131, 148, 195; in Jackson, 38, 42, 46; in Mississippi high schools, 15–16, 54, 146, 150, 163–66, 176, 271n.37; in northern schools, 35, 165, 176–77, 241n.59, 257n.79
Branch, Taylor, 225
Brandeis Afro-American Organization (Brandeis University), 169–70
Brandeis High School (New York City), 168
Brandeis University (Massachusetts), 125, 169–70
Breakaway School (San Francisco), 215
Brinkley High School (Jackson), 45–46
Brooks, Owen, 187
Brown, John, 114
Brown, Joyce, 135–36, 144–45
Brown, Millicent, 270n.17
Brown v. Board of Education (1954), 8, 20, 28–51, 155, 218, 223, 238n.24, 240n.47
Brown v. Board of Education (1955), 31
Bryant, C. C., 52–53, 246n.51
Bryant, Roy, 8
Burger, Warren, 205
Burgland High School (McComb), 52, 221–22, 246n.57
Burnside v. Byars (1966), 164
busing, 218

Campbell, James, 179

Campbell College (Jackson), 42, 55–56

campus ministries, 80

canvassing, 96, 120–22, 132–34, 150, 188, 201

Carleton College (Minnesota), 85

Carmichael, Stokely, 152–53, 167, 178, 182, 273n.59

Carson, Clayborne, 10

Carter, David, 278n.122

Carter, Eloise, 54–55

Carthan, Eddie James: background of, 50; Freedom School experience of, 1, 4, 98, 118, *130*, 136–37; political activity and career of, 132–34, 159–60, 201–3, *202*, 206

Casin, Hilda, 135, 246n.52

CBS News, 102

Central High School (Liberty), 162

Chaffe, Lois, 92, 273n.62

Chaney, Ben, 37–39, 64, 157

Chaney, James, 64, 70, 104–5, 109, 135–36, 144

Charleston Freedom Schools (South Carolina), 228

charter schools, 227

Chicago Defender (newspaper), 62

Chicago Freedom Schools, 35, 176, 220

Chilcoat, George, 11

Children's Defense Fund (CDF), 16, 219, 226

Children's Development Group of Mississippi (CDGM), 192, 278n.117

churches: burnings of, 40, 105, 135, 176; as safe meeting places, 39, 49, 98, 113, 188. *See also* religion

Citizens' Councils, 30–31, 43, 47, 58, 238n.36

citizenship education, 71, 92, 94, 109, 117

Citizenship Schools, 34, 48, 92, 240n.55

Citizens' League (Holly Springs), 61–62

civil disobedience, 41, 53

Civil Rights Act (1964), 71, 131, 152, 159, 161, 186, 217. *See also* federal education policy

Civil Rights Cases (1883), 236n.14

civil rights education, 39, 68, 109–10, 127, 146, 176, 191–92, 198

civil rights movement: and black power movement, 167, 268n.6; and conservatism, 153; and education, 4, 7, 16–17, 163, 195, 199; and federal legislation, 186; history

of, 2, 71, 129, 221–22, 224–27, 245n.31, 251n.4; leadership training in, 14, 94–95, 120–22; local and national movement interplay, 2, 38–39, 49, 51, 153, 185–86; and segregationist reprisals and firings, 27, 31, 47, 63, 134; theater and drama in, 115–16, 162, 174, 274n.66; whites in, 14–15, 75, 81, 110, 137, 142, 144; women in, 77–79, 181–82, 216–17, 243n.15, 252n.27, 266n.95. *See also* Freedom Schools; Mississippi Freedom Summer; schools, desegregation of; student activism; violence; voting rights

Civil War, 1, 20, 22–23, 114, 140

Clarion-Ledger (Jackson), 44

Clark, Gloria Xifaras, 88, 137, *138*, 175, 213–14

Clark, Septima, 92

Clarksdale, Mississippi, 47–51

Clarksdale Freedom School, 11, *99*

class, 32, 66, 68, 70–71, 77, 126, 189, 192–93, 212

Cleveland Freedom Schools (Mississippi), 132

Coahoma Agricultural High School (Clarksdale), 236n.17

Coahoma County Federated Council of Organizations (CCFCO), 48

Coahoma County Negro Citizens Association, 48

Coahoma County Progressive Voters League, 48

Cobb, Charles, 5, 68, 71–73, 93–95, 172–73, 176–77, 225

Coffin, William S., 75

colleges and universities: historically black, 33, 40–42, 46–47, 60–61, 98, 239n.46; recruitment for Freedom School volunteers at, 75, 80, 92; as safe meeting places, 98, 113; as sites of protest, 7, 46, 171. *See also individual colleges and universities*

Collier, Jo Etha, 200, 218

Colom, Wilbur, 61–62, 66, 115, 120, 160, 168–69, 171, 175–76, 205–6

Columbia University (New York), 7, 169, 171

Colvin, Claudette, 285n.4

common school model, 23

community centers, 35, 188

community control of schools, 179, 209, 280n.22

community organizing: and careers of
volunteers, 5, 16, 183, 197–98, 203, 208,
217; and education for freedom, 13, 34,
72; and Freedom Schools, 38–39, 77, 92,
102, 128–29, 131–34, 165–66, 221; and
permanent outreach projects, 77, 92, 102,
137–39
Compromise of 1877, 24
Congress of Racial Equality (CORE), 7, 58,
64, 69, 89, 105, 112–13, 193
conservative and neoconservative politics, 191,
218–19
Coopwood, Sam, 130–31
Cotton, Willie Mae, 135
Council of Federated Organizations (COFO),
69–76, 94, 96, 112, 135–36, 155, 174, 177–78
Counts, George, 26
critical pedagogy, 198, 211–12, 219. *See also*
pedagogy
critical thinking: and academic success, 26, 218,
223; and Freedom Schools, 14, 92, 94, 117,
136, 159, 168, 183, 223; and humanities-
based curriculum, 109–10
Cronkite, Walter, 102
Crosby, Emilye, 10
Crossroads at Clarksdale (Hamlin), 245n.31,
245n.33
Cultural and Activist Agitation Committee
(Jackson), 42
Cunningham, Charles J., 26
Curry, Constance, 10

Dahmer, Vernon, 58–59
Darden, C. R., 63
data-driven teaching strategies, 223
Day, Noel, 35, 92, 257n.79
Dayton, Cornelia H., 266n.97
DeBerry, Roy, 115, 160, 169–70
Debs, Eugene V., 89
De La Beckwith, Byron, 43
Delta Ministry (National Council of
Churches), 156, 187, 271n.37
Democratic Party: and black voter registration,
73–74, 132; and discussion in Freedom
Schools, 123; and Mississippi Freedom
Democratic Party, 268n.2; National

Convention of (1964), 151, 173, 193, 205,
268n.2
Dennis, Dave, 16, 74–75, 144–45, 220, 225–26
Derby, Doris, 115–16
de Sousa, Ronnie, *85*
Detroit, unrest in, 152
Detroit Freedom Schools Project, 174
Dewey, John, 26
Diamond, Dion, 55
Dittmer, John, 10, 28, 177
"Does the Negro Need Separate Schools?"
(Du Bois), 273n.59
Donaldson, Ivanhoe, 88
double taxation, 24
Douglass, Frederick, 21–22, 115, 179, 210
Dream Defenders, 225
Du Bois, W. E. B., 23–25, 236n.17, 273n.59

economic status of blacks: debt accumulation
and protracted servitude, 50–51; and
federal programs, 15, 50, 153, 186–94,
201, 213, 276n.96; and independent
employment, 34, 40, 50, 66; and literacy
and education, 3, 26, 145, 214, 220–21, 223;
in Mississippi, 1, 19; in rural areas, 47, 57,
142. *See also* poverty
Edelman, Marian Wright, 219, 225
education: adult, 11, 145; alternative, 56; black
educators' role in, 26, 28, 32–33, 181,
239n.45; and black liberation, 19, 26, 33–34,
75, 145, 150, 153, 211–12, 223, 226, 234n.1,
236n.17; and *Brown* decision, 28–29; in
citizenship, 71, 92, 94, 109, 117; and civil
rights, 8–10, 12–13, 16–17, 20, 220–21,
226; early childhood, 8, 15, 186–94, 214;
federal policy on, 3, 8, 155–57, 186–94,
197, 213, 217–19, 226, 276n.96, 278n.117;
of freedmen, 23, 34, 235n.8, 251n.12; for
freedom concept, 19–23, 109, 111, 122–23,
179; in Liberation Schools, 15, 153, 179–81,
273n.59, 275n.82; and literacy, 19–23,
220–21, 223; in Mississippi, 4–5, 27, 30,
91, 235n.8, 236n.18; multicultural, 211,
281n.32; in Progressive era, 26, 237n.20;
public system of, 3, 23–24, 145–46, 186,
211, 218, 227; reform of, 157, 194, 198–99,

226–28; and segregated schools, 16, 19, 25, 35, 217–18; sex, 222, 261n.8; special, 145, 210; vocational, 25, 75, 145, 236n.17. *See also* Civil Rights Act; Freedom Schools; schools, desegregation of

Edwards, Don and Len, 143–44

Eisenhower, Dwight, 63

elementary, middle, and high school students: and Black Panther Party, 180; and civil rights movement, 2, 5–6, 12; expulsion from school of, for political activity, 35, 54–55, 64, 162–64, 169–70, 206; in Freedom Schools, 5, 7, 15, 65, 95, 109, 122–23. *See also* student activism

Elementary and Secondary Education Act (ESEA, 1965), 186, 197, 217–19. *See also* federal education policy

Ella Baker Child Policy Training Institute, 219

Emmanuel AME Church (Charleston), 228–29

employment: of black educators, 31–32, 62, 163, 240n.47; and civil rights activity retaliation, 27, 31, 34, 62, 119, 157; and gender roles, 181; and Great Migration, 95–96; and independence from whites, 47–49, 58, 66, 98, 157; and urban unemployment, 206

enslaved communities, 19–20, 111. *See also* slavery

environmental justice, 226

Esquire (magazine), 84

Eubanks, Thelma, 114

Evans, Earnestine, 61, 274n.66

Evers, Medgar, 38, 42–43, 61, 63, 67, 116, 174, 206–7

Eyes on the Prize (television documentary), 10

Fairclough, Adam, 28

Falconer, Emridge, 119

Falk, Gail, *114*, 260n.7

family, 56, 58, 62–63, 65, 134

Farm Security Administration, 50

Fast, Howard, 114

Federal Bureau of Investigation (FBI), 70–71, 143–44, 267n.107

federal education policy: Civil Rights Act, 131, 152, 159, 161, 186, 217; Elementary and

Secondary Education Act, 186, 197, 217–19; Head Start, 8, 15, 153, 186–94, 197, 213, 276n.96, 278n.117; No Child Left Behind Act, 226; and school desegregation, 155–57

Fifth Avenue Peace Parade Committee, 212

Fire Next Time, The (Baldwin), 114–15

First Children (oral-history project), 270n.17

Florida, 20–21

Flynn, Deborah, 174, 274n.66

Fondren, Elnora, 159

Forman, James, 75, 152

Forrest County, Mississippi, 57–59

Forrest County Voters League, 59

42 (film), 10

Foster, W. B., 165

Freedmen's Bureau, 23

Freedom Ballot Campaign, 73

Freedom Day (Cleveland, Mississippi), 132

Freedom Day (Hattiesburg), 59, 155

Freedom Houses, 5, 61, 98, 111–12

Freedom News (Holly Springs Freedom School), 130–31

Freedom of Choice in the United States (FOCUS), 218

"freedom of choice" plans, 155–56, 218, 226

Freedom Registration, 122

Freedom Rides: attacks on, 43–44; college students in, 7, 80; and desegregation of interstate transportation, 43, 53; impact of, on civil rights movement, 13, 37, 44, 53, 66, 112, 188

Freedom Schools: careers of volunteers in, 196–211; civil rights education in, 108–9, 146, 220; and community organizing, 38–39, 77, 92, 102, 128–29, 131–34, 165–66, 221; and contemporary education, 197–98, 220, 223, 226–27; curriculum of, 5, 71–72, 92–97, 109–10, 113, 117–18, 122–23, 261n.8; and direct-action nonviolent protest, 49, 51–55, 61, 86, 160–61, 175–76; educational goals of, 4, 72, 113, 173–74, 190; and educational reform, 16, 172, 194; enrollment in, 111–14, 147, 260nn.6–7, 273n.62; fiftieth anniversary conference celebrating, 224–27; financial, legal, and political resources of, 69–70, 88, 142–43, 174–75;

Freedom Schools (*continued*)
  gender roles in, 11, 78, 182; interracial
  dialogue in, 71, 136–44; leadership training
  in, 14, 94–95, 109–10, 120–26, 195; locations
  of, 6, 11, 64, 97–98, 113; marginalization of,
  219, 227–28; origin of, 34–35, 56, 176–77,
  219–20, 241n.59; pedagogy of, 9, 11, 71–72,
  128–29, 136, 195, 206, 228, 257n.78; political
  socialization in, 62, 65, 117, 123–24, 129,
  206; professional teacher volunteers in,
  87–88, 125–26, 183, 185; role of, in civil
  rights movement, 153, 177, 197, 229; status
  of, in Mississippi Freedom Summer, 69, 74,
  78, 147–48; student newspapers in, 119–20,
  129–31; and student political activism,
  39, 96–97, 147, 150–51, 156, 165; student
  recruitment for, 66, 111–12, 124–25; teacher
  autonomy and relationships in, 35–36,
  90–91, 97, 124–28; teacher orientation
  and training for, 79–80, 93, 97, 101–7, 211,
  258n.102; and teacher political activism,
  110, 150, 156, 182–85, 208; and teacher racial
  attitudes, 80, 86, 103–4, 124–26; teacher
  recruitment for, 9, 34, 88–90, 96, 261n.8;
  threat of violence against, 105, 138; white
  volunteers in, 14, 36, 59–60, 69–70, 73–77,
  177, 250n.2, 252n.22, 267n.107
Freedom Schools Curriculum Conference,
  92–94, 256n.71
Freedom Schools Student Conference, 144–46,
  155, 158, 161
Freedom Schools Teachers Manual, 97
Freedom's Journal (McComb Freedom School),
  129
Freedom's Journal (Meridian Freedom School),
  120
Freedom Star (Meridian Freedom School), 129
Freedom Summer (film), 10, 225
Freedom Train (Benton Freedom School), 129
Freedom Vote (registration campaign), 49,
  73, 75
Freedom Writers (film), 10
Free Southern Theater, 115–16, 175
Free Space (Allen), 215
free speech, 164, 182–83
Free Speech Movement (Berkeley), 182–83

Free University of New Bedford
  (Massachusetts), 214
Freire, Paulo, 211, 220
Friends of SNCC, 80, 213
Friends of the Mississippi Summer Project
  (Oxford, Ohio), 142–43
Fusco, Liz: background of, 87, 90; Freedom
  School experience of, 9, 122, 148,
  177–78, 273n.62; political activity of,
  91, 154, 173–74; teaching career of, 126,
  208–9, 211
Futorian, Aviva, 125, 169

Gaines v. Canada (1938), 27
Gaston, A. G., 60
Gaston, Hattye, 187
Gavin, Joanne, 87, 260n.7
gender roles, 71, 78–79, 140, 181–82, 215,
  252n.27. *See also* sexuality; women
Gibbs, Phillip Lafayette, 199, 270n.23
Goldwater, Barry, 191
Goodman, Andrew, 71, *101*, 104–5, 109,
  135–36
grassroots organizing, 2, 10, 14, 153, 187, 197
Gray, Victoria, 59, 188
Great Migration, 95–96, 257n.86
Great Society (legislation), 153, 186, 213, 217
Green, James Earl, 199
*Green v. County School Board of New Kent
  County* (1968), 218
Greenwood Freedom School, 121–22
Gregory, Dick, 48
Greyhound, sit-ins at terminal of, 43, 53
Griffin, Ida Ruth, 187
Gronemeier, Dale, 142–43
Guardian (newspaper), 87, 143, 216
Guyot, Lawrence, 72, 75

Hall, G. Stanley, 5
Hamer, Fannie Lou, 75, 172, 176, 179, 200
Hamlin, Françoise N., 10, 245n.31, 245n.33
Hampton Normal and Industrial Institute
  (Virginia), 25
harambee, 226
Harlem, 35, 169
Harlem Freedom School (New York), 35

Index

Harper's Weekly (magazine), 143

Harring, Bossie Mae, 108–9

Harrington, Michael, 276n.96

Harris, Anthony: career of, 201, 206; Freedom School experience of, 116, 120, *121*, 139, 141; political activity of, 57–58, 133

Harris, Daisy, 58

Harvard University (Massachusetts), 75, 80

Hattiesburg, Mississippi, 57–59, 131–32

Hattiesburg Freedom School, 11, 112–13, 127, *128*, 149

Haven Methodist Church (Clarksdale), 49, 98

Hayden, Casey, 181–82, 215–16

Hayes, Curtis, 53, 56, 58–59, 135

Hayes, Rutherford B., 24

Headrick, Rita, 118–19

Head Start, 8, 15, 153, 186–94, 197, 213, 276n.96, 278n.117. *See also* federal education policy

health care, 189, 226

Hendrick, Jim, 189

Henry, Aaron, 47–49, 51, 59–60, 73, 98, 200, 245n.33

Herenton, Willie, 204

Higgins, C. D., 246n.57

Higgins, Walter A., 32–33

Highlander Folk School (Monteagle, Tennessee), 34, 92, 240n.55, 257n.78

High School Coalition Against the War in Vietnam, 168–69

high school students: political activism of, 55–56, 72, 155–57, 162, 166, 168–69, 205–6, 221; school protests and walkouts by, 32, 45–46, 51, 54–56, 63, 157, 159, 165, 170, 200

Hill, Homer: background of, in civil rights movement, 19, 32–33, 37–39, 46–67; Freedom School experience of, 4, 98, 114–15, 118, 158, 196–97; on interracial dialogue, 108, 136

Hillegas, Jan, 178–79

historically black colleges and universities, 33, 40–42, 46–47, 60–61, 98, 239n.46. *See also* colleges and universities; *individual colleges and universities*

historiography: of black power movement, 268n.6, 272n.47; of civil rights movement,

7, 151; of interracial dialogue, 250n.2; of Mississippi Freedom Summer, 11, 16–17, 70; oral history, 142, 269n.16, 270n.17; women's history, 266n.97

Hogan, Joe, 205

Holly Springs Freedom School, 11, 60, 174–76

Holmes County, Mississippi, 1

Holt, John, 213

Horton, Myles, 34, 92, 273n.62

"House of Liberty, The" (Brown), 135

Houston, Charles Hamilton, 26

Howard University (Washington, D.C.), 16, 26, 72, 169, 205

Howard Zinn Education Project, 284n.63. *See also* Zinn, Howard

Howe, Florence, 9, 156, 260n.7

Hoyt, Phyllis, 102

Hughes, Langston, 115

Hurst, E. H., 54

Illinois State University, 143

immigration, 226

imperialism, 172

Indianola, Mississippi, school boycott in, 164–65, 271n.39

integration: of colleges and public places, 7, 42, 243n.10; and quality education debate, 4, 110, 152, 158, 180; and school desegregation, 28–29, 142; and school resegregation, 15–16, 211, 227; and whites in civil rights movement, 14–15, 75, 110, 137, 142, 144

interracial dialogue, 14, 71, 110–11, 136–44, 177, 206, 250n.2

interracial marriage and relationships, 140–41, 266n.94, 266n.97. *See also* sexuality

Interstate Commerce Commission, 43

interstate transportation, 43, 53. *See also* Freedom Rides; Greyhound, sit-ins at terminal of

"Islamic Law of Personal Status and Its Contemporary Impact on Women in Jordan" (Simmons), 216

Issaquena-Sharkey Counties, Mississippi, boycott in, 164–65, 176, 271n.37

Jackson, Denis, 133

Jackson, Mississippi: black colleges in, 55–56, 60, 73, 98; civil rights activity in, 31–32, 40–47, 51, 56, 63, 65–66, 161–62, 166–67; and Freedom Rides, 38, 53; and Freedom Schools, 11, 106–7, 229, 260n.7; school desegregation in, 155–57, 218

Jackson Freedom School, 11, 260n.7

Jackson State College, 41–42, 199–200, 270n.23, 278n.2

Jet (magazine), 52

Jim Crow: and education, 12–13, 62; and interracial relationships, 141; legal challenges to, 27; in Mississippi, 3, 5, 7, 10, 25, 50–51, 57, 66, 142; and public schools, 162, 273n.59; and voter registration, 126–27

Jim Hill High School (Jackson), 45–46

Job Corps, 213

jobs. *See* employment

Johnson, Derrick, 225

Johnson, Laura, 187–88

Johnson, Lyndon B., 15, 73, 186, 213, 217, 268n.2; administration of, 192, 194, 278n.122

Jones, Roscoe, 63–65, *100*, 144–45, 149, 155, 158, 163–64

Joseph, Peniel, 153, 268n.6

journalism, 197, 203, 208, 214–15

Justice Department, 53, 58, 76

Kennard, Clyde, 57–58

Kennedy, Robert, 123

Kent State University (Ohio), shootings at, 199, 278n.2

King, Ed, 73

King, Martin Luther, Jr., 46, 153, 167, 182, 206–7, 211, 227, 245n.36

King, Mary, 181–82, 215–16

Klopfer, Donald, 279n.10

kneel-ins, 42, 49. *See also* churches

Ku Klux Klan (KKK), 43, 105, 178

labor movement, 35, 88–89, 174, 205, 208, 212–13, 245n.36

Ladner, Joyce, 41

Lanier High School (Jackson), 45–46

Lee, Herbert, 54–55, 116

Levenstein, Lisa, 266n.97

Levin, Tom, 278n.117

Levy, Betty Bollinger, 84, *85*, 89, *100*, 185, 280n.22

Levy, Mark: background of, 83–85; career and political activism of, 185, 212–13, 280n.22; Freedom Schools experience of, *85*, 99, *100*, 102, 111, 113, 117, 183, 260n.7

Lewis, Joe, 54

Lewis, John, 8, 73, 75, 152, 172

Lewis, Oscar, 278n.122

Liberation Schools (Black Panther Party), 15, 153, 179–81, 273n.59, 275n.82

liberation theology, 228–29

Liberty, Mississippi, 53

Life (magazine), 102

Ligon, Jerry, 11

literacy, 19–23, 115, 220–21; tests of, 25, 53. *See also* education

Little Rock High School, Arkansas, desegregation of, 63

Los Angeles, 152

Loving v. Virginia (1967), 141

Lowenstein, Allard, 73, 75

Lowndes County, Alabama, 167, 282n.47

Lowndes County Freedom Organization, 282n.47

Lucifer (newspaper), 89

Lynch, John Roy, 23, 235n.8

Lynd, Alice, 87

Lynd, Staughton: and Freedom School activism, 127, 136, 146, 173; and Freedom School administration, 86–87, 99, 112–13, 147; and Freedom School educational goals, 9, 78–80, 97, 117, 253n.31; and Vietnam War and black power movements, 168

Lynd, Theron, 58

Malcolm X, 123, 172, 179

March Against Fear, 167

Marshall, Thurgood, 26–28, 205

Marshall County, Mississippi, 60–61, 175–76

Martin, Larry, 112

Martin, Trayvon, 204–5

masculinity, 252n.27. *See also* gender roles

Index

Masonic Temples, 27, 44, 55

mathematics and science, literacy in, 220–21, 223. *See also* education

May-Pittman, Ineva, 32

McAdam, Doug, 10, 78, 89, 102

McComb, Mississippi, 34–35, 52–56, 64, 161–62, 166, 182, 246n.50, 247n.62. *See also* Burgland High School

McComb Freedom School, 11, 135–36, 141

McDew, Charles (Chuck), 55–56, 225

McEvans High School (Bolivar County), 163

McLaurin v. Oklahoma (1950), 27

McMillen, Neil, 10

McRee, James F., 189

Medical Committee for Human Rights, 69

Memphis, Tennessee, 245n.36

Memphis Magazine, 204

Meredith, James, 38, 167, 200

Meridian, Mississippi, 63–64, 99

Meridian Baptist Seminary, 99

Meridian Freedom School, 99–100, 105, 112–13, *114*, 115, *115*, 117–20, 123, 260n.7

Miami University of Ohio, 224

middle class, 66, 70, 77, 193. *See also* class

Mid-South Tribune (Memphis), 203

Milam, J. W., 8

Mileston, Mississippi, 1, 50–51, 98, *100*

Mileston Freedom School, *100*, 118, *130*, 132, 136

military–industrial complex, 169

military service, 168, 170–71, 185, 206

Millsaps College (Jackson), 42, 243n.10

Minnis, Jack, 215, 282n.47

miscegenation laws, 141, 266n.94, 266n.97. *See also* interracial marriage and relationships

Missionary Union Baptist Church (Jackson), 40

Mississippi: legislature of, 29–30, 158, 192, 235n.8, 238n.36, 270n.18; neoconservative politics in, 191; poverty and living conditions in, 3, 49–51, 142; public schools in, 5, 15, 23–24, 125, 146, 155–58, 160–66; school desegregation in, 30, 151, 155–58, 218; statewide student movement in, 15, 51–56, 111, 150–51, 154–56, 161, 163–66

Mississippi Action for Progress, 193

Mississippi Burning (film), 10, 70

Mississippi Council on Human Relations, 41, 156

Mississippi Freedom Democratic Party (MFDP): and Mississippi Freedom Summer voter registration drive, 69, 73, 110, 123, 132, 197, 268n.2; protest of, at Democratic National Convention, 151, 173, 268n.2; and school desegregation in Jackson, 156; youth platform of, 145

Mississippi Freedom Summer: components of, 2, 78; fiftieth anniversary conference celebrating, 224–27; fund-raising for, 142–43; and gender roles and sexuality, 78–79, 140–41; local staff and leadership of, 104; and Mississippi Freedom Democratic Party, 69, 73, 110, 123, 132, 197, 268n.2; and NAACP, 63, 69, 73–74, 103, 112–13, 166, 225; and SCLC, 69; segregationist threats against, 101, *104*, 138–39; and SNCC, 5, 60, 69–76, 80–88, 96, 112–13, 137, 152, 256n.71; strategic importance of, 14, 38, 70–71, 122, 154, 182, 220; volunteer training and recruitment for, 74–75, 77, 80–90, *101*, 101–7; and voter registration drive, 14, 38, 57, 61, 69–74, 94, 121–22, 146, 159, 220; white volunteers in, 70–71, 74, 77

Mississippi Legal Education Advisory Committee, 29

Mississippi Plan, 24

Mississippi Southern College (University of Southern Mississippi), 57

Mississippi Student Union (MSU), 15, 111, 150–51, 154–56, 161, 163–65

Mississippi Teachers Association, 27

Mississippi University for Women, 203, 205–6

Mississippi University for Women v. Hogan (1982), 205–6

Mitchell, Arelya: background of, 60–62; Freedom Schools experience of, 4, 98, 137; journalism career of, 130–31, 203–6, *204*, 214, 279n.10

Mitchell, W. B., 60, 188

Mobilization for Survival, 212

mock elections, 73

Montgomery, Alabama, 186, 285n.4

Index

Montgomery Bus Boycott, 227, 285n.4
Moore, Amzie, 52–53
Moore, Edith Marie, 119–20
Morris, Aldon, 41
Moses, Bob: and black power movement, 168, 172–73, 179; and Children's Defense Fund, 16; and direct-action protest, 52–53, 55–56; on education, 220–21, 226, 273n.59; and Freedom Schools, 73–76, 88, 92–93, 225
Moses, Gilbert, 116
Moss Point Freedom School, 118–19
Moynihan Report ("The Negro Family: The Case for National Action," Daniel Patrick Moynihan), 91, 194, 278n.122
Mt. Zion Freedom School, 133
Murrah High School (Jackson), 157, 200, 269n.16, 279n.6
music and dancing, 83, 113, 118, 123, 171

National Association for the Advancement of Colored People (NAACP): and Head Start, 194; legal challenges of, to segregation, 26–28, 30–31, 91; in Mississippi Freedom Summer, 63, 69, 73–74, 103, 112–13, 166, 225; retaliation against members of, 62; strength of, in Mississippi, 2, 39, 42–43, 46, 59–64, 243n.12; and youth activism, 48–49, 51–54, 58, 61, 159, 166, 213, 225; Youth Councils of, 43, 48–49, 61, 63, 159, 213, 243n.14
National Council of Churches (NCC), 69, 92, 156, 187, 271n.37
National Council of Negro Women, 216
National Student Association, 85
National Tenants Association, 205
National Welfare Rights Organization, 205
Nelson, Stanley, 225
neoconservatism, 191, 218
Newark, New Jersey, 152
New Deal, 2, 50
New Jerusalem Church (Mileston), 100
New Jerusalem Church (Tchula), 98
New Right, 187, 191, 195
Newsweek (magazine), 106
New York City, schools in, 35, 176, 179, 209, 280n.22

New York City Board of Education, 179
New York Freedom Schools, 35, 176
New York Radical Women, 215
No Child Left Behind Act (2001), 226. See also federal education policy
nonviolence, 7, 66, 103, 120–21, 131, 151, 153
Nonviolent High (Mississippi), 34–35, 55–56
Northern Mississippi Voters' League, 60
Norvell, Aubrey James, 167
"Notes on Teaching in Mississippi" (Mississippi Freedom Schools), 97
"Now Is the Hour" (Moore), 119–20
nuclear arms, protest against, 212

Obama, Barack, 204
Oberlin College (Ohio), 80, 176
O'Brien, Frances, 82, 82–83, 89, 209–11
Ocean Hill–Brownsville, teachers' strike in, 179, 209, 280n.22
Office of Economic Opportunity, 192, 278n.117
Old Salem Attendance Center, 165
Old Salem School (Benton County), 62
O'Neal, John, 79, 88, 115–16
O'Neal, S. Bernard, 246n.52
One Voice, 225
oral history, 142, 269n.16, 270n.17. See also historiography
Orangeburg Massacre (South Carolina), 152
Organization of African Unity, 179
Organization of Afro-American Unity (OAAU), 179
Other America, The (Harrington), 276n.96
Oxford, Mississippi, 38
Oxford, Ohio, 101, 103, 142, 224

Pachella, Diane, 118
Pacific Lutheran University (Washington), 83
Parchman Farm (Mississippi State Penitentiary), 44, 46, 57
Parks, Rosa, 227, 285n.4
Parks, Wesley, 200
participatory democracy, 128–29
Pascoe, Peggy, 266n.97
Patterson, James, 29
Patterson, Shirley Porter, 100
Paulo Freire Freedom Schools (Tucson), 220

Payne, Charles, 10, 139–40

Peacock, Willie, 61

Pease, H. R., 235n.8

pedagogy: critical, 198, 211–12, 219–20; of Freedom Schools, 9, 11, 71–72, 128–29, 136, 183, 195, 206, 228, 257n.78; and Head Start, 187, 194; and protest, 14–15, 34, 71, 109–10, 122–25, 180–81, 275n.82; traditional, 263n.40

Pedagogy of the Oppressed (Freire), 211

Perlstein, Daniel, 10, 273n.59, 275n.82

Philadelphia, Mississippi, 105, 164

Philadelphia Freedom Schools (Pennsylvania), 220

Pigee, Vera Mae, 48–49, 51, 59–60, 98, 159, 243n.15

Plessy v. Ferguson (1896), 25–28

poetry, 119–20, 279n.10

police brutality, 42, 165

political socialization, 38, 62, 117, 123–24, 129–31, 137, 190, 206

Polk, Jo Lynn, 119

poll taxes, 24–25, 235n.12, 246n.52

Porter, Richard, *100*

positivist-oriented measurement, 198

poverty, 8, 15, 186–94, 213, 221, 249n.97, 276n.96, 278n.122. *See also* economic status of blacks

Prince Edward County, Virginia, school shutdown in, 35, 88, 96, 241n.57

private academy system (Mississippi), 30, 158, 238n.36, 270n.18, 271n.39, 283n.59

Project Keep Hope Alive, 201

Project Women Power, 216

"Prospectus for a Summer Freedom School Program" (Cobb), 68, 73

Providence Journal (newspaper), 215

public accommodations, 25, 42, 46, 57, 61, 146, 159–61. *See also* segregation

public education, 3, 19, 23–24, 145–46, 186, 211, 218, 227; privatization of, 15, 218, 226–27. *See also* black education; education

public spaces: desegregation strategies for, 16–17, 46, 131, 159; student protests in, 7, 61, 134, 150, 160, 195

public speaking, 120, 184

Queens College (New York), 35, 80, 83

race, 15, 71, 90–91, 136–44, 177–78, 266n.97. *See also* interracial dialogue

Race Mixing (Romano), 266n.97

racialized other, 15, 144

racial purity, 140–41

Ray, Kay, *100*

Reconstruction: and black education, 13, 20, 23–24, 29, 74–75; and black voting rights, 235n.12; and Freedmen's schools, 34, 235n.8, 251n.12; in Freedom School curriculum, 114; and presidential politics, 191

Redeemers, 24

Reese, Arthur, 127, *128*, 174

Reese, Carolyn, 127

Reeves, Genevera, 62

religion, 41, 90, 119, 216, 219. *See also* churches

Remember the Titans (film), 10

Republican Party, 24, 191, 205

Ricks, Willie, 167

Ripley, Mississippi, 62, 160, 270n.23

Roberts, Wally, 80–81, *81*, 127, 129, 142, 196, 208, 214–15

Robertson, David E., 247n.75

Rochester (Eddie Anderson), 116

Romano, Renee C., 266n.97

Roosevelt, Franklin Delano, 50

Rothschild, Mary Aickin, 10, 176

Ruleville Freedom School, 129

Rust College (Holly Springs), 60–61, 98, 165, 175, 242n.7

Rustin, Bayard, 92–93, 251n.4

safe meeting places, 34, 40–41, 48–49, 60, 64, 77, 97–98, 113, 175, 188

sanitation workers, strike by (Memphis), 245n.36

Saturday Review (magazine), 215

Savio, Mario, 182–83

schools, desegregation of: and debate on integration and quality education, 15, 75, 146, 157–59, 270n.17, 279n.6; federal legislation on, 217–18; and "freedom

schools, desegregation of (*continued*)
of choice" plans, 155–56, 218, 226; and
Freedom School students' activism,
39, 96–97, 145, 147, 156, 165; and high
school protests, 32, 45–46, 51, 54–56, 63,
159, 170, 200; legal challenges to, 8, 20,
26–51, 155, 218, 223, 238n.24, 240n.47; and
Mississippi elementary schools, 151, 156–57;
Mississippi history of, 270n.17, 283n.59;
and Mississippi school boycotts, 15–16, 146,
150, 163–66, 176, 271n.37; state and local
attacks on, 217–18; visibility of protests
about, 160–66; white opposition to, 218–19.
See also education; integration

schools, resegregation of, 15–16, 211, 227. *See
also* schools, desegregation of

Schwerner, Mickey, 64, 71, 83, 104–5, 109, 113,
135–36

Schwerner, Rita, 64, 113

Schwerner, Stephen, 83

Scott, Walter, 228

Seeds of Freedom (Flynn et al), 116, 162, 174,
274n.66

segregation, 27–28, 34, 70, 118, 196, 217–18,
257n.86. *See also* integration; schools,
desegregation of

Sellers, Cleveland, 151

Selma to Montgomery March, 186

Service Employees International Union, 213

"Sex and Caste" (King and Casey), 215–16

sexuality, 139–41, 182, 261n.8, 266nn.93–94,
266n.97. *See also* gender roles

sharecropping, 66. *See also* black land
ownership

Sharkey-Issaquena Counties, Mississippi,
boycott in, 164–65, 176, 271n.37

Shaw Freedom School, 163

Siegel, Sandy, 83, *84*, 89–90, 106, 122–23, *124*, 184

Sillers, Walter, 29

Simmons, Gwendolyn Robinson, 86–87, 89,
149, 152, 216–17

Simon, Paul, 143

Slaughter House Cases (*The Butchers'
Benevolent Association of New Orleans v.
The Crescent City Live-Stock Landing and
Slaughter-House Company*, 1873), 236n.14

Slave Codes, 21

slavery, 3, 12, 19–23, 111, 114, 226, 237. *See also*
education: of freedmen

slaves, rebellions by, 20–21

Smith, Frank, 61

Smith, Lillian, 114

"Somebody Had to Do It" (Brown), 270n.17

South Carolina State University, 7

Southern Christian Leadership Conference
(SCLC), 48, 52, 58, 69, 205, 249n.97

Southern Educational Communications
Association, 204

Southern Poverty Law Center, 227

Southern Student Organizing Committee
(SSOC), 7, 77, 252n.22

South Reporter (Holly Springs), 130

Sovereignty Commission, 33

Spelman College (Georgia), 79–80, 85–87

Spofford, Tim, 278n.2

standardized tests, 226

standards-based assessment, 198

Stanford University (California), 75, 80

Stennis, John, 192, 217–18, 278n.117

Stephanie B. (Freedom School student), 133

Stepin Fetchit (Lincoln Perry), 116

Steptoe, E. W., 53

St. James Church (Clarksdale), 98, *99*

St. Louis Argus (newspaper), 203

St. Mary's High School (Holly Springs), 162

St. Paul Freedom Schools (Minnesota), 220

student activism: arrest and incarceration for,
44–46, 53–55, 57, 131–34, 165, 223; coerced
military enlistment for, 170–71; of college
students, 7, 52–53, 80–90, 199–200,
231n.4; economic reprisals against families
for, 134; expulsions for, 35, 54–55, 64, 162–
64, 169–70, 206; as high school protests
and walkouts, 32, 45–46, 51, 54–56, 63,
155–57, 159, 165–66, 168–70, 200; of high
school students, 72, 162, 205–6, 221;
impact of, on interracial dialogue, 137; in
Mississippi schools, 131–34, 150, 154–66;
in northern schools, 35, 169–71, 176, 181,
199, 220, 257n.79, 278n.2; obstacles to
participation in, 124–25. *See also* Freedom
Schools

student newspapers, 11, 110, 119–22, 129–31, 203

Student Nonviolent Coordinating Committee (SNCC): and black power movement, 152–53, 167, 172–73; campus and community activism of, 7, 55–56, 58, 96, 137–38, 156; and federal education policy, 193; and Mississippi Freedom Summer, 5, 60, 69–76, 80–88, 96, 112–13, 137, 152, 256n.71; retreat of, in Waveland, 177, 181, 215–16; whites in, 74–75, 177–78

Students' Bill of Rights, 226

Students for a Democratic Society, 213

Sudsofloppen, 215

Supreme Court, 25, 27, 164, 205, 218, 236n.14

Sweatt v. Painter (1950), 27

taxation, 24–25, 235n.12, 246n.52

Tchula, Mississippi, 1–2, 11, 98, 159, 201–2

Tchula Freedom School, 11

Tchula Seven, 202

teachers: education programs for, 26, 125, 183, 211, 281n.32; firings and unemployment of, 31–32, 62, 163; and gender roles, 14, 78–79, 182; political rights of, 62, 134, 145–46; salary equalization for, 27–29, 31, 145; unions of, 87–88, 102, 174. *See also* black educators; Freedom Schools

Teachers Committee for Peace in Vietnam, 185, 212

Ten Point Program (Black Panther Party), 179–80

test scores, 198, 223

theater and drama, 115–16, 162, 174, 274n.66

theory of parallel institutions, 172

Thompson, Allen C., 106, 218

Thompson, Hymethia Washington Lofton: background of, 40–46; and black power movement, 167–68, 171; career and political activity of, 37–39, 44–46, 157, 200–201, 206, 279n.6; Freedom Schools experience of, 4, 98, 108, 121, 147

Till, Emmett, 8, 47, 50, 58, 109, 134, 205

Tinker v. Des Moines (1969), 164

Tippah County, Mississippi, 175

Tonkin Bay Resolution, 168

"To Our President, a Former Teacher" (Teachers Committee for Peace in Vietnam), 185

Totten, Bernice, 188

Tougaloo College (Jackson), 7, 40–41, 59–60, 73, 87, 98, 116, 167, 224–28

Tougaloo Nine, 41

Trammell, Theodore, 49, 98

Travis, Brenda: background of, 52–56, 59–60; Freedom Schools experience of, 4, 39, 65; recognition of, for activism, 247n.62

Tubman, Harriet, 210

Tuskegee Normal and Industrial Institute (Alabama), 25

unemployed and working class, 66, 189, 206

Unica Junior College (Jackson), 170

Union WAGE (newspaper), 215

Union Women's Alliance to Gain Equality (Union WAGE), 215

United Campus Christian Fellowship (Pacific Lutheran University), 83

United Federation of Teachers (UFT), 35, 87–88, 102, 255n.52

United Nations, 216

United States v. Lynd (1961), 58

University of California, Berkeley, 7, 80, 83, 182–83

University of California, Davis, 83

University of Illinois, 7

University of Kansas, 60

University of Michigan, 80

University of Mississippi, 7, 38

University of Wisconsin, 80

urban unrest, 152–53

Vardaman, James K., 25

Vietnam War, 9, 15, 164, 167–71, 183–85, 199, 205, 212

violence: church burnings, 40, 105, 135, 176; directed at youth and students, 134–35, 200; formation of militia groups, 24; and Freedom Schools volunteers, 77, 83, 102–5, 135, 138, 199–200, 210–11; murder of Chaney, Goodman, and Schwerner, 104–5, 109, 135–36; murder of Till, 8, 47,

violence (*continued*)
50, 58, 109, 134, 205; as retaliation for civil
rights activity, 27, 31, 49, 63, 76, 134–25,
139, 156; shootings, at Emmanuel AME
Church, 228–29; shootings, at Jackson
State College, 199; shootings, at Kent State
University, 199. *See also* Freedom Rides
Voters League, 160
voting rights: and Citizenship Schools, 34;
federal legislation on, 71, 152, 186, 201, 220;
and Freedom School students' activism,
53, 110, 121–22, 132–33, 268n.2; history of,
in Mississippi, 1–2, 25, 59, 73, 159, 235n.12;
legal obstacles to, 24–25, 53, 235n.12,
246n.52; and Mississippi Freedom Summer
registration drive, 7, 57, 61, 94, 146, 159,
220, 226; and Reconstruction, 235n.12
Voting Rights Act (1965), 71, 152, 186, 201, 220

W. A. Higgins High School (Clarksdale), 32
Walker, Rita, 112
Walker, Vanessa Siddle, 26
Walker, W. T., 133–34
Wallace, George, 123
War on Poverty (legislation), 15, 185–94, 213,
276n.96
War Resisters League, 212
Washington, Booker T., 25, 114, 131, 236n.17
Waterhouse, Patricia, *100*
Watkins, Hezekiah, *45*, *207*; career of, 206–7;
forced enlistment of, in military, 170–71;
Freedom Schools experience of, 4, 65, 120;
political activity of, 44–46
Watkins, Hollis, 53, 56, 58–59
Watson, Daisy, 119
Watson, Lauren, 180
Weiss, Mark, 90
"We Shall Overcome" (song), 113

Western College for Women (Ohio), 101, 224
Westinghouse Report ("Impact of Head
Start: An Evaluation of the Effects of
Head Start on Children's Cognitive and
Affective Development," Westinghouse
Learning Corporation and Ohio
University), 193
White, Hugh, 30
White Folks Project, 77, 252n.22
white supremacy, 191–92
Wilkins, Roy, 123
women, 77–79, 181–82, 216–17, 243n.15,
266n.95, 266n.97. *See also* gender roles;
sexuality
women's liberation movement, 9, 183–84,
215–16
women's suffrage movement, 89
Woodson, Carter G., 33
Woolworth (store), protests at, 49, 53, 72
workers' rights, 226
Wright, Richard, 114–15

Yale University, 75, 80
Young People's Project, 221, 225
youth: arrest and incarceration of, 44, 46, 53,
57, 107, 131–34, 165, 223; family support
of activism of, 58; local networks and
political socialization of, 38, 42–43, 51,
111. *See also* elementary, middle, and high
school students; Freedom Schools; student
activism
"Youth Go Churchy" (Mitchell), 130

Zellner, Bob, 56, 84
Zellner, Dorothy, 84
Zimmerman, George, 204–5
Zinn, Howard, 9, 80, 87, 125, 198, 260n.7,
284n.63